Lecture Notes in Computer Science 4718

Commenced Publication in 1973
Founding and Former Series Editors:
Gerhard Goos, Juris Hartmanis, and Jan van Leeuwen

Jeffrey Hightower   Bernt Schiele
Thomas Strang (Eds.)

Location- and Context-Awareness

Third International Symposium, LoCA 2007
Oberpfaffenhofen, Germany, September 20-21, 2007
Proceedings

 Springer

Volume Editors

Jeffrey Hightower
Intel Research Seattle
1100 NE 45th St., Seattle, WA 98105, USA
E-mail: jeffrey.r.hightower@intel.com

Bernt Schiele
TU Darmstadt
Computer Science Department
Hochschulstrasse 10, 64289 Darmstadt, Germany
E-mail: schiele@informatik.tu-darmstadt.de

Thomas Strang
German Aerospace Center
Institute of Communications and Navigation
82234 Wessling/Oberpfaffenhofen, Germany
E-mail: Thomas.Strang@dlr.de
and
Digital Enterprise Research Institute (DERI)
University of Innsbruck, 6020 Innsbruck, Austria

Library of Congress Control Number: 2007934918

CR Subject Classification (1998): H.3, H.4, C.2, H.5, K.8

LNCS Sublibrary: SL 3 – Information Systems and Application, incl. Internet/Web
and HCI

ISSN   0302-9743
ISBN-10   3-540-75159-9 Springer Berlin Heidelberg New York
ISBN-13   978-3-540-75159-5 Springer Berlin Heidelberg New York

Springer is a part of Springer Science+Business Media

springer.com

© Springer-Verlag Berlin Heidelberg 2007
Printed in Germany

Typesetting: Camera-ready by author, data conversion by Scientific Publishing Services, Chennai, India
Printed on acid-free paper   SPIN: 12162987   06/3180   5 4 3 2 1 0

Preface

These proceedings contain the papers presented at the 3rd International Symposium on Location- and Context-Awareness in September of 2007.

Computing has become mobile, wireless, and portable. The range of contexts encountered while sitting at a desk working on a computer is very limited compared to the large variety of situations experienced away from the desktop. For computing to be relevant and useful in these emerging situations, computers will need to take advantage of users location, activities, goals, abilities, preferences, interruptibility, affordances, and surroundings. With this contextual awareness, we can expect computers to deliver information, services, and entertainment in a way that maximizes convenience and minimizes intrusion.

This symposium presented research aimed at sensing, inferring, and using location and context data in ways that help the user. Developing awareness involves research in sensing, inference, data representation, and design. We sought technical papers describing original, previously unpublished research results including:

- Sensing location and context
- Inference techniques for context from low-level sensor data
- Privacy and sharing of location and context information
- User studies of location- and context-aware systems

Our call for papers resulted in 55 submissions, each of which was assigned to members of our Program Committee. After reviews and e-mail discussions, we selected 17 papers for publication in these proceedings.

We extend a sincere thank you to all the authors who submitted papers, to the 33 hard-working members of our Program Committee, and to our external reviewers.

September 2007

Jeffrey Hightower
Bernt Schiele
Thomas Strang

Organization

Program Committee

Gregory Abowd	Georgia Tech
Witold Abramowicz	Poznan University of Economics
Alessandro Acquisti	CMU
Michael Beigl	TU Braunschweig
Carlos Bento	University of Coimbra
Gaetano Borriello	University of Washington
Jim Crowley	INRIA, France
Eyal de Lara	University of Toronto
Anind Dey	CMU
Alois Ferscha	University of Linz
Hans Gellersen	Lancaster University
Robert Harle	University of Cambridge
Mike Hazas	Lancaster University
Jaga Indulska	University of Queensland
Minkyong Kim	IBM Research
John Krumm	Microsoft Research
Reto Krummenacher	DERI Innsbruck
Anthony LaMarca	Intel Research
Marc Langheinrich	ETH Zurich
Claudia Linnhoff-Popien	LMU Munich
Paul Lukowicz	University of Passau
Max Mühlhäuser	TU Darmstadt
Kurt Partridge	PARC
Shwetak Patel	Georgia Tech
Alex Pentland	MIT
Matt Reynolds	ThingMagic Inc.
Kay Roemer	ETH Zurich
Chris Schmandt	MIT
Albrecht Schmidt	Fraunhofer IAIS and University of Bonn
Tim Sohn	UC San Diego
Hiroyuki Tarumi	Kagawa University
Alex Varshavsky	University of Toronto
Andy Wilson	Microsoft Research

External Reviewers

Mohammed Al-Loulah	Lancaster University
Philippe Golle	PARC

Sponsoring Institutions

German Aerospace Center (DLR)
Intel

Table of Contents

WiFi Location Technology

Activity and Situational Awareness

Taxonomy, Architectures, and a Broader Perspective

The Meaning of Place

Radio Issues in Location Technology

New Approaches to Location Estimation

Bootstrapping a Location Service Through Geocoded Postal Addresses

Gayathri Chandrasekaran, Mesut Ali Ergin, Marco Gruteser,
and Richard P. Martin

WINLAB, Electrical and Computer Engineering Department
Rutgers, The State University of New Jersey
North Brunswick, NJ 08902-3390
{chandrga,ergin,gruteser}@winlab.rutgers.edu, rmartin@cs.rutgers.edu

Abstract. We analyze the feasibility of boostrapping a location service through geocoded postal addresses rather than the common wardriving technique. A location service that contains the MAC addresses and geographic position of wireless LAN access points enables positioning services for WLAN devices and location-aware networking protocols. This work thus compares the accuracy of access point position estimates obtained based on RF signal strengths readings (wardriving) with the accuracy of the geocoded postal address. The results show similar accuracy for geocoding in comparison to typical wardriving studies, with significantly reduced effort if postal addresses of access point positions are known.

1 Introduction

WiFi localization promises to complement satellite positioning in two key areas that frequently experience poor satellite coverage, indoor environments and urban canyons. Wide area WiFi localization techniques as provided by Place Lab [1] or commercial providers [2], however, rely on a location service that provides geographic position of third-party WiFi access points identified by their MAC address.

Obtaining the data to initialize and subsequently maintain the records of such a location service requires significant effort. Typically, data is collected via *wardriving*, whereby a vehicle sweeps the area of interest and recording periodically its position and the signal strength of nearby access points (the vehicle can determine its position with a Global Positioning System receiver). From this dataset, the position of access points can then be estimated using a number of heuristics such as position of maximum signal strength, or centroid of all access point sightings.[1] This process is inaccurate [4] and it is laborious, since it requires physically driving a vehicle through the road network in the intended coverage area. It needs to be repeated periodically to update the dataset, since owners of access points upgrade their hardware (resulting in a change of MAC address),

---

[1] See Wigle.net [3] for example wardriving datasets.

J. Hightower, B. Schiele, and T. Strang (Eds.): LoCA 2007, LNCS 4718, pp. 1–16, 2007.
© Springer-Verlag Berlin Heidelberg 2007

or move with the access point to a different geographic location. To reduce this updating effort [5] proposes self-mapping, wherein users of the location service contribute updates to its records. Still, bootstrapping a location service to the point where it is useful for early adopters is necessary.

This paper studies the feasibility of an alternate method, initializing location service records through geocoded postal addresses. This approach is motivated by the realization that large Internet service providers already maintain a directory of postal addresses (i.e., billing addresses) and could easily add MAC addresses to these records. To evaluate this approach, we compare the accuracy of access point position estimates obtained through wardriving with those from postal address geocoding. Specifically, we study the effect of building and road densities, wardriving road coverage, and geocoding databases on these results.

The remainder of this paper is organized as follows. The terms and metrics are introduced in section 2. The methodology is described in detail in section 3. Section 4 describes the results and section 5 has discussions related the ideas presented. The related work is summarized in Section 6. Finally, section 7 concludes the paper.

2   Terms and Metrics

In this section, we define the various terms and metrics used in the paper. Definitions are as follows:

- **Actual Location of the AP:** It is the geographic location where the AP is physically installed. This was found using the Orthophoto-based geocoding explained in the next section.
- **Full Coverage War-Driving Location of the AP:** It is the geographic location of the AP reported by war driving through both the main and side roads. The inference of the location of the AP in this experiment is based on the location at which the strongest SNR was received. *Full Coverage War Driving Error* is then defined as the Euclidean distance between the actual location of the AP and the full coverage war driving location of the AP, measured in feet.
- **Main Road War-Driving Location of the AP:** It is the geographic location of the AP reported by war driving only through the main roads. *Main Road War-Driving Error* is then defined as the Euclidean distance between the actual location of the AP and the main road war driving location of the AP, measured in feet.
- **Postal Address Geocoded Location of the AP:** It is the geographic location of the AP reported by geocoding the postal address of the building in which the AP is installed. *Postal Address Geocoding Error* is then defined as the Euclidean distance between the actual location of the AP and the postal address geocoded location of the AP, measured in feet.

3   Methodology

In this section, we define our goals and explain our experimental techniques used to achieve these goals. Our goals were to:

1. Quantify the errors due to different kinds of war driving efforts. In our experiments, we compare two different kinds of war-driving - *Full Coverage War Driving* which involves driving through both main roads and side roads surrounding the area of interest to get a comprehensive coverage of the APs, and the *Main Road War-Driving*, which is typically similar to the kind one can find in the public war driving databases, where only the major roads around the area of interest are traversed.

2. Analyze the postal address geocoding error for two different map data sources, namely the Navteq and TIGER/Line. Navteq [6] serves as the main data source for Yahoo Maps, Google Maps, and Mapquest. TIGER/Line [7] map data source is being developed by the US Census Bureau for supporting imaging needs of the Decennial Census and other bureau programs.

3. Quantify the errors incurred with various bootstrapping techniques in three different environments: A sparse residential area (Figure 1), a relatively dense residential area (Figure 2), and a highway (Figure 3). The sparse residential area consisted of single family houses which had long walkways between the roads and the houses. The relatively dense Residential area had single family houses closer to the roads. Highway had three lanes on each direction with 80 km/h speed limit and mostly consisted of commercial buildings. All areas were within central New Jersey region.

4. Study our claim that postal address geocoding techniques could complement or partially replace the war driving efforts while still giving comparable results in terms of accuracy.

Fig. 1. Sparse Residential Area. The white line represents the route driven for Main Road War Driving.

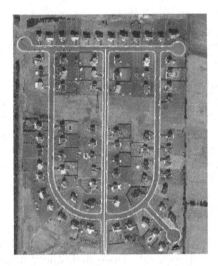

Fig. 2. Relatively Dense Residential Area. The white line represents the route driven for Main Road War Driving.

Fig. 3. Highway Route. The white line represents the route driven in the highway.

Towards achieving stated goals, we first need to know the actual postal addresses where the access points are installed in our selected areas. Our final dataset consisted of all these APs for which we were able to determine the corresponding postal address of their installation location. The total number of such APs are 167 in this paper. For each of these APs, orthophoto-based geocoding was accomplished, where we visually identified each of these postal address on Google Earth [8] and geocoded the address to a location centered on the building related to the address. Then, the corresponding errors for the different

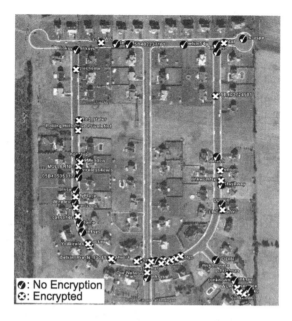

Fig. 4. The positions of the APs reported from war driving with a directional antenna

bootstrapping techniques were determined by comparing them to the data obtained in this step. We summarize the steps involved in this process as:

1. Locate the access points and the postal address of the place where the APs were deployed with the help of a directional antenna.
2. Create an orthophoto-based geocoding for each of the postal addresses that we determined in the first step to establish the ground truth about the actual geographic location of the AP.
3. War drive on main and small roads with an omni-directional antenna to obtain a comprehensive coverage of the region and determine the geographic locations of the APs as reported by war driving.
4. War Drive only on main roads with an omnidirectional antenna and determine the geographic locations of the APs as reported by war driving.
5. Geocode all the postal addresses collected in Step 1 using the Navteq and the TIGER/Line databases.

3.1 Actual Location of the AP

Identifying the postal address where the APs were deployed was challenging due to the dense deployment of the 802.11a/b/g Access points.

Figure 4 illustrates the war driving data obtained with a typical omnidirectional antenna in the relatively dense residential area. We can see from the figure that it is difficult to determine in which buildings the access points are placed.

Hence, in addition to the external USB-driven Pharos iGPS-360 GPS unit, we decided to use a 2.4 GHz, 15 dBi, Die Cast Mini-Reflector Grid Wireless LAN directional antenna for war driving. The directional antenna was connected to a Hermes chipset based Orinoco Silver PCMCIA wireless card in the laptop using an N-Male to MC converter. We pointed our directional antenna towards the outer edge of the circular area. The sniffed frames were fed into the stumbling software (Network Stumbler [9]) and the locations of the APs were plotted. The new plot looked similar to 4 but the SNR readings in each of the plotted APs gave an insight about the direction from which the signals were captured.

We could see that each AP plotted on the linear-segment of the road in Figure 4 could correspond to one of the two houses on either sides of the road (because we are plotting APs on points where the best signal strength was received). We then looked at the SNR of the each of these APs to determine whether the AP signal came from the direction in which the directional antenna was pointed to or from the other side. According to the specification, the antenna has a differential gain between front and back lobes of 20 dB and a horizontal beamwidth of 16 degrees. Therefore, we were able to observe peak RSSI values above 80 when the antenna pointed directly at the home containing the access point, and RSSI values dropped by about 10 points when the antenna faced backwards. We determined these thresholds through a calibration procedure on several freestanding houses (where we were certain about the AP position). Based on this calibration, we decided to map an AP onto the house facing the antenna, if its maximum RSSI values lies above 80, map it onto the house in the opposite direction if its value lies between 75 and 80, and drop all other points to reduce mapping uncertainty. In the dense area, we also verified a sample of 3 access point locations with residents of the community, all of which were correctly mapped by this procedure.

The highway mostly had commercial buildings like hotels, restaurants, coffee-shops, book-stores, whose SSIDs were more meaningful and matched with the commercial spot's name. Table 1 summarizes a few of our observations of the common SSIDs used by these commercial spots.

Since multiple APs were installed in hotels with the same SSIDs, it was usually simple to identify the correspondence between the AP name and the location at which it was installed by looking at the war driving data.

Thus for the highway area, we drove once with an Omni-Directional Antenna to capture the wireless signals and extracted the SSIDs that we were able to

Table 1. Correlation between the enterprise trademark names of the commercial buildings and their Wireless SSIDs

Commercial Name	SSID
Barnes and Nobles	BNDEMO
Holiday Inn	HOLIDAY INN
Best Western	ethostream
Extended Stay America	goesh
Panera Bread	PANERA
Red Roof Inn	tmobile
Midas Auto Services	MIDASWIRELESS

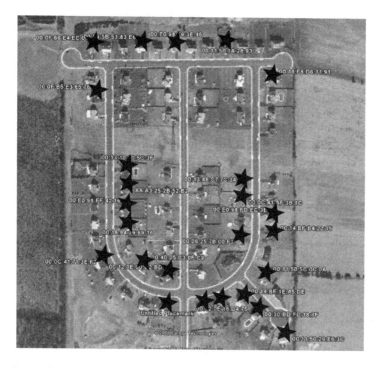

Fig. 5. Orthophoto-based geocoding for the postal addresses along with the MAC address of the AP installed in that address

correlate with the commercial spot. We then drove once again to note down the postal addresses of the commercial spots that we identified in the first run. Thus the ground truth of the location/postal address of the APs in the highway was established.

3.2 Orthophoto-Based Geocoding

For each of the postal addresses collected in the previous step, we did an orthophoto-based geocoding. In this process, we visually identified each of these postal address on Google Earth [8] and geocoded the address to a location centered on the building referenced by the address. Thus for each of the postal addresses, we extracted the actual geocodes.

Figure 5 represents the orthophoto-based geocoded postal addresses along with the MAC address of the AP installed at that particular postal address. Each star in Figure 5 is placed on the center of the house and is labeled with the MAC address of the AP installed in that house.

3.3 War Driving

War driving is widely used to estimate access point locations. War driving is the process of gathering statistics about wireless networks in a given area by listening to the broadcast beacons emitted by the APs. These beacons contain information regarding the SSID, MAC, and encryption capabilities. Along with a GPS unit, these beacons can be used to log available networks using various freely available war driving software such as NetStumbler [9] or Kismet [10]. We used Network Stumbler to collect our logs.

There are various algorithms to infer the actual location of the AP from war driving logs. Centroid, weighted-centroid, and particle filters [11] are examples to those algorithms used in tools like [12,13]. However, since most paths that we drove were approximately linear, the approximated location of the APs fell on this linear segment. Hence, we used the point at which maximum signal to noise ratio was achieved as an estimate of the location of the AP in our war driving data.

Full Coverage War-Driving. For the full coverage war driving data, we drove on all the main roads and small roads at speeds less than 45 km/h. As explained before, the points of best signal strength for each of the APs were used and the Euclidean distance between the location of the AP reported by the full coverage war driving and the actual location of the AP (found using step 2) was calculated.

Main Road War-Driving. Public war driving repository like Wigle.net [3] allow users of the community to upload their war driving data, containing information about the BSSID and locations of the APs encountered. The serious drawback of this data is that the APs are primarily located near the main roads and commercial areas due to the community members' driving patterns. It is impractical to achieve the accuracy of full coverage war driving by using the data from these repositories. Therefore, in our evaluations of the residential areas, we considered driving only on main roads (as shown by the white lines in Figures 1 and 2) and quantified the Euclidean distance between the AP location reported by main road war driving and the actual location of the AP.

3.4   Geocoding Postal Addresses

In general, the postal address geocoding is accomplished by

- Geocoding the end points of the road segments
- Noting down the address range in each of these segments
- Extrapolating the geographic co-ordinates for the remaining addresses in that segment.

Thus there is some error introduced due to the extrapolation step. If the road segments are long and if the houses/commercial buildings are not equispaced, the error introduced due to extrapolation of the geographic co-ordinates of the addresses would be high. Similarly, small road segments introduce less extrapolation error. In our experiment, the US1 highway roads had long road segments whereas the residential areas had shorter road segments.

In our evaluations, we have considered two different Address Map Databases Navteq [6] and TIGER/Line [7] for the characterization of the accuracy of the postal address geocoding. Navteq serves as the data source for Yahoo Maps, Google Maps, Google Earth and MapQuest. So, we evaluate only the geocodes for the postal address generated by the Yahoo Maps among the other alternatives that use the same data source.

The TIGER/Line system (Topologically Integrated Geographic Encoding and Referencing) is a different digital database developed at the U.S Census Bureau to support its imaging needs for the Decennial Census and other Bureau programs. The median accuracy of this data is claimed to be around 167ft. Thus, we also evaluate the geocoding accuracy of this database for the postal addresses that have been generated.

We report the postal address geocoding error for the mentioned two address map databases in our evaluations.

4   Results

Figure 6 shows the error distributions for the sparse and the relatively dense residential areas. The sparse residential area that we considered had single family houses that were far from the roads with huge walkways. Thus the full coverage war driving results in Figure 6(a) show a median error of around 300ft. The relatively dense residential area had single family houses close to the roads. Hence the median error for the full coverage war driving in relatively dense residential area is about 110ft, as shown in 6(b). Similar patterns in the sparse and dense residential areas are observed for the main road war driving where the median error for sparse residential area ($\sim$1000ft) is much higher than median error for the relatively dense residential area ($\sim$500ft).

The error due to postal address geocoding is not very much affected by the type of region. Median error exhibited by both the Yahoo Maps and TIGER/Line database in either case is around 300ft to 350ft. However, we observe from

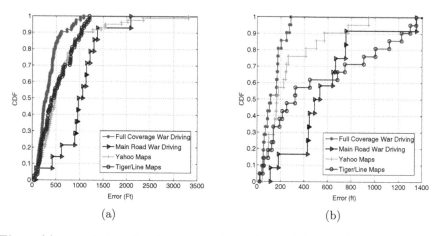

Fig. 6. (a) Error distribution in sparse residential area, (b) Error distribution in relatively dense residential Area

Figure 6(b) that Yahoo Maps have a much better geocoding compared to the TIGER/Line maps. The median error for Yahoo maps in the case of relatively dense residential area is around 180ft as opposed to TIGER/Line database, which is around 300ft.

In Figure 7, we only plot one type of war driving result (i.e., main road war driving), since highway road is indeed considered to be the only road surrounding the area. In other words, there is no difference between the full coverage war driving and main road war driving for the highway area. Obviously, we could have driven in the parking lots to improve the accuracy, however, this is beyond the scope of our experiment and also considered trespassing for some of the buildings. We also do not show the error distribution of the TIGER/Line database in this figure, because the US-1 Highway addresses that we have considered in this experiment do not yet appear in the TIGER/Line Maps.

Our observations from the experiment highlight the fact that the accuracy of the highway postal address geocoding is low (with median errors of 750ft). These high errors could be attributed to the long road segments in highways as discussed in the previous section. Although some of the popular highways have been subject to war driving, many others can still benefit from postal address-based bootstrapping. Also, data from already covered highways can be refined further through the postal address-based approach, since quality of the map databases are continuously being improved for many other purposes.

Figure 8 summarizes the data for all three areas we had considered. Our overall observations follows:

- As expected the time-consuming full coverage war driving method provides the least AP position estimation error, a median error of 250ft.
- Main road war driving, which is less time consuming than full coverage war driving, reduces accuracy to a median of 350ft.
- Both Yahoo Maps and the TIGER/Line maps exhibit similar error characteristics for most addresses. However, Yahoo geocoding shows more serious outliers with errors up to 3300ft. In general, 95% of the geocoded postal addresses generated using either of the databases have errors less than 1200ft.

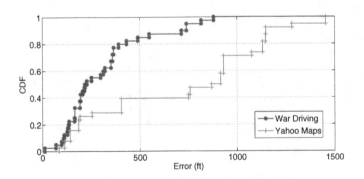

Fig. 7. Error Distribution in Highway Scenario

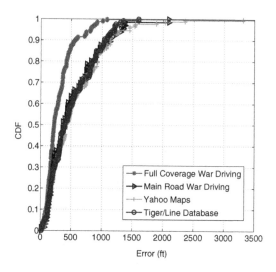

Fig. 8. Summary of the Error Distribution for Various Bootstrapping Procedures

– Postal address geocoding shows a median error of 350ft, similar to the accuracy of main road war driving technique in the areas that we have considered. (However, main road war driving can be less accurate if sufficient coverage is not achieved, as in the residential areas shown earlier).

Table 2 summarizes the number of APs detected through various bootstrapping procedures in the three areas we considered – Sparse residential area, relatively dense residential area and highway. In total, we analyzed a sample of 167 access points from all three areas. The bottleneck for extending this sample of access points was our inability to identify without ambiguity the ground truth about the postal addresses of many other locations APs were deployed. Of 167 APs, 106 APs were selected from the sparse residential area due to the ease of identification of the actual locations of the APs.

We observe that full coverage war driving has a detection rate of 100% in all three areas. However, this result is biased because the ground truth for the

Table 2. Number of APs detected in various bootstrapping procedures

	Full Coverage War Driving	Main Road War Driving	Yahoo Maps	TIGER/Line Database	Total APs Analyzed
Sparse Residential Area	106	14	106	106	106
Relatively Dense Residential Area	21	12	21	21	21
US Highway 1 Area	40	-	38	0	40

Table 3. Time taken (in mins) for full coverage and main road war driving

	Time taken for War Driving in Mins	
	Full Coverage War Driving	Main Road War Driving
Sparse Residential Area	30	3.5
Dense Residential Area	6	2
Highway	45	45

presence of APs was established with the help of war driving with a directional antenna. APs which were not detected in war driving were not included in the experiment. The significance of this table is that main road war driving detects a far lesser number of APs than the full coverage war driving in the residential areas. The number of APs detected in the sparse residential area is only 14 out of 106 APs that were considered in that area. The number of APs detected in the relatively dense residential area is 12 out of 21. The very low AP detection rate in the sparse residential area is due to the presence of a large residential community located far from the main roads as shown in Figure 1. The relatively dense residential community, however, is small and we traversed a path along the center of the community as shown by the white line in Figure 2. As a result, 57% of the APs have been detected in this area. The number for main road war driving in the highway case is not different than the full coverage war driving case. The table also shows that both Yahoo Maps and TIGER/Line database have the geocodes for all of the residential addresses we have used. For the US1 highway, TIGER/Line Map does not have geocodes for any of the 40 addresses, whereas Yahoo Maps have geocodes for the 38 addresses out of these 40. The absence of TIGER/Line data for the US1 highway should not be generalized for other highways without further investigation.

Table 3 summarizes the time taken (in Mins) for full coverage war driving and main road war driving in both of the residential areas.

We see that full coverage war driving, which took 30 mins in sparse residential area, is about nine times more time consuming than the main road war driving, which took around 3.5 minutes. Similarly, the full coverage war driving in relatively dense residential area took thrice as much time as that of main road war driving in the same area. In highways, our route of 25 miles took nearly 45 minutes of war drive time.

5 Discussion

In this section, we elaborate on accuracy considerations and methods for obtaining databases with MAC and postal addresses.

A key issue to make the geocoding approach feasible is obtaining a database that maps (wireless interface) MAC addresses to the postal addresses of their deployment locations. We envision several ways of obtaining such a database. First, access point software configuration wizards could be programmed to ask the end user or the installation technician for the postal address of the deployment location and report both to a location service. Due to the nature of the wireless communications at public frequencies, access points already contain a software face for installing and efficiently operating an AP at a certain location already require manual intervention (e.g, configuring channel, SSID and encryption settings). This approach would require participation of access point manufacturers. Alternatively, this software could be integrated into any downloadable software (presumably providing a service of interest to users to encourage downloading). This software can query the MAC address of the associated access points from the local wireless interface, and ask the user for the postal address (with appropriate disclosure). In both approaches, some users may be unwilling or unable to provide the postal address information. Some may either deliberately or accidentally enter incorrect information, a source of inaccuracy that was outside the scope of our study.

A different approach to obtaining such a database, relies on Internet service providers to record the MAC addresses of provided access points and the postal addresses where the Internet service is provided. Many current ISP contracts include a free wireless access point and a significant number of users is likely taking advantage of such offers. Similarly, major online retailers could combine wireless MAC and shipping addresses of access points. Again, these approaches introduce inaccuracies not considered in this study, when access points are moved to and used at a different address than the original shipment address. (ISP may be able to detect this via a change in MAC address connected to their network, but retailers can not). However, this approach may at least provide enough data to seed (or bootstrap a location service) in certain areas whereby wardriving may still be needed in others.

To reduce privacy concerns of users, the location service database should not contain the real identities of users and should not contain the postal addresses, only the geographic coordinates. If users harbor further concerns about an AP linked to their home locations, perturbations of the access point position could be introduced, although this would reduce accuracy.

Note also that the accuracy of geocoding continues to improve. High accuracy of this process is essential for many vital services (e.g. emergency response, law enforcement, planning delivery routes, etc.). Therefore, parallel attempts from both government and private sector exist to increase the fidelity of geocoding. In particular, the E911 Phase-II requirement is a driving force for geocoding. While it mainly concerns the accuracy of cellular positioning systems (requirement of less than 50 to 300 m error [14]), these coordinates usually must be translated into postal addresses with which emergency responders are more familiar. Thus, the accuracy of this translation process is also important and future location services can benefit from these continuing geocoding refinements.

The postal-address-based techniques are likely not very accurate in the enterprise domain, because a significant number of such APs are deployed within campus locations, where the whole campus is referenced by a single street address to the external world. However, wardriving is still unnecessary if installation location information from conventional enterprise asset tracking or network management systems can be provided to the location service. This would, of course, require participation of the campus network administrators.

Last but not least, the accuracy implications of access point location errors on a client positioning service are dependent on the positioning algorithms used and remained outside the scope of this paper. While some indoor positioning services such as RADAR [15] do not rely on actual AP positions, to our knowledge, wide-area services such as Place Lab [1] would be affected by AP position errors.

6   Related Work

War driving has gained importance with the launch of the Place Lab [1] initiative for the outdoor localization. Projects like Wigle.net maintain user contributed datasets containing the SSID, MAC and locations of the APs discovered through war driving. War driving is time consuming and it is desirable to look at alternatives to complement war driving efforts for efficient bootstrapping.

Authors of [16] characterize the error in location inference when localization is done using AP locations discovered from war driving. They, however, do not propose any alternative solutions to war driving and their evaluations are limited to a single campus network.

In [17], authors study accuracy and efficiency of wardriving process using three different methods: *on foot, on bicycle, in car.* Experiments show the position estimation's strong dependence on the particular means used for wardriving (e.g., wardriving on bicycle allows up to three times more APs to be discovered compared to wardriving in car).

Initial studies on the probability distribution of errors incurred by geocoding residential address using the TIGER/Line [7] data source appeared in [18]. The authors have also had access to the (non-public) E911 database through the Iowa county officials and have reported the median geocoding error to be 145ft. This result motivated us to evaluate geocoding for bootstrapping a location service, it can, however, not be directly compared to the accuracy results from previous wardriving studies, since these results are very dependent on the locale. Our work provided a direct comparison of wardriving and geocoding accuracies in the same areas. There are also other attempts to evaluate geocoding accuracy for various domains of study, like public-health [19] and transportation [20].

Also, [4] analyzed the Skyhook Wireless War Driving Database and has briefly illustrated the arterial bias involved in inferring the AP's location through war driving. Comprehensive wardriving on surrounding roads has been pointed out as a means to reduce this bias.

7   Conclusion

In this paper we have considered geocoding of postal addresses as an alternative method to populate a location service with WiFi access point positions. Specifically, we compared the accuracy of AP position estimations obtained through geocoding with that of wardriving. We found that in the considered areas, estimation accuracy through geocoding matched that of wardriving arterial roads. Accuracy through wardriving can be improved, however, by covering a larger fraction of the road network.

Based on these results we believe that geocoding postal address is a viable alternative to populate location services. Even partial postal address datasets might reduce wardriving effort in a hybrid approach involving both geocoding and wardriving. We hope that organizations in possession of large numbers of addresses (for installed AP locations) can use these insights to bootstrap WiFi localization services.

References

1. LaMarca, A., Chawathe, Y., Consolvo, S., Hightower, J., Smith, I., Scott, J., Sohn, T., Howard, J., Hughes, J., Potter, F., Tabert, J., Powledge, P., Botriello, G., Schilit, B.: Place lab: Device positioning using radio beacons in the wild. In: Proceedings of the third International Conference on Pervasive Compiting Pervasive, May 2005, pp. 116–133. Munich, Germany (2005)
2. Skyhook Wireless, http://www.skyhookwireless.com/
3. Wigle.net, http://www.wigle.net/
4. Jones, K., Liu, L.: What where wi: An analysis of millions of wi-fi access points. Tech. Rep., Georgia Institute of Technology, Atlanta, GA, USA (2007)
5. LaMarca, A., Hightower, J., Smith, I., Consolvo, S.: Self-mapping in 802.11 location systems. In: Beigl, M., Intille, S.S., Rekimoto, J., Tokuda, H. (eds.) UbiComp 2005. LNCS, vol. 3660, pp. 87–104. Springer, Heidelberg (2005)
6. Navteq, The Map Database provider for Yahoo/Google/MapQuest, http://www.navteq.com/
7. Tiger/Line - Topologically Integrated Geographic Encoding and Referencing - A digital map database developed at the U.S. Census Bureau, http://www.census.gov/geo/www/tiger/tigerua/uatgr2k.html
8. Google Inc., Google Earth Release 4.1 (2007), http://earth.google.com/
9. Network Stumbler, http://www.netstumbler.com
10. Kismet, http://www.kismetwireless.net/
11. Hightower, J., Borriello, G.: Particle filters for location estimation in ubiquitous computing: A case study. In: Davies, N., Mynatt, E.D., Siio, I. (eds.) UbiComp 2004. LNCS, vol. 3205, pp. 88–106. Springer, Heidelberg (2004)
12. Earth Stumbler, http://www.earthstumbler.net/
13. Kismet Earth, http://www.kismetearth.net/
14. Enhanced 911 - Wireless Services, (February 2006), http://www.fcc.gov/911/enhanced/
15. Bahl, P., Padmanabhan, V.N.: RADAR: An in-building user location and tracking system. In: Proceedings of IEEE Infocom, March 2000, vol. 2, pp. 775–784. IEEE Computer Society Press, Los Alamitos (2000)
16. Kim, M., Fielding, J.J., Kotz, D.: Risks of using AP locations discovered through war driving. In: Fishkin, K.P., Schiele, B., Nixon, P., Quigley, A. (eds.) PERVASIVE 2006. LNCS, vol. 3968, pp. 67–82. Springer, Heidelberg (2006)
17. Yoshida, H., Ito, S., Kawaguchi, N.: Evaluation of pre-acquisition methods for position estimation system using wireless LAN. In: Proceedings of the Third International Conference on Mobile Computing and Ubiquitous Networking (ICMU 2006), London, UK, October 2006, pp. 148–155 (2006)

18. Zimmerman, D., Fang, X., Mazumdar, S., Rushton, G.: Modeling the probability distribution of positional errors incurred by residential address geocoding. International Journal of Health Geographics 6(1) (2007)
19. Kravets, N., Hadden, W.C.: The accuracy of address coding and the effects of coding errors. Health and Place (Elsevier) 13(1), 293–298 (2007)
20. Indech-Nelson, J., Zuehlke, K.K., Guensler, R.: A comparison of geocoding methodologies for transportation planning applications. In: Proceedings of 11th TRB National Transportation Planning Applications (May 2007)

Deployment, Calibration, and Measurement Factors for Position Errors in 802.11-Based Indoor Positioning Systems

Thomas King, Thomas Haenselmann, and Wolfgang Effelsberg

Department for Mathematics and Computer Science
University of Mannheim Germany
{king,haenselmann,effelsberg}@informatik.uni-mannheim.de

Abstract. Indoor positioning systems based on 802.11 and fingerprints offer reasonably low position errors. We study the deployment, calibration, and measurement factors for position errors by systematically investigating (1) the number of access points, (2) the number of samples in the training phase, (3) the number of samples in the position determination phase, and (4) the setup of the grid of reference points. Further, we bring out the best of the positioning system by selecting advantageous values for these parameters. For our study, we utilize a test environment with a size of about 312 square meters that is covered with 612 reference points arranged in an equally spaced grid.

1 Introduction

During recent years, we have seen considerable improvements in down-sizing computer hardware and in increasing the capacity of rechargeable batteries, as well as the advent of wireless networks for the mass markets. These technologies allowed manufacturers to build mobile devices that have a similar performance as desktop computers had several years ago. The benefit of these mobile devices can be leveraged by so-called *location-based services*: Applications that act differently depending on the position of the user or, even better, pro-actively offer location-dependent information to the user. Location-based services are currently a hot topic in research, and are considered to be a promising market.

Nowadays, the *Global Positioning System* (GPS) [1] is the predominant outdoor positioning system. Though GPS works well in many outdoor scenarios, it suffers from obstacles such as skyscrapers creating shielded street canyons or walls and ceilings blocking the radio signals indoors. One of the most promising technologies that could be an equivalent to GPS for indoor applications are *802.11-based positioning systems* (e.g., [2] and [3]). Lately, 802.11 hardware is readily available and installed nearly everywhere where people live and work. Another important fact is that 802.11 can be used for communications as well as for positioning purposes at the same time [4]. Even better, almost all modern PDAs, smartphones and laptops are capable to communicate with the 802.11 infrastructure because they are shipped with built-in 802.11 hardware.

J. Hightower, B. Schiele, and T. Strang (Eds.): LoCA 2007, LNCS 4718, pp. 17–34, 2007.

The most promising 802.11-based positioning systems utilize the so-called *fingerprint* approach [2]. This technique comprises two stages: An offline training phase and an online position determination phase. During the offline phase, the signal strength distributions are collected from access points at pre-defined reference points in the operation area. They are stored in a table together with their physical coordinates. An entry in this dataset is called a fingerprint. During the position determination phase, mobile devices sample the signal strengths of access points in their communication range and search for similar patterns in the fingerprint data. The best match is selected, and its physical coordinates are returned as the position estimate.

Recent research has mainly focused on algorithms that compute the best match (e.g., [5], [6], and [7]). Although, the authors of these papers provide experimental results and compare their own work to existing approaches, they neglect an in-depth analysis of the impact of different factors for position errors. To our knowledge, this paper is the first to present a detailed analysis of the deployment, calibration, and measurement factors causing position errors. The questions we seek answers to are the following:

- How does the number of access points influence position errors?
- What is the impact of the number of training set samples on position errors?
- What is the impact of the number of online samples on position errors?
- How does the grid spacing and offset of the grid of reference points contribute to position errors?
- What is the lower bound of the average position error achievable with a 802.11-based positioning system if all parameters are set to the best possible values?

Answers of the above questions have implications on the planning, deployment and administration of 802.11-based positioning systems. Furthermore, our analysis will also be helpful for the research area of position determination algorithms.

We use our test environment on the entire floor of an office building on the campus of the University of Mannheim to carry out our study. Although we have worked with only one test environment, the consistency of parts of our results (e.g., number of samples) with results published by other researchers indicates that the conclusions we draw are indeed meaningful. Further, we selected the position determination algorithm proposed by Haeberlen et al. [7] because it shows the best performance. However, we also performed tests with other algorithms (e.g., [2] and [8]) and our spot checks indicate that the results are also applicable to these algorithms.

Our results are as follows:

- The number of access points is a primary factor which affects position errors.
- For the training phase, 20 samples at each reference point are sufficient.
- For the number of samples in the position determination phase, no single value can be determined. The trade-off here is about improved position errors and the time required to calculate a position fix. Thus, for a positioning

system running in tracking mode, a high frequency of position updates is required and hence we recommend three samples. Otherwise, we recommend the use 15 samples as 15 samples show a reasonable price-performance ratio.
- Although, a grid spacing of 0.5 meters leads to the best results, the amount of time required to collect the data for the training phase is hardly bearable if carried out by humans. Again, we have to trade position error against time. So, we recommend a grid spacing between 1.0 and 2.5 meters. An operator can select a grid spacing in this range depending on the amount of time he is willing to spend and the position accuracy he is expecting. To find a suitable offset for a given grid spacing we provide an algorithm.
- We observed a bottom line of 2.0 meters for the average position error, even if we select advantageous values for the parameters.

The rest of the paper is organized as follows. The next section (Sec. 2) presents the related work. In Sec. 3 we describe our experimental setup and methodology in-depth. Subsequently, Sec. 4 presents a detailed analysis of various values for particular parameters we have identified as factors for position errors. In Sec. 5, we discuss the implications that can be drawn from the results we observed. We conclude the paper in Sec. 6.

2   Related Work

In their preliminary work Bahl et al. proposed the first 802.11-based indoor positioning system [2]. In this paper, the authors provided a few experimental results and mainly focused on position determination algorithms. A few months later, Bahl et al. released a technical report [9] that offers additional experimental results and more position determination algorithms. Although the authors provide results from a second test environment they mainly focus on a tracking algorithm.

In contrast to the algorithms presented by Bahl et al., Castro and Muntz came up with the idea of using probabilistic algorithms [3]. In [8] and [7], two groups from Rice University have embraced this idea and proposed two probabilistic algorithms. The first algorithm requires a histogram of signal strength samples at each reference point resulting in huge piles of data. In their second approach, the histograms are replaced with Gaussian distributions to alleviate the burden of handling large amounts of data. Furthermore, the Gaussian approximation makes their system more accurate.

Moustafa and Agrawala show in a mathematical analysis that probabilistic approaches outperform deterministic position determination algorithms [10]. Further, Moustafa et al. propose different algorithms for the position determination and for the tracking of users ([11] and [5]).

King et al. [6] also use a probabilistic algorithm to determine the position of the user, however, they additionally utilize a digital compass to determine the orientation of the user. The orientation of the user is required because their research shows that depending on the orientation of the body radio signals are differently blocked.

One of the largest research projects in the area of positioning systems in the last few years is PlaceLab [12]. PlaceLab focuses not only on 802.11-based systems, instead it utilizes a wide range of already existing Beacons to compute a position estimate (e.g., Bluetooth, GSM). Furthermore, PlaceLab mainly investigate outdoor scenarios and not indoor environments.

Although all these papers mainly focus on the algorithms to determine the position of users and most of them provide experimental results, none of them systematically investigates the deployment, calibration, and measurement factors for position errors.

3   Experimental Setup and Measurement Methodology

In this section, we first briefly describe our experimental environment (Sec. 3.1). We then present the hardware and software setup (Sec. 3.2). Subsequently, we report how we collected the data used in the experiments. Finally, we describe the overall experimental methodology (Sec. 3.4).

3.1   Local Test Environment

We deployed the positioning system on the second floor of an office building on the campus of the University of Mannheim. The operation area is nearly 15 meters in width and 36 meters in length, covering an area of approximately 312 square meters. The floor plan of the operation area is shown in Fig. 1. The large hallway in the left part of the map is connected by two narrow hallways that are separated by rooms such as a copier room, an archive and a kitchen. The rooms depicted on both sides of the narrow hallways are mainly used as offices, and due to access restrictions they could not be included into the operation area.

3.2   Hardware and Software Setup

Initially, the test environment was covered by one Linksys / Cisco WRT54GS and two enterasys RBT-4102-EU access points administered by the computer center of our university. We additionally installed 11 access points: Two D-Link DWL-G700AP, three NETGEAR WG102, and six Linksys / Cisco WRT54G access points. All access points support 802.11b and 802.11g. Except of one enterasys access point, all access points are located on the same floor as our operation area. This particular enterasys access point is placed on a lower floor, however, it covers the operation area completely. The position of this access point is marked by an orange ring and the positions of the other access points are marked by orange circles (see Fig. 1).

As a client, we used a Lucent Orinoco Silver PCMCIA network card supporting 802.11b. This card was plugged into an IBM Thinkpad R51 running Linux kernel 2.6.13 and Wireless Tools 28pre. To collect signal strength samples, we implemented a framework that contains two parts: A library that cooperates with the network card driver to perform scans and capture internal driver information [13], and an easy-to-use application that stores these information in a

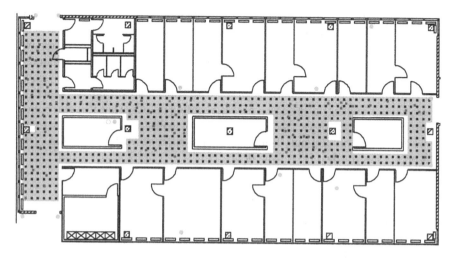

Fig. 1. Floor plan of the local test environment. The operation area is painted in gray. The blue markers represent the offline reference points and the purple markers show the randomly selected online points. The access points are marked by orange circles and an orange ring.

file together with additional data such as the physical position and a timestamp. Further, the application configures the library to select a scan frequency and scan technique for the signal strength measurements. For our experiments we used active scanning. Active scanning is defined in the 802.11 standard[1] and it is a technique to find a suitable gateway to the Internet by measuring the signal strength of access points within communication range.

From the driver our library collects the following information for each device that replies to an active scan:

- MAC address of the device
- received signal strength
- noise level
- mode of the device (i.e. access point or ad-hoc)
- frequency used for the communication

Although only the MAC address, mode and received signal strength values are required by 802.11-based positioning systems, we stored the additional information for further analysis and debugging purposes.

3.3   Data Collection

The grid of reference points applied to the operation area includes 612 points with a spacing of 0.5 meter (see the blue markers in Fig. 1). During the offline phase, we collected 110 signal strength samples at each reference point, resulting

---

[1] http://standards.ieee.org/getieee802/

in 72,600 samples in total. We spent over ten hours to collect all the data, however, we want to point out that for a productive deployment of a positioning system 20 signal strength samples and a grid with grid spacing of 1.5 meters will be sufficient (see Sect. 4), cutting down the expenditure of time to less than half an hour.

For the online phase, we randomly selected 83 coordinates. The only condition to select a point inside the operation area as a online point is that it is surrounded by four reference points of the grid. Again, we collected 110 signal strength samples for each online point, leading to 9,460 samples in total. In Fig. 1 the online points are marked by purple dots.

3.4 Experimental Methodology

Metrics and Parameter Space. For our experiments, we consider a two-dimensional operation area. We define *position error* as the Euclidian distance between the real physical position and the estimated position. Based on this definition, we consider two metrics during our experiments:

- average position error
- standard deviation of the position error

The former metric is also called accuracy, the latter is sometimes named precision. Both metrics are important because users need highly accurate and precise position estimates.

We have identified the parameter space for our measurements as follows:

- *Number of access points:* To study the impact of the number of access points, we vary the number of enabled access points between one and 14.
- *Number of training set samples:* The time required to collect the training set can be approximated by the number of reference points times the number of signal strength samples at each reference point. To lower the deployment burden of fingerprint-based positioning systems, time requirements should be minimized. For this, it is mandatory to know how many samples at each reference point are required during the training phase to produce stable position estimates. Therefore, we varied the number of signal strength samples from one to 110.
- *Number of online samples:* The number of online samples required to calculate a position estimate determines the time how often position updates are available to the user. Typically, a wireless network card requires at least 250 milliseconds to perform an active scan, so, the time between two position updates is a multiple of 250 milliseconds, depending on the number of samples used. For this, we also varied the number of online samples between one and 110.
- *Grid spacing:* As previously mentioned, the time required to collect the training set depends on the number of reference points. For a given operation area, the number of reference points depends on the grid spacing and the offset of the grid. If the grid spacing is doubled, the number of reference points is

approximately square rooted. The grid of reference points that covers our operation area has a grid spacing of 0.5 meters, allowing us to vary the grid spacing between 0.5 and 4.0 meters in 0.5 meter steps.

– *Offset of the reference grid:* As mentioned in the last item, the number of reference points also depends on the offset of the reference grid. Especially, in obstacle indoor areas, different offsets might lead to various ways the operation area is covered with reference points. To study the impact of the offset, we varied the offset for grids with a spacing larger than 0.5 meters.

Experiments. To investigate each parameter of the parameter space we use the data we have collected as described in Sect. 3.3. We developed a software-suite called Loceva [13] to switch off different values of particular parameters, so that we are able to quickly emulate various scenarios. This approach allows us to study scenarios that could otherwise hardly be investigated due to the enormous amount of time it would take to carry them out.

We define a *basic experiment* that is used as a basis for the subsequent studies. If a study of a particular parameter requires an extension of the basic experiment, the changes are described in the according section. The basic experiment is defined as follows:

– Nine access points are used.
– For each reference point, 20 offline samples are randomly selected out of the 110 samples.
– For the online phase, three samples are randomly chosen from the 110 samples for each coordinate.
– A grid spacing of 1.0 meter is applied.
– The offset of the grid is set 0.5 meters north (relative to the point of origin).

This basic experiment is repeated 1000 times to achieve statistically stable results. We now present the various experimental results.

4   Experimental Results

In this section, we first present the impact of the number of access points on position errors (Sec. 4.1). Subsequently, we discuss the influence of the number of samples in the training phase as well as in the position determination phase on position errors. In Sec. 4.4, we present the results of the experiments with various grid spacings and offsets. The best is brought out of the positioning system in the last subsection.

4.1   Number of Access Points

To investigate the effect of different numbers of access points on position errors, we extend the basic experiment by varying the number of access points between one and 14. For this, we randomly select the particular number of access points out of the 14 access point covering the operation area.

Figure 2(a) shows the average position error and its standard deviation with respect to the number of access points. As expected, the average position error decreases with an increasing number of access points. Furthermore, we see a marginal utility for each access point added. For instance, the position error drops from about 7.2 meters to about 4.8 meters if the number of access points is increased from one to two. This corresponds to a reduction of more than 2.4 meters or 33 percent. If the number of access points is further increased the reduction is about one meter (from 4.77 to 3.74 meters). If we make a large step and add the 10th access point we see that the average position error is reduced by about only nine centimeters (from 2.65 to 2.56 meters). Furthermore, not only the average position error decreases, but also does the standard deviation. For example, the standard deviation is about 4.6 meters when two access points are used; it is reduced by about 1.4 meters to 3.1 meters in case three access points are available. And again, the standard deviation shows an similar diminishing utility as seen by the average position error.

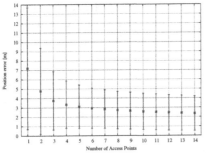

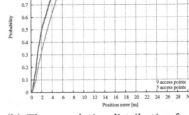

(a) The effect of the number of access points on position errors.

(b) The cumulative distribution function of position errors for 3 and 9 access points.

Fig. 2. The impact of the number of access points on position errors

From the literature we know that in areas of the developed world where people live and work it is common to see on the average three access points ([12] and [14]). So, with three access points, an average position error of about 3.7 meters is achievable. If we are trying to reduce the average position error by 33 percent (that corresponds to 1.2 meters), at least an additional six access points are required. Unfortunately, in the scenarios described in the literature, such a high number of access points is quite uncommon, however, in some environments such as multi-story buildings or universities, it is typical to see dozens of access points. Even better, access points are quite cheap nowadays, allowing a positioning system operator to deploy additional access points just for the matter of positioning accuracy.

To get a deeper understanding of what the position error distribution for the three and nine access points scenarios look like, we printed the cumulative distribution function in Fig. 2(b). From this figure we see that in 95 percent of all cases the position errors are smaller than 6.5 meters if nine access points are used. If only three access points are utilized, position errors are smaller than 8.7 meters in 95 percent of all cases. It is important to note that not only the average position error is of interest if we compare positioning systems. Important is also the length of the tail of the distribution. Thus, we see that the largest position error is about 12.85 meters for nine access points and 33.23 meters for three access points.

For the basic experiment we have chosen nine access points. Nine access points are more than what we usually encounter, however, we selected this number because we think operators may install extra access points for the sake of position accuracy. We selected the eight access points located in the hallways of both floors because this is the place where network operators usually install these devices. The ninth access point is the one installed in the large office in the south-west part of the map. However, the location of the access points is of minor importance because our results show that a particular selection of the nine out of the 14 access points influences position errors only slightly (about a few centimeters).

4.2   Training Set Size

In the training phase, an operator walks from reference point to reference point and collects signal strength samples. Therefore, two factors mainly determine the time required to collect the training data: The number of reference points and the number of offline samples taken at each reference point. The impact of the former on position errors is discussed below. The latter is the objective of this section.

Usually, active scanning is used to collect signal strength samples of access points within communication range. A typical wireless network interface requires 250 milliseconds to complete a scan. Thus, decreasing the number of samples required at each reference point directly reduces the time required to gather the training data.

To see how the training set size affects the positioning accuracy we conducted an experiment that extended the basic experiment by varying the number of offline samples. We start with one offline sample. Next we select five samples. Further, we increase the samples in steps of five up to 110.

As we see from Fig. 3(a), the average position error drops from 4.36 meters to 2.78 meters in case the number of offline samples is increased from one to five. Further, we see a constant decrease of the average position error if the number of offline sample is increased. However, at around 20 samples the marginal utility of adding five additional samples is less than one centimeter, or in other words the average position error only decreases by less than one centimeter if another five samples are added. Not only the average position error is saturated at around 20 samples, also the standard deviation decreases only slightly in case additional samples are collected. This being said, we see that taking more than 20 offline samples is not worth the effort. This is why, we selected 20 samples for the training set size of the basic experiment.

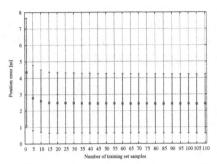
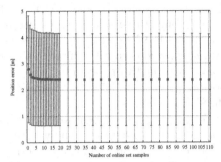

(a) Varying the number of samples in the training phase.

(b) Varying the number of online samples.

Fig. 3. Average and standard deviation of position errors depending on the number of online and offline samples, respectively

4.3   Online Set Size

In this section, we focus on the online phase and analyze the impact of the number of signal strength samples on position errors. This is interesting to know because the number of samples determines the time required to calculate a reliable position estimate. As mentioned in the previous section, a common 802.11 wireless network card takes 250 milliseconds to measure the signal strength of access points within communication range and hence the time to calculate a position fix is a multiple of 250 milliseconds.

The basic experiment is extended in such a way that we vary the number of online samples from one to 110 for this experiment. In the range between one and 20 we investigate every single step, whereas we use an increment of five in the range of 20 to 110.

Figure 3(b) depicts position errors with respect to the number of online samples. We present average and standard deviation because we want to see if an large number of online samples impacts these two measures. Unfortunately, the standard deviation is more or less unaffected by the number of samples. With one signal strength sample the standard deviation is about 2.03 meters and it drops to 1.82 meters if the signal strength is sampled four times. In the range of four to 110 samples, the standard deviation varies only between 1.82 and 1.73 meters.

We see a similar behavior with the average position error. With only one signal strength sample the average position error is about 2.79 meters, but it drops down to 2.49 meters if three signal strength samples are collected. If the number of signal strength samples is further increased the average drops only slightly and we see a diminishing marginal utility. For instance, with 20 samples an average position error of about 2.4 meters is achievable and with 110 samples the position error is on average 2.37 meters.

For the default online set value in the basic experiment, we have to make a trade-off. On one hand, we are interested in the best possible position estimate and on the other hand we want position updates as often as possible. Especially, if the positioning system is running in tracking mode, position updates should be offered quite frequently. For this, we select three samples as the default value because it trades time against position error in such a way that waiting another 250 milliseconds improves the average position error by only about two centimeters whereas the last scan improved the error by about nine centimeters.

4.4   Grid Setup

As stated in Sect. 4.2, one of the factors that determines how much time it takes to collect the training data is the number of reference points. In the literature, most authors utilize an equally spaced grid of reference points to cover the operation area. This makes the whole process quite easy and does not require any further operator interaction. An equally spaced grid is defined by a offset, the grid spacing, and the angle of the grid alignment. To simplify the scenario we assume that the grid is aligned in the same way as the building that comprises the operation area.

Although the grid spacing is a relevant factor, it is also important to pay attention to the offset of the grid. Especially, in indoor scenarios we usually face a lot of obstacles (e.g., cabinets, tables or locked rooms) that fragment a floor into subareas. Therefore, the offset of a grid may determine the size of the area a reference point is associated with. For instance, our test area contains three connected hallways. The small rooms (the copier room, the kitchen, and the archive) in the middle of the virtual large hallway chop it into two narrow hallways that are linked by spaces between the rooms. So, if we overlay such fragmented areas with a grid that utilizes a given grid spacing, it may occur that different numbers of reference points can be deployed depending on the offset of the grid. Figure 4 illustrates an example of two grids with a grid spacing of 2.0 meters using different offsets. The grid in Fig. 4(a) covers the operation area with 51 reference points, whereas the grid in Fig. 4(b) comprises only 19 reference points. The offsets for these grids are shifted 0.5 meters north, 1.0 meters east and 1.5 meters north, 0.5 meters east, respectively.

An investigation of the impact of the offset and the grid spacing on position errors is the subject of this section.

Offset. We define the point of origin by selecting the bottom left reference point of the 0.5 meter spaced grid (see Fig. 1). Based on this point of origin and the 0.5 meters spaced grid of 612 reference points we derive grids with different offsets and grid spacings between 1.0 and 4.0 meters. For instance, four different 1.0 meter spaced grids can be created by selecting only every other reference point and by moving the offset 0.5 meters north, east or both.

In the following we selected a grid spacing of 2.0 meters because this scenario can easily be described and shows a tendency that is valid for all other grid spacings as well. With such a grid spacing, 16 offsets can be selected. Depending on the offset, different numbers of reference points can be applied to the operation area. Table 1 lists the various offsets and the corresponding number of reference points.

From the table we see that the number of reference points varies between 19 and 51, or in other words, depending on the offsets of the grid up to 37 percent

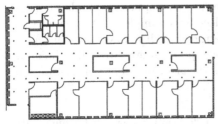 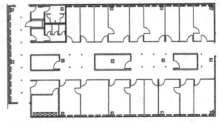

(a) This grid contains 51 reference points. The offset is moved 0.5 meters north and 1.0 meters east compared to the point of origin.

(b) This grid contains 19 reference points. The offset is moved 1.5 meters north and 0.5 meters east compared to the point of origin.

Fig. 4. Two grids of reference points with a grid spacing of 2.0 meters but different offsets

Table 1. This table shows the number of reference points for different offsets of 2.0 meter spaced grids. The first value of the offset column represents the north offset, the second value the east offset.

Offset	# reference points	Offset	# reference points
0.0, 0.0	41	1.0, 0.0	34
0.0, 0.5	26	1.0, 0.5	21
0.0, 1.0	50	1.0, 1.0	43
0.0, 1.5	47	1.0, 1.5	42
0.5, 0.0	44	1.5, 0.0	33
0.5, 0.5	30	1.5, 0.5	19
0.5, 1.0	51	1.5, 1.0	42
0.5, 1.5	48	1.5, 1.5	41

of the maximum number of reference points are available. Examples for these extremes are depicted in Fig. 4(a) and Fig. 4(b), respectively.

Although a small number of reference points means that the time required for the data collection phase can be reduced, we expect position errors to increase because each reference point is responsible for a larger region of the operation area. In the following, we investigate this question. For this, we extend the basic experiment by selecting a grid spacing of 2.0 meters and select offsets as listed in Table 1. Figure 5 shows the average position error grouped by the number of reference points. The average position error is between 2.71 and 3.23 meters. 2.71 meters are achieved in case of 50 reference points and 3.23 meters in case of 43 reference points. Furthermore, from the graph we see that the average position error slightly improves if the number of reference point is increases. This tendency is not strictly consistent. For instance, the case of 43 reference points is an outlier.

If we look at different grids of reference points and how they fit into the operation area we see that for some grids there are large areas that are not covered

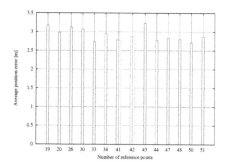

Fig. 5. Average position error vs. number of reference points

by any reference point. Other grids cover the operation area more "smoothly". For instance, in Fig. 4(b) we see that the two horizontal hallways are not covered at all by any reference points whereas in Fig. 4(a) the operation area is more evenly covered. If we further relate the average position error to the smoothness of arrangement of reference points it follows that smoother grids achieve better position errors. For example, the smooth grid of Fig. 4(a) achieves an average position error of 2.87 meters in contrast to the rough grid of Fig. 4(b) that achieves on 3.17 meters on the average.

It is relatively easy for a human to decide which scenario shows the smoother arrangement of reference points if two scenarios are given. To let the computer take the same decision, we conceived the following algorithm: Randomly select 312 points inside the operation area and add up, for each of these points, the distance to its closest reference point. The scenario with the smaller result is the one with the smoother grid arrangement. We selected 312 points for our 312 square meter operation area. We achieved great results by sticking to the one point for one square meter rule during our tests.

This algorithm can be used to determine which offset leads to the smoothest grid and therefore to a small average position error. We verified the practicability of this approach by letting the algorithm select the offset of the smoothest grid and then we compare the average position error of this grid with the other grids. For all grid spacings between 1.0 and 4.0 meters, the algorithm selected a offset that leads to a grid that achieved at least the third best average position error.

In many real-world deployments there will be no pre-defined offsets to choose from (as in our case). The operator can manually select a few possible offsets and use the approach described above to find the best suitable offset for the operation area in question.

Grid Spacing. In this section, we focus on the grid spacing and how it impacts the precision and accuracy of the positioning system. For this, we vary the grid spacing of the basic experiment from 0.5 meters stepwise by 0.5 meters until a spacing of 4.0 meters is reached. For all grid spacings larger than 0.5 meters we applied the technique described in the previous section to select a suitable offset.

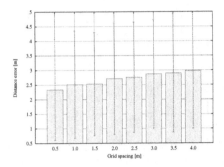

Fig. 6. Average and standard deviation of position errors w.r.t grid spacing

From Fig. 6 we see that with a grid spacing of 0.5 meters an average position error of 2.33 meters and a standard deviation of 1.73 meters is achievable. In case a grid spacing of 4.0 meters is applied the average position error goes up to 2.97 meters and the standard deviation increases slightly to 1.98 meters. Each time the grid spacing is increased by 0.5 meters the average position error increases between 3 and 11 centimeters. This is interesting to notice because if we assume a perfect positioning system that always finds the closest reference point then the average position error should increase 19 centimeters each time the grid spacing is increased by 0.5 meters[2]. We call this error the *inherent position error*. Real-world positioning systems are usually not perfect and this is why a second kind of error adds to the position error: the error caused by selecting a reference point that is not closest to the user's real position. This second part is dubbed the *real position error*. Coming back to the observed position errors, it follows that the real position error decreases if the grid spacing is increased. Or in other words, the positioning system is getting better in finding the closest reference point if the grid spacing is increased.

Figure 7 shows the average signal strength at each reference point for one access point. We selected grid spacings of 0.5 and 2.0 meters to exemplify why it is getting easier for the positioning algorithm to find a closer reference point if the grid spacing is increased. From the figures we see that the number of at least two reference points that share the same average signal strength is decreasing if the grid spacing is increased. If we count only the reference points that do not share their signal strength value with other reference points, we see that in our sparse example nine such reference points can be found. This corresponds to 18 percent of all reference points. In contrast, the example with the 0.5 meter spaced grid contains only five such reference points or 0.008 percent of all reference points.

As already mentioned, the number of reference points is one factor that mainly determines the time require to collect the data in the offline phase. From the previous section we know that the exact number of reference points depends on the shape of the operation area as well as on the inside the operation area.

---

[2] Let x and y be random variables $\in [0, \ldots, a = \frac{gridspacing}{2}]$ then the average positioning error can be determined by: $E(\sqrt{x^2 + y^2}) = \frac{1}{a^2} \int_0^a \int_0^a \sqrt{x^2 + y^2} \, \mathrm{d}x \, \mathrm{d}y$.

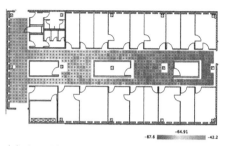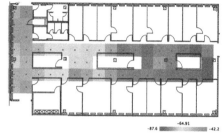

(a) A grid spacing of 0.5 meters is used in this scenario.   (b) In this scenario a grid spacing of 2.0 meters is applied.

Fig. 7. Two maps with different grid spacings show the average signal strength at each reference point for one access point. The position of the access point is marked by an orange circle.

However, for an operator it might be interesting to get a rough estimate of the number of reference points that might cover the operation area. Especially in large deployments this information is helpful to assess the time requirements for the training phase. To simplify the calculation we assume that the operation area is rectangular and we omit obstacles that should not be covered by reference points. These assumptions are valid because a rectangle can be drawn around every shape an operation area might have and omitting obstacles does not increase the actual number of reference points. Instead, the actual number of reference points would be smaller and so our approach yields to a upper bound. Let l be the length of the rectangle approximating the operation area and w its width. Furthermore, let d be the selected grid spacing of the equally spaced grid of reference points. Then the maximum number of reference points m that cover this area can be calculated as:

$$m = (\frac{l}{d} + 1) * (\frac{w}{d} + 1)$$

For instance, if we approximate our operation area of 312 square meters by a rectangle of 36 times 9 meters and select a 2.0 meter spaced grid the area can be covered with at most 105 reference points. From Table 1 we know that in practice the maximum number is 51. The difference here is caused by obstacles and a non-rectangular operation area.

For the basic experiment we selected a grid spacing of 1.0 meter because this is the size used by other researchers in the literature (e.g., [6] and [9]). For the offset, we used our aforementioned algorithm to find the smoothest grid resulting in a offset moved 0.5 meters north compared to the point of origin.

4.5   Best Case Scenario

In this section, we bring the best out of the positioning system. For a few application areas, it sounds quite feasible to deploy a few extra access points and to spend a few more minutes for the collection of the training data, especially

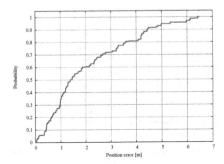

Fig. 8. Cumulative distribution function for the best case scenario

if in return the accuracy and precision of the positioning system increases. To exploit the potential of 802.11-based positioning systems, we selected all the parameters that produced the best results in the previous sections: 110 samples for the offline set, 110 samples for the online set, a grid spacing of 0.5 meters, all 14 access points.

As expected, the average position error as well as the standard deviation achieve the best results presented so far: 2.06 meters on the average with a standard deviation of 1.65 meters. Compared to best results presented in the previous sections the average position error drops by about 27 centimeters, corresponding to an improvement of 14 percent (see Sec. 4.4). The standard deviation improves by about five percent, from 1.73 to 1.65 centimeter.

In Fig. 8 we present the cumulative distribution function of this experiment because we are interested in the 95th percentile and in the long tail of the distribution. As you see, we achieve position errors of less than 5 meters in 95 percent of all cases. Furthermore, the maximum position error is less than 6.5 meters. Compared to the results presented in the previous sections, we see that with this experiment, the long tail of the position error distribution can be reduced by more than 5.5 meters (see Sec. 4.1). This is an interesting and important result which makes 802.11-based positioning systems more robust.

5   Discussion

After we have presented the key factors for position errors in the previous sections, we want to discuss the interesting and surprising implications that are caused by this results. First, we are going to stress the importance of the number of access points for 802.11-based positioning systems. Second, we will discuss the bottom line of the average position error we have observed.

Our results in Sec. 4.1 already show the importance of the number of access points. We want to emphasize their importance here again. Although the other parameters of the parameter space are also important factors to influence position errors, they all come with the drawback that decreasing position errors by using these parameters increases the amount of time required to get the system to work considerably. Instead, adding an extra access point to the operation area requires only a fixed amount of time for the installation. During the training phase as well as during the position determination phase, an additional access point does not influence the time requirements in any way. Increasing the number of access points leads to a decrease of the average position error and its standard deviation or in other words makes the position system more accurate and robust. These two facts make extra access points highly appealing for performance improvements of 802.11-based positioning systems.

In all of our experiments we have seen a "hidden" bottom line for the average position error of 2.0 meters. Even if we select the most advantageous values for the parameters of the positioning system, we are not able to under-run the lower bound of 2.0 meters. This is consistent with the results published by other researchers (e.g., [2], [9], and [5]). From this, we draw the conclusion that an average position error of 2.0 meters is the lower bound for 802.11-based positioning systems.

To further improve position errors of 802.11-based positioning systems researchers came up with the idea of sensor-fusion [12]. This means that additional sensors such as Bluetooth or a digital compasses are used in combination with 802.11. First publications proof that the average position error can be reduced to 1.65 meters in case a digital compass is used [6]. However, this approach lessens the advantage that every 802.11-enabled device can be used for positioning purposes out of the box.

6   Conclusion

In this paper, we have presented a measurement study of deployment, calibration, and measurement factors for position errors in 802.11-based positioning systems. Our results show that for the training phase 20 samples at each reference point are enough. For the position determination phase at least three samples should be selected to achieve reasonable position errors. If the positioning system is not used to track users, better results are achievable with 15 samples. How the grid of reference points should look like cannot be definitely said because there is a trade-off between position errors and time. Therefore, we recommend a grid spacing between 1.0 and 2.5 meters depending on the time the operator is willing to spend to gather data for the training phase. To find a suitable offset for the reference grid, we have presented an algorithm. The number of access points is a great means to improve position errors for many reasons. Access points are cheaply available nowadays and can be easily installed. Further, the number of access points does not influence the time requirements of the training and position determination phase.

All our experiments as well as the results presented by other researchers show that on average position errors of less than 2.0 meters is not achievable. Thus, we draw the conclusion that there is a "hidden" bottom line of 2.0 meters for the average position error that cannot be under-run.

Acknowledgments

We would like to thank Alexander Biskop and Andreas Färber for their help collecting data for the experiments. Furthermore, the authors acknowledge the financial support granted by the *Deutsche Forschungsgemeinschaft* (DFG).

Availability

The research tools Loclib and Loceva are described in [13]. The tools as well as our trace data will be available under the terms of the GPL on our website [15].

References

1. Kaplan, E., Hegarty, C. (eds.): Understanding GPS: Principles and Applications, 2nd edn. Artech House Incorporated (2005)
2. Bahl, P., Padmanabhan, V.N.: RADAR: An In-Building RF-Based User Location and Tracking System. In: Proc. IEEE InfoCom, pp. 775–784 (2000)
3. Castro, P., Muntz, R.: Managing Context Data for Smart Spaces. IEEE Personal Communications, 44–46 (2000)
4. King, T., Haenselmann, T., Kopf, S., Effelsberg, W.: Overhearing the Wireless Interface for 802.11-based Positioning Systems. In: Proc. IEEE PerCom, pp. 145–150 (2007)
5. Youssef, M., Agrawala, A.: The Horus WLAN Location Determination System. In: Proc. ACM MobiSys, pp. 205–218 (2005)
6. King, T., Kopf, S., Haenselmann, T., Lubberger, C., Effelsberg, W.: COMPASS: A Probabilistic Indoor Positioning System Based on 802.11 and Digital Compasses. In: Proc. ACM WiNTECH, pp. 34–40 (2006)
7. Haeberlen, A., Flannery, E., Ladd, A.M., Rudys, A., Wallach, D.S., Kavraki, L.E: Practical Robust Localization over Large-Scale 802.11 Wireless Networks. In: Proc. ACM MobiCom, pp. 70–84 (2004)
8. Ladd, A.M., Bekris, K.E., Rudys, A., Marceau, G., Kavraki, L.E., Wallach, D.S: Robotics-Based Location Sensing using Wireless Ethernet. In: Proc. ACM Mobi-Com, pp. 227–238 (2002)
9. Bahl, P., Padmanabhan, V.N.: Enhancements of the RADAR User Location and Tracking System. Technical Report MSR-TR-2000-12, Microsoft Research, Microsoft Corporation One Microsoft Way Redmond, WA 98052 (2000)
10. Youssef, M., Agrawala, A.: On the Optimality of WLAN Location Determination Systems. In: Proc. CNDS (2004)
11. Youssef, M., Agrawala, A., Shankar, A.U: WLAN Location Determination via Clustering and Probability Distributions. In: Proc. IEEE PerCom, pp. 143–150 (2003)
12. LaMarca, A., Chawathe, Y., Consolvo, S., Hightower, J., Smith, I., Scott, J., Sohn, T., Howard, J., Hughes, J., Potter, F., Tabert, J., Powledge, P., Borriello, G., Schilit, B.: Place Lab: Device Positioning Using Radio Beacons in the Wild. In: Proc. IEEE PerCom, pp. 116–133 (2005)
13. King, T., Lemelson, H., Haenselmann, T., Effelsberg, W.: Loc{lib,trace,eva,ana}: Research Tools for 802.11-based Positioning Systems. In: Proc. ACM WiNTECH (2007)
14. Bychkovsky, V., Hull, B., Miu, A., Balakrishnan, H., Madden, S.: A Measurement Study of Vehicular Internet Access Using In Situ Wi-Fi Networks. In: Proc. ACM MobiCom, pp. 50–61 (2006)
15. King, T., Kopf, S.: Loclib - A Location Library. Website (January 2007), http://www.informatik.uni-mannheim.de/pi4/projects/loclib/

LifeTag: WiFi-Based Continuous Location Logging for Life Pattern Analysis

Jun Rekimoto[1,2], Takashi Miyaki[3], and Takaaki Ishizawa[4]

[1] Interfaculty Initiatives in Information Studies, The University of Tokyo
7-3-1 Hongo, Bunkyo-ku, Tokyo 113-0033, Japan
[2] Interaction Laboratory, Sony Computer Science Laboratories, Inc.
3-14-13 Higashigotanda, Shinagawa-ku, Tokyo 141-0022, Japan
[3] Graduate School of Frontier Sciences, The University of Tokyo
7-3-1 Hongo, Bunkyo-ku, Tokyo 113-0033, Japan
[4] Keio University Graduate School of Media and Governance
5322 Endo, Fujisawa-shi, Kanagawa 252-8520, Japan

Abstract. Continuous logging of a person's geographical position is required for various "life-log" applications, such as memory aids, automatic blog generation, and life pattern analysis. GPS is one way of logging, but it is unable to track movements indoors, and hence cannot track peoplefs ordinary activities. We propose a WiFi-based location detection technology for location logging. It detects a device's location from received WiFi beacon signals. It works indoors and outdoors, and its estimated accuracy is often comparable to that of GPS. We built WiFi-based location logging systems based on a smart phone and a keychain-like device using custom hardware. These prototypes record WiFi information every few minutes, and this information is converted into actual location logs. We describe some life patterns created by analyzing these location logs. We also discuss various application examples and ideas for when continuous location logging becomes commonplace.

1 Introduction

"Life-logging" or "reality mining" is a technology that records personal activities by using various sensing devices [6,1,5]. Such archived information can be used for supporting people's memories, organizing information, and helping communications.

Of the various data types for life logging, one of the simplest and most usable is location data. If a person had a perfect record of time-stamped location logs, it would become possible to assign a location to any time-stamped data, such as pictures or voice notes. A location log can also represent personal preferences (e.g., frequently visited places), and activity patterns [4] (e.g., commuting from home to the office, working, and holidays). By accumulating the logs of many users, it would also become possible to detect communication patterns in a community.

The realization of location logging requires a technology that can precisely and continuously record person's locations without too much effort from users. GPS (global positioning satellite) can track location, and there are already commercial GPS loggers, such as SONY GPS-CS1, and life-log projects using GPS [2]. However, we consider

J. Hightower, B. Schiele, and T. Strang (Eds.): LoCA 2007, LNCS 4718, pp. 35–49, 2007.

that GPS is not adequate (or, at least not enough) for continuous location life-logging for the following reasons:

- People's activities, especially in urban environments, are mostly indoors, and GPS works very poorly (or does not work at all) in indoor environments. Even outdoors, GPS's accuracy becomes worse in urban areas with limited sky views and building signal reflections.
- GPS sensing requires a certain amount of time to starts from a "cold-start" mode. To periodically record a person's location (e.g., every 5 minutes), the GPS device must always be "on" in order to track the GPS satellites. This feature consumes a lot of battery power and thus makes it difficult to construct a long-life logging device.
- For life-logging purposes, it is often not enough to record the latitude and longitude when a person is in a building. More precise information in a building, such as "floor" and "room" level information would often be required. Although GPS can detect height information, its accuracy is not enough to distinguish individual floors.

For these reasons, location logging using GPS is not always effective. In fact, the GPS-logger devices on a market are mainly designed for outdoor activities such as mountain climbing.

Instead of GPS-based solutions, we propose a WiFi-based location logging system called "LifeTag". LifeTag uses a WiFi access point location database to detect its location [3,8,7,9]. Unlike other WiFi-based positioning systems, LifeTag simply records the nearby access points' signal strength with access point IDs. Later, this recorded information is converted into actual location information by referring to the access point location database. This feature greatly simplifies the location-logging device's hardware, and makes it possible to develop a logging device as small as a keychain.

This paper presents the LifeTag device and its applications. First, we briefly introduce our WiFi-based location platform called PlaceEngine. Then we explain how the LifeTag device works and how recorded logs can be used for various applications.

2 PlaceEngine: Location Estimation Using WiFi Signal Strength

We developed a WiFi-based location platform service called "PlaceEngine" [9]. This is a web service[1] that estimates a userfs location and sends him or her location information after receiving a query consisting of WiFi signal information (or WiFi "fingerprints") including MAC addresses and the received signal strengths (RSSI) of nearby access points.

For this service, we also constructed an access point database that covers major cities in Japan. This database stores more than half a million access points and their estimated locations. Access point locations are estimated by combining various methods, including:

- *War Driving:* Driving a car throughout the city, collecting WiFi signal fingerprints and also recording GPS information as reference location information.

---

[1] www.placeengine.com

- *Warwalking:* WiFi signal fingerprint collecting by walkers who spot locations indicated on maps.
- *End User Register:* End users of this system explicitly register locations by using a map interface.
- *Access Log Analysis:* Analyzing end users query logs.

Figure 1 shows the results of access point database estimation around the Tokyo metropolitan area. As shown in this map, almost all of the downtown area is covered by WiFi access points. Figure 2 shows a typical location-aware application using PlaceEngine.

Fig. 1. WiFi access point locations estimation (Tokyo metropolitan area). It contains information on over half a million access points.

Position estimation using WiFi works both indoors and outdoors. Figure 3 compares the estimation results of GPS (Sony's VGP-BGU1 GPS device) and WiFi (PlaceEngine) location logs. The accuracy of GPS estimation is affected by surrounding environments, such as building shadows or roofs. GPS accuracy is greatly reduced in indoor environments, whereas WiFi location estimation is not affected in building shadows and indoors.

PlaceEngine also provides a unique feature that estimates floor or room information. The idea is similar to social tagging. Each end user can attach symbolic tag names, such as "2F" or "meeting room A" to a particular location. The attached name information is stored with WiFi signal fingerprints in the database. Later, when a user asks

Fig. 2. Example of position sensing application using PlaceEngine WiFi location platform

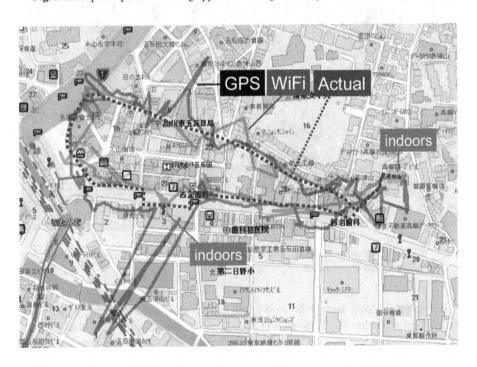

Fig. 3. Example of WiFi location estimation and comparison with GPS

for a location, the PlaceEngine service compares the current WiFi signal fingerprint and stored fingerprints in the database, and also conducts tag "voting" to determine which symbolic name is most appropriate for the current WiFi situation. When the first choice

Fig. 4. Example of indoor position estimation

of voting is significantly stronger than the second choice, the system replies with the symbolic floor or room name as well as with the estimated geographical location (i.e., latitude and longitude) and address.

3   LifeTag Location Logging System

We developed a personal location-logging system called "LifeTag" that is based on the PlaceEngine location platform. The user of this system carries a small WiFi sensing device that periodically records surrounding WiFi fingerprint information (WiFi access point IDs and received signal strength). Later, this recorded information is converted into actual location logs by accessing the PlaceEngine's WiFi location database. We think this approach is suitable for location life-logging, especially in urban areas, because:

- It works both indoors and outdoors. It is also possible to detect the floor number of a building by analyzing WiFi signal information.
- The device only has to sense and record WiFi fingerprint information so it can be made simple and small. In particular, the logging phase does not require any network communication or access to a large database. Recorded information turns into actual locations (longitude, latitude, etc.) when the device connects to a network.
- WiFi signal recording is quick. The device simply receives and records WiFi beacon packet information for a short period (typically less than one second). Unlike GPS, there is no "cold-start" phase to find the satellites. This is a useful power saving feature, because the device can normally be in a sleep mode and only has to wakeup periodically for signal logging.
- WiFi access points are already very densely deployed in many urban areas (Figure 1). Thus, WiFi signals can almost always be detected in cities in order to track onefs location.

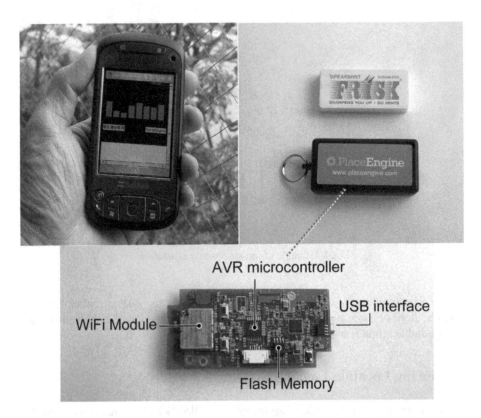

Fig. 5. LifeTag: two hardware configurations (left: smart phone version, right: keychain version with custom logging hardware)

- While WiFi-location technology such as the PlaceEngine mainly focus on a WiFi access point managed by anonymous owners, careful calibrations with exact access point location information can give even better estimation accuracy (Figure 4). Since infrastructure often exists in offices or campus environments, location log for people in such areas will be extremely accurate.

Based on the above design principles, we prototyped location logging devices with two hardware configurations. The first prototype uses an existing smart mobile phone with WiFi capability (Figure 5-left). The logging function is implemented as a software module. During the logging phase, this device is normally in a sleep mode. The software module periodically (typically in every 3 minutes) wakes up the device and records nearby WiFi access point signal information. The entire logging phase takes 3 seconds and the device goes back into sleep mode after the signal information is recorded. Battery power consumption is greatly reduced because of this intermittent feature. As a result, the device runs for 4 to 5 days without recharging.

Figure 5-right shows the LifeTag keychain prototype built with our custom hardware. It consists of a WiFi module, flash memory, a real time clock, USB interface, and an AVR 8bit microcontroller. The device is significantly smaller than the smart phone

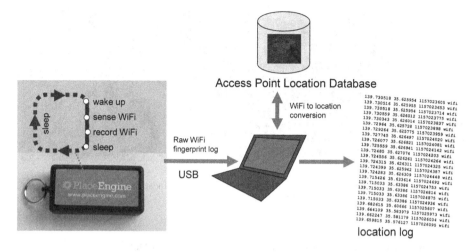

Fig. 6. LifeTag operation cycle: logged WiFi fingerprint data is translated into actual location logs by referring to the WiFi access point location database

version, and it intended to be used as an object like a keychain (Figure 7, left). People simply carry this device in their pocket, and the device automatically records WiFi signal fingerprints.

The logged data of both prototypes is a list of timestamped WiFi signal fingerprints and is not itself a location log. This data is later translated into actual location information by referencing the PlaceEngine WiFi access point database. Figure 6 shows the overall architecture of the LifeTag system and sample location logs.

3.1 Location Bookmaking

The LifeTag keychain has an additional feature besides logging: a button to explicitly "bookmark" the place (Figure 7). The user presses the button when he/she would like to bookmark the current location, and the LifeTag wakes up and records the WiFi signal information. Later, this information can be used as a part of location history charted with special bookmark tags.

4   Location Logging Applications

The method and devices described in the previous section enable anyone to record very dense and continuous location logs. As an initial experiment, we asked three volunteer users (including one of the authors of this paper) to carry devices and record location logs for about four months. The log interval varies from 1 minute to 5 minutes. The total number of location records was 271,000 (90,269 per person).[2]

This section explains various application possibilities of personal location logs.

---

[2] The location bookmarking feature described in the previous section was not completely implemented during the trial phase. Thus, the discussion in this section focuses on automatic and implicit location logging.

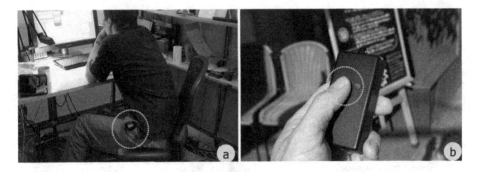

Fig. 7. Using LifeTag on a daily basis: (a) continuously logging locations in indoor and outdoor environments. (b) manually bookmarking a place of interest.

4.1 Assigning Location Tags to Time-Stamped Data and Day Playback

Figure 8 shows two typical applications using location log data. Figure 8 (left) is a photo sharing service (Flickr) with automatically assigned location tags (called "geotags") to pictures. Pictures are taken with a digital camera, and a software module automatically matches the picturefs timestamp and location log's time stamp and assigns a geotag to each picture. After that, pictures can be organized by location with a Flickr map services based on geotags. Although the camera itself has no location sensors, such as GPS, all the pictures can be given location tags.

Figure 8 (right) is a "day playback" application. This application takes location log data and plays it back by moving a map according to the log's locations. This application also automatically shows pictures according to location by analyzing timestamps and geotags assigned to the pictures. This combination of map animation and pictures helps users to recall past activities.

4.2 Activity Pattern Visualizations

In addition, by analyzing the location information, a person's activity patterns and preferred places in the city can be ascertained. We generated map visualizations based on such location history patterns.

Figure 9 is a "heatmap" that represents a person's probability density. In this map, frequently visited places, such as the office, become brighter than other areas. This map is a fingerprnt (life pattern) of the person's overall activity.

More precisely, Figure 10 shows the result of location log clustering. We used the k-means clustering algorithm and detected the clusters it gave. The two topmost clusters are marked "A" and "B", and they represent this person's home and office.

4.3 Life Pattern Arithmetic: Comparison of Two Location Logs

By analyzing the location logs of two persons, it is possible to find a "common place" for them. Figure 11 shows the result of performing an "and" operation on the location logs of two persons. The right map in Figure 11 represents places where both user A

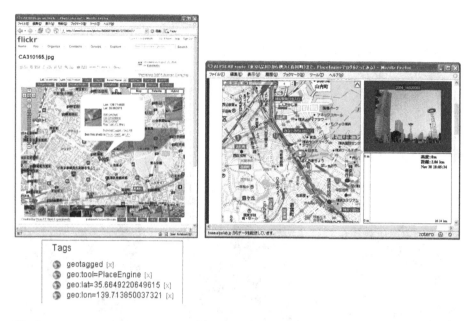

Fig. 8. Two applications using location logs: (left) A Flickr photo browser enhanced by location tags. (right) Route "playback" software to review activities of recent days.

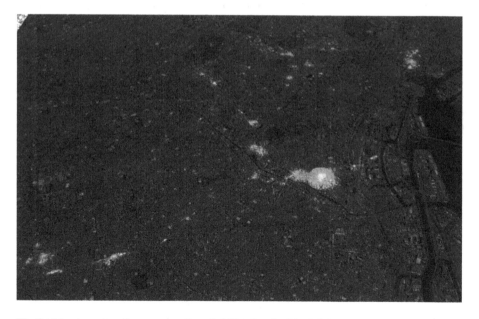

Fig. 9. A heatmap based on a person's probability density. The brightest spot is the user's office, and other frequently visited places are bright spots.

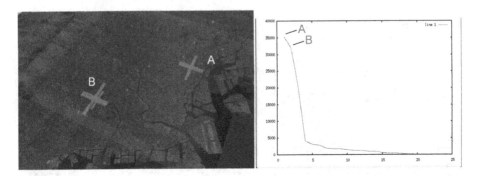

Fig. 10. Location activity log clustering result: Two major clusters (A and B) are detected using k-means clustering. Note that the number of cluster elements follows a power law distribution.

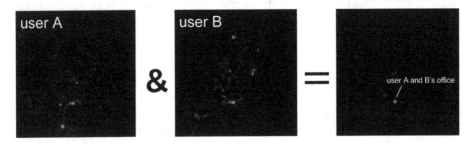

Fig. 11. Example of life pattern arithmetic operations: logs of two different users (A and B) are shown. By applying the "and" operation upon these logs, common areas can be extracted.

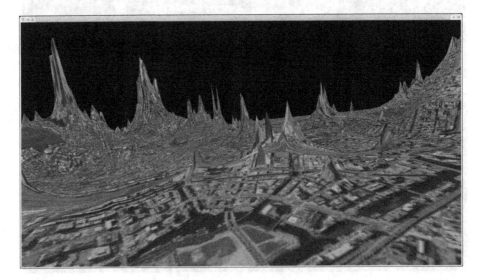

Fig. 12. Tokyo city landscape based on a person's location history. The z-axis is not height, but reflects the probability density of person's location. Frequently visited areas become hills or mountains.

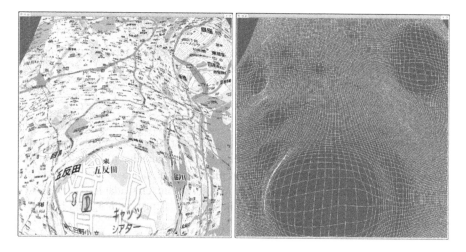

Fig. 13. A person's "cognitive" map based on his or her location history. Areas are distorted to reflect the person's location probability density. Frequently visited areas become larger on the map.

and user B exist at (almost) the same time. Since these two users work in the same office building, there is one brightest spot (marked as "user A and B's office" in this map), while other smaller areas are also detected.

4.4 Personalized Geographical Visualization Based on Activity Patterns

Figure 12 is a city map deformed with a person's location history. The map's height (z-axis) reflects the person's probability density (how likely it is that this person is at this position in the city). If this person visits a particular place more frequently, that place is given a higher altitude. The resulting landscape may differ from person to person, and it reflecte each person's activity pattern. Figure 13 also shows the location history by using a multiple fisheye deformation technique. In this case, the areafs size reflects the person's location probability density. If we assume that the importance of a place can be determined from a person's location density, such a visualization will resemble a "cognitive map" that people may have in their minds.

These views are our initial attempts on how a city view can be changed according to individual life patterns. As expected, these city views differ from person to person, and it can be said they are visualizations of the lives of the persons in question. City views also reflect a person's life status (daytime-map and night-map, or weekday-map and holiday-map are also quite different from each other).

5 Browsing Support for Location Logs

The previous section shows various visualization examples of location logs. These visualizations are useful for getting overall impressions of activity patterns. On the other hand, browsing and searching of the location history is also useful for recalling activities on a particular day.

Since the raw location log is merely a list of (timestamped) latitude and longitude values, it is not understandable without some system support.

5.1 Activity Lists by Reverse Geocoding

Figure 14-a shows a simple location history using street addresses. Addresses are obtained from a reverse-geocoding database (a database that converts latitude and longitude values into street addresses). This is more readable than a list of latitudes and longitudes, and by applying simple substitution rules, such as (Higashigotanda 3 chome, Shinagawaku to "Office"), the list can be made more understandable (Figure 14-b). These text logs can be automatically generated and used for searching and browsing. They are also useful for writing blogs.

```
00:00-12:25 Home
12:30    Kosugi Nakahara-ku Kawasaki-shi
12:35    Higashitamagawa Setagaya-ku Tokyo
12:45    Shimomeguro Meguro-ku Tokyo
12:50-13:25 Kami-Oosaki Shinagawa-ku Tokyo
13:30-15:15 Higashigotanda Shinagawa-ku Tokyo
15:30    Kamioosaki Shinagawa-ku Tokyo
15:35    Ebisu-nishi Shibuya-ku Tokyo
15:40    Jinguumae Shibuya-ku Tokyo
15:45    Tomigaya Shibuya-ku Tokyo
15:50-16:45 Tomigaya Shibuya-ku Tokyo
17:35-19:50 Higashigotanda Shinagawa-ku Tokyo
19:50-20:10 Higashigotanda Shinagawa-ku Tokyo
20:15    Kamioosaki Shinagawa-ku Tokyo
20:20    Kamioosaki Shinagawa-ku Tokyo
20:30    Okusawa Setagaya-ku Tokyo
20:35    Shinmaruko Nakahara-ku Kawasaki-shi
20:40    Hiyoshi Kohoku-ku Yokohama
20:45-23:55 Home                        (a)
```

```
00:00-12:25 at home
12:30-13:30 commuting to office
13:30-15:15 Office
15:30-15:45 moving to Shibuya Office
15:50-16:45 Shibuya Office
17:35-19:40 Office
19:50-20:45 going home
20:45-23:55 at home                (b)
```

Fig. 14. Textual representation of location logs (a) Results of simple reverse-geocoding (b) Applying location name substation rules (e.g., Higashigotanda → Office)

5.2 "Place Cloud"

Figure 15 is another textual representation using a variant of a tagcloud. A tagcloud is a commonly used technique in social tagging applications. It shows the frequency of attached tag words by changing the word sizes.

In our case, address words, such as "品川区 (Shinagawa-ku)" or "東五反田 (Higashigotanda)" are regarded as tags attached to days. We call this a "placecloud". If a person stays in one place longer, the corresponding placetag frequency also increases. As a result, each day has placetags with frequency counts. Figure 15-(a) is a simple tagcloud based only on tag frequency. The tag size represents the time in which a person stays in a corresponding location. It is useful, but the same places, such as office or home, tend to constantly become bigger than other placetags, and the resulting visualizations become similar over the course of many days.

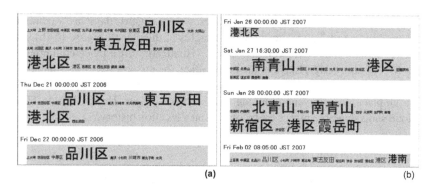

Fig. 15. PlaceCloud: a tagcloud variant of a location history. (a) tag size is determined simply by duration spent at the location. (b) tag size is determined by TF/IDF.

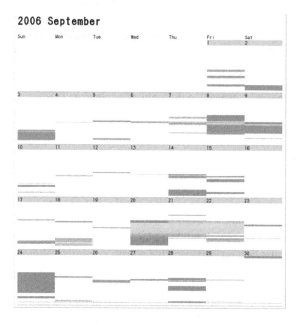

Fig. 16. Automatic "Event" detection from personal history: dark areas represent unusual events for this person

Figure 15-(b) is a placecloud using "TF/IDF" [10] to determine tag importance. TF/IDF is a populartext mining technique to determine the importance of words based on word frequency and word distribution among documents. Using TF/IDF, $w_{i,j}$, which is the weight (importance) of the word j in document i, can be determined as:

$$w_{i,j} = tf_{i,j} \times log(\frac{N}{df_i}) \tag{1}$$

where $tf_{i,j}$ is the number of occurrences of word i in document j, df_i is the number of documents containing word i, and N is the total number of documents.

By applying the TF/IDF idea to location logs, we can regard "days" as "documents" and "places" as "words" and determine the weights of the places. Figure 15-(b) shows placeclouds based on TF/IDF weights. In this visualization, if a place commonly appears in lists of many days, like a home or an office, the tag size becomes smaller even when a person stays a long time in these places. On the other hand, if a person visits an uncommon place, the corresponding tag size becomes bigger. Therefore, this TF/IDF placecloud shows notable places based on person's location history.

5.3 "Event" Detection

By extending the idea of picking up notable days, it is also possible to detect a point in time that is "special" to each person. Normally, life is "routine"; we wake up at home, commute to the office, and go back home. By accumulating personal location logs, it becomes possible to predict a person's location probability density. Thus, if the user is at an unlikely location at a particular time, it is likely that this is a special occasion for the person.

For example, it might be considered usual for a person to be in his/her office at 3 PM, but not in the same office at 3 AM. The unlikely situation would thus be an important event. It is possible to detect such "events" from the person's location log automatically. Figure 16 visualizes such "events" in the form of a calendar. This event information can be used to assist memory and automatic creation of blogs.

6   Conclusion

We described a system that continuously and precisely records one's location history. Unlike a GPS-based system, our system can detect and record indoor positions. This feature is essential for logging location histories because most daily activities are in indoor environments. The underlying WiFi location platform, called PlaceEngine, provides a location estimation service using a database consisting of more than half a million estimated access point locations. It covers the major cities in Japan and it has proven to be useful for the life-logging purposes described in this paper.

Our LifeTag device is a keychain-like device that automatically senses and records WiFi fingerprint information around a user. We showed various applications and visualization techniques exploiting the obtained location logs.

Although we mainly focused on the uses of WiFi location detection technology, other location technologies such as GPS and UWB could be used as well. Using other kinds of sensors, such as motion or orientation sensors, to assist in life-logging is also possible, although there is a tradeoff between benefit and hardware complexity.

As described in this paper, it is now possible to record an accurate location history of a person's whereabouts. This means any time-stamped data, such as digital pictures, can automatically be "location-stamped" by matching timestamps. Hence, it can be said that "when" and "where" data are now interchangeable. We may also be able to make "who" data interchangeable with "when" and "where" data, by analyzing the location logs of multiple users. It is often said that daily events have five main attributes of "when," "where," "who," "why," and "how". Location logging is a simple but effective technology because it has a potential to merge three of the "W"s (when, where, and who) into one.

Acknowledgement

We thank Shigeru Tajima for his hardware design and construction supports.

References

1. CARPE, research.microsoft.com/CARPE2004 (2004)
2. Ashbrook, D., Starner, T.: Learning significant locations and predicting user movement with GPS. In: Proceedings of IEEE Sixth International Symposium on Wearable Computing (ISWC02) (2002)
3. Bahl, P., Padmanabhan, V.N.: RADAR: An in-building RF-based user location and tracking system. INFOCOM 2, 775–784 (2000)
4. Clarkson, B.: Life patterns: structure from wearable sensors. Ph.D thesis, MIT Media Laboratory (2002)
5. Eagle, N., Pentland, A.: Reality Mining: Sensing complex social systems. Personal and Ubiquitous Computing 10(4) (2006)
6. Gemmell, J., Belland, G., Luederand, R., Drucker, S., Wong, C.C.: MyLifeBits: Fulfilling the Memex vision. In: ACM Multimedia 2002, pp. 235–238 (2002)
7. Ito, S., Yoshida, H., Kawaguchi, N.: Studies on collection method of access point in metropolitan-scale 802.11 location systems. In: Dourish, P., Friday, A. (eds.) UbiComp 2006. LNCS, vol. 4206, Springer, Heidelberg (2006)
8. LaMarca, A., Chawathe, Y., Consolvo, S., Hightower, J., Smith, I., Scott, J., Sohn, T., Howard, J., Hughes, J., Potter, F., Tabert, J., Powledge, P., Borriello, G., Schilit, B.: Place Lab: Device positioning using radio beacons in the wild. In: Proceedings of Pervasive 2005 (2005)
9. Rekimoto, J., Shionozaki, A., Sueyoshi, T., Miyaki, T.: PlaceEngine: A wifi location platform based on realworld-folksonomy. In: Internet Conference 2006, pp. 95–104. Japanese (2006)
10. Salton, G., Buckley, C.: Term weighting approaches in automatic text retrieval. Technical Report TR87-881, Cornell University (1987)

Scalable Recognition of Daily Activities with Wearable Sensors

Tâm Huỳnh, Ulf Blanke, and Bernt Schiele

Computer Science Department
TU Darmstadt, Germany
{huynh,blanke,schiele}@mis.tu-darmstadt.de

Abstract. High-level and longer-term activity recognition has great potentials in areas such as medical diagnosis and human behavior modeling. So far however, activity recognition research has mostly focused on low-level and short-term activities. This paper therefore makes a first step towards recognition of high-level activities as they occur in daily life. For this we record a realistic 10h data set and analyze the performance of four different algorithms for the recognition of both low- and high-level activities. Here we focus on simple features and computationally efficient algorithms as this facilitates the embedding and deployment of the approach in real-world scenarios. While preliminary, the experimental results suggest that the recognition of high-level activities can be achieved with the same algorithms as the recognition of low-level activities.

1 Introduction

Activity recognition has been an active area of research in recent years due to its potential and usefulness for context-aware computing. Current approaches typically rely on state-of-the-art machine learning ranging from unsupervised to supervised techniques and from discriminant to generative models. Most research however has focused on low-level and short-term activities. While this focus has advanced the state-of-the-art significantly we strongly believe that activity recognition should move forward to address the important and challenging area of longer-term and high-level activity recognition. In many applications ranging from medical diagnosis over elderly care to modeling of human behavior, the analysis and recognition of high-level activities is an important component.

There are various reasons why only a few researchers have worked on longer-term, complex and high-level activities (with some notable exceptions as discussed in Section 2). For example it is often argued that the recognition of low-level activities is a prerequisite to recognize more complex and high-level activities. Besides being tedious and time-consuming, the recording of high-level activities is a non-trivial task, as the data should be as realistic and representative as possible. So fundamental problems such as the inherent difficulties and the large variability as well as more practical reasons seem to have prevented most researchers to address the recognition of complex and high-level activities.

J. Hightower, B. Schiele, and T. Strang (Eds.): LoCA 2007, LNCS 4718, pp. 50–67, 2007.

The explicit goal of our research is to enable the recognition of longer-term and high-level activities. Therefore, an essential first step is to record an interesting and realistic dataset of high-level activities. As we are interested in long-term activities it is essential to use long-term recordings which is why this papers uses over 10h worth of data. The paper then compares four algorithms both for the recognition of low-level activities as well as high-level activities. For each of the algorithms, we analyze and discuss different parameters such as feature length and sensor placement. The results suggest that the recognition of high-level activities may be achievable with the same algorithms as for low-level activities. In particular, our results indicate that recognition of high-level activities can be achieved using features computed from raw sensor data alone, without building up any intermediate representation such as a grammar of low-level activities.

Let us briefly define – for the purpose of this paper – the difference between low-level and high-level activities. Low-level activities are e.g. *walking, sitting, standing, hoovering, eating, washing dishes*, etc which typically last between 10s of seconds to several minutes. High-level activities, on the other hand, are longer-term as e.g. *cleaning the house*, which will typically last more than 10s of minutes and could last as long as a few hours.

The main contributions of the paper are as follows. First, the results of our experiments suggest that today's activity recognition algorithms are quite capable to address the problem of high-level activity recognition. Second, we record and provide an interesting and realistic dataset of high-level activities which we plan to make publicly available upon publication of this paper. Third, we analyze and compare different algorithms for the recognition of low-level and high-level activities. Fourth, we systematically analyze important parameters such as sensor placement, feature length and classification window.

The paper is structured as follows: In the next section we will put our work into context by discussing related work. In Section 3, we introduce the dataset and hardware for our experiments. Section 4 presents the algorithms we use for recognition of both high- and low-level activities. Sections 5 and 6 report on the results for low- and high-level activities, respectively. Section 7 presents the summary and conclusion.

2   Related Work

Current research in activity recognition from wearable sensors covers a wide range of topics, with research groups focusing on topics such as the recognition of activities of daily living (ADLs) in the context of healthcare and elderly care (e.g. [1]), automated discovery of activity primitives in unlabeled data (e.g. [2]), semi- or unsupervised learning of activities (e.g. [3,4]), or the combination of several sensor modalities to improve recognition performance (e.g. [5,6]). The majority of this work is concerned with single activities over relatively short timescales, ranging from limb movements in dumbbell exercises [2] over postures and modes of ambulation such as *sitting, standing* and *walking* [7,8], to household activities such as *making tea, dusting, cleaning the windows* or *taking a shower*

[6,9]. To our knowledge, little work has been done in using wearable sensors to recognize activities on larger time scales, i.e. by recognizing higher-level scenes such as *cleaning the house* or *going shopping*. A notable exception is the work by Clarkson et al. [10], who used wearable vision and audio sensors to recognize scenes such as a user visiting a supermarket or a video store. However, since cameras and microphones are considered intrusive by many people, such an approach is unlikely to be adopted in everyday life. There has been work in identifying daily routines in the lives of users (e.g. [11]) or inferring a user's high-level intentions during his daily movements through urban environments (e.g., [12,13,14]). However, these works mainly focus on the location of the user or have a different understanding of the term 'high-level', more referring to a user's abstract goals in terms of traveling destinations than to a collection of related low-level activities. On a smaller scale, [6] proposed to break down activities such as *cleaning the windows* into small movements called *actions*, such as *wipe horizontally* and *wipe vertically*. In this work we follow a different approach, by summarizing a collection of activities into scenes measured in hours rather than in minutes.

3   Experimental Setup

An important first step towards the recognition of high-level activities is a realistic and representative recording of sensor-data. We formulated four requirements and considerations as the basis of our data recording. First, as the primary aim is the recognition of high-level activities, we explicitly started with the recording of such activities and later defined, named and annotated those low-level activities that occurred and were performed during these high-level activities. As we will see below, this leads to quite a different set of low-level activities than one may obtain when starting from low-level activities. Second, the recording should be as realistic as possible so that the activities should be performed "in the field" – that is in an unconstrained and natural setting – and not in a laboratory or staged setting. Third, the usefulness and the usability of high-level activity recognition strongly depends on the price and form-factor of the final device. Therefore we decided to keep the algorithms, features and the sensor-platform as simple and power-efficient as possible so that the embedding into a simple self-contained device is feasible in the future. Forth, we decided to start with the recording of data for a single user, as our primary aim in this paper is to analyze and show the feasibility of high-level activity recognition first. Even though that might seem like a limitation, we rather expect that the execution of high-level activities varies greatly between individuals so that one might need to use a personalized device. If this holds true or one can enable person-independent high-level activity recognition remains an open research question and is beyond the scope of this paper.

One requirement formulated above was to base our recognition on simple sensors and easy-to-compute features which is why we decided to use the mean and variance of acceleration signals. Accelerometers are especially appealing in

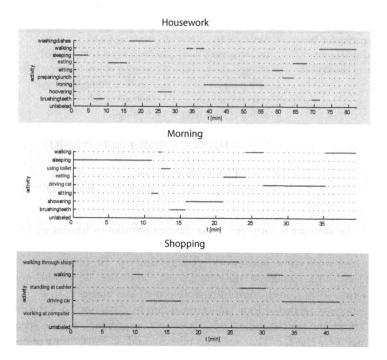

Fig. 1. Ground truth for recordings of the three scenes *Housework*, *Morning* and *Shopping*. Each scene was performed four times by the user, here we show only one instance of each scene.

this context, since they are cheap and can be increasingly found in everyday objects such as mobile phones, cameras, wrist watches and even shoes. The use of simple features for recognition would allow the computation to take place online on a miniature mobile device without draining the battery or slowing down other applications. Computing the features on the device and discarding the raw signals can also help to save memory and allow for longer recordings.

Dataset. During the recordings the user was wearing three sensors. One sensor was attached to the right wrist, one to the righthand side of the hip, and one to the right thigh, as illustrated in Figure 3(a). The ground truth labels were mainly added and edited offline, using a separate video recording (from a passively mounted video-camera used during the *housework* and *morning* scenes) and some optional online annotations from a PDA.

The dataset consists of three different high-level activities or *scenes* performed by one user. The first scene consists of a typical morning routine one might perform before going to work, which, for one of the recordings, looked as follows (see Figure 1 for the corresponding ground truth annotation). After some time of sleeping, the user gets up, walks to the bathroom, uses the toilet and brushes his teeth. After having breakfast, he leaves the house and drives to work by car. The second scene is a shopping scenario which might look as follows: after

Highlevel Activities	Lowlevel Activities	
a Preparing for Work	1 (unlabeled)	9 walking [a, b]
b Going Shopping	2 brushing teeth [a, c]	10 working at computer [b]
c Doing Housework	3 taking a shower [a]	11 waiting in line in a shop [b]
	4 sitting [a]	12 strolling through a shop [b]
	5 driving car [a, b]	13 hoovering [c]
	6 eating at table [a,c]	14 ironing [c]
	7 using the toilet [a]	15 preparing lunch [c]
	8 sleeping [a]	16 washing the dishes [c]

Fig. 2. Overview of the low- and high-level activities in the recorded dataset. Each high-level activity consists of a set of low-level activities, as indicated in brackets.

working at the computer for some time, the user walks to his car and drives to a nearby shopping center, buys groceries and heads back in his car. In the third scene, the user does some housework after getting up. He might first brush his teeth and have some breakfast, may then wash the dishes, hoover his apartment and iron some clothes, and eventually walk out of the house.

Each scene was recorded four times, on different days and in a natural environment, i.e. at the user's home and in a nearby supermarket. The scenes were loosely defined by the fact that each activity should at least occur once in each instance. The length of the scenes varies between 40 and 80 minutes; the total length of the data is 621 minutes. Figure 1 shows the ground truth for one instance of each scene, and Figure 2 gives an overview of all activities. The scenes consist of 15 different activities (plus one garbage class for unlabeled data), some of which are shared between two or three scenes. For evaluation, we created four sets, each consisting of three concatenated scenes. We used these sets to perform a 4-fold leave-one-out crossvalidation on the data.

Hardware. Figure 3(b) shows the sensor platform that was used for recording the data for our experiments [15]. It features a 2D accelerometer (ADXL202JE) and nine binary tilt switches for sensing motion and orientation of the user. The sensor board is stacked onto a BSN node [16] with 512 kb of EEPROM storage for logging sensor data, followed by a third board for the power supply.

Feature Computation. During recordings, the platform stores all sensor data on the EEPROM storage, from which it can later be retrieved via an rs232 connection. As we aimed for recordings of several hours, the limiting factor for our experiments was the size of the 512 kb on-board memory rather than battery lifetime. To save memory, we compute and store only the mean and variance of the acceleration signal at 2 Hz and discard the raw (80 Hz) acceleration data. This allows us to record about five hours of sensor data on the chip. The next generation of the platform will have a larger on-board memory and allow for recordings of several days or even weeks.

(a)	(b)

Fig. 3. Left: User wearing sensors on wrist, hip and thigh. Right: The sensor platform, consisting of the power supply (bottom), the BSN node for logging (middle) and the sensor board (top).

4   Algorithms

We use four different approaches for recognition of activities – three of them are based on a discrete representation that we obtain by clustering the sensor data, and one approach is based on training HMMs on continuous data. All approaches have in common that they use the mean and variance of the acceleration signal over a sliding window as the underlying features. These features are cheap to compute and are known to yield high recognition rates in settings comparable to ours (e.g. [8,17,18,19]).

Related work has shown that it is possible to recognize movements or activities based on low dimensional models learned in a semi- or unsupervised fashion (e.g., [2,19]). Such models can also be thought of as an alphabet of symbols, a vocabulary in which activities are formulated as 'sentences'. Compositions of such sentences could later serve as a tool for recognizing more abstract and high-level behavior. The first three of the following approaches are inspired by this idea, but as we do not assume that human motion follows a strict grammar, we only consider the occurrences of symbols over intervals, without modeling their temporal order. We use k-means clustering as a simple yet effective unsupervised method to map features to a set of discrete symbols, i.e. to one of the k cluster centers. We represent each feature by the closest cluster center. As a result, the input data is transformed into a one-dimensional sequence of cluster assignments. Based on this representation, we employ three different learning methods which we describe in the following. The fourth method is based on HMMs and uses a vector of mean and variance values as features. Figure 4 illustrates the different representations we use for recognition.

K-means. As a baseline method, we label each cluster with the activity that occurs most often among the training samples belonging to the cluster. Classification is then performed by assigning to each test sample the label of the closest

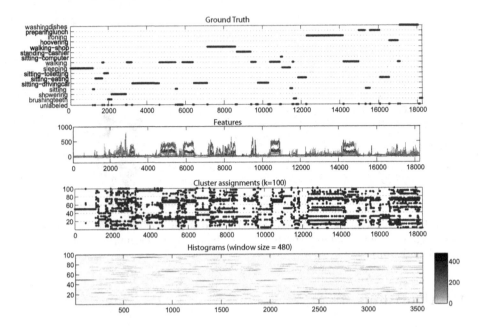

Fig. 4. Examples of the different representations used for recognition. From top to bottom: ground truth; features (mean & variance over 4 sec); cluster assignments (each feature is assigned to one of k=100 clusters); histograms of cluster assignments (over windows of 480 samples).

cluster center. During experiments we vary the size of k and the length of the window over which the features are computed.

Occurrence Statistics + NN. In this approach, rather than using individual symbols as features, we compute histograms of cluster assignments over a sliding window of the training sequence. Each histogram is labeled with the activity that occurs most often in the window of samples that it covers. For evaluation, we perform a nearest neighbor (NN) classification on the histograms computed from a test sequence.

Occurrence Statistics + SVM. This approach is also based on histograms of cluster assignments. However, instead of using a nearest neighbor classifier, we train a support vector machine (SVM) using the histograms as features.

HMMs. The fourth approach is based on Hidden Markov Models (HMMs). HMMs belong to the class of generative statistical signal models, and they have been successfully used in activity recognition tasks before (e.g. [20,10,21]). They lend themselves to a hierarchical classifier design, which makes them interesting candidates for modelling activities on different levels of abstraction.

As for the first three approaches, we use the mean and variance of the acceleration signal over a sliding window as features. We then partition the data into N

equal parts and train a separate HMM on each part. We use left-right models with one gaussian per state, and we vary the number of states in our experiments. In order to assign activity labels to the models, we use a sliding window over the features as observation sequence, and compute the likelihood of the window for each of the N models. The model with the highest likelihood is then assigned the label of the activity that occurs most often in the window. Classification is performed similarly, i.e. by computing the likelihood of each model over a sliding window starting at a certain sample, and subsequently assigning to the sample the label of the model with the highest likelihood.

5   Low-Level Activities

In this section we report on the performance of our proposed approaches with respect to the fifteen low-level activities listed in Figure 2. As mentioned earlier, the definition of those low-level activities came after the recording of the high-level activities. That way, a somewhat obvious but important observation is that the definition of low-level activities is not as well-defined as one might expect. E.g., for the following activities, it is not clear if they belong to the same or to different low-level activities: *walking down a corridor* vs. *walking in a super-market while collecting items*; *sitting in a car* vs. *sitting at a table while eating* vs. *sitting on the toilet* vs. *sitting at a desk and working on a computer*; etc. It should be clear that this is not simply a question of a hierarchical and temporal decomposition of concurrent activities but that this is rather an inherent diffi-culty linked to the context of the particular activity (e.g. *sitting on the toilet* vs. *sitting at a table*). So we decided to define the low-level activities within each high-level activity as they occurred within the context of the high-level activity. That way we have a range of activities which occur across multiple high-level activities such as *walking, eating at table* and *brushing teeth* and others which are more specific such as *driving a car* or *strolling through a shop*.

Based on these definitions of low-level activities, this section compares he recog-nition performance of our four approaches. For each of the algorithms we also iden-tify and discuss suitable parameters such as the number of clusters, the length of the feature window, and also appropriate on-body locations for the sensors.

K-means. Figure 5(a) shows the accuracy[1] for different numbers k of clusters and different window lengths for the features. One can observe that values of k below 50 have a negative impact on the recognition performance. For values of $k >= 50$, accuracy lies roughly between 60 and 70%. The best result of 69,4% is obtained for $k = 500$ and a feature length of 64 seconds. Surprisingly, the best results are obtained for relatively long window lengths. Lengths between 16 and 256 seconds perform best, and there is a visible drop in performance for shorter and longer window lengths. Figure 6 shows the confusion matrix for the best parameter combination. One can clearly see that the recognition performance varies strongly between the different activities. Seven of the 15 activities have

---

[1] We use the term *accuracy* to refer to the number of correctly classified samples divided by the number of all samples.

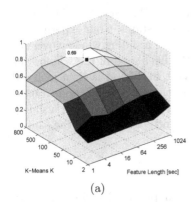 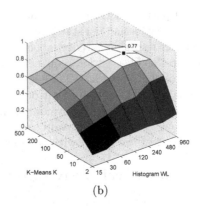

(a)   (b)

Fig. 5. Accuracy of classification for low-level activities; using assignments to cluster centers as features (left) vs. using histograms of such assignments in combination with nearest neighbor classification (right)

		Classified Activity																Sum	Recall
		1	2	3	4	5	6	7	8	9	10	11	12	13	14	15	16		
	1 unlabeled	1314	148	188	64	567	136	81	103	540	85	10	428	317	993	707	158	5839	22.5%
	2 brush teeth	146	1258	310	0	0	0	0	0	9	0	16	0	71	302	2	51	2165	58.1%
	3 shower	83	249	1710	0	0	13	17	0	58	0	0	47	54	270	40	70	2611	65.5%
	4 sit	287	4	6	684	424	168	267	5	68	19	0	49	7	26	19	0	2033	33.6%
	5 drive car	334	0	0	343	9743	301	84	26	62	0	0	73	0	0	0	0	10966	88.8%
Ground Truth	6 eat	192	5	21	127	938	4253	26	11	42	0	0	25	2	3	21	13	5679	74.9%
	7 use toilet	83	14	46	41	324	106	224	7	14	16	0	0	12	53	4	0	944	23.7%
	8 sleep	260	14	21	45	116	34	0	7016	111	36	0	55	0	0	10	22	7740	90.6%
	9 walk	614	12	105	29	66	0	7	0	8988	0	0	1285	139	153	32	40	11470	78.4%
	10 work at comp.	99	0	3	22	52	35	15	36	26	1325	0	24	9	21	21	0	1688	78.5%
	11 stand at cashier	14	0	0	0	0	0	0	0	0	0	798	717	23	145	92	15	1804	44.2%
	12 walk in shop	193	14	37	7	2	0	0	0	836	0	297	3260	109	201	342	14	5312	61.4%
	13 hoover	74	44	74	0	0	0	0	0	128	0	0	135	785	456	66	149	1911	41.1%
	14 iron	122	76	155	0	0	0	0	0	38	0	162	53	267	7009	438	263	8583	81.7%
	15 prep. lunch	331	4	2	0	0	20	0	0	14	0	37	349	49	499	731	95	2131	34.3%
	16 wash dishes	240	29	54	13	0	0	0	0	11	0	3	37	23	350	255	2554	3569	71.6%
	Sum	4386	1871	2732	1375	12232	5066	721	7204	10945	1481	1323	6537	1867	10481	2780	3444	74445	
	Precision	30.0%	67.2%	62.6%	49.7%	79.7%	84.0%	31.1%	97.4%	82.1%	89.5%	60.3%	49.9%	42.0%	66.9%	26.3%	74.2%		

Fig. 6. Aggregate confusion matrix for the best parameter combination when using k-means cluster centers as features. $k = 500$, mean & var computed over 64 seconds, shift $= 0.5$ seconds. Overall accuracy is 69%.

recall or precision values above 70%, the best being *sleeping* (97.4/90.6), *working at the computer* (89.9/78.5), *walking* (82.1/78.4) and *driving car* (79.7/88.8). During four activities the user was sitting (*sitting, driving car, eating at table, using the toilet*), and from Figure 6 one can see that these activities are often confused with each other during classification.

Occurrence Statistics + NN. Figure 5(b) shows the recognition results for the histogram-based approach combined with a nearest neighbor classifier. We vary the number of clusters and the length of the histogram windows (the windows are always shifted by 5 features at a time). The underlying mean and variance features are computed over windows of 4 seconds with a shift of 0.5 seconds (in contrast to the k-means approach, we observed that small feature windows performed better here). The highest accuracy of 77% is obtained for $k = 100$ and a histogram window of 480 samples, covering about 4 minutes of data. For larger

		1	2	3	4	5	6	7	Classified Activity 8	9	10	11	12	13	14	15	16	Sum	Recall
	1 unlabeled	79	79	24	0	7	4	34	50	53	0	0	0	10	208	11	66	625	12.6%
	2 brush teeth	73	142	86	0	0	8	8	1	0	0	0	3	0	0	0	59	380	37.4%
	3 shower	0	0	558	0	0	0	0	0	0	0	0	0	0	0	0	3	561	99.5%
	4 sit	0	0	0	0	67	0	68	0	26	0	0	0	0	0	27		188	0.0%
	5 drive car	0	0	0	0	2134	0	0	0	102	0	0	54	0	0	0		2290	93.2%
Ground Truth	6 eat	0	10	13	0	104	1033	25	0	0	0	0	47	5	0	11	23	1271	81.3%
	7 use toilet	0	81	5	0	71	28	26	10	13	0	0	0	0	0	0		234	11.1%
	8 sleep	15	26	0	0	0	4	7	1498	7	0	0	0	0	0	0		1557	96.2%
	9 walk	46	0	6	0	90	0	17	7	1632	18	0	303	10	69	0	3	2201	74.1%
	10 work at comp.	0	0	0	0	127	0	0	0	17	180	0	0	0	0	0		324	55.6%
	11 stand at cashier	0	0	0	0	0	0	0	0	3	0	125	120	0	0	139		387	32.3%
	12 walk in shop	0	0	0	0	23	0	0	0	52	0	60	886	0	0	75		1096	80.8%
	13 hoover	10	0	0	0	0	0	0	0	0	0	0	0	365	8	10	21	414	88.2%
	14 iron	0	0	0	0	0	0	0	0	10	0	0	0	0	1676	45	10	1751	95.7%
	15 prep. lunch	0	0	8	68	0	17	30	0	5	0	30	53	13	14	156	109	503	31.0%
	16 wash dishes	0	0	12	0	0	17	0	0	6	0	0	0	0	14	6	715	770	92.9%
	Sum	223	338	712	68	2623	1121	215	1566	1926	198	215	1480	409	1975	474	1009	14552	
	Precision	35.4%	42.0%	78.4%	0.0%	81.4%	92.1%	12.1%	95.7%	84.7%	90.9%	58.1%	59.9%	89.2%	84.9%	32.9%	70.9%		

Fig. 7. Aggregate confusion matrix for the best parameter combination when using histograms of cluster centers as features. $k = 100$, histogram windows over 480 features (about 4 min.) shifted by 5 features each, mean & var computed over 4 sec., shift = 0.5 seconds. Overall accuracy is 77%.

histogram windows the accuracy visibly decreases. Similarly to the k-means results, values of k below 50 lead to a sharp drop in performance, implying that too much information is lost from the discretization. Figure 7 shows the confusion matrix for the best parameter settings. Except for the activities *taking a shower*, *sitting*, *using the toilet* and *washing the dishes*, the precision increases for all activities compared to the previous approach. Notably, the confusion between the activities *ironing* and *hoovering* is much lower in this approach. The overall gain in accuracy of 8% indicates that the use of histograms of symbols rather than individual symbols does indeed help to improve recognition performance.

Occurrence Statistics + SVM. When using an SVM for classification in combination with the histogram features, the recognition results can be slightly improved compared to the nearest neighbor approach. Figure 8(a) shows the accuracy for different values of k and different window lengths for the histograms. The best result of 78% is obtained for $k = 50$ and a histogram window of 480 samples, covering about 4 minutes of data. One can observe that accuracy decreases with higher number of clusters and smaller window lengths. For window lengths between 240 and 960 samples, corresponding to about 2 to 8 minutes of data, and values of k between 50 and 200, we obtain the highest accuracies.

HMMs. Figure 8(b) shows recognition results for the HMM approach. We vary the feature length and the number of models N; in this particular example, the number of states is fixed to 8, and the observation window for classification covers 16 samples. The number of models N directly affects the length of data that each HMM models, since the data is equally partitioned into N parts. Thus, N is inversely related to the length of the histogram windows of the previous approaches. From the plot one can observe that using less than 200 models (i.e. each model sees about 2.5 min of data or more) leads to a visible decrease in performance. We obtained the best result of 67% for $N = 200$ models and a feature length of 64 sec, an observation length of 16 and models with 32 states. When varying the number of states we found that they only marginally

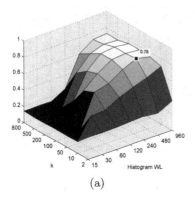
(a)

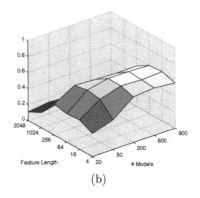
(b)

Fig. 8. Accuracy of classification for low-level activities; using histograms of cluster assignments in combination with an SVM (left) vs. using HMMs (right)

		Classified Activity																Sum	Recall
		1	2	3	4	5	6	7	8	9	10	11	12	13	14	15	16		
	1 unlabeled	288	337	654	849	323	497	533	49	879	458	65	833	103	485	151	98	6602	4.4%
	2 brush teeth	0	1565	32	77	21	32	46	0	20	32	0	0	0	159	183	0	2167	72.2%
	3 hoover	0	75	1070	523	0	33	32	0	120	50	0	0	0	0	0	0	1903	56.2%
	4 iron	0	0	182	6732	1211	41	0	0	117	166	0	0	0	0	130	0	8579	78.5%
	5 prep. lunch	0	0	0	365	927	105	27	0	131	162	66	35	130	33	54	33	2068	44.8%
Ground Truth	6 sit	10	81	0	61	142	577	84	13	273	212	33	257	0	0	0	196	1939	29.8%
	7 eat	0	0	20	43	70	80	3615	0	130	252	0	1327	0	33	19	32	5621	64.3%
	8 sleep	533	16	0	0	11	283	29	6638	56	0	33	127	0	0	0	65	7791	85.2%
	9 walk	33	130	196	145	7	463	310	0	8399	171	0	493	13	903	0	33	11296	74.4%
	10 wash dishes	0	9	0	167	98	69	206	0	2	2740	0	0	0	0	262	0	3553	77.1%
	11 work at comp.	0	0	0	0	0	65	24	0	178	0	1307	33	0	86	0	0	1693	77.2%
	12 drive car	0	0	0	0	0	99	524	0	440	0	33	9670	0	33	0	98	10897	88.7%
	13 stand at	99	0	0	0	200	0	0	0	0	0	0	0	1285	212	0	0	1796	71.5%
	14 walk in shop	0	98	0	0	197	66	0	0	862	0	0	68	429	3581	0	0	5301	67.6%
	15 shower	0	254	0	205	0	0	0	0	0	130	0	0	0	0	1982	0	2571	77.1%
	16 use toilet	20	16	0	25	0	206	328	0	28	2	0	295	0	0	0	0	920	0.0%
	Sum	983	2581	2154	9192	3207	2616	5758	6700	11635	4375	1537	13138	1960	5525	2781	555	74697	
	Precision	29.3%	60.6%	49.7%	73.2%	28.9%	22.1%	62.8%	99.1%	72.2%	62.6%	85.0%	73.6%	65.6%	64.8%	71.3%	0.0%		

Fig. 9. Aggregate confusion matrix for the best parameter combination when using the HMM-based approach. The parameters were: window length for features = 64 sec., 200 models, 32 states per model, observation length = 16. Overall accuracy is 67.4%.

effected the results. Figure 9 shows the confusion matrix for the best parameter combination. Overall, results of the HMM approach suggest that the temporal aspect – at least for the features we employed – is not dominant enough to allow for higher recognition rates.

Sensor placement. The results so far were based on the data of all three sensors the user was wearing on wrist, hip and thigh. It turns out that using only subsets of these sensors for recognition reveals some interesting relations between the placement of sensors and the recognition of individual activities. For instance, we found that the overall accuracy of the k-means approach slightly improved from 69 to 70% when we used only two sensors, namely the sensors on wrist and thigh. These results are consistent with the findings from [8], who also found that when using only two sensor locations, wrist and thigh are the most suitable locations. Using these locations even leads to better results when recognizing

Activity	K-means		Occ./NN		Occ./SVM		HMM	
	p	r	p	r	p	r	p	r
(unlabeled)	30,0	**22,5**	**35,4**	12,6	7,9	3,0	29,3	4,4
brush teeth	**67,2**	58,1	42,0	37,4	23,0	21,1	60,6	**72,2**
shower	62,6	65,5	78,4	**99,5**	**86,7**	91,8	71,3	77,1
sit	**49,7**	**33,6**	0,0	0,0	0,0	0,0	22,1	29,8
drive car	79,7	88,8	81,4	93,2	**86,9**	**95,4**	73,6	88,7
eat	84,0	74,9	**92,1**	81,3	82,3	**87,3**	62,8	64,3
use toilet	**31,1**	**23,7**	12,1	11,1	15,0	9,4	0,0	0,0
sleep	97,4	90,6	95,7	96,2	91,2	**97,2**	**99,1**	85,2
walk	82,1	**78,4**	**84,7**	74,1	79,5	77,6	72,2	74,4
work at computer	89,5	78,5	90,9	55,6	**93,3**	**94,8**	85,0	77,2
stand at cashier	60,3	44,2	58,1	32,3	**75,9**	47,3	65,6	**71,5**
walk in shop	49,9	61,4	59,9	**80,8**	**70,7**	80,1	64,8	67,6
hoover	42,0	41,1	89,2	**88,2**	**98,3**	82,6	49,7	56,2
iron	66,9	81,7	84,9	95,7	**89,0**	**95,9**	73,2	78,5
prep. lunch	26,3	34,3	32,9	31,0	**45,7**	**54,3**	28,9	44,8
wash dishes	74,2	71,6	70,9	**92,9**	**79,0**	89,9	62,6	77,1
Mean	62,0	59,3	63,0	61,4	**64,0**	**64,2**	57,5	60,6
Accuracy	69,4		77,0		**79,1**		67,4	

Fig. 10. Summary of the results for low-level activities. Each column shows the precision (p) and recall (r) values for each activity, as well as the accuracy, i.e. the number of correctly classified samples divided by all samples. The highest values in each row are highlighted.

the activities *brushing teeth, driving car, preparing lunch* and *washing dishes*. When only using the wrist sensor, performance for *brushing teeth* and *taking a shower* improves, likely because these activities are mainly characterized by hand and arm movements. For *sleeping* and *walking*, using only the hip sensor already yields precision and recall values up to 95%.

5.1 Discussion

Figure 10 shows a summary table comparing the best results of the four approaches. Generally, the approach *Occurrence Statistics + SVM* achieves the highest accuracy of 79.1%. For most activities, the use of histograms instead of single cluster assignments as features leads to better precision and recall values. However, there are two stationary (*sitting, using the toilet*) and two dynamic activities (*brushing teeth, walking*) in which the use of single cluster assignments yields higher results in either precision, recall or both. The HMM approach achieves the lowest accuracy of 67.4%, slightly less than the *k-means* approach. In summary, we conclude that using histograms of symbols as features and combining them with a strong classifier is a promising and competitive approach for recognizing the type of daily activities we recorded in our study.

It is worth noting that the overall recognition scores seem low compared to the published state-of-the-art. However, in contrast to most other recordings and as discussed above, we explicitly defined the low-level activities after the recording of the high-level activities, and therefore both the larger variability within single low-level activities (such as *walking*) and the high similarity between different low-activities (such as *walking* and *walking through shop*) pose a more challenging recognition problem than is usually addressed.

6   High-Level Activities

In this section we report on how well our proposed approaches can deal with the recognition of high-level scenes comprising a collection of low-level activities. More specifically, we evaluate how well our algorithms can classify the three different scenes *Morning*, *Housework*, and *Shopping*. Each scene has a length of at least 40 minutes and consists of at least six different activities. The evaluation was performed in the same fashion as for the low-level activities: we constructed four datasets, each containing one instance of each of the three scenes, and then performed a leave-one-out crossvalidation.

K-means. Figure 11(a) shows the accuracy for different numbers of clusters and different window lengths for computing mean and variance of the signal. As for the low-level activities, one can observe that for values of k below 50 performance decreases rapidly. In terms of feature windows, there is a visible tendency that longer window lengths lead to a better performance. For the parameter values that we sampled, the best result of 84.9% was obtained for $k = 50$ and a feature window of 768 sec., i.e. about 13 min. (We comment on the feature length below in the paragraph 'Sensor Placement'.) The confusion matrix for this configuration is shown in Figure 12 (upper left). Precision and recall range between 74 and 94%.

Occurrence Statistics + NN. In this experiment, as for the low-level activities, we vary the number of clusters and the length of the histogram. The results can be seen in Figure 11(b). The mean and variance features are computed over 4 sec. windows with a shift of 1 second. The best results are obtained for values of k between 50 and 500, and histogram windows between 512 and 2048 samples, i.e. between about 8 and 32 minutes. Figure 12 (upper right) shows the confusion matrix for $k = 500$ and a histogram window of 512 samples; the accuracy for this run was 83.4%, which is slightly lower than for the k-means approach. In terms of precision and confusion there is no clear difference to the k-means approach. However, the results improve substantially when using an SVM for classification instead of a nearest neighbor classifier, as is described in the next section.

Occurrence Statistics + SVM. Figure 11(c) shows the accuracy for different values of k and different window lengths for the histograms when using an SVM as classifier. The best results are obtained for histogram windows between 1280 and 2048 samples, i.e. between 20 and 32 min. Interestingly, the number of clusters for discretization only has a minimal influence on the recognition performance, the dominating parameter is the length of the histogram window. Even when using only $k = 10$ clusters, the accuracy stays above 90%. Figure 12 (lower left) shows the confusion matrix for the best result of 91.8% accuracy, which is an improvement of about 7% compared to using the nearest neighbor classifier as described in the previous paragraph.

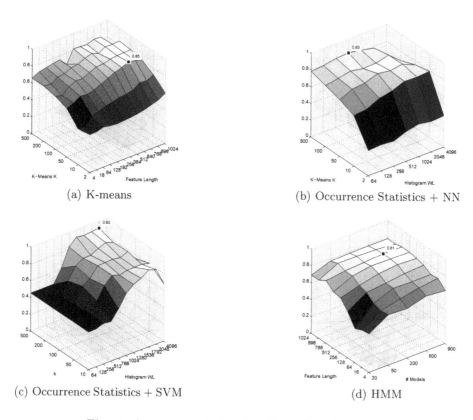

(a) K-means

(b) Occurrence Statistics + NN

(c) Occurrence Statistics + SVM

(d) HMM

Fig. 11. Accuracy of classification for high-level activities

		Classification (k-means)					Classification (Occ. Stats + NN)				
		preparing for work	going shopping	doing housework	Sum	Recall	preparing for work	going shopping	doing housework	Sum	Recall
GT	preparing for work	7652	921	916	9489	80.6%	1568	336	72	1976	79.4%
	going shopping	1030	6683	1310	9023	74.1%	86	1669	101	1856	89.9%
	doing housework	741	263	14764	15768	93.6%	354	224	2651	3229	82.1%
	Sum	9423	7867	16990	34280		2008	2229	2824	7061	
	Precision	81.2%	84.9%	86.9%			78.1%	74.9%	93.9%		

		Classification (Occ. Stats + SVM)			Sum	Recall	Classification (HMM)			Sum	Recall
GT	preparing for work	1383	132	0	1515	91.3%	8220	753	515	9488	86.6%
	going shopping	62	1359	126	1547	87.8%	1042	4962	930	6934	71.6%
	doing housework	14	143	2612	2769	94.3%	1156	536	7334	9026	81.3%
	Sum	1459	1634	2738	5831		10418	6251	8779	25448	
	Precision	94.8%	83.2%	95.4%			78.9%	79.4%	83.5%		

Fig. 12. Aggregate confusion matrices for the best parameter combinations of the four approaches for recognizing high-level activities

HMMs. Figure 11(d) shows the recognition results for the HMM approach. As for the low-level activities, we vary the feature length and the number of models N. The number of states is fixed to $s = 2$ (we did vary the number of states but found only small changes in performance), and the length of the observation

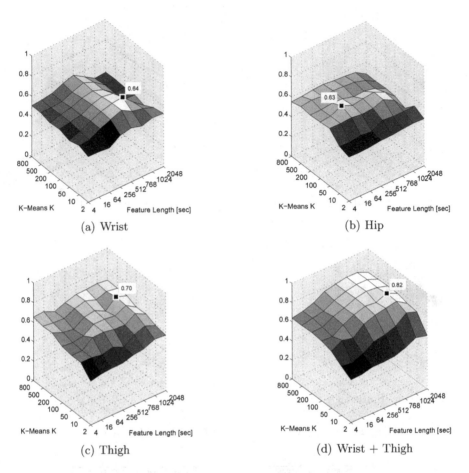

Fig. 13. K-means based recognition accuracy of high-level activities for subsets of sensor locations. The best values of each combination are highlighted.

	K-means		Occ./NN		Occ./SVM		HMM	
	p	r	p	r	p	r	p	r
Scene								
Preparing for Work	81.2	80.6	78.1	79.4	**94.8**	**91.3**	78.9	86.6
Going Shopping	84.9	74.1	74.9	89.9	**83.2**	**87.8**	79.4	71.6
Doing Housework	86.9	93.6	93.9	82.1	**95.4**	**94.3**	83.5	81.3
Mean	84.4	82.8	82.3	83.8	**91.1**	**91.2**	80.6	79.8
Accuracy	84.9		83.4		**91.8**		80.6	

Fig. 14. Summary of the results for high-level activities. The columns show the precision (p) and recall (r) values for each activity, as well as the accuracy.

window for each HMM is set to 16 samples. From the figure one can observe that values of N below 200 lead to a decrease in performance. The best results of slightly above 80% are obtained for feature lengths above 256 seconds (4 min) and $N = 200$ models or more. Figure 12 (lower right) shows the confusion matrix for $N = 200$ and a feature length of 768 seconds.

Sensor Placement. We also investigated the influence of different sensor locations on the recognition of high-level activities. Figure 13 shows the differences in performance when applying the k-means approach to subsets of sensors. Figure 13(a) shows the results for the wrist sensor. One can observe that for this sensor, the size of the feature window strongly influences the recognition rate – there is a distinct peak for relatively large windows between 512 and 1024 seconds. Obviously, for shorter windows the wrist movements are not discriminative enough for recognition. This might be due to the fact that the three scenes share some of the low-level activities, and that of these, many involve similar wrist movements, as for example *brushing teeth* or *showering*. The results for hip (Figure 13(b)) and thigh (Figure 13(c)) sensor do not exhibit such a clear tendency towards specific window lengths. Thus it appears that it is mainly the wrist sensor that is responsible for the good performance of relatively long windows when using all three sensors. The result for the hip sensor indicates that the performance at this location is more influenced by the number of clusters than the feature length; the best results are obtained for $k = 100$. Similarly as for the low-level activities, the combination of wrist and thigh sensor also performs very well for high level activities. For $k = 100$ and a feature length of 1024, the accuracy is 82%, i.e. only 3% worse than when using all three sensors.

6.1 Discussion

Figure 14 shows a summary table comparing the best results of the four approaches. As for the low-level activities, one observes that the approach *Occurrence Statistics + SVM* achieves the highest accuracy, in this case 91.8%. Combining the histogram features with an SVM instead of a nearest neighbor classifier leads to higher precision and recall values for all activities. Generally, the accuracy of all four approaches is over 80%, which is significantly higher than the chance level of about 33%. Even though the results might not generalize due to the small number of high-level activities in our set, we find that the high recognition rates are remarkable, considering the use of simple and easy-to-compute features in combination with a relatively large and challenging dataset.

7 Conclusion

The main goal of this paper was to investigate how well current approaches in activity recognition can be applied to the recognition of high-level activities, which happen on the order of hours rather than minutes and consist of a diverse set of small scale activities. To this end, we recorded a naturalistic dataset with a user wearing three sensors on wrist, hip and thigh performing several instances of three different high-level scenes. We evaluated four different algorithms with respect to their ability to recognize both the low- and high-level activities contained in the dataset. One important aim of our research is to investigate to which extent current approaches for recognition of low-level activities can be directly applied to the recognition of high-level activities – i.e. using the same simple features without adding any intermediate levels of representation. We believe that in the future such an approach would allow for scalable and efficient activity recognition systems based on simple sensors.

The results indicate that our algorithms can achieve competitive recognition rates for many of the low-level activities. The best results of slightly below 80% were achieved when using histograms of cluster assignments as features, combined with a support vector machine for classification. We investigated different window lengths and numbers of clusters and found that mapping the data to 50 clusters already leads to good results. In terms of sensor placement, using only two sensors at wrist and thigh resulted in equal or even better rates than using all three sensors.

When classifiying high-level activites, we achieve recognition rates of up to 92%, which is clearly above the chance level of about 33%. We achieve these results with the same algorithms that we used for the low-level activities, merely by changing parameters such as the feature length and classification window. The best results were again obtained by the histogram-based approach in combination with an SVM. For all our approaches we use simple mean and variance features derived from accelerometer readings at 2 Hz. Considering the relatively simple sensors and features, as well as the challenging dataset, we find that the results for the high-level activities are surprisingly good.

We conclude that recognizing activities on such scales using only small and unobtrusive body-worn accelerometers is a viable path worth pursuing. Yet we are aware that our work is but a first step towards recognition of high-level activities, and that more sophisticated models might yield better results. An obvious extension would be an hierarchical approach, using the outcome of the low-level classification as basis for the high-level inference, e.g. by defining a grammar of low-level activities. High-level activities however are often unstructured and may contain seemingly unrelated low-level activities, as e.g. observed in the data collection of this paper (e.g. when the user decided to eat during his housework). Therefore such an hierarchical approach is beyond the scope of this paper and will be explored in future work. In addition, we intend to validate our results on larger and more diverse sets of high-level activities, as well as across different users, in order to find out how well our approach generalizes.

Acknowledgements. This work is supported by the European Commission funded project MOBVIS (FP6-511051). Ulf Blanke gratefully acknowledges the scholarship provided by the DFG research training group "Topology of Technology".

References

1. Lester, J., Choudhury, T., Borriello, G.: A practical approach to recognizing physical activities. In: Proc. Pervasive (2006)
2. Minnen, D., Starner, T., Essa, I., Isbell, C.: Discovering characteristic actions from on-body sensor data. In: Proc. ISWC (2006)

3. Wyatt, D., Philipose, M., Choudhury, T.: Unsupervised Activity Recognition Using Automatically Mined Common Sense. In: Proc. AAAI 2005 (2005)
4. Huynh, T., Schiele, B.: Unsupervised discovery of structure in activity data using multiple eigenspaces. In: Proc. LoCA, Dublin, Ireland (2006)
5. Stiefmeier, T., Ogris, G., Junker, H., Lukowicz, P., Tröster, G.: Combining motion sensors and ultrasonic hands tracking for continuous activity recognition in a maintenance scenario. In: Cruz, I., Decker, S., Allemang, D., Preist, C., Schwabe, D., Mika, P., Uschold, M., Aroyo, L. (eds.) ISWC 2006. LNCS, vol. 4273, Springer, Heidelberg (2006)
6. Wang, S., Pentney, W., Popescu, A.M., Choudhury, T., Philipose, M.: Common Sense Based Joint Training of Human Activity Recognizers. In: Proc. IJCAI (2007)
7. Laerhoven, K.V., Gellersen, H.W: Spine versus porcupine: A study in distributed wearable activity recognition. In: McIlraith, S.A., Plexousakis, D., van Harmelen, F. (eds.) ISWC 2004. LNCS, vol. 3298, Springer, Heidelberg (2004)
8. Bao, L., Intille, S.: Activity recognition from user-annotated acceleration data. In: Proc. Pervasive, Vienna, Austria, pp. 1–17 (2004)
9. Patterson, D., Fox, D., Kautz, H., Philipose, M.: Fine-grained activity recognition by aggregating abstract object usage. In: Gil, Y., Motta, E., Benjamins, V.R., Musen, M.A. (eds.) ISWC 2005. LNCS, vol. 3729, pp. 44–51. Springer, Heidelberg (2005)
10. Clarkson, B., Pentland, A.: Unsupervised clustering of ambulatory audio and video. In: icassp (1999)
11. Eagle, N., Pentland, A.: Reality mining: sensing complex social systems. Personal and Ubiquitous Computing 10(4), 255–268 (2006)
12. Liao, L., Kautz, H., Fox, D.: Learning and inferring Transportation Routines. In: Proc. AAAI (2004)
13. Krumm, J., Horvitz, E.: Predestination: Inferring Destinations from Partial Trajectories. In: Dourish, P., Friday, A. (eds.) UbiComp 2006. LNCS, vol. 4206, Springer, Heidelberg (2006)
14. Marmasse, N., Schmandt, C.: Location-Aware Information Delivery with ComMotion. In: Thomas, P., Gellersen, H.-W. (eds.) HUC 2000. LNCS, vol. 1927, pp. 157–171. Springer, Heidelberg (2000)
15. Laerhoven, K.V., Gellersen, H., Malliaris, Y.: Long-Term Activity Monitoring with a Wearable Sensor Node. Body Sensor Networks Workshop (2006)
16. Lo, B., Thiemjarus, S., King, R., Yang, G.: Body Sensor Network–A Wireless Sensor Platform for Pervasive Healthcare Monitoring. In: Proc. Pervasive (2005)
17. Kern, N.: Multi-Sensor Context-Awareness for Wearable Computing. PhD thesis, TU Darmstadt (2005)
18. Ravi, N., Dandekar, N., Mysore, P., Littman, M.: Activity recognition from accelerometer data. In: Proc. IAAI (2005)
19. Huynh, T., Schiele, B.: Towards less supervision in activity recognition from wearable sensors. In: Cruz, I., Decker, S., Allemang, D., Preist, C., Schwabe, D., Mika, P., Uschold, M., Aroyo, L. (eds.) ISWC 2006. LNCS, vol. 4273, Springer, Heidelberg (2006)
20. Oliver, N., Horvitz, E., Garg, A.: Layered representations for human activity recognition. In: Proc. ICMI (2002)
21. Lester, J., Choudhury, T., Kern, N., Borriello, G., Hannford, B.: A hybrid discriminative/generative approach for modeling human activities. In: Proc. IJCAI, Edinburgh, United Kingdom, August 2005, pp. 766–772 (2005)

Information Overlay for Camera Phones in Indoor Environments

Harlan Hile and Gaetano Borriello

Dept. of Computer Science and Engineering
University of Washington
Box 352350
Seattle, WA 98195-2350 USA
{harlan,gaetano}@cs.washington.edu

Abstract. Increasingly, cell phones are used to browse for information while location systems assist in gathering information that is most appropriate to the user's current location. We seek to take this one step further and actually overlay information on to the physical world using the cell phone's camera and thereby minimize a user's cognitive effort. This "magic lens" approach has many applications of which we are exploring two: indoor building navigation and dynamic directory assistance. In essence, we match "landmarks" identified in the camera image with those stored in a building database. We use two different types of features – floor corners that can be matched against a floorplan and SIFT features that can be matched to a database constructed from other images. The camera's pose can be determined exactly from a match and information can be properly aligned so that it can overlay directly onto the phone's image display. In this paper, we present early results that demonstrate it is possible to realize this capability for a variety of indoor environments. Latency is shown to already be reasonable and likely to be improved by further optimizations. Our goal is to further explore the computational tradeoff between the server and phone client so as to achieve an acceptable latency of a few seconds.

1 Introduction

As someone walks through a building, he may want help navigating to the right room or accessing dynamic directory information related to his current location. Both of these tasks would benefit from the environment directly providing personalized information. Current approaches to this problem use location systems to help the user index into the information. However, the retrieved information must be put into context. We use a camera phone to provide the contextual framework by having the act of pointing the camera form the query into the information. The phone's display can then be used to overlay information directly onto the image and provide the user information in context. The crucial element of this approach is in determining the precise camera pose (location in 3D and orientation - a full 6 degrees of freedom).

J. Hightower, B. Schiele, and T. Strang (Eds.): LoCA 2007, LNCS 4718, pp. 68–84, 2007.

We are working on two applications of this capability. The first is motivated by an ongoing project to help individuals with cognitive impairements navigate in indoor spaces. This user population often has difficulty navigating complex buildings such as medical centers and shopping malls. In essence, we are trying to provide customized "painted lines on the floor" for users to follow to their destination. Our goal is to overlay directional arrows and navigation instructions onto the image as it is easier to understand directions when they are overlaid directly on the user's own view of his environment, especially for people with cognitive impairments [1]. The inability to get around efficiently can limit integration into the community or affect their ability to be gainfully employed. We are building a system that supports both indoor and outdoor navigation; here we focus only on the indoor portion. The second application targets a more general population that may be interested in finding out information about a building such as what events are taking place, which resources are reserved and by whom, and when someone was last in their office. This is what we mean by "dynamic directory information". As people walk down hallways, they should be able to see customized "dynamic name plates" that provide this data. Examples of information overlay for both of these uses are shown in Figure 1.

Our approach to finding the camera pose is based on a simple concept: we determine the "landmarks" in the image and their correspondence to previously cached landmarks of the space. By matching enough landmarks we can precisely compute the camera pose and thereby accurately overlay information onto the display. This simple idea is complicated by the fact that different spaces have different types of landmarks. We use "micro-landmarks" such as floor/wall transitions, corners, and door/floor edges when we are in spaces that have a high degree of homogeneity, such as hallways. We use "texture-landmarks" in larger and richer spaces such as open areas (e.g., an atrium or large room).

In the case of hallways, we can determine a user's location on the floorplan of a building by comparing the camera image to the floorplan. Our image processing targets micro-landmarks likely to be found on the floorplan, e.g., position of doors, hallway intersections, etc. We compare those found in the image to a floorplan provided by the building's infrastructure. We use a building server to hold this floorplan data as well as provide the computation cycles for extracting the micro-landmarks and performing the matching. Communication between the client and server is realized through a Wi-Fi connection supported by many newer phone models. We prune the search of the best correspondence by using the Wi-Fi fingerprint to coarsely locate the user (we only expect a location estimate that is accurate to within 5-10 meters - easily attainable with several of today's Wi-Fi-based positioning systems [2,3]).

The problem of determining useful landmarks is complicated in large open spaces as it is much more difficult to discern floorplan features. In this case, we use an approach developed by Snavely, Seitz, and Szeliski named Photo Tourism [4] which uses texture features of the images computed by SIFT [5] which are mapped to 3D locations through the use of multiple images. This stored structure allows a similar correspondence to be computed between the landmark database

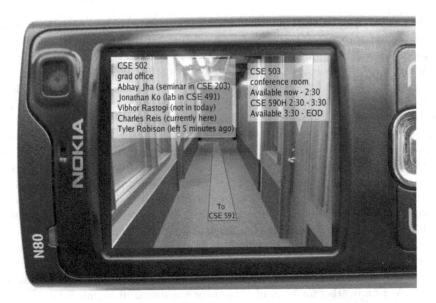

Fig. 1. Sample of possible information overlay on an image of the environment. Image shows both an overlaid navigation aid and a magic lens-type application with dynamic information about the current surroundings.

and new images. These texture-landmarks do not rely on specific structural elements. It is important, however, to ensure that the landmark database used for feature correspondence is an accurate reflection of the current space.

Thus, our system works as follows: (0) the phone captures the image, (1) sends it to the server along with Wi-Fi fingerprints and the type of information requested, (2) the server performs feature extraction and (3) finds the correspondence to the building's floorplan or to previously captured images, (4) from this correspondence the camera pose can be computed, and finally, (5) the server returns an information overlay for display to the phone client. Figure 2 provides a diagram of how our system operates (focusing on the micro-landmarks used for hallways). Our challenge is to ensure that all this computation and communication can be performed in under 5 seconds to support reasonable user interaction speeds. Although we currently do all the processing on the building's server our goal is to explore different partitions of tasks and evaluate their performance. Moreover, we can further explore the types of features/landmarks we extract from the image and consider several hybrid approaches. We also plan to investigate the use of video (as the user moves the phone) as this may provide more cues than a static image. Video processing is likely to be better suited for this type of "magic lens" or augmented reality application. We expect that the current single image technique can be extended with refinement techniques to support video.

In the following sections of this paper, we discuss work on similar problems and how they relate to our system. Then we examine the steps of processing an

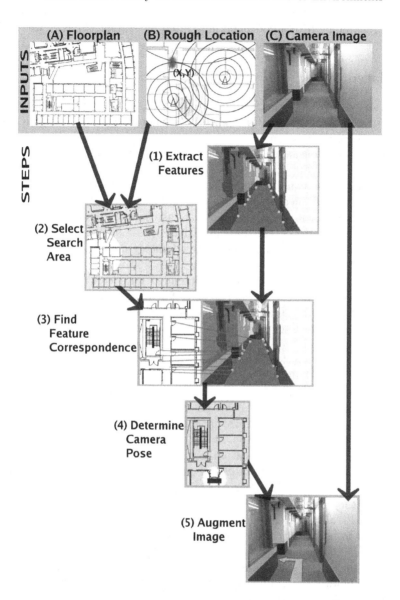

Fig. 2. System diagram for calculating camera pose and overlaying information on an image from a camera phone. The inputs to the system are the following: (A) a floorplan with relevant features marked on it, (B) a rough location estimate (which includes floor information), and (C) an image from the camera. Using this information, the first step is to extract relevant features from the image. Step two is to choose a region of the floorplan and a set of features to match against. In step three, a mapping between the features in the image and features on the floorplan must be assigned and evaluated. In step four, this information can then be used to find a more precise location and orientation on the floorplan. Lastly in step five, location of objects and features on the floorplan can then be transferred onto the image, along with data relevant to the user. A similar methodology exists for texture landmarks.

image and matching it to a floorplan, illustrated by examples. Lastly we discuss remaining issues and extensions to our system.

2   Related Work

A variety of systems exist that can localize a device in its environment with the use of an image. Many of these are designed for robot navigation, and make use of odometry data and rely on many images to localize accurately. Early work shows that matching building features to refine location is feasible [6], but requires a highly accurate estimate of current position and orientation. More recent work makes use of robust image features such as those produced by SIFT [5]. The vSLAM system simultaneously builds a map and localizes images features within that map [7]. Other robotic navigation systems use many images along a path and visibility information to calculate likely locations [8,9]. None of these systems are suitable for our desired scenario where odometry data and multiple images are not available.

Image analysis systems that are not intended for localization also provide useful components. Photo Tourism can solve for 3-D locations of feature points in a scene and calculate camera positions from a large group of images [4]. New images can be matched to the current model, producing an accurate camera pose in relation to the scene. Annotations can be transferred between images by using the underlying 3-D structure. Photo Tourism relies on distinct SIFT features which most hallways lack, and it is not designed for quickly finding a camera position in a large area given a location estimate. For this reason, the approach of Photo Tourism plays an important role in our system, but is not sufficient. Systems to recognize landmarks in outdoor environments and provide annotations also exist [10]. This also relies on SIFT features, and does not actually generate a refined location, but merely identifies what objects might be in the image. Providing a database of geocoded features is also much higher cost than providing a building floorplan. Although these systems support similar interactions, they are not suitable for use on hallway images.

Augmented reality systems share a similar goal of information overlay. These systems tend to be object centric, and often tag objects with special markers to facilitate their location in an image [11,12,13]. Other systems actively project structured light on the environment to aide in localization [14], but would have difficulty in a hallway environment. Existing augmented reality systems provide a variety of examples of information overlay and may be a source for applications of this system, but do not currently support hallway environments without special tagging or special hardware. Although some systems seek to augment existing maps [15], our system aims to bring the map information to the user's current environment.

3   System

As previewed in Figure 2, the steps of the system will be first to extract possible relevant features from a given 640x480 cell phone camera image. Next a relevant section of the floorplan (or other feature database) must be chosen, and then the matching will be performed. Once the correspondence is found, it can be used to find location and orientation of the camera. Lastly, the location of objects and other relevant information can be transferred back into image space. The following sections will discuss these steps in more detail, illustrated by examples from work on the problem. Although the bulk of our current work focuses on hallway images and building features, we also discuss the use of image-based features that will support environments other than hallways.

3.1   Features in Homogeneous Environments (Hallways)

Feature Detection. The first step in finding how an image matches to a floorplan is to locate the features in the image. There is limited information on a standard floorplan, but any floorplan should include location of doorways and corners of walls. These features, or micro-landmarks, will be visible in the image too, and the goal is to find them. The concept is simple: to locate the lines that define the edge of the floor and the lines that define the edge of each doorway or corner. Intersecting these sets of lines will give points that correspond to the features on the floorplan.

We have implemented a basic feature detection method based on segmenting the image. Instead of looking for the edges of the floor directly, we locate the entire floor and then use the edges of that region. We have chosen the Mean Shift method to perform image segmentation [16]. The floor will then likely be the segment that is at the bottom center of the image. It is difficult to take a picture of a hallway where this is not the case, but this requirement could be included in the interface that prompts users to take pictures. The edge of this region is then traced and the corners are identified using a "cornerity" metric [17]. This will not locate all the places along the floor where there is a doorway, but it finds many of them. More can be located by intersecting vertical lines found in the image with the floor boundary, but this is not done in these examples. Additionally, this tracing method finds some false corners that do not correspond to anything in the floorplan. False corners that are at the top of a vertical line of the floor edge can be discarded as points likely caused by occlusion of the floor. The results of segmentation and corner finding are shown in Figure 3. These are points that can now be used to match to the floorplan.

Although this basic feature detection gives results suitable for demonstrating the system, we are looking at other methods to improve it. This will be discussed more in Section 4. Our current method is similar in spirit to other work done on natural indoor scene analysis for local robot navigation [18].

Feature Matching. Once the features in the image are found, they must be matched to the floorplan. The first step of this is to choose a set of points from the floorplan to match against. This is done both to remove ambiguous cases and to reduce the search space. The rough location estimate provides a center for the region to be tested, and a radius can be estimated based on the accuracy of the location system and some idea of the camera's useful visibility range. Figure 4

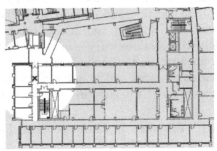

Fig. 3. The hallway image is first segmented with Mean Shift, then the edge of the floor traced and corners located. Corners marked with orange circles are candidates for matching to floorplan features.

Fig. 4. The region of the floorplan considered for matching. The estimated location is marked with an X, and the feature points are marked with small red dots.

shows the floorplan, an estimate of the location, and the features that will be considered for matching for the hallway image shown in Figure 3. It is possible to include other information when calculating the region to consider, such as visibility calculations, or priors for direction, either from direction of motion or an external sensor, but we currently do not include these.

Once the two sets of features are defined, they must be matched up. This is a challenging problem because of the number of possible ways to match. A transformation between the image space and the map space can be defined by four sets of correspondences. For the examples presented here, there are an average of 10 image points and an average of 27 map points, resulting in over 2 billion possible four-point correspondences. In order to make this problem tractable, we perform this matching using a RANSAC approach that intelligently selects and prioritizes the hypotheses. The hypotheses are generated by randomly choosing two points from the image and two points from the map. These two points define a line in each space, and the next two points must have consistent placement with respect to that line across the image and map space. This selection eliminates approximately 90% of the hypotheses that would be generated purely randomly. Hypotheses are also prioritized based on the area covered by the four points in the image. The larger the distance between the points, the more likely it will produce a stable homography. The area of the bounding box of the four points is used as a measure of spread, and a threshold is slowly lowered in order to implement priority. Lastly, the search is terminated early if the estimate has not improved in a "long time" (for example, 5,000 samples) because it unlikely to improve further as the threshold lowers. Our examples obtain good results testing less than 100,000 hypotheses.

Hypotheses are evaluated by solving for a homography that maps from the image points to the floorplan points, and looking at the sum of squared distance between the two point sets. Weights for points closer to the camera (lower in the

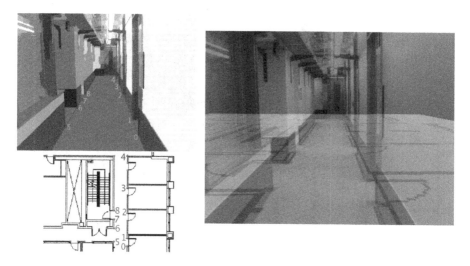

Fig. 5. Results of point correspondence algorithm. Upper left: the detected points on the image labeled by number. Lower left: the points on the floorplan that were matched to the image, labeled with corresponding numbers. Right: the floorplan warped into the image space and overlaid on top of the original image, which matches very well. This example has 10 image points and 32 map points, and completes matching in about 15 seconds.

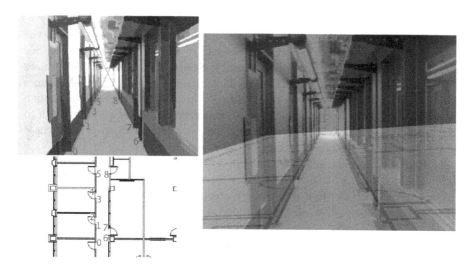

Fig. 6. Results of point correspondence algorithm. Upper left: the detected points on the image labeled by number. Lower left: the points on the floorplan that were matched to the image, labeled with corresponding numbers. Right: floorplan warped into the image space and overlaid on top of the original image. This example has 11 images points and 31 map points and completes matching in about 12 seconds. The view the opposite direction down the hallway is visually similar, so this is not a trivial example.

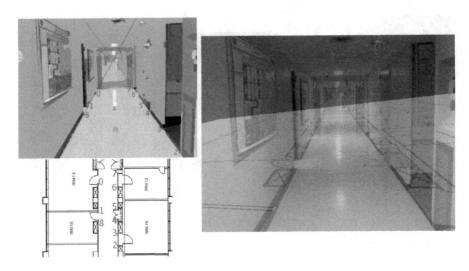

Fig. 7. Results of point correspondence algorithm. Upper left: the detected points on the image labeled by number. The detected points of this example required some manual filtering to get a good match. Lower left: the points on the floorplan that were matched to the image, labeled with corresponding numbers. Right: floorplan warped into the image space and overlaid on top of the original image. This example has 9 image points and 19 map points and completes matching in about 8 seconds.

image) are higher because they are likely to be detected more accurately in the image. The highest ranking solution at the end of the search is then used. See Figure 5 and 6 for results from our Computer Science building. Figure 7 shows results from our Health Sciences Center. This image presented more challenges due to the lower contrast, reduced brightness, and reflective floors. Although some manual filtering of the image features was required to get good a match to the floorplan, we believe it is possible to refine the algorithms to process these images correctly, as discussed in Section 4.

The RANSAC method returns results in 5 to 30 seconds on a 2.8GHz desktop machine, which is approaching the speed necessary for use in a live application. We believe that further improvements are possible that will increase both speed and robustness. This will be discussed more in Section 4.

3.2 Features in Heterogeneous Environments (Open Areas)

The system described above is tailored specifically to hallways and areas that have micro-landmark building features visible, but a lack of other distinct visual features. Images of rooms besides hallways often do not show many building features, but have a richness of other features, as in Figure 8. In order to support areas like this, a system like Photo Tourism can be used [4]. This requires a database of SIFT image features reconstructed from many images of the area and then aligned with the floorplan. New images can then be matched to this data and localized, providing a camera location and orientation. An example of this is shown in Figure 9, where the atrium of a building is analyzed using about 50 high quality (7 megapixel) images, and then a cell phone image is localized within this structure. The example shown here took about 7 seconds to match the cell phone image to the database of image features.

Approaches like Photo Tourism work well in open areas with many distinct image features, but have difficulty in more confined and uniform spaces like hallways. Additionally, it requires significant effort to take enough pictures to provide a database to localize new images. For this reason, we think a mixture of our hallway and floorplan micro-landmark system with an image feature texture-landmark database system will provide the most coverage at a lower startup cost. Integration of these systems may be done in a variety of ways, and is discussed further in Section 4.

Fig. 8. An atrium of a building. This lacks easily detectable building structure making it difficult to match directly to a floorplan. However, it has an abundance of distinct image features, making it possible to use other methods based on an image feature database.

3.3   Augmenting Images

The correspondence between the image features and the landmarks (from the floorplan or feature database) allow the camera pose can be estimated. This will give both the location and orientation of the camera in the space of the floorplan. The camera pose can be solved after finding the correspondence or the pose and correspondence can be solved simultaneously. It is also possible to use the simple homography calculated by our RANSAC matching method to map regions between the image and floorplan without further calculation.

The mapping between the image and floorplan can then be used to overlay information onto the camera image. Arrows to give navigation directions can be drawn on the floor by drawing the arrow on the floorplan and warping it into the image space. Tips of arrows can even disappear behind corners to give

Fig. 9. This shows the reconstructed structure of a building atrium using Photo Tourism. The colored dots show the location of detected image features. The black triangles show the camera positions for images used in the reconstruction. The red triangle shows the location of the cell phone image within the reconstruction. Above: the reconstruction has been manually aligned with the building floorplan. Below: a view of the image is shown overlaid on the reconstruction.

an added sense of depth by clipping to the area segmented as floor, without requiring additional knowledge of the 3D structure. An example of this is shown in Figure 10. Since the location of doors is known in the image, the doors can be marked with additional labels, as suggested in Figure 1.

Fig. 10. This shows an arrow overlaid to match the perspective of the floor. The calculated homography was used to place the arrow.

4 Remaining Issues

We have demonstrated the feasibility of an image based localization system for overlaying information. However, many improvements are necessary in order to build a live application. Different areas of future work will be discussed in the following sections.

4.1 Robustness

This would not be an interesting problem if the simple methods proposed here worked for all situations. Indeed, there are many cases it does not work for that must be overcome. Figure 11 shows some possible problem areas. Transitions in floor covering can easily cause problems in segmenting the floor. Additionally, reflective floors make it difficult to segment the floor and produce reflected copies of relevant features. Combining information from probable floor edges as well as color and texture may help both problems, as could including information about floor types in the floorplan. Additionally, providing a small number of training examples may enable a customized doorway-corner feature detector while still maintaining low startup cost. Buildings with different types of doors or flooring in different areas could use a marked floorplan to select the appropriate detectors based on the rough location estimate.

Breaking assumptions about floor shape, for example hallways that curve, may cause problems with fitting lines to these edges, so the algorithms should not rely on this. Areas with few features, such as stretches of hallway without doors, or areas with unusual features, such as a catwalk, must be dealt with. Including floor edge lines as features in addition to points may provide more op-portunity for matching, as would training specific doorway or corner detectors for each building. Estimates of user motion may also provide additional infor-mation about current location. These estimates may come from the location system, from the camera in a video mode, or even from external sensors, such as accelerometers and gyroscopes. Additionally, images that contain clutter will cause problems with simple segmentation. A box sitting on the floor may cause spurious features, as could a person walking by. In addition to improving the image analysis component, the point correspondence component should be robust to both spurious and missing features. Making more direct use of a camera model when matching between the image and the map should result in better constrained and more robust solutions. We are investigating the requirements of the matching system in order to inform the development of the feature detectors.

To cover a wider range of environments, a mixture of floorplan-based features and image based features can be used. Although navigation instructions are not as useful in a room, there are applications that could use this feature. There are few features in the floorplan that are visible in an average room, however the presence of objects in these rooms provides features that are more likely distinguishable with SIFT [5] and Photo Tourism [4]. In order for a system that uses SIFT image features to be robust to matching a wide variety of images, a large volume of pictures are necessary. In addition to variance in lighting at different times of day, camera quality also influences matching. For this reason, it may be necessary to include pictures of the environment across a range of lighting and a range of cameras. It may also be possible to use the floorplan feature system to bootstrap the SIFT feature collection, giving a lower startup cost but the ability to leverage SIFT features. Outdoor environments could also make use of SIFT features, but would not be able to leverage map information, instead requiring a large volume of images of the environment.

Even with robust algorithms, there are likely some images that will cause failure. It is important to be able to recognize these failures automatically and possibly provide a measure of uncertainty. Relaying this back to the user with information about what went wrong will increase their trust of the system by not giving obviously wrong results. It will also allow them to take this information into account when taking a new picture.

4.2   Speed

It is also important to consider response time in order to use this approach in an application. A user will likely not want to wait more than a few seconds for a response, so our goal is a response time of 5 seconds or less. If all the processing is done on a server and not on the phone, the time to send the image across a network must also be included. We assume a Wi-Fi enabled phone for the location system, and use 640x480 images, but other scenarios may take significantly more network time. Even for our case, algorithms must be chosen to meet this time goal. Our current bottleneck is finding correspondence between the features in the image and the map, but we believe this can be improved further. New methods for image analysis will also need to be chosen with speed in mind. It is also possible that some or all of the processing could be done on the phone as the processing power of phones continues to increase.

Fig. 11. Examples of images that pose problems for simple segmentation. Changes in floor material, reflective floors, and unusual structures such as curved walls and catwalks break simple assumptions, but they should all be handled properly. Additionally, people or clutter in the hallways will cause problems detecting features, as will environments with low contrast difference between floors and walls.

The Photo Tourism system is not designed to provide quick camera pose estimation within a large space given a new image and location estimate. It will be necessary to design the feature database to return a small number of features in the area around the location estimate in order to support our live user interaction model. Additional optimizations may be necessary to increase speed and improve handling of lower quality cell phone images. Additional work will be necessary to integrate both the floorplan-based landmarks and the image-based landmarks into one cooperative system. A simple geographic based approach could be used to dictate using one approach in hallways and the other in open areas, or the two types of features could be detected in parallel and then used together to solve for camera pose.

Video based "magic lens" or augmented reality type applications are also an area requiring optimization. Even if the initial camera pose takes some time to compute, assuming relatively small motion between frames it should be possible to compute an update to camera pose in a fraction of the time required for the general case. Since this system uses data in the image itself to calculate where to show things on the image, it should not be subject to the disconcerting lag in systems that use separate sensors to determine where the camera is aimed. An example of such a system is Nokia's MARA, which relies on GPS and compass sensors [19].

4.3   Applications

A system like this would make developing and using augmented reality applications for indoor environments much easier. Environments would not need to be instrumented with additional features; at a minimum a floorplan is required in order to deploy the system, although additional information such as photographs or property tags may be provided to improve robustness. Users would only need to have a camera phone to take advantage of the applications. Navigation applications could provide much clearer directions by overlaying directions on images of the current environment. Navigation applications could also make use of the improved location accuracy, again without the need for additional markers as proposed in other navigation systems [20]. Using images of the environment instead of words or maps is more effective for people with cognitive disabilities [1], and would be a pleasant interface for most users. The ubiquity of cellphone usage would not make users requiring assitance stand out. Pausing to take a picture of the current location also seems like a natural way to ask for help in deciding where to go next. This interface may also be a convenient way to retrieve timely information about the current environment. Linking information from a calendar system would enable it to show the availability of the nearby conference room, without requiring data entry on the phone. An X-Ray Vision-type application could use more detailed information about the building to show plumbing or similar structures within the walls. Overlaying those details on images of the walls will allow servicemen to more accurately predict where work might be needed.

Outdoor environments would also benefit from navigation instructions tailored to the current view, and we believe a similar approach will work in outdoor environments. It could also be used as a way to identify landmarks and index into information about them. For example, it could find the name or address of a building, hours of operation, reviews from other people about that location, and other information–all without requiring users to do complex lookups on their phones. There is a wealth of opportunities for building applications on top of a system like this.

5 Conclusion

We have presented early results that demonstrate it is possible to provide the capability of information overlay on camera phones for a variety of indoor environments. Our system tailored to hallway environments currently provides reasonable latency, and still has room for further improvement. We have also demonstrated that a system based on SIFT image features can work in more open environments, and that these two systems complement each other. Although there are significant improvements necessary to achieve a workable system, we have developed a framework to support localization from images and allow applications such as navigation and dynamic directory assistance to overlay information on a user's camera phone with minimal infrastructure cost.

Acknowledgements

This work is supported by NIDRR under our ACCESS project. Thanks to Noah Snavely, Steve Seitz, Linda Shapiro, Alan Liu, and Dan Goldman for their assitance on this project.

References

1. Liu, A.L., Hile, H., Kautz, H., Borriello, G., Brown, P.A., Harniss, M., Johnson, K.: Indoor wayfinding: developing a functional interface for individuals with cognitive impairments. In: Assets '06: Proceedings of the 8th international ACM SIGAC-CESS conference on Computers and accessibility, pp. 95–102. ACM Press, New York, USA (2006)
2. Ekahau Wi-Fi positioning engine, a commercial location product, http://www.ekahau.com/
3. Ferris, B., Haehnel, D., Fox, D.: Gaussian processes for signal strength-based location estimation. In: Proceedings of Robotics: Science and Systems (August 2006), Philadelphia, USA (2006)
4. Snavely, N., Seitz, S.M., Szeliski, R.: Photo tourism: exploring photo collections in 3d. ACM Trans. Graph 25(3), 835–846 (2006)
5. Lowe, D.G.: Distinctive image features from scale-invariant keypoints. Int. J. Comput. Vision 60(2), 91–110 (2004)
6. Kosaka, A., Pan, J.: Purdue experiments in model-based vision for hallway navigation. IEEE/RSJ International Conference on Intelligent Robots and Systems (IROS) 1, 87–96 (1995)
7. Karlsson, N., di Bernardo, E., Ostrowski, J., Goncalves, L., Pirjanian, P., Munich, M.: The vslam algorithm for robust localization and mapping. In: Proceedings of the 2005 IEEE International Conference on Robotics and Automation (April 2005), pp. 24–29 (2005)
8. Dellaert, F., Burgard, W., Fox, D., Thrun, S.: Using the condensation algorithm for robust, vision-based mobile robot localization. In: Proc. of the IEEE Computer Society Conference on Computer Vision and Pattern Recognition (1999)
9. Wolf, J., Burgard, W., Burkhardt, H.: Robust vision-based localization for mobile robots using an image retrieval system based on invariant features. In: Proceedings of the IEEE International Conference on Robotics and Automation (2002)

10. Fritz, G., Seifert, C., Paletta, L.: A mobile vision system for urban detection with informative local descriptors. In: ICVS '06: Proceedings of the Fourth IEEE Intl Conference on Computer Vision Systems, IEEE Computer Society, Los Alamitos (2006)
11. Rekimoto, J., Ayatsuka, Y.: Cybercode: Designing augmented reality environments with visual tags. In: Proceedings of DARE (2000)
12. Hile, H., Kim, J., Borriello, G.: Microbiology tray and pipette tracking as a proactive tangible user interface. In: Ferscha, A., Mattern, F. (eds.) PERVASIVE 2004. LNCS, vol. 3001, pp. 323–339. Springer, Heidelberg (2004)
13. Caudell, T., Mizell, D.: Augmented reality: an application of heads-up display technology tomanual manufacturing processes. Proceedings of Hawaii International Conference on System Sciences. 2, 659–669 (1992)
14. Köhler, M., Patel, S., Summet, J., Stuntebeck, E., Abowd, G.: Tracksense: Infrastructure free precise indoor positioning using projected patterns. In: Pervasive Computing (2007)
15. Hecht, B., Rohs, M., Schöning, J., Krüger, A.: Wikeye - using magic lenses to explore georeferenced wikipedia content. In: 3rd International Workshop on Pervasive Mobile Interaction Devices (PERMID 2007) (2007)
16. Comaniciu, D., Meer, P.: Mean shift analysis and applications. In: ICCV '99: Proceedings of the International Conference on Computer Vision, vol. 2, IEEE Computer Society, Los Alamitos (1999)
17. Guru, D., Dinesh, R., Nagabhushan, P.: Boundary based corner detection and localization using new 'cornerity' index: A robust approach. In: CRV '04: Proceedings of the 1st Canadian Conference on Computer and Robot Vision (CRV'04), pp. 417–423. IEEE Computer Society, Los Alamitos (2004)
18. Rous, M., Lupschen, H., Kraiss, K.: Vision-based indoor scene analysis for natural landmark detection. In: IEEE International Conference on Robotics and Automation, pp. 4642–4647 (April 2005)
19. Nokia mobile augmented reality applications (MARA), http://research.nokia.com/research/projects/mara/index.html
20. Muller, H.J., Schoning, J., Kruger, A.: Mobile map interaction - evaluation in an indoor scenario. In: Workshop,Mobile and Embedded Interactive Systems (MEIS'06), part of Informatik (October 2006)

SocialMotion: Measuring the Hidden Social Life of a Building

Christopher R. Wren[1], Yuri A. Ivanov[1], Ishwinder Kaur[2],
Darren Leigh[1], and Jonathan Westhues[1]

[1] Mitsubishi Electric Research Laboratories, Cambridge, MA, US
[2] M.I.T. Media Laboratory, Cambridge, MA, US

Abstract. In this paper we present an approach to analyzing the social behaviors that occur in a typical office space. We describe a system
consisting of over 200 motion sensors connected in a wireless network
observing a medium-sized office space populated with almost 100 people
for a period of almost a year. We use a *tracklet graph* representation of
the data in the sensor network, which allows us to efficiently evaluate
gross patterns of office-wide social behavior of its occupants during expected seasonal changes in the workforce as well as unexpected social
events that affect the entire population of the space. We present our experiments with a method based on Kullback-Leibler metric applied to
the office activity modelled as a Markov process. Using this approach we
detect gross deviations of short term office-wide behavior patterns from
previous long-term patterns spanning various time intervals. We compare
detected deviations to the company calendar and find and provide some
quantitative analysis of the relative impact of those disruptions across
a range of temporal scales. We also present a favorable comparison to
results achieved by applying the same analysis to email logs.

1   Introduction

The social fabric of an organization is largely hidden from direct observation. It
is not the same as the organizational structure. It is not completely defined by
email or phone communication. The social fabric is the interpersonal connectivity
in a group that is largely created and maintained by physical interactions in the
space [1]. Measuring the structure and dynamic evolution of these connections
is essential to understanding the health and productivity of an organization. At
the same time, the details of these interactions are very sensitive from a personal
privacy standpoint, so it is important to treat them with respect [2].

This social fabric is embedded within the architectural structure of a building.
There will be social spaces such as lounges or kitchens. There may be specific
associations between individuals and particular places in a building, such as
offices. There are likely to be organizational functions that are concentrated in
particular locations, such as departments and work groups. We are motivated by
these facts to take a building-centered approach to measuring the social fabric.
By measuring the way the social fabric drapes over the physical structure of the
space we indirectly measure the structure of the social fabric itself.

J. Hightower, B. Schiele, and T. Strang (Eds.): LoCA 2007, LNCS 4718, pp. 85–102, 2007.
© Springer-Verlag Berlin Heidelberg 2007

This space-centric perspective has several advantages. By trying to understand the way the building is being used we can avoid the need to instrument or catalog each person in the space. This is a significant advantage in cost, reliability, and the impact on privacy. One of the insights that we gained during the experiments with the data that we collected is that in order to find events that disrupt the established patterns of social interactions, we do not need to look at every individual participant of the daily routine of the office space, but rather at how all together the inhabitants behave differently in response to a socially disruptive event. This implies that all analysis can be done *en masse*, without resorting to finding patterns in behavior of each individual, nor establishing his/her identity. This approach also makes it possible to fluidly handle visitors and other transient populations.

We have installed a 200 node sensor network in a corporate facility and have used it to collect the data for the period of over 10 consecutive months. Each sensor node has the ability to sense motion when a moving object appears in its field of view. We consciously tried to avoid using video cameras in order to accommodate the sense of comfort among the people populating the office. This on one hand made the problem of data collection easier, as the occupants felt that their privacy was respected, but on the other hand, made the task of data analysis harder, as no ground truth can be derived from the sensor data.

However, it should be pointed out that even with the use of the video cameras, it would be nearly impossible to obtain ground truth for the data on such scale. Video storage issues aside, a simple review of the recorded videos could take a very long time. In view of this we opted for using other means for analysis - company calendar and email logs. This approach inevitably leads to questions of quantitative validity of the analysis. In the light of this argument we would like to emphasize that it is not a classification approach that we present, but rather a ranking system. We attempt to explain found irregularities in the behavior patterns the best we can, but it is nearly impossible to frame the experiments in a purely quantitative fashion for lack of exact transcription of a year worth of movements of 100 people.

Using a tracklet graph representation that we have developed in our earlier work [3] this paper focuses on the statistics calculated over a large population of these graphs. The graphs record the possible destinations for a person leaving his/her office. Aggregating these graphs over extended periods of time allows us to estimate Markov models of the connectivity of the space. The Kullback-Leibler Divergence (KLD) is then used to compare models from different time periods. This technique enables analysis of the time-varying patterns of social behavior of the entire organization.

During the ten months of observation the organization experienced several disruptive events: the arrival and departure of a large transient worker population, a change in the senior management structure within the organization, a change in management in the parent company, and other events such as holidays, etc. We will present evidence that the sensitivity of this building-centered social analysis to disruptions compares favorably to a classical email-based approach.

2   Background

Social relationships in organizations have been studied for quite some time [4]. The methods developed for the analysis of these relationships have ranged from conducting individual surveys and handing out questionnaires to mining data in online communities and using wearable sensors to monitor the social activities of the people. The analysis of the social dynamics and understanding roles of individuals in social networks [5] may help organizations to improve their productivity by leveraging the groups naturally forming among their staff.

In the recent years, data gathered from the company email communications has been used to identify social networks in an organization [6,7]. The success of this approach is largely due to a directed and unambiguous nature of point-to-point email communications, as well as to the convenience of the centralized storage of this data. When compared to traditional surveying techniques this approach is both cheaper and less prone to human reporting error. Though most such analyses use the To and From data fields in the email to form directed graphs of social relationships, some scholars have gone further and included the content and topic of message to allow determination of expertise and social roles of the correspondents [8]. More detailed analyses are made possible by fusing of informationfrom multiple data sources, such as web pages [9].

Recently swarms of simple sensors have been used as perceptual tools for living and office spaces. Much of this work has its focus on prediction of motion [10] and monitoring activity [11,12,13]. That body of work so far has avoided the question of social network analysis.

In another very different approach, wearable electronic sensors have been used to gather information about social networks in organizations [14,15]. In order to gather information about verbal interactions and the nature of the conversational dynamics in social networks, people in the organization wore sensors on their bodies over extended periods of time. The goal of this analysis was to understand the social network in an organization and identify the people informally entrusted with leadership roles in various groups and subgroups. The authors found that conversational cues such as turn-taking pattern strongly correlates with the speakers' roles in the organization.

Up until recently the research in this area has been focusing on the roles of individuals, viewing social networks from the perspective of the individual participants. By necessity such analysis can be privacy invasive. All measurements that carry identity or cognitive information such as emails or voice recordings can be viewed as compromising individual's privacy and are subject to strict regulations and limitations on the scale of deployment. In contrast, measuring less descriptive information in a process that allows a person to preserve his or her anonymity enables massive deployments, that can be rich sources of information about social dynamics without having to sacrifice significant individual privacy. This data can be freely distributed, analyzed and reported on. An extensive discussion of privacy is beyond the scope of this paper hoeever. We invite th interested ereader to see our prior work in this area [16].

The social network of any organization is not a fixed immutable feature to be discovered through a one-time effort. The network, like the community that it describes is alive and changes over a period in time. It is affected by the influx of workers, by top down management changes or directives and in response to physical factors such as building space reallocations. This paper is a step towards developing methods that can be used to identify and quantify the effects of such interruptions and activities on social relationships between people. Our hope is that this information could help planning such moves more effectively to minimize their disruptive impact.

3   Models

A gross estimate of the level of activity in a space can be cheaply and easily obtained from a collection of motion sensors. Even the most basic such measurements will reveal the patterns of usage in a space. This point is clearly illustrated in Figure 1, which shows the total activity observed in a space over many months. It can be seen that there is a dominant weekly pattern that governs the behavior of this group of people. It is also possible to see the added activity contributed by a pulse of seasonal workers from approximately June 1 through August 31. Finally, there is a clear depression of activity around the winter holidays.

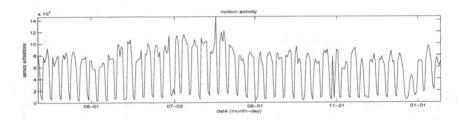

Fig. 1. Gross activity in the experimental space, as measured by the number of raw motion sensor activations

While these are interesting results, they are very coarse. There are a number of more subtle, though no less significant events that have been missed. For example, the plot in Figure 2 shows the number of people who are out of the office, as recorded in the company calendar. It is easy to see that there are periods of time in late August and late December when many people are away from the office (the two primary peaks in that plot). The August travel pulse, with a third of the people away, is not represented in the simple motion analysis of Figure 1 . The absences are masked by some other activity in the space.

Capturing more subtle events in the space requires a more sensitive model. In this section we focus on modeling the structure of the interconnections between parts of the space. To do this we extract the trips that people take in the space and model how those trips connect the various parts of the space.

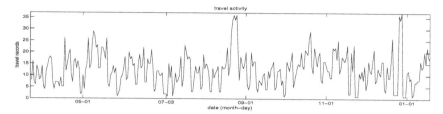

Fig. 2. A plot showing the number of people away from the facility on a particular day

It is not possible, with the very little information provided by motion detectors, to flawlessly extract the tracks of individuals in the space. To compensate for this perceptual shortcoming we instead use a representation that encodes the inherent ambiguities in the data efficiently. We briefly review a method introduced in [3] that allows us to extract a structure called a *tracklet graph*.

One of the main contributions of this paper is in embedding these tracklet graphs into a new probabilistic framework. This embedding results in a Markov chain model that describes the probability of seeing a trip between any two points in the space, even if we never see a single, unambiguous example of such trip. This model captures the social fabric of the space.

Finally we end the section with a description of the Kullback-Leibler Divergence (KLD) formulation for Markov chains that we use to detect changes in that social fabric over time.

3.1   Tracking

Classical tracking accommodates ambiguity by maintaining a set of hypotheses that describe every consistent explanation of the data. This is referred to as multiple hypothesis testing [17]. The problem with approaches similar to that is that with each new ambiguity the hypothesis set may grow exponentially. The goal of the tracking algorithm is to use new observations to prune away the ambiguities and arrive at a single, true explanation for the data.

Most of the tracking literature focuses on the use of high-quality sensors such as cameras [18]. Since we only use motion detectors we cannot prune our hypotheses: all motion activations look the same. Unlike a camera-based system, we cannot prune hypotheses by noticing a blue shirt, or a particularly tall person, or recognizing a face. All the data collected by the system is therefore inherently ambiguous about the person's identity. A person may emerge from a particular office, but there is no way to tell who that person is, or even that it is in fact a single person. And when that person or group of people passes other people in the hallway there is no way to tell with any certainly who went where.

Conversely, we *do* need to know where people go in order to model the social fabric. Maintaining an exponentially growing hypothesis set is not feasible. To circumvent this we utilize a representation that folds the hypotheses set into a graph structure that does not grow exponentially.

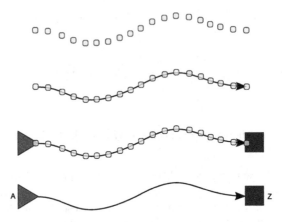

Fig. 3. The Tracklet derived from a sequence of observations

Rather than requiring perfect tracking from high-quality sensors, or settling for low-quality inference from low-quality sensors, we show one possible method that allows us to draw inferences from these collections of imperfect graphs.

Tracklets. The idea of a *tracklet* [3] was developed as a way to represent ambiguity in tracking for forensic applications. It allowed a system to efficiently query a human operator for input to refine the imperfect tracking results.

The basic concept of a tracklet is that it aggregates observations that are unambiguously related to each other. This is illustrated in Figure 3 where at the top we see a collection of observations strung out through space and time. If the observations are sequential in time, come from sensors that are close to each other is space, and are isolated from other distracting observations, then a simple model of movement in the space will allow us to aggregate those observations into a single chain (the second line of Figure 3). Further, if the collection of observations is itself isolated in space and time, then we say that the tracklet begins or terminates (third line of Figure 3). In subsequent figures we will drop the observations themselves, only showing the high-level tracklet abstractions, such as the bottom line of Figure 3.

We shall refer to the simple directed graph in Figure 3 as γ_0. The graph γ_0 shows that the probability of the terminating event Z being generated by the same individual (or group of individuals) that generated the originating event A is high, without loss of generality we will say

$$P(A \prec Z | \gamma_0) = 1$$

the probability that Z flows from the same cause as A, given graph γ_0 is unity.

The Tracklet Graph. Ambiguities in the environment will generate more complicated graphs. All observations that share a possible common cause will

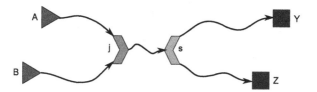

Fig. 4. A simple tracklet graph with a single split s

be linked together in the same connected graph. In Figure 4 we see a more complicated graph representing two or more individuals crossing paths in the space.

The new symbols represent a split and a join. The brown chevron represents a join. The green chevron represents a split. That is, several observations follow the split, s, within a small enough temporal and spatial neighborhood to generate ambiguity. In the case of a split, there must be several individuals moving together or very near each other to be considered as joint actors in a tracklet. After the split, the fate of each individual that traversed the tracklet from j to s is ambiguous: did they move along the tracklet from s to Z or from s to Y.

Given this graph, which we shall call γ_1, we do not know the fate of an individual originating at node A, this ambiguity is expressed as

$$P(A \prec Z | \gamma_1) = p \tag{1}$$
$$P(A \prec Y | \gamma_1) = q \tag{2}$$

It is worth noting that $p+q$ only equals unity if we are told that individuals are moving in isolation. Otherwise it is possible that a small group (indistinguishable from individuals by these sensors) could have originated at A and split, some to Y and some to Z.

Observed graphs may become arbitrarily complex. The graph γ_2 in Figure 5 is a much more complicated graph with several splits an joins.

By tracing the directed links in the graph we can see that it is possible to connect the origin A with any destination $\{W, X, Y, Z\}$.

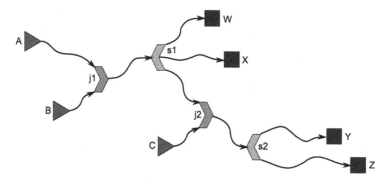

Fig. 5. An example tracklet graph, called γ_2

The tracklet graph in Figure 5 folds onto a single representation all the ambiguity in the situation that would have required several dozen separate hypothetical outcomes to cover all the possible combinations of destination and possible group sizes.

3.2   Populations of Graphs

Imagine that several individuals are moving about a space at a particular instant in time. If they happen to cross paths they will generate ambiguities, and thereby will contribute to a particular tracklet graph instance, γ_i. The framework above allows us to model the fate of those individuals at that moment in time. We now extend that framework by considering collections of graphs, Γ that describes the behavior of a population of individuals over a longer span of time.

We can ask questions of the form, "What does this collection of graphs tell us about the probability that individuals travel from one place to another within a building." We can answer this question by retrieving all the graphs that contain an origin at location A and then counting the number of graphs that contain a possible connection between A and Z:

$$P(A \prec Z | \Gamma) = \frac{\sum_{i=0}^{N} P(A \prec Z | \gamma_i)}{M}$$

where N in the number of graphs in Γ, and M is the number of graphs in Γ that contain the node A as an origin.

It is possible to accumulate evidence for a repeated behavior even if there is not one unambiguous tracklet showing the behavior in its entirety. It is easy to see that if traffic originating at A *always* terminates at Z then all the graphs in Γ that contain A as an origin will contain a plausible path from A to Z and therefore a significant quantity of evidence. The $P(A \prec Z | \Gamma)$ will end up being the average over the evidence $P(A \prec Z | \gamma_i)$ from the graphs in the collection. That will be a smaller number than if every example of that behavior were completely unambiguous, then $P(A \prec Z | \Gamma)$ would be identically unity.

The maps in Figure 8 demonstrates the output of this form of analysis. The illustrations show $P(A \prec Z | \Gamma)$ as a line between A and Z which are the sensors arranged on the circumference of the circle. Darker links represent higher probabilities. These maps illustrate the social fabric of the building.

3.3   Trip Model

We want to extract models from graph populations captured over different periods of time and then compare those models to find changes in the social fabric. If we interpret these models as Markov chains [19], then we can use known formulations of the Kullback-Leibler Divergence to measure the differences between two models [20].

The probabilities $P(A \prec Z | \Gamma)$ between all pairs A and Z in the space represent an estimate of the probability that, given an origin at the point in space A

then there will be a trip that ends at point Z. We interpret this as the transition probability between states in a Markov chain where each element is:

$$T_{A,Z} = P(A \prec Z|\Gamma)$$

A complete Markov model also requires a stationary probability that captures the likelihood of seeing the beginning of a chain in a particular state. The elements of this vector can be trivially estimated from data:

$$S_A = \frac{N_A}{N\omega}$$

where N_A is the number of tracklets that originate at A and $N\omega$ is the number of all tracklet originations. Taken together S_A and $T_{A,Z}$ describe a Markov chain that is a generative models of the social fabric during a window of time.

3.4   Comparing Models

The Kullback-Leibler Divergence is a way to measure the "distance" between two probability distributions. Rached, et. al. showed that the calculation of the divergence when the probability distributions take the form of Markov processes [20] can be done as follows:

$$D(i,j) = \sum_r S_i(r) \sum_c T_i(r,c) \log \frac{T_i(r,c)}{T_j(r,c)}$$

where r are the rows and c are the columns of the matrices.

The plots in Figure 6 are examples of the KLD applied to the analysis of the social fabric of an organization. For each instant in time two models are extracted: one describing the social structure prior to that time, and one describing the structure after that time. The value of the plot is the divergence between these two models.

3.5   The Cyclostationarity of Humans

Figure 6 illustrates a problem with our model as stated. Human social behavior is periodic. In particular the top plot in Figure 6 shows that the model is overwhelmed by the weekly rhythms of the social system. It is not fruitful to blindly compare weekdays to weekends. There has been significant work on cyclostationary processes, for example the work of Kuhl [21]. In our analysis we will generally exclude weekends and assume that weekdays are relatively homogeneous. It is possible to see in the lower plot of Figure 6 that this simplification greatly improves the analytic results. It is now easy to find significant events such as holidays that were largely obscured by the variations induced by the weekly rhythm.

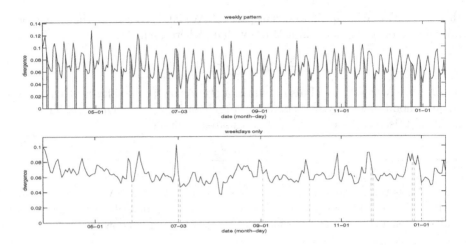

Fig. 6. Human patterns are cyclo-stationary. The top plot shows a comparison of all days, including weekends (marked). The bottom plot shows a comparison of weekdays only (holidays marked).

4   Data Collection

We present results on two datasets: motion data from a sensor network, and a collection of email extracted from user archives. Both datasets cover the 10 months from March 22, 2006 to January 22, 2007.

4.1   Motion

The motion dataset is a record of 10 months of activity at a corporate facility. The facility hosts 80 full-time employees and at least as many transient workers. The site hosts a large number of visitors who may be at the site only a few days a year. The facility also hosts janitorial staff, maintenance staff, electricians, plumbers, carpenters, couriers, caterers and other workers who are not under the administrative control of the organization. Each and every one of these individuals contributed data to this experiment because there was no need to outfit individuals with any kind of tag or hardware.

The data was collected with a motion-based sensor network. The network is built of over 200 nodes that communicate over a wireless radio link to 10 base stations that copy data to the wired local area network. Each node is comprised of an off-the-shelf passive infrared motion detector module and a combination microprocessor and radio board designed at the Massachusetts Institute of Technology[12]. When the nodes observe motion, they broadcast their serial number. The base stations timestamp the data and then inserts a record into a datlabase. The database used to generate our results contains nearly 21 million motion events.

The output of the tracklet building process is a list of tracklets, a list of joins and splits, and a membership map that associates the raw motion events with the tracklets. The list of tracklets in the database contains 3.4 million entries. The average length of a tracklet in the database is 8.5 seconds. This is a meansure of the crowdedness of the building, and implies that even short walks through the space are likely to encompass several ambiguities.

Extracting the tracklet graphs from the raw data takes a few hours to process a database covering over 7000 hours of data. All of this processing is causal, so it can occur during collection. The sensor network is designed such that it can easily be scaled up. In contrast, storage and computation requirements of a network of video cameras can be extremely complicated and costly.

4.2 Email

The email database was built through voluntary participation. Building occupants were asked to visit a web page and provide authentication credentials to a script. The script used those credentials to access the participants' email archives. From each email in the desired time window the script extracted sender and recipient information from the headers. Each unique address was assigned a random integer as a token. Sender and recipient token pairs were then recorded in a database, along with the time of the message. In this way a single email may generate more than one pair, since emails may have multiple recipients. Email lists were treated as distinct entities. Email addresses outside the organization were assigned to a single special token, and so are indistinguishable to the analysis. Once data collection was complete the mapping between tokens and addresses was destroyed. This creates a sanitized view onto the structure of the email habits of the organization. The database contains over 37,000 address pairs. There is no noise in this data, the origin and destination of each communication is explicit, so it is trivial to extract Markov models from this data[19].

4.3 Ground Truth

Ubiquitous computing has struggled with the concept of ground truth. Even the best methods are intrusive, inturrupting the user with intrusive questionnaires many times per day [22]. It is difficult to see how to scale these methods to year-long trials. There is also a long-standing concern over the reliability of self-reporting, particularly on the subject of interpersonal communication [23]. In this study we rely on the corporate calendar as a source of lables for disruptions.

5 Results

The plot in Figure 7 shows the result of the Kullback-Leibler divergence analysis described in Section 3. It is possible to process at different time scales by estimating models from larger temporal spans of data. The four plots in that figure show models ranging from roughly a day to roughly a week. We use an exponential window to create differentiable plots. However sinc ethe windows have

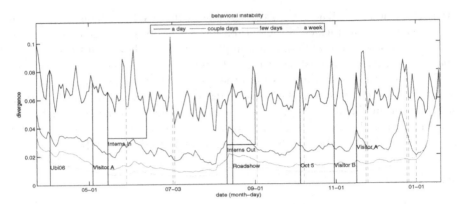

Fig. 7. Responses over a range of temporal scales from a day to a week

theoretically infinite extent, it is difficult to precisely specify the time windows. The "a week" window mixes 10% of the current day distribution with 90% of the estimated distribution to form the new estimate. For comparison, the "couple days" window mixes 40% of the current day with 60% of the estimated distribution. Hard windows are equivalent to convolving with a boxcar filter, and induce similar aliasing artifacts into the results. The Black (dark) vertical lines indicate disruptive events. Green (light) vertical lines indicate holidays.

The events chosen on the plots as disruptive events include things we have taken from the company calendar. It's not possible to record the daily activity of each individual every day for a year. We are instead looking for group events: events that likely affect the whole group. Those can be externally driven: such as holidays. They can also be internally driven, such as staff changes or large corporate events. By insuring that all the major events are represented in the data, with a statistically significant degree of confidence, and further that all the statistically significant peaks in the data are explained by these events, we demonstrate that our tool is sensitive to these macroscopic patterns of behavior.

The time window indicates the amount of data used to build the models that will be compared. So on the daily time scale we compare a model of today with a model of yesterday. On the weekly timescale we compare the model of this week with a model of last week, in a sliding fashion. The weekly model is not simply a filtered version of the daily model. This can be seen in practice by comparing the holiday behavior. For example, July 4th is the single most disruptive event at a daily timescale (top plot). However it completely disappears with only a slight expansion of the time window. In contrast the winter holidays are associated with extended leaves from the office by many people, as can be seen in Figure 2. This holiday has less of an impact at the daily level because people depart in a staggered fashion: no two days taken in isolation are very different from each other. However the flow of people has a significant impact on the longer time scales since the week before the winter holidays is very different from a week during the winter holidays.

The largest long-term disruption is in August when summer vacations, a major pulse of business travel, and the reduction in seasonal staff typically occur. This creates a massive disruption that has a significant impact even at the weekly time scale. It is interesting to note that this major disruption is not even noticeable in the gross activity plot in Figure 1. This indicates that it is not a simple matter of there being less people in the space: it is a sustained, *structural* change in the social fabric of the organization.

The final peaks to notice are the ones labeled "Visitor A". In addition to the senior management termination in October, another disruptive development was a change in management above the organization. It is interesting to note that the May visit is associated with a daily spike but not a lasting disruption. However the late November visit is associated with one of the largest spikes in the entire "couple days" plot. While the visit is proximate to the traditional US holiday, it is clear form the travel records in Figure 2 that this holiday does not induce a pulse of travel similar to the August or December pulses. We hypothesize that this visit was itself massively disruptive due to lingering sensitization after the October 5th event. "Visitor A" is a highly placed corporate executive who is visiting a little over a month after the sudden termination of a senior manager at the site on October 5th.

5.1 Details

We visually explore some of the Markov models in Figure 8. The three rows in the figure illustrate three different points in time. The top row shows July 17th, a day in the middle of the summer when the organization is enjoying relative stability. The second row illustrate October 5th, the day of a disruptive event: the termination of a senior manager. The third row centers on a major holiday.

In each case two models are presented. The divergence plots, such as Figure 7, compare two models. In Figure 8 the left column is the model of past history. The parameters are set so that these models are estimated from approximately one week of data. The right column is a model of the near future. These models are estimated from approximately a day of data.

The Markov model describes the probability of seeing a trip starting at one sensor and ending at another. This is represented graphically by arranging the sensors on a circle and connecting them with straight lines. Line brightness corresponds to probability, with darker lines showing more probable transitions.

Midsummer represents a period of stability. The left and right models at the top of Figure 8 are estimated from non-overlapping data. There are small differences in the plots. However it is visually apparent that the structure of the social connections in the space are stable. This is reflected in the relatively low divergence rates from this period of time on the plots in Figure 7.

There are some features that are worth noticing. The markers around the outside of the plot indicate important locations in the building. The kitchen is a key resource and is marked with a circle on the right side of the plot. The restrooms are marked with squares at the top of the plot. The elevator and

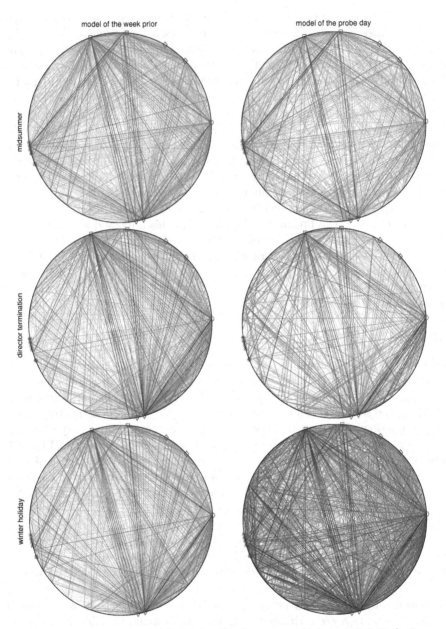

Fig. 8. Example transition probabilities (darker means higher probability). Squares mark bathrooms. Stars mark seasonal employees. Triangles mark elevators and stairs. The circle marks the kitchen. Diamonds mark executive offices.

stairways are marked with triangles at the bottom of the plot. On the left are stars that mark a range of sensors that are near cubicles typically occupied by seasonal staff. Finally the diamonds in the upper right mark a range of sensor associated with the administrative group in general, and the senior managers in particular. Staff offices are mostly near the lower right and left side of the plot.

Early October is a period of organizational disruption for the group. A senior manager who leads about a third of the organization is unexpectedly terminated. This causes a wave of fear and gossip to sweep through the organization. This disruption shows up in Figure 7 both as a spike in the daily model and as an extended ridge in the longer-scale plots. In the model view on the middle right we can see significantly less connectivity between the administrative wing in the upper right and the rest of the building. At the same time we see many more strong links among the staff offices on the left and lower right.

It is also interesting to compare the structure of the top left plot to the structure of the middle left plot. These are both models of relatively stable periods. However the top plot includes a much larger fraction of seasonal staff. The top model shows a dominant quadrilateral marking the interactions of the seasonal employees with the central resources of the bathrooms, the kitchen, and the elevators. In the middle plot the left side of the quadrilateral has largely disappeared as those areas of the building have become depopulated. This shift is responsible for the long timescale disruptions in June (addition of seasonal staff) and August (subsequent reduction).

Holidays marked with light (green) vertical lines in Figure 7, are some of the most disruptive events. The plot on the bottom right of Figure 8 appears much darker than the rest. This is because of the normalization of the transition matrix. Where there is no dominant path then there are many more paths that appear nearly dominant. As a result a much higher proportion of lines are drawn dark. It is also interesting to note that the characteristic quadrilateral reasserts itself in the lower right. Even though there are far fewer temporary employees in the winter than there are in the summer, they do not receive vacation time, so the few who are present during the winter comprise a disproportionate fraction of the population during holidays.

5.2   Email Comparison

A more classical approach to social network analysis is to instrument communication media such as email systems or telephones. We have collected an email database and performed the same analysis on that data. Once the transition and prior probability distributions are estimated from the data, the exact same code computes the Kullback-Leibler divergence for the plots. In Figure 9 we present a side-buy-side comparison of the stability of email behaviors and the more physical behaviors observed by the sensor network. The red triangles on the peaks indicate that a data point has a high confidence of being an outlier, with a p-value of $p < 0.05$ according to a χ^2-test. The significance testing helps us objectively differentiate meaningful peaks from the noise in the plot that our eye may find interesting.

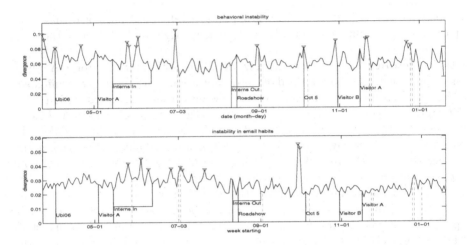

Fig. 9. Physical behaviors (top) show more sensitivity to disruptive events than email behaviors (bottom)

The most stunning thing about the email plot is how insensitive it is to disruption. The major winter holidays and the presence of the seasonal employees generate significant peaks. The rest of the disruptive events that were detected by the motion system, including most holidays, are completely buried in the noise. It could be that people do not, in fact change their email habits while traveling. It could be that there are simply too many distracting emails in the system that are hiding the informative structures in the data in a haze of entropy. Since these results are extracted from emails that people save, we expact that very few of these emails are spam.

There is also no significant reaction to a change in email habits after the termination in October. It could be hypothesized that people did not change their email traffic patterns but merely changed the topics of conversation. We did not do content analysis so we cannot discount that hypothesis. However it is clear from the right middle plot in Figure 8 that there was a significant increase in staff visiting each other in their offices. It seems safe to assert that they may have been discussing topics that did not seem prudent to commit to email. This finding highlights an important power of social network tools based on physical behavior since people may use different modalities for different purposes.

6   Summary

We have looked inside an organization of several hundred people and watched it react to disruptions over the course of almost a year in a way that has never been done before. We attempted to formulate a quantitative measure of the level of social disruption in such a building-centered setting. It is virtually impossible to obtain the exact transcription of daily events for the data set collected on this scale. Instead we focused on a sort of a ranking system that allows us to identify time periods where the dynamics of the group behavior significantly deviated from the "usual".

These results demonstrate that it is possible to measure and model the dynamics of social structures within an organization without instrumenting individuals or installing invasive sensors in the environment, although much works is left to be done refining this method. This building-centered, non-invasive approach allows us to collect comprehensive datasets that seamlessly include everyone in an organization: including transient staff and visitors. By focusing on the building we have created a system that is very human-centered: inclusive while remaining economical, and sensitive to the social fabric without sacrificing the privacy of the individuals who weave that fabric.

References

1. Allen, T.: Architecture and communication among product development engineers. In: Proceedings of the Engineering Management Society, pp. 153–158. IEEE, Los Alamitos (2000)
2. Reynolds, C., Picard, R.: Evaluation of affective computing systems from a dimensional metaethical position. In: First Augmented Cognition International Conference, Las Vegas, NV (2005)
3. Ivanov, Y., Sorokin, A., Wren, C., Kaur, I.: Tracking people in mixed modality systems. In: Visual Communications and Image Processing. Volume EI123., IS&T/SPIE (2007)
4. Scott, J.P.: Social Network Analysis: A Handbook. SAGE Publications, Thousand Oaks (1991)
5. Tichy, N.M., Tushman, M.L., Fombrun, C.: Social network analysis for organizations. The Academy of Management Review 27 (1979)
6. Tyler, J., Wilkinson, D., Huberman, B.A.: Email as Spectroscopy: Automated Discovery of Community Structure within Organizations. In: Communities and Technologies, Kluwer Academic, Dordrecht (2003)
7. van Alstyne, M., Zhang, J.: Emailnet: A system for automatically mining social networks from organizational email communication. In: Annual Conference of the North American Association for Computational Social and Organizational Sciences (2003)
8. McCallum, A., Corrada-Emmanuel, A., Wang, X.: Topic and role discovery in social networks. In: 19th Joint Conference on Artificial Intelligence (2005)
9. Culotta, A., Bekkerman, R., McCallum, A.: Extracting social networks and contact information from email and the web. In: Conference on Email and Spam (2004)
10. Aipperspach, R., Cohen, E., Canny, J.: Modeling human behavior from simple sensors in the home. In: Proceedings Of The IEEE Conference On Pervasive Computing (2006)
11. Wilson, D.H., Atkeson, C.: Simultaneous tracking & activity recognition (star) using many anonymous, binary sensors. In: The Third International Conference on Pervasive Computing, pp. 62–79 (2005)
12. Munguia Tapia, E., Intille, S.S., Lopez, L., Larson, K.: The design of a portable kit of wireless sensors for naturalistic data collection. In: Fishkin, K.P., Schiele, B., Nixon, P., Quigley, A. (eds.) PERVASIVE 2006. LNCS, vol. 3968, Springer, Heidelberg (2006)

13. Abowd, G., Bobick, A., Essa, I., Mynatt, E., Rogers, W.: The aware home: Developing technologies for successful aging. In: Proceedings of AAAI Workshop on Automation as a Care Giver (2002)
14. Eagle, N., Pentland, A.: Reality mining: Sensing complex social systems. Personal and Ubiquitous Computing 10(4), 255–268 (2006)
15. Choudhury, T., Pentland, A.: Characterizing social networks using the sociometer. In: Proceedings of the North American Association of Computational Social and Organizational Science (NAACSOS) (2004)
16. Reynolds, C.J., Wren, C.R.: Worse is better for ambient sensing. In: Pervasive: Workshop on Privacy, Trust and Identity Issues for Ambient Intelligence (2006)
17. Athans, M., Chang, C.B.: Adaptive estimation and parameter identification using multiple model estimation algorithm. Technical Report, 1976-28, Massachusetts Institute of Technology Lincoln Laboratory, Lexington, Massachusetts, USA (1976) Group 32 (1976)
18. Moeslund, T.B., Granum, E.: A survey of computer vision-based human motion capture. Computer Vision and Image Understanding 81, 231–268 (2001)
19. Stark, H., Woods, J.W: Probability, Random Processes, and Estimation Theory for Engineers, 2nd edn. Prentice Hall, Englewood Cliffs (1994)
20. Rached, Z., Alajaji, F., Campbell, L.L.: The kullback-leibler divergence rate between markov sources. IEEE Transactions on Information Theory 50(5) (2004)
21. Kuhl, M.E., Wilson, J.R.: Modeling and simulating poisson processes having trends or nontrigonometric cyclic effects. European Journal of Operational research 133, 566–582 (2001)
22. Consolvo, S., Walker, M.: Using the experience sampling method to evaluate ubicomp applications. In: Pervasive Computing, IEEE, pp. 24–31 (2003)
23. Bernard, H.R., Killworth, P.D.: Informant accuracy in social network data ii. Human Communications Research 4(1), 3–18 (1977)

A Unified Semantics Space Model*

Juan Ye, Lorcan Coyle, Simon Dobson, and Paddy Nixon

System Research Group, School of Computer Science and Informatics,
UCD, Dublin, Ireland
juan.ye@ucd.ie

Abstract. Location-aware systems provide customised services or applications according to users' locations. While much research has been carried out in developing models to represent location information and spatial relationships, it is usually limited to modelling simple environments (cf. [13,19,3]). This paper proposes a unified space model for more complex environments (e.g., city plan or forest). This space model provides a flexible, expressive, and powerful spatial representation. It also proposes a new data structure – an integrated lattice and graph model – to express comprehensive spatial relationships. This structure not only provides multiple graphs at different abstraction levels, but it also collapses the whole map into smaller local graphs. This mechanism is beneficial in reducing the complexity of creating and maintaining a map and improving the efficiency of path finding algorithms.

1 Introduction

The development of location-aware systems has become commonplace recently. This was encouraged by the availability of numerous available location sensing devices [11] and by a popular demand for location-aware applications. A huge number of location models have been developed – however most of them tend to either service particular sensing abilities or application requirements.

Consider a complex real-world environment, such as a city or forest. It can be partitioned through multiple hierarchies (e.g., postcode areas, districts or compass directions) and involve a huge number of places (e.g., hundreds of streets or thousands of buildings). In this environment, it may be necessary to describe the location of a certain entity in various ways depending on the available location sensors. Most of existing space models only provide traditional types of spatial representations, such as symbolic and geometric representations. Especially some of these models support a single coordinate reference system, because they only have one or two precise sensors that provide location data in a coordinate format. As such, the ability of these models to flexibly express location information is limited.

Our space model aims to support a powerful and expressive spatial representation. It absorbs the best practices from existing models so as to support the traditional spatial

---

* This work is partially supported by Science Foundation Ireland under grant numbers 05/RFP/CMS0062 "Towards a semantics of pervasive computing" and 04/RPI/1544 "Secure and predictable pervasive computing".

J. Hightower, B. Schiele, and T. Strang (Eds.): LoCA 2007, LNCS 4718, pp. 103–120, 2007.

representations, and makes improvements over them. This model supports multiple co-ordinate systems from two perspectives: different global coordinate systems to support different sensing technologies; and user-defined local coordinate systems to support customised representations of environment instead of forcing all the spatial representa-tions in a uniform coordinate system. Furthermore, this space model also supports *relative* location representation [15]. Relative locations are necessary when the location cannot be exactly specified or defined, or if the location is dynamic or moving. For example, 'a place 500m east of this building", or "I am in the canteen of this train". Our approach can flexibly define a local reference system to describe these locations in different directions by combining various kinds of spatial representations, while not being limited to coordinates.

In complex environments it may also be necessary to construct a detailed map that can provide a path to a destination for an entity among a large number of places (with varied levels of granularity). There are two underlying models to organise spaces: hier-archical and graph models, which represent *containment* and *connectedness* relation-ships respectively. The typical approach to constructing a location map is to build a single huge graph for the whole environment, while fixed at a certain granularity (e.g., room-leveled spaces). This graph cannot be flexibly extended into coarser-grained spaces (e.g., buildings or streets), or into finer-grained spaces (e.g., desks). Although additional graphs may be built for these spaces, it is complicated to build a mapping between them or coordinate them in applications. Most research experiments usually take place in a building, so a single graph is easy to build and maintain. However, a sin-gle graph for larger-scaled environments will take much effort and time to build and to maintain its consistency and integrity. Also, existing models do not provide an approach to collapse this graph so as to reduce the construction complexity.

In our space model, we propose a new data structure - a lattice integrated with graphs to represent spatial relationships for complex environments. This space model applies the lattice model to represent the *containment* relationship and applies the graph model to represent the *adjacency* and *connectedness* relationships between spaces at the same abstraction level. The integrated model builds a lattice model for all the spaces under a certain partition approach. The graph models are embedded in the lattice model where each node is associated with a graph whose vertices are the immediate sub spaces of the node and whose edges are the adjacency and connectedness relations between these vertices.

With this space model, system designers can build a single model to express all the spatial relationships at once. They do not need to maintain separate hierarchy and graph models and mappings between them. Furthermore, users can build graph models at different abstraction levels whose hierarchies are managed in a lattice model. Even at a certain abstraction level, the whole graph can be further divided into smaller graphs that are associated with sibling nodes in the lattice. That is, each sibling node manages a local graph that is part of the whole map. These local graphs can also be integrated to form the whole map through a special space – a *sensitive space* – in the lattice model. For a given set of spaces, a sensitive space is the largest of their common sub spaces, whose detailed discussion will be in Section 3. This approach makes the graph model easy to create and maintain. In addition, our space model improves the efficiency of path finding algorithms. In existing models, the path finding algorithm usually works on a large amount of location data. Heuristic approaches are applied in the algorithm. Also, our space model has the ability to reduce the initial searching space for path finding, which potentially improves search efficiency.

This paper is organised as follows. Section 2 reviews the mature location models and distills the best practices from them. Section 3 introduces our space model in representing location information and spatial relationships. Section 4 will demonstrate the implementation of relative location representations and the path finding based on the integrated model. Finally, in Section 5 we conclude the paper and point to future research problems in this work.

2   State of the Art of Location Models

This section will review the main types of location models including geometric, symbolic, hybrid, and semantic models. Their novel ideas and techniques will be introduced at the aspects of representing location information and spatial relationships.

At the aspect of representing location information, Jiang's model [13] proposes a detailed method to represent geometric location in multiple coordinate reference systems. A sub space's coordinate system is specified by defining its *origin point* and *axes* within its super space's coordinate system. The origin point is specified as a displacement vector in the super space's coordinate system, while axes are specified as three unit vectors in the form of a matrix, called *rotation matrix*. A simple linear algebra is applied to convert coordinates under different reference systems. This approach is built on a sound mathematical foundation. However, a sub space's coordinate system is defined only under its super space's coordinate system, which is too restricted and not flexible. Our space model will borrow the basic idea of this approach and make improvement on the flexibility of defining local coordinate systems.

When it comes to describing the shape of a three-dimensioned space, Coschurba's model [6] proposes a 2.5-dimensioned approach to describe a three-dimensional (3D) shape by specifying its base as a two-dimensioned (2D) and its height as a numeric value (0.5D). Only the coordinates for the space's base shape are recorded, which can reduce the amount of coordinate data and allow applying geometric computations on each shape. This approach for defining shapes and representing coordinates is borrowed to our space model and is further extended to more shapes.

Korkea-aho [15] introduces a common data set and an extensible framework of expressing location information in the Internet. He proposes a relative location as a specific type of descriptive location, that is, the location of an object is described relative to some other objects, such as, "10 meters North to the shop", or "the area centered around the building in a 100-meter arm". The relative location representation is very useful, and is not introduced in existing location models. Our space model will extend the spatial representations to cover this relatively spatial expression.

The HP Cooltown project [18] introduces a semantic representation, which is orthogonal to symbolic and geometric representations. The semantic representation provides other information around its place, such as a bus route or a snapshot of interest. In our space model, a space object may describe the spatial features corresponding to the location of an entity, but other non-spatial features will necessarily be assigned to the corresponding entity object. For example, a building entity has its location described by a space object, whose symbolic representation is "science building". The building entity can be extended with other non-location contextual information including its functions, reception, activities, or services. The information expressed in a semantic representation of the Cooltown project is part of this extended contextual information.

At the aspect of representing spatial relationships, Becker [2] has analysed and summarised different types of symbolic location models: set-based, hierarchical, and graph-based models.

A set-based model organises symbolic locations into sets according to the spatial containment relationship. A typical example of the set-based model is the EasyLiving project at Microsoft [4]. It applies simple, computable set operators to evaluate the overlapping relationship, and to compare non-quantitative distances. A set-based model also can express the connectedness relationship by defining *neighbourhood* sets into pairs of directly connected locations. Set-based models can provide an explicit semantics of containment and overlapping relationships; however, the connectedness relationship results in tremendous number of sets and the notion of distance is not quantitatively computable.

A hierarchical model is a special case of set-based models. Similarly, a hierarchical model can express the explicit containment relationship, and it fails in supporting the connectedness relationship and the quantitative notion of distance. It is a most popular model applied in current location models such as Jiang's model [13], Schmidt's model [20], Durr's model [8], and MiddleWhere [19]. There are two hierarchical structures: a tree to organise non-overlapping locations, and a lattice to organise overlapping locations. Compared to a set-based model, a hierarchical model can represent the structure of locations more explicit and more intuitive. Moreover, these characterised structures support more efficient and optimised computations, such as a traversing algorithm in a tree, and the join and meet operations in a lattice. Compared to a tree model, the lattice model has more flexible expressivity and has been widely applied to location models such as Kainz' model [14], the Geocost model [6], and MiddleWhere [19].

A graph-based model is applied to express the connectedness relationship and the notion of distance. Hu's model [12] proposes a semantics graph model called *exit hierarchy*. In a graph, each node represents a symbolic location, and each edge represents the connectedness relationship, which quantitative distance can also be assigned on as a weight. Furthermore, nodes or edges can be attributed to more contextual information, such as passability limits, or transportation restrictions. A graph-based model provides an explicit and extensible semantics for the connectedness relationship and a quantitative notion of distance. It benefits in navigating an environment and answering the shortest path queries. However, its deficiency exists in the limited description level of locations (e.g., at the room level), and in the difficulty of expressing the containment relationship.

From the above analysis, none of the three models can have the adequate capability of representing all the spatial relationships. The set-based and hierarchical models are good at expressing containment and overlapping relationships, while the graph-based model is good at expressing connectedness relationships and the quantitative notion of distance. We take all these best practices and improve them in our unified formal model of space.

3   A Unified Formal Model of Space

This section will build a formal semantics to richly express and model spatial information and relationships. The space model can provide multiple representations for any space in reality. It also can describe various spatial relationships, including containment, adjacency, connectedness, disjointness, overlapping, and distance.

3.1   Representation of Spatial Information

There are diverse ways to represent location information, however, the elementary types of spatial representations are geometric and symbolic representations. A *geometric representation* characterises a space with its geometric shapes and a set of coordinate points under a certain Cartesian Coordinate Reference System (CCRS). A *symbolic representation* characterises a space with a human-friendly descriptive label. A *hybrid representation* is introduced, if a space has a symbolic and geometric representation, both of which map to each other.

The space model supports a resolute or relative representation (Figure 1). A resolute representation can be a geometric, symbolic, or hybrid representation of the former two types. A resolute representation is usually used to describe an explicit space, such as "a conference room", or a coordinate $[4.50, 2.09, 3.87]$. A relative representation is used to represent an implicit space by specifying a base and an offset representation, both of which are directly or indirectly related to a resolute representation. In the following, we will detail the resolute representation first.

A space is physically featured by different geometric shapes. A geometric shape can be regular, which is portrayed through a mathematically computable way. A regular shape can be a primitive 2D or 3D shape, or a composite shape of primitive shapes. A

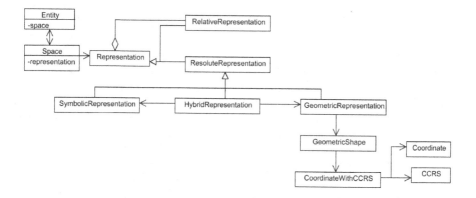

Fig. 1. Space Representation

few of primitive shapes have been listed, such as point, line segment, polygon, and sphere. If a shape cannot be depicted using a regular shape, then it is regarded as irregular.

The shape structure can be extensible to more sophisticated shapes in particular applications. For each space, coordinates are chosen and organised in a characteristic format in terms of the space's geometric shape. Typical shapes and their associated coordinate formats are listed as follows.

- *Point*: one coordinate;
- *Line segment*: two coordinates for two ends of a line segment;
- *Polygon*: a set of coordinates for each vertex of a polygon; especially, *Rectangle* is described by a pair of coordinates for diagonal points;
- *Circle or sphere*: a coordinate for a center and a numeric value for its radius;
- *Cube*: a set of coordinates for its base polygon and a numeric value for its height.
- and so on.

Coordinates for a composite shape can be obtained by integrating characteristic coordinates from the primitive shapes that it is composed of. However, an irregular shape cannot be easily described. A simplified solution is either to convert an irregular shape to a set of similar regular shapes or to pick up a few characterised coordinate points.

The coordinate representation is closely related to the geometric shape of a space. This approach can reduce the number of coordinate data and help organise them in a computable way. It is easy to do some spatial computations, such as computation of area or volume, and evaluation of whether a coordinate is in a space or not. For example, if a coordinate point and a sphere space are given, the evaluation can be computed by comparing its radius with the distance between this point and its center. If the distance is longer than the radius, then this point is considered out of the sphere-shaped space.

The space model supports multiple Cartesian Coordinate Reference Systems (CCRS), including global (such as WGS84, Gauss-Kruger, and UTM) and user-defined coordinate reference systems. The global system is applied according to different positioning sensors. For example, GPS provides coordinates under WGS84. Local reference systems are applied in terms of sensors and customised representation of an environment or a space. The Ubisense provides coordinates under a user-defined CCRS at the beginning when it is set up and configured. In a local environment, especially a dynamical environment, a user-defined CCRS is usually applied, when only relative location information is required. For example, in a train or ship, only relative location information in the train space is concerned, so a CCRS can be created locally in a train.

This space model supports multiple CCRSs and conversion of coordinates between these different CCRSs. Each space can be described with a set of coordinate sets, and each coordinate set is defined under a certain CCRS. A local CCRS is defined by specifying its origin point and axes, both of which can be referred to any existing CCRS, not necessarily its super space's CCRS. A default CCRS is defined as a primitive reference system that can be directly or indirectly referred to by all the other CCRSs. The conversion techniques has been borrowed from Jiang's model [13].

A symbolic representation for a space is a human-friendly, string-based descriptive label. A label can be a real name of a space like country's name, city's name, university's name, and so on. A space can be labeled in terms of its functionality like "conference room", "foyer", and "registration office", etc. A space can also be named with its owners like "Waldo's house", "secretary's office" and so on. If a space has geometric and symbolic representations, then a bi-literal link can be built between them. For spatial computation, the geometric properties can be obtained from a symbolic representation; for expression, a symbolic label can be acquired according to the corresponding geometric representation.

So far, we have discussed the resolute representation for explicit location information, and now we will introduce a relative representation. A relative representation consists of a base and offset representation. Both base and offset representations can be any type of representation, and they are associated by a certain structural relation.

An offset representation can be adjacent to or centered around a base representation. If it is centered around a base representation and is specified in a given distance, a relative representation can be expressed as a circle (or sphere) by taking the base one as an origin point, and the distance as a radius (Figure 2). If it is adjacent to a base representation and is specified with a distance to the base and a list of degree to each direction. The direction is a standard compass direction description, including "East", "West", "South", "North", "Upper", and "Lower". The relative representation is defined in a similar approach of a local CCRS. This local CCRS is specified by taking the base location as an origin point, and taking the compass direction as the axes' direction. A relative representation will be located by projecting the associated distances and degrees in each direction to the corresponding axe in this standard compass coordinate system. For example, the relative representation using laser range finding of "3.62m 35° South-East and 45° elevation", can be projected to a local CCRS (Figure 3).

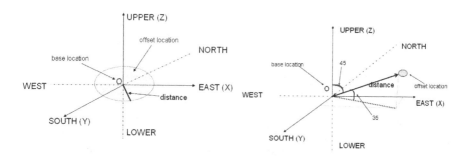

Fig. 2. A centered relative representation   **Fig. 3.** A adjacent relative representation

3.2   Representation of Spatial Relationships

We have shown that different models (set-based, graph-based, and hierarchical models) have their particular strength on expressing spatial relationships. However, none of them can work individually to express all the spatial relationships well. Our space model unifies a lattice and graph model. It describes *containment*, *disjointness*, and *overlapping* relations using its lattice model; and the *adjacency* and *connectedness* relations, and notions of *distance* using its graph model.

A Lattice Model. Among hierarchical models, a lattice model has better expressivity and flexibility than a tree model. In the following, we will introduce a tractable way to organise symbolic spaces in a lattice model according to the containment relation.

Definition 1. *All the symbolic spaces in a real world are organised into a set S with the containment relation $\leq$.*

- *The space set $S = \{s_1, \ldots, s_n\}$;*
- *Containment relationship: $s_i \leq s_j$ means that a space s_i is contained by s_j. The containment relation is a partial order:*
    - *Reflexivity: $s \leq s$ means a space s contains itself;*
    - *Antisymmetry: $s_i \leq s_j \land s_j \leq s_i \Rightarrow s_i = s_j$;*
    - *Transitivity: $s_i \leq s_j \land s_j \leq s_k \Rightarrow s_i \leq s_k$.*

In Figure 4, the left side simulates part of the real world space, and the right side organises its symbolic spaces.

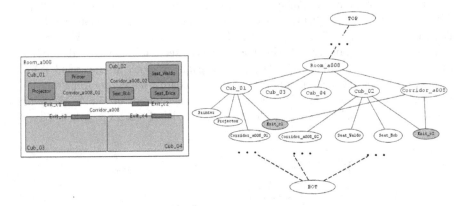

Fig. 4. An example of a lattice model for a real world space

A particular containment relationship $s_i \preceq s_j$ means that a space s_i is immediately contained by s_j. The *immediate containment* $\preceq$ is the basic operation to construct *containment* $\leq$. In building a spatial model, only the immediate containment is specified for spaces, while the general containment can be derived transitively. Their conversion relation is defined as follows:

- If $s_i \preceq s_j$ and whenever $s_i \leq s_k \leq s_j$, it follows that $s_k = s_i$ or $s_k = s_j$.
- $s_i \leq s_j$ holds iff there exists a finite sequence of spaces $s_{k1}, \ldots, s_{km}$ such that $s_i \preceq s_{k1} \ldots s_{km} \preceq s_j$.

According to both containment relationships, we derive (immediate) sub / super spaces. For any space $s \in S$,

- its immediate sub spaces: $s.isub = \{s_i \in S | s_i \preceq s\}$;
- its sub spaces: $s.sub = \{s_i \in S | s_i \leq s\} \supseteq s.isub$;

- its immediate super spaces: $s.isup = \{s_i \in S | s \preceq s_i\}$;
- its super spaces: $s.sup = \{s_i \in S | s \leq s_i\} \supseteq s.isup$.

After discussing the containment relation, we start analysing the way to construct the space set. That is, how the whole space is partitioned into spaces with varying levels of granularity step by step. In the space set S, there are two special spaces: one is the universal space $s_\top$ that represents the whole world; another is the null space $s_\bot$ that represents non-existing space. That is, $\forall s \in S$, $s \leq s_\top$ and $s_\bot \leq s$.

Proposition 1. *For a space $s \in S$, its immediate sub spaces are $s.isub = \{s_i \in S | s_i \preceq s\}$, satisfying*

- *the union of $s.isub$ covers the whole space represented by s.*
- *the intersection of any two of its immediate sub spaces s_i and s_j can be*
  - $s_\bot$, *if they are disjoint;*
  - *a unique space $s' \in S$, if they are overlapping. s' is the common space with the coarsest granularity, which follows that $s_k \leq s'$, where $s_k \in s_i.sub \cap s_j.sub$.*

Proposition 1 provides a tractable top-down approach to divide a space into finer-granularity spaces gradually. A space can be partitioned into a set of spaces in different orthogonal planes. For example, a building can be partitioned into floors in a vertical plane; and it also can be partitioned into wings in a horizontal plane. Both the vertical plane and the horizontal plane are orthogonal to each other. It's obvious that floors overlap with wings. An overlapped space is the unique space among the intersection of sub spaces of the corresponding floor and wing, e.g., "wing A at the ground floor".

In this lattice model, the overlapping relationship has a general meaning, which includes overlapping in the same plane and that in different orthogonal planes. The overlapping in the same plane can be slightly overlapping and partially overlapping. The slightly overlapping happens when a space is neighboring to another, while these spaces cannot be simply separated. There usually exists a common space that is hard to decide which space it belongs to. From figure 4, if a cubicle Cub_{01} is adjacent to a corridor $Corridor_{a008}$ and another cubicle Cub_{02}, there is an exit $Exit_{c1}$ and a wall between them respectively, which can not be simply decided which room the exit or wall should exactly belong to. However, there is not a delicate approach to determine whether overlapping is slight or partial. To simplify, both overlapping is regarded as the same, and it is only necessary to evaluate whether the overlapping spaces are passable or not. When two spaces are connected through a third space, this space is called a *sensitive space*.

Definition 2. *For a space $s \in S$, if any two of its immediate sub spaces s_i and s_j overlap in the same orthogonal plane, then a **sensitive space** is the unique space s_* that is the overlapping space with the coarsest granularity among the intersection of sub spaces of s_i and s_j.*

The semantics of a sensitive space is to traverse coarser-granularity spaces, labeled as $s_i \Leftrightarrow s_j$. Across a sensitive space, an object can pass through the coarser-granularity spaces. There are many types of sensitive spaces. For example, a hall traverses two wings, a lift traverses floors, and so on.

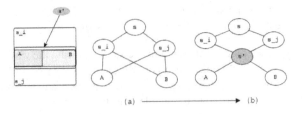

Fig. 5. A special case in partitioning

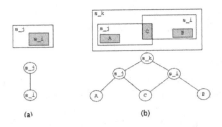

Fig. 6. Simple examples of spatial relationships in a lattice model

A poset (partially ordered set) can be a complete lattice if there exist the greatest lower bound (meet $\sqcap$) and the least upper bound (join $\sqcup$) for any subset A of S. For any two spaces, join is defined as the unique space with the finest granularity that covers both of them; meet is defined as the unique common space with the coarsest granularity that is covered by both. According to the above construction procedure, the partially-ordered spatial set S can be constructed into a lattice model. Proposition 1 makes sure the existence of the join and meet for any two spaces. The leftmost in Figure 5 is a real space, where s_i and s_j overlap at two finer spaces A and B, as the figure (a) shows. According to the proposition, only one overlapping space is allowed, so a common space s' is created to be an immediate super space of A and B (see Figure 5 (b)). In the following, we give a formal definition for join and meet. Given two spaces s_i and s_j,

- *join operation*: $s_i \sqcup s_j = s$, where $\forall s' \in s_i.sup \cap s_j.sup$, $s' \le s$;
- *meet operation*: $s_i \sqcap s_j = s$, where $\forall s' \in s_i.sub \cap s_j.sub$, $s \le s'$.

Figure 6 shows typical relations between spaces in a lattice model. Some examples of the join and meet operations between these spaces are computed as follows. In Figure 6 (a), $s_i \sqcap s_j = s_i$, and $s_i \sqcup s_j = s_j$. In Figure 6 (b),

$$s_i \sqcap s_j = c, \qquad\qquad s_i \sqcup s_j = s_k;$$
$$A \sqcap s_i = s_\perp, \qquad\qquad A \sqcap B = s_\perp;$$
$$A \sqcup s_i = s_k, \qquad\qquad A \sqcup B = s_k.$$

In the above, a lattice model is constructed for symbolic spaces according to the containment of architectural design, which portrays the physical view of an environment.

For the same environment there may be multiple lattice models with respect to different partition principles. For example, another lattice model can also be built in terms of the administrative functions, such as lab area, lecture area, or office area, which portrays a conceptual view of an environment. Both lattice models present various views of an environment, which can be beneficial in serving customised queries. Take an example of a query: "a reception office in this building". It is more efficient to execute this query in the latter lattice model that will only look for the reception office in the administration area, rather than search the whole space in the former lattice model.

So far, this section has described how to organise the symbolic spaces into a partial order set according to the spatial containment relationship. The proposition 1 provides a top-down approach to dividing the whole space $s_\top$ with the coarsest granularity into spaces with finer granularities. It also helps to constrain the constructed poset S to be a lattice model that is bound by the universal space $s_\top$ and the null space $s_\perp$.

A Graph Model. The above lattice model is used to explore the spatial containment, overlapping, and disjointness relationships, while the following graph model will help to make the adjacency and connectedness relationships explicitly.

Faced with the huge complexity of spaces in reality, it is difficult to build a large graph for the entire space and maintain the integrity of the graph. Some adjacent spaces may be ignored or missing when drawing the adjacency relation for a certain space. The large graph needs lots of effort to maintain when a space is changed (such as enlarged, detracted, or deleted). Instead, our approach collapses a large graph into smaller graphs, each of which represents a separate region. These small local graphs are associated with the immediate sub spaces of each node in the lattice model. Therefore, when needed, these smaller graphs can be composed together as well.

Definition 3. *For any* $s \in S$, *a corresponding* **graph** $G_s = (V, E, E_c)$ *is a directed and weighted graph, where*

1. *V is the immediate sub spaces of s; that is, $V = s.isub$, where $s \neq s_\perp$ and $\forall s' \in s.isub, s' \neq s_\perp$;*
2. *E represents the adjacency relation. $s_i - s_j$ means s_i and s_j is neighboring to each other;*
3. *E_c represents the connectedness relation. $s_i \rightarrow s_j$ means that an object can go from s_i to s_j;*
4. *d on each edge represents a distance between spaces.*

If spaces are disjoint to each other or overlapping in different orthogonal planes, there are no edges between them; otherwise, they are considered *adjacent* to each other. Further, if a space is passable to another directly, the relationship between them is regarded as *connectedness*. Particularly, the connectedness relation implies direction. When an object can go from a space s_i to s_j, then s_i is connected to s_j, labeled as $s_i \rightarrow s_j$. In some circumstances, it is forbidden to go from s_j to s_i (e.g., an escalator).

A local graph for a node in a lattice model reflects a certain abstraction level of spaces, which is a certain scale of observing the real space. For example, Figure 7 presents two graphs with varying granularities, which correspond to the spaces in Figure 4. The graph mapping to $room_{a008}$ reflects the adjacency of cubicles, while

Table 1. Evaluation of different spatial relationships

Spatial Relationship	Evaluation
containment	$s_i \sqcap s_j = s_i$ (or s_j)
	$s_i \sqcup s_j = s_j$ (or s_i)
disjointness	$s_i \sqcap s_j = s_\perp$
overlapping	$s_i \sqcap s_j \neq s_\perp$
adjacency	$s_i \sqcap s_j \neq s_\perp$ and $s_i - s_j$
connectedness	$s_i \sqcap s_j \neq s_\perp$ and $s_i \rightarrow s_j$

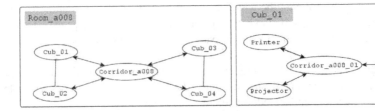

Fig. 7. An example of two graphs at different abstraction levels

the graph mapping to Cub_{01} reflects the adjacency of finer spaces within a cubicle. It is convenient for applications to flexibly load graphs in different scopes. For example, when an object is in the ground floor, the application only needs to present the graph of rooms that are located in the ground floor; when an object moves into the room $room_{a008}$, it presents a more detailed graph of cubicles; furthermore, when the object enters a cubicle, a graph with finer granularity is presented.

This approach decreases the complexity of loading a huge graph in the beginning, and it reduces the amount of information because it does not need to load unnecessary graphs such as Cub_{02} when only the graph Cub_{01} is needed. This approach makes it advantageous to maintain a relatively small graph, because a graph is part of the whole world. It also makes less effort to reconfigure the graph without affecting other graphs.

This approach also keeps the spaces at the same abstraction level in the same graph. It makes more sense when we discuss the adjacent relation between the spaces at the same level of abstraction (such as among rooms or among buildings). However, it is hard to discuss the adjacency between a room and a floor.

Distance is a complicated and application-specific notion. A distance is a physical length between two spaces; however, sometimes it is related to other contextual information (such as transportation, or path restriction) in real applications. However, this graph model will only consider a general definition for *physical distance*, while other contextual information on distance can be extended in customised applications. A physical distance can be classified into *absolute* and *accessible* distances. An absolute distance is a direct length between two spaces, while an accessible minimal distance is a length along a path through which a space is connected to another space. An accessible minimal distance is related to path finding, and it can be computed by accumulating a series of absolute distance. Therefore, absolute distances are fundamental for the distance concept.

In the graph model, an absolute distance d on each edge is a tuple $< d_e, d_l >$, which corresponds to the Euclidean and path distance respectively. The Euclidean distance is the shortest straight line length between centers of two spaces, while the path distance is the length of a path from the center of one space to the center of another space. This approach to describe distance is borrowed from MiddleWhere [19].

Path finding is an important issue in a location-aware system. That is, how a path is located from a source space to a target space. There exists a set of paths between two given spaces.

Definition 4. *A **path** consists of some finite space sequence following the connectedness relation, which starts from a source space s and ends at a target space t.* $p(s, t) = s \rightarrow s_1 \rightarrow \ldots \rightarrow s_n \rightarrow t$.

Local graphs cannot satisfy the requirements of path finders if the given source and target spaces are not in the same local graph. Thus a larger graph is required, making it necessary to combine a set of local graphs. If all the spaces in the graphs have geometric representations, then these spaces can be projected into a uniform Cartesian coordinate reference system (CCRS). Thus a combined graph is produced by computing their coordinates. If not all of the spaces have geometric representations, we propose an alternative approach to integrate graphs through sensitive spaces. In a lattice model, coarser-granularity spaces are traversed by their sensitive space. If two coarser spaces s_i and s_j have a sensitive space s_* between them, when two graphs G_{s_i} and G_{s_j} are required to be merged, s_* will be located and serve as a connection of two graphs. Section 4 will give a description of the path finding algorithm.

4 Demonstration

To demonstrate the applicability of our space model, it is applied to build a map for our computer science building. All the spaces are represented in a resolute hybrid representation. They are organised in a lattice model, and then a graph model is built for

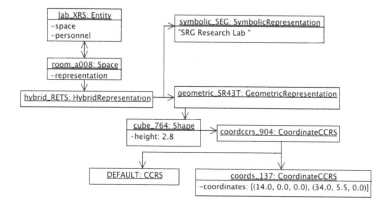

Fig. 8. A typical example of representing an entity's space

each node in a lattice. In the following, we will describe how spaces are expressed in hybrid and relative representations. Later, we will detail how the space model helps in path finding algorithms.

4.1 Spatial Representation

Each space has a hybrid representation. A symbolic representation assigns a human-understandable name for the space, while a geometric representation characterises the space's geometric shape and a list of coordinates under a certain CCRS. For example in Figure 4, a space $room_{a008}$ is represented in Figure 8. The space object deals with all location-related information, which is a property of an entity. The entity lab_{XRS} carries with other contextual information like its included persons, calendar, and research areas.

Section 3.1 has provided a general way to express a relative representation; however, its typical applications are simple, like "a place 500m east of this building". This is represented as follows, and a resolute location can be computed in applications by building a local CCRS with the base as an origin point and the standard compass direction as three axes' direction. The offset representation can be projected into this CCRS according to the distance to the base representation, and degree to each direction axis.

Base Representation	Offset Representation		
	distance	direction	degree
$building\_space\_SRES$	5.0	EAST	0.0

4.2 Path Finding

In this section, we will describe how the lattice model integrated with graphs helps to improve the efficiency of a typical path finding algorithm, while a concrete path finding algorithm is out of the scope of this paper.

Our space model is used to partition the world into small sub graphs that are organised and managed under the lattice model. Different levels of the lattice model determine the abstraction levels of each sub graph. At a certain abstraction level, each sub graph is further partitioned into smaller local graphs that are connected to each other through sensitive spaces. We propose that the path finding algorithm will be executed on each local graph, rather than throughout a huge graph for the whole environment.

Given two spaces s_{source} and s_{target}, their immediate super spaces are located from the lattice model, labelled as G_s and G_t. If G_s and G_t are the the same graph, the searching will be only executed on the spaces in that graph, while ignoring all the other spaces and spatial relationships out of that graph. If G_s and G_t are different graphs, a series of sensitive spaces, called *sensitive path*, will be located as follows: $G_s \xrightarrow{s_1} G_1 \quad \cdots \quad G_{m-1} \xrightarrow{s_m} G_t$, where $s_1, ..., s_m$ are sensitive spaces, and $G_1, ..., G_{m-1}$ are the graphs connecting G_s and G_t. This shows the higher level hints of searching: sensitive spaces are the key spaces between the given source and target spaces. In each local graphs, the paths will be searched, such as $s_{source} \rightarrow s_1$, $..., s_i \rightarrow s_{i+1}, ..., s_m \rightarrow s_{target}$.

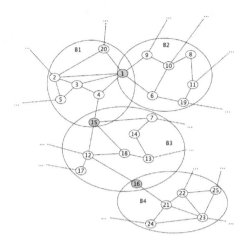

Fig. 9. A simple example of path finding

For example in Figure 9, a path from a space s_2 to s_{23} is required. The smallest local graphs for s_2 and s_{23} are located as B_1 and B_4, both of which are not directly connected to each other. By examining the sensitive space set, a series of sensitive spaces sensitive spaces and the intermediate graphs will be determined: $B_1 \xrightarrow{s_{15}} B_3 \xrightarrow{s_{16}} B_4$. Following this, paths will be searched only in each local graph , such as $s_2 \rightarrow s_{15}$ in B_1, $s_{15} \rightarrow s_{16}$ in B_3, and $s_{16} \rightarrow s_{23}$ in B_4.

It is worth noting that a given source or target space may be contained in more than one smallest local graphs, if it is a sensitive space. In the above figure, the sensitive space s_1 has two immediately super spaces B_1 and B_2. Besides, there are multiple possibilities of sensitive paths. Assume that the space B_2 is directly connected to B_3 through the sensitive space s_7. For the above example, another series of sensitive spaces will be produced: $B_1 \xrightarrow{s_1} B_2 \xrightarrow{s_7} B_3 \xrightarrow{s_{16}} B_4$. Correspondingly, another path finding will be carried out: $s_2 \rightarrow s_1$ in B_1, $s_1 \rightarrow s_7$ in B_2, $s_7 \rightarrow s_{16}$ in B_3, and $s_{16} \rightarrow s_{23}$ in B_4. As the path finding is executed separately on local graphs, the local results can be shared between different series of sensitive paths. For example, the path $s_{16} \rightarrow s_{23}$ in B_4 can be shared from the above example.

The path finding procedure may be complicated by the above factors such as multiple immediate super spaces and multiple possibilities of series of sensitive spaces. However, the number of immediate super spaces is usually small, and the searching of sensitive paths is the procedure of finding a path between the immediate super spaces. The computation cost is relatively small, compared to searching a huge graph covering the whole space. This space model not only reduces the searching space for possible paths, but it also provides a higher level view of searching by locating a series of sensitive spaces.

Besides this path finding algorithm, the model also can answer nearest neighbor queries (e.g. finding the nearest printer [13]) by considering the distance on each edge. It is difficult for hierarchical location models to carry out path finding, but it is possible for them to answer the nearest neighbor query. This query is carried out by searching all the printers, computing the distances between the user and all the candidate printers and choosing the closest printer. This approach ignores the potential path inherent during searching. It is obvious that the shortest absolute physical distance between two coordinate points is not the shortest accessible distance along the available path. Besides, the simple computation of distances will not help a stranger who is not familiar with that space. However, our model can find the nearest neighbor through choosing the shortest accessible distance along a path.

Compared to other graph models, this space model can reduce the searching space largely during a path finding. A typical graph model would carry out searching a huge graph that consists of all the spaces in the entire environment. In the above example, the searching probably starts from all the spaces connected to s_2 in the whole graph. However, the path finding algorithm based on our space model will always be executed on the limited number of spaces in local graphs, and connected spaces in other local graphs are transparent. Only when the searching fails, it will be extended to other local graphs through sensitive spaces. The searching space is only the number of spaces in potentially local graphs and sensitive spaces, which is relatively small compared to searching all the spaces in the whole graph at once.

5   Conclusion and Future Work

This paper has proposed a unified space model to service the requirement of spatial representation and relationships for a large-scaled and complex environment. This model provides a powerful and expressive representations of location information for any space. It supports traditional symbolic and geometric representations, and relative location representations, which is more comprehensive than existing models.

This space model takes the advantages of both lattice theory and graph theory, and combines them in a novel way. This single model supports comprehensively spatial relationships such as containment, adjacency, and connectedness. It offers multiple graphs at various abstraction levels that are distributed at different nodes in a lattice model. The demonstrations in Section 4 suggest that this will potentially improve the efficiency of path finding algorithms.

This space model is comprehensive, for it involves all the details that are needed to represent location-related information. It can be simplified to suit to simpler applications. When graph models are not needed, developers can only construct a lattice model without building the connectedness relationship. When a hierarchical model is not needed, developers can just build a typical graph model while adding a universal space to be the immediately super spaces for all the spaces in this graph. Considering the natural complexity of real environments, it always takes a huge effort to build a detailed space model, no matter based on our model or existing models. However, our model tries to reduce the complexity of construction by collapsing a whole graph into manageable local graphs, and linking and organising them into a lattice model. Moreover, this approach can reduce the cost of maintenance. When spaces in the environment have been updated (e.g., adding or removing spaces), it will be easier to track down a few of local graphs that are required to be revised correspondingly, rather than check and affect the whole graph. However, if the spaces being updated are (or will be) sensitive spaces, it may cause inconsistency. This will increase the complexity of maintenance in our model.

To make better use of this model, developers must have a good knowledge of the target environment, including partition principles, levels of granularity, and particularly the sensitive spaces being chosen. Developers should build a lattice model for all the spaces in an environment with the help of Proposition 1 to locate sensitive spaces. Then they can build connectedness relationships between immediately sub spaces for each node in the lattice so as to form local graphs. This ensures the consistency of spatial relationships between all the spaces. In our initially simple experiment, this space model can be easily constructed for the spaces in one floor. However, to attain the goals of the model, it should be applied and evaluated in a larger-scaled and more complicated environment. In parallel, the path finding algorithm must be properly evaluated and refined as the space set grows.

Furthermore, the space model could be extended with extensions that constrain the accessability of locations, e.g. opening hours for public spaces, highway restrictions for roads, or gender restrictions for bathrooms [5]. Further constraints could be set to determine security and privacy characteristics of location information.

References

1. Bauer, M., Becker, C., Rothermel, K.: Location models from the perspective of context-aware applications and mobile ad hoc networks. Personal Ubiquitous Computing 6(5-6), 322–328 (2002)
2. Becker, C., Durr, F.: On location models for ubiquitous computing. Personal Ubiquitous Computing 9(1), 20–31 (2005)
3. Beigl, M., Zimmer, T., Decker, C.: A location model for communicating and processing of context. Personal Ubiquitous Computing 6(5-6), 341–357 (2002)
4. Brumitt, B., Shafer, S.: Topological world modeling using semantic spaces. In: Proceedings of the Workshop on Location Modeling for Ubiquitous Computing, Atlanta, Georgia (September 2001)
5. Chen, H., Finin, T., Joshi, A.: An Ontology for Context-Aware Pervasive Computing Environments. Special Issue on Ontologies for Distributed Systems, Knowledge Engineering Review 18(3), 197–207 (2004)
6. Coschurba, P., Rothermel, K., Durr, F.: A fine-grained addressing concept for geocast. In: Schmeck, H., Ungerer, T., Wolf, L. (eds.) ARCS 2002. LNCS, vol. 2299, pp. 101–113. Springer, Heidelberg (2002)
7. Domnitcheva, S.: Location modeling: State of the art and challenges. In: Abowd, G.D., Brumitt, B., Shafer, S. (eds.) Ubicomp 2001: Ubiquitous Computing. LNCS, vol. 2201, Springer, Heidelberg (2001)
8. Durr, F., Rothermel, K.: On a location model for fine-grained geocast. In: Dey, A.K., Schmidt, A., McCarthy, J.F. (eds.) UbiComp 2003. LNCS, vol. 2864, pp. 18–35. Springer, Heidelberg (2003)
9. Glassey, R., Ferguson, R.I.: Location modeling for pervasive environments. In: Proceedings of the 1st UK-UbiNet Workshop (September 2003)
10. Graumann, D., Hightower, J., Lara, W., Borriello, G.: Real-world implementation of the location stack: The universal location framework. In: Proceedings of the 5th IEEE Workshop on Mobile Computing Systems and Applications (WMCSA 2003), 00:122 (2003)

11. Hightower, J., Borriello, G.: Location systems for ubiquitous computing. IEEE Computer 34(8), 57–66 (2001)
12. Hu, H., Lee, D.L.: Semantic location modeling for location navigation in mobile environment. In: 5th IEEE International Conference on Mobile Data Management (MDM 2004), pp. 52–61, Berkeley, CA, USA (January 2004)
13. Jiang, C., Steenkiste, P.: A hybrid location model with a computable location identifier for ubiquitous computing. In: Borriello, G., Holmquist, L.E. (eds.) UbiComp 2002. LNCS, vol. 2498, pp. 246–263. Springer, Heidelberg (2002)
14. Kainz, W., Egenhofer, M.J., Greasley, I.: Modeling spatial relations and operations with partially ordered sets. Geographical Information Systems 7(3), 215–229 (1993)
15. Korkea-aho, M., Tang, H.: A common data set and framework for representing spatial location information in the internet. Cluster Computing 5(4), 389–397 (2002)
16. Marmasse, N., Schmandt, C.: A user-centered location model. Personal Ubiquitous Computing 6(5-6), 318–321 (2002)
17. Patterson, C.A., Muntz, R.R., Pancake, C.M.: Challenges in location-aware computing. IEEE Pervasive Computing 2(2), 80–89 (2003)
18. Pradhan, S.: Semantic location. Personal Ubiquitous Computing 4(4), 213–216 (2000)
19. Ranganathan, A., Al-Muhtadi, J., Chetan, S., Campbell, R., Mickunas, M.D.: Middlewhere: a middleware for location awareness in ubiquitous computing applications. In: Proceedings of Middleware '04, New York, USA, pp. 397–416 (2004)
20. Schmidt, A., Beigl, M., Gellersen, H.-W.: A location model for communicating and processing of context. Personal Ubiquitous Computing 6(5-6), 341–357 (2002)

Federation and Sharing in the Context Marketplace

Carsten Pils[1], Ioanna Roussaki[2], Tom Pfeifer[1], Nicolas Liampotis[2],
and Nikos Kalatzis[2]

[1] Telecommunications Software and Systems Group, Waterford Institute of Technology,
Carriganore, Waterford, Ireland
`cpils@tssg.org, t.pfeifer@computer.org`
[2] School of Electrical and Computer Engineering, National Technical University of Athens,
9 Heroon Polytechneiou Str, 157-73 Zographou, Athens, Greece
`{nanario,nliam,nikosk}@telecom.ntua.gr`

Abstract. The emerging pervasive computing services will eventually lead to the establishment of a context marketplace, where context consumers will be able to obtain the information they require by a plethora of context providers. In this marketplace, several aspects need to be addressed, such as: support for flexible federation among context stakeholders enabling them to share data when required; efficient query handling based on navigational, spatial or semantic criteria; performance optimization, especially when management of mobile physical objects is required; and enforcement of privacy and security protection techniques concerning the sensitive context information maintained or traded. This paper presents mechanisms that address the aforementioned requirements. These mechanisms establish a robust spatially-enhanced distributed context management framework and have already been designed and carefully implemented.

Keywords: Context Distributed Database Management System, context databases & query languages, federation, spatially-enhanced distributed context management, mobile physical object handling, context privacy & security.

1 Introduction

Network operators capture valuable information such as device location and status, user profiles and movement patterns, network performance, etc., in order to provide telecommunication services to their clients. This data is considered to be vital context information [1] that can be exploited to customize services, to anticipate user intentions and to ultimately reduce human-to-machine interactions [2]. In case this information is mashed-up with context data collected by other sources, such as sensor networks and web resources it becomes a commodity that can be traded with other operators and third party services providers. However, even though context information holds out the prospect of enhancing user experience and increasing revenues, trading it is not straightforward: First, the data is highly sensitive and a security breach could easily prove to be catastrophic for both users and operators. Second, the various infrastructures that store and manage context data are heterogeneous, while there is no standardized interface that supports context information exchange. Third, information, which can not

J. Hightower, B. Schiele, and T. Strang (Eds.): LoCA 2007, LNCS 4718, pp. 121–138, 2007.

be retrieved when necessary, is valueless. In an open context marketplace, where a wide variety of information types is traded, context consumers are challenged by the discovery of the required data. Finally, timely delivery of context information is crucial, due to the fact that most data sources provide real-time information.

On a business level, information exchange is regulated by federation agreements. They specify the information that can be accessed by consumers, its quality and penalties for breach of contract. A context marketplace must implement and enforce these agreements based on efficient monitoring and access control mechanisms. Moreover, such marketplaces must provide mechanisms to store, advertise and discover information in a secure, distributed, scalable and standardized manner. Thus, technically speaking, the core of a context marketplace is a distributed heterogeneous spatial database management system. Yet, none of the database management systems meet these requirements. This paper presents the Context Distributed Database Management System (CDDBMS), an efficient distributed heterogeneous spatial database management system that caters for the needs of a context marketplace.

The rest of this paper is structures as follows. Section 2 outlines the basic approach and details the requirements imposed by federation agreements. The CDDBMS architecture, database schema and query languages are presented in Section 3, while the implemented approach to handle mobile physical objects is described in Section 4. Section 5 presents the security and privacy approach implemented by the CDDBMS. Finally, in Section 6, conclusions are drawn and plans for future work are exposed.

2 Federation and Basic Context Management Approach

The CDDBMS is a peer-to-peer database comprising of node servers, each of which stores information about at least one predefined information domain. Such domains include for instance: user profiles, accounting information of a telecommunication operator, service advertisements or information related to a specific geographical area. Context producers store their data with respect to domains and consumers query information accordingly. Two domains are distinguished: Logical (Logic-D) and geographic domains (Geo-D). Logic-Ds contain non-spatial information like for example user profiles and are rather independent from other domains. Geo-Ds, however, carry strong spatial inclusion relationships. For example, the suburb is geographic specialization of the city domain and thus, there is an inclusion relation between the City-Node and the Suburb-Node. Fig. 1 shows example Geo-Ds and their inclusion relations. Inclusion relations span a directed tree on the Geo-D space, where each CDDBMS is a node and each inclusion relation is a vertex. This graph structure perfectly matches an R-Tree [3], an indexing structure of spatial databases. As a result, the geographic inclusion dependencies imply a structure which perfectly caters for spatial queries [4]. However, this structure requires a tight coupling of nodes and has thus a strong impact on federation agreements. For example, the two operators depicted in Fig. 1 maintain a CDDBMS infrastructure including sensor networks, which is only accessible to the customers of the individual operators. Particularly, in densely populated areas such as capitals or major cities, the two operators compete heavily, and thus, there is no federation agreement which allows any information

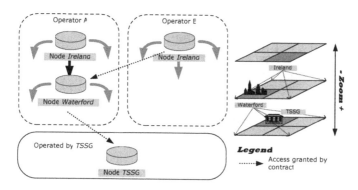

Fig. 1. Federation scenario example

exchange. Yet, in less populated areas, infrastructure investments are less profitable and therefore the two operators share information, i.e. Operator B customers have access to the "Waterford" Node maintained by Operator A. In order to support seamless information roaming, operators can make federation agreements with other stakeholders, such as SMEs like TSSG (see Fig. 1) and users that act as sources of context information. Employees and users can thus access their premises' and intelligent houses' context information wherever they are. Provisioning of context information is not only a business of telecommunication companies. Medium and small enterprises could also offer and share context information and complement the Operators' data. A thorough analysis of secure large-scale federation solutions for mobile service platforms is provided in [5].

3 CDDBMS Architecture and Query Languages

The infrastructure exploited by the stakeholders of the context marketplace is heterogeneous. Different database management systems, which store context information, are deployed. Though, all databases implement the SQL standard, they provide different extensions or do not fully comply with it. Moreover, these systems do not address federation and the lack of a standardized database schema makes it almost impossible to find entries. To solve this problem, CDDBMS nodes have both a standardized database schema and a standardized query interface.

3.1 Architecture

Fig. 2 illustrates the CDDBMS architecture. Each CDDBMS node comprises a Node-Manager and an off-the-shelf database management system (DBMS). The Node-Manager implements the management logic and the interfaces required for exchanging information with other nodes. Synchronous and asynchronous communication of context data is supported by the Query and the Event interfaces.

The DBMS is the actual repository of the node's context data. Basically any of-the-shelf relational database engine meets the requirements of the CDDBMS. However, as spatial queries are a major feature of the CDDBMS, all CDDBMS nodes that cover a

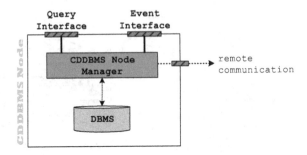

Fig. 2. Architecture of the CDDBMS

Geo-D must implement the Simple Feature Standard SQL (SFS) of the Open Geospatial Consortium (OGC) [6]. This standard specifies SQL-like spatial query statements and 3-dimensional shapes that are used to describe geographic areas. All major database management systems, such as Oracle (www.oracle.com), DB2 (www-306.ibm.com/software/data/db2), PostGis extension of PostgreSQL (www.postgresql.org) or MySQL (www.mysql.com), are shipped with an SFS extension.

Access to the DBMS is managed by the Node Manager. Applications can either provide context query statements to the Node-Manager via the Query interface or they can subscribe for context data update events via the Event interface. When the Node-Manager receives a context query statement or an event subscription, it first examines whether the relevant data item is stored in the local repository. If this is the case, query execution and subscription are rather straightforward. If the required context information is maintained by a remote node, the local Node Manager communicates the request to a so called Home-Node. Each context data item is associated with a Home-Node that stores its latest state (i.e. the master copy) and synchronizes its updates. To facilitate fast update and easy look-up of the latest state, the address of the Home-Node is encapsulated in the data item's identifier.

3.2 Database Schema and Query Languages

As the information traded at the context marketplace is heterogeneous, only a very simple database schema, which is yet perfectly aligned to the major query uses cases, suits the CDDBMS. Key-value pairs, subsequently called Attributes, which are the simplest form of storing information therefore constitute the core of CDDBMS schema. Attributes are grouped by Entities that are interconnected by Associations [7]. The CDDBMS is thus quite similar to the World Wide Web: Attribute sets correspond to the content of a web page, Entities to web pages and Associations to sets of hyperlinks. This design perfectly caters for two major query use cases:

- *Navigation queries/Browsing*: Starting from a known context data item, applications (or context consumers in general) can follow Associations to discover new information, i.e. Entities and Attributes. For example, when a user's entity is known, an application can follow the "myPreferences" Association to discover the user's service preferences.
- *Spatial queries*: As spatial inclusion relations can be directly mapped to Associations, navigational queries can also be used to look-up spatial data.

However, the burden of evaluating spatial information is put on the query client. Spatial queries are a simpler way of discovering spatial information. A query client must just provide a spatial description. The databases analysis this description and returns the data accordingly. To this end, the distributed spatial query processing algorithm utilizes inclusion relations.

Navigational queries require previous knowledge about the content of the database (the context data item entry) and its structure (Associations). When only the semantics of the target context data item are known, both navigational queries and spatial queries are useless. Semantic queries are therefore considered to be the third major context query use case:

- *Semantic Queries*: The context consumer is only aware of the semantics of a context data item. An application, for example, that discovers a printer in a building, just creates a query which couples the printer's OWL description and the spatial description of the building.

Processing of semantic queries is challenging as it involves first order logic reasoning or graph matching algorithms. Both mechanisms are not well supported by of-the-shelf databases. Section 4.4 describes the approaches for semantic query processing that are supported by the CDDBMS.

Like the database schema, the query language is also inspired by web technology. Each context Model Object is identified by a URL structured as follows:

```
NDQL://hostname:port/database/ModelType/type/number
```

The schema, NDQL, stands for Navigational Database Query Language. Hostname and port identify the Home-Node, while database is the name of the DBMS database that stores the context object. ModelType is one of the following: "Entity", "Association" or "Attribute". Type is an arbitrary type descriptor and number is a unique index. Queries can be applied to an object by simply adding a question mark and an NDQL query statement to its identifier. NDQL query statements are basically a subset of SQL and can be directly translated into SQL statements. The language is designed to provide a view on the database which supports the integrity of the schema. An NDQL projection/selection query is expressed as follows:

```
GET Entity FROM [assoc-id] WHERE Association type=[entity-type]

GET Entity FROM LOCATION=[coordinates] WHERE sem=[OWL-desc]
```

The first query looks-up all Entities of type [entity-type] that belong in the association-set of Association [assoc-id]. The second query looks-up all Entities that match the specified OWL description [OWL-desc] and are located in the spatial area [coordinates]. Note, that for the first query the reference to Home-Node is encapsulated in the Association identifier, while for the second it is described by the Location constraint (actually this might refer to multiple Nodes). Modification queries, i.e. inserts, updates and deletes, have the following format:

```
(UPDATE | ADD | DELETE) :[reference]
```

where [reference] is a reference to an instantiated context Model Object.

4 Dealing with Mobile Physical Objects

The CCDBMS is designed to manage spatial models of the physical world that cover large areas or even the entire physical world. To this end, the nodes, Geo-Ds respectively, are ordered in an R-Tree structure. Fig. 3 illustrates such a structure. Each Geo-D, depicted on the right side, is associated with a node (corresponding domain node) of the distributed spatial database. A domain context data object stored at each node specifies the geographical coverage. When a node receives a query, it first checks whether one of the queried context objects is within the coverage domain, Geo-D respectively. If the query is relevant to the domain, either the corresponding context data items are instantly retrieved, or the query is passed on to the appropriate child Geo-D. If the query is not relevant to the Geo-D, it is passed on to the parent node (given it did not originate there). Finally, it traverses the spatial CDDBMS node hierarchy down to the responsible Geo-D Nodes. As more than one Node might be responsible for the target Geo-D, the query might be duplicated and forwarded to all responsible Node-Managers. Result sets are directly forwarded to the requesting Node-Server, which is also responsible of orchestrating join operations.

The outlined routing of spatial queries is not without consequences for the security and storage approach. The security protection measures are detailed in Section 5. To

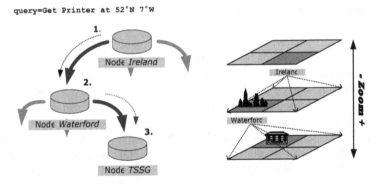

Fig. 3. Distributed spatial database: Spatial search for a printer in Waterford, Ireland

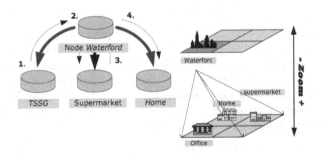

Fig. 4. Data manipulation in the CDDBMS. An example: Driving home from office and stopping at the supermarket.

facilitate efficient spatial query processing, spatial data objects must be maintained by the node that manages the corresponding Geo-D. Fig. 4 illustrates how the CDDBMS manages context information of physical mobile objects. A TSSG employee leaves his/her office and drives home, making a stop at a local supermarket on his/her way. In total, he/she crosses Geo-D boundaries five times. Consequently, a context data object representing the employee within the distributed spatial database should be moved across the four nodes five times.

Table 1. Parameters of scalability equation

Parameter	Description
N	Number of user profiles stored in the user profile database.
λ	Movement rate per user in seconds, i.e. rate at which a user changes Geo-Ds.
p	Probability that a Geo-D change affects only the parent Geo-D. With respect to graph G, p is the probability that a node change affects only its parent node.
L	Height of graph $G=(V,E)$
M	Maximum degree of a vertex of G, i.e. maximum number of sub Geo-Ds per Node Server.

Basically, moving data items between domains is perfectly scalable as most changes are performed within local network domains. Yet, any changes to mobile objects must be synchronised with the master copy at the Home Node. Frequent synchronisations increase the network traffic considerably and thus constitute a critical problem compromising the scalability of the system, as indicated by the following analysis.

The location hierarchy of Node Servers is a directed, acyclic graph $G=(V,E)$, where each vertex $v \in V$ corresponds to a Node Server and each edge $e \in E$ is an inclusion relation with respect to the Geo-Ds. In fact, G is considered to be a tree with a vertex degree of m. Given the parameters described in Table 1, the number of updates $U_C(N)$ to the Home-Node (induced by location updates) can be expressed as follows:

$$U_C(N) = \lambda \cdot N$$

Most updates are propagated across the entire network and impose considerable load on the backbone network. It would be much more efficient if most updates were kept locally, i.e are not propagated across the backbone. In such a distributed storage and synchronisation approach changes are only propagated to the parent Node Server. A distributed approach would have $U_D(N)$ updates per second:

$$U_D(N) = \lambda \cdot N \cdot (1 - p)^L$$

G is an R-Tree. To simplify the calculations, it has been assumed that the users are randomly distributed among the m^L leafs; thus each leaf node maintains N/m^L users. The performance gain of the distributed approach with respect to the centralised one is given by the following expression:

$$Gain(N) = \frac{U_c(N)}{U_d(N)} = \frac{m^L}{m^L \cdot (1 - p)^{L-1}}$$

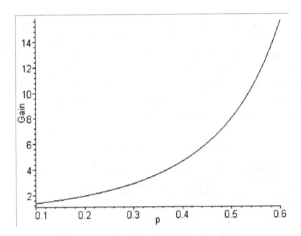

Fig. 5. Performance gain of the distributed over the centralised synchronisation approach. For parameter settings refer to Table 1.

The gain just depends on the graph structure (height and vertex degree) and probability p. Fig. 5 illustrates G for a rather flat hierarchy with 4 levels, i.e. L=4 and rather moderate $p<0.6$. The distributed approach clearly outperforms the centralised. Consequently, with respect to mobile physical objects, frequent synchronisations with the Master Copy should be avoided.

4.1 Mobile Node Server

Location sensors provide coordinates of devices. It is assumed that each of these devices runs a CDDBMS Node Server that should be attached to the hierarchy of the spatial database. A mobile device's Node Server will be hereafter referred to as a Mobile Node Server or just Mobile Node.

The Geo-D of a Mobile Node is the mobile device itself. For small devices this is just a logical domain, but for large devices such as cars, aircrafts or even ships, Geo-Ds cover geographic areas, which are however mobile with regards to the outside world. The current context of a mobile device is stored by its Mobile Node Server. Thus, finding the context of a mobile device is equivalent to finding its Mobile Node Server.

The approach implemented by the CDDBMS for handling mobile objects is depicted in Fig. 6. Each Mobile Node is represented by an Entity. The Home Node is a Node Server in the fixed network and thus, the route to this server never changes. When a Mobile Node moves into a different Geo-D, a Visited-Parent Entity is created at the Node that manages the domain. The Visited-Parent Entity inter-links the Mobile Node and the Home Node. Processing of non-spatial statements is thus similar to mobile IP [8]. The Home Node re-directs query statement to the Visited Parent, which finally dispatches it to the Mobile Node.

As the Home Node stores the Master Copy of the Entity that models the Mobile Node, all statements related to the Mobile Node are sent to the Home Node first. The latter looks-up the Entity and extracts the URL of the Visited Parent or one of the

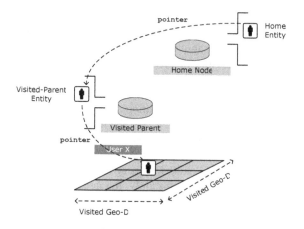

Fig. 6. Visited Parent approach

Visited Parent's parent Nodes (pointer chain). Since statements are directed to the actual Mobile Node, data synchronization with the Home Node is no longer necessary. Instead the copy at the Visited Parent may serve as the synchronization copy comprising all updates and the Home Node is only used for re-direction and as static data storage.

4.2 Mobile Handover Procedure

When a Mobile Node Server changes the Geo-D, the routing entries, the pointer chain respectively, must be updated. To this end, Node Managers implement a simple handover procedure that is illustrated in Fig. 7: Two CDDBMS Nodes manage adjacent Geo-Ds, each Geo-D has its own location sensor. Initially, user X has just a

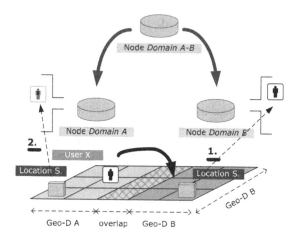

Fig. 7. Mobile physical data object handover procedure

location entry at Node A, the location value is frequently updated by the location sensor of Geo-D A. (1) When the user moves into Geo-D B, thus getting into the sensor range of this domain's location sensor, a new location entry is created in Geo-D B. Both location entries (at Node A and B) might virtually contain the same sample data, but since different location sensors have captured the samples, an aggregation of the two is not possible (at least not in the CDDBMS). (2) When user X leaves Geo-D A, thus getting out of sensor range, the location sensor signals that the location entry is invalid. The CDDBMS Node removes it, and the handover is then completed. If the location sensor fails to signal that the entry is invalid, the location entry is removed when no updates are received within a predefined timeframe.

The handover sets new routing paths for query statements. Since neither handover nor statement processing are executed instantly, the handover protocol must take into account delayed query statements. For example, let's examine the case where a statement is issued at time t, while a handover is performed at time $t+h$, and the completion of the re-routing is finished at time $t+h+k$. Thus, when the statement is routed to the destination Visited Parent in the time interval $[t+h, t+h+k]$, it ends up at the old Visited Parent rather than at the new one. To solve this problem, Geo-Ds are required to overlap. While the Mobile-Node is within the overlapping region, both old and new Visited Parent still refer to the Node.

The CDDBMS implements also another handover procedure, the soft handover procedure, that supports a graceful handshake between two Node Managers. It is applicable to mobile devices that are equipped with a location sensor. In such a setup there are no ambiguities about the Geo-D and the context data object can be exchanged in a handshake between the two databases whenever a mobile device crosses the border of a Geo-D. Range-monitoring queries allow keeping track of these events. Cai et al. propose efficient mechanisms for range-queries based on safe regions [9]. With the help of these queries, location sensors are only required to send updates when they leave a safe region, thus reducing the power consumption of the mobile device.

4.3 Distributed Semantic Database Management

Taxonomies are a simple approach of describing semantics. Given the fact that they imply just planar graphs, efficient matching algorithms for relational data models can be implemented. Let $G_T=(V_T, E_T)$ be a taxonomy, where V_T is the vocabulary and E_T are the tag relationships. To process the taxonomy with a relational database the graph G_T is decomposed into a database table as illustrated in Fig. 8. The taxonomy with root tag name *"device"* is decomposed into *taxonomy table*. Each tag is associated with a unique identifier (id column) and a parent tag name (parent column). The relationships between semantic tag names and Entities are described by the *entity table*. It comprises the columns cid (which is the unique context entity identifier in the CDDBMS), type (reference to id column of *taxonomy table*) and entity name. A semantic query is a graph $G_Q=(V_Q, E_Q)$ with $V_Q \subseteq V_T$ and a semantic match is a sub-graph isomorphism between G_Q and G_T. Unfortunately, the general sub-graph isomorphism problem is NP-complete [10]. However, the sub-graph matching of planar graphs can be computed in polynomial time [11].

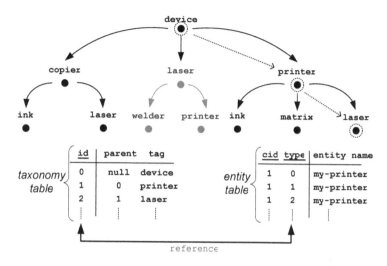

Fig. 8. Semantic Entity retrieval example

A simple matching algorithm between G_Q and G_T is just a set based match, i.e. the structure of the graphs is ignored, while only the semantic tags associated with the query and the entities are compared. Given $V_Q = \{a_1, \ldots, a_n\}$ and $\{cid, (t_1, \ldots, t_m)\} \in$ *entity* (t_i is the tag name implied by column `type`) a set match is $\{cid \mid V_Q \subseteq \{t_1, \ldots, t_m\}, \{cid, (t_1, \ldots, t_m)\} \in$ *entity*$\}$. That is, the entities returned are the ones associated with the same tag names as the semantic query. In terms of SQL, this corresponds to a self-join of table *entity*:

```
SELECT cid, name FROM entity A₁,... entity Aₘ WHERE
      A₁.cid=...=Aₘ.cid and A₁.type=a₁ and ... Aₘ.type=aₘ
```

Given that the attributes `cid` and `type` are indexed, the computational complexity of the statement is $O(|\text{entity}| \cdot \log(|\text{entity}|)^{m-1})$. The efficiency of the set-based query comes at the cost of retrieval performance. For example, a set-based query {*device, printer, laser*} returns both laser printers and laser devices which are used for engravings (see Fig. 8). This is due to the fact that set-based queries do not take the graph structure into account. Hierarchical queries are not supported by SQL. The Oracle 10g database, however, implements an SQL extension which supports such queries. CONNECT BY describes hierarchical relationships between Oracle table rows. Thus a query $a_1/a_2/.../a_m$ (a_1 is parent of a_2 and so on) can be matched as follows:

```
SELECT id FROM taxonomy
            connect by prior id=parent start with tag=a₁      (1)
INTERSECT (SELECT id FROM taxonomy...start with tag=aᵢ), i=1...m

SELECT cid, name FROM entity WHERE type=id                    (2)
```

"`Prior`" specifies row parent/child relationships and "`start with`" specifies the root of the sub-graph. Each SELECT statement in (1) specifies a sub-graph of the taxonomy with root a_i. By intersecting the graphs, only the minimum graph is returned. Finally, in (2), the Entities that match the tags are returned. Apparently, this algorithm takes the tag relationships into account. Moreover, it can be extended to match arbitrary query graphs. Similarly to semantic queries, *XPath* queries [12] have a graph structure. Yet, the latter comprise just parent/child relationships, yielding simpler matching approaches. In [13], Grust *et al.* present efficient *XPath* matching algorithms.

OWL semantic descriptions are more powerful than simple taxonomies. They support first order logic reasoning and thus, they are expected to further increase the retrieval performance. Logic based matching is supported by deductive databases like ConceptBase [14] and XSB [15]. They implement logic based query languages such as Datalog [16]. Yet, none of-the-shelf database support these queries. The Node-Manager is foreseen to deal with this issue by maintaining two databases: a deductive database and a conventional one. It could thus merge the results of the two databases. OWL-based matching is a subject of future work.

5   Privacy and Security

Privacy is defined in [17] as *"the claim of individuals, groups, or institutions to determine for themselves when, how, and to what extent information about them is communicated to others"*. As already stated, the CDDBMS supports the trade of sensitive context information and thus, privacy protection formulates one of most critical requirements to be addressed. The need to disclose a large volume of personal data to various operators and service providers introduces further implication, thus making access control mechanisms indispensable for ensuring the protection of privacy-sensitive information in the CDDBMS. But there are also other means applied by the CDDBMS to deal with security and privacy of context information, such as query tunnelling, context data encryption and anonymisation, etc. The relevant mechanisms established are briefly described in the remainder of this section.

5.1   Anonymisation, Pseudonymisation and Partitioning of Personal Context

As already mentioned, users disclose personal and hence privacy-sensitive data to the CDDBMS. This information should per se not be generic, in which case the user could "hide" in a group of users with same attributes/preferences and situations (see the definition of anonymity set in [18]), but highly specialized for each user in order to tailor the functionality in the best possible manner.

The intended disclosure of personal data and the magnitude of providers in the context marketplace lead to an increase of privacy threats for users. Personal information is disclosed to unknown – thus often not trustworthy– providers and a lot of sensitive personal information is to be handled by services and the CDDBMS. This is especially dangerous if the user's identity is known. Roughly stated, the privacy threat grows stronger as the amount of known context information increases.

This is the point, where the privacy protection approach gets a grip. The huge set of personal context data is partitioned in smaller sets with much lower sensitivity. A user is enabled to use several pseudonyms, thus building several virtual identities (VIDs) in the system. A VID [19] is a kind of user identity consisting of an artificial name (pseudonym) for the user, augmented by a set of attributes under which the user appears in the system. Each VID only comprises a partition of the user's overall context data set, thus resembling a restricted view on the user presented to external parties. This information set is a partial view on the user's overall context hierarchy. Fig.9 illustrates an example of this approach. We are currently investigating the design of a mechanism for context-partition formulation that aims to eliminate the possibility of generation of thematic clusters and avoid the case where relations between the attributes within a cluster may threaten the user privacy.

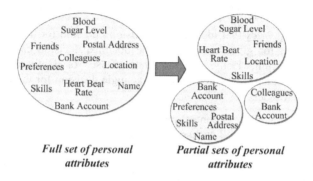

Fig. 9. Partitioning of personal context information

Another advantage of controlling access to VIDs rather than to plain data is the fact that escalated revealing of knowledge about the real user identity is enabled. For instance, if people are involved in public affairs, they often need to trade anonymity for a service. This also means that the disclosure of private data is proportional to the number of parties that share the awareness of one only real identity. In our VID approach, involving personal information in public affairs does not necessary mean trading anonymity. This is due to the fact that, in case a virtual identity is carefully selected, then the possibility of revealing a true identity by inspecting the disclosed information is drastically reduced or even eliminated. Of course, each VID must still be accountable for the user's actions (for charging purposes as well as for the case of misuse by the user). How this is realized is described in [19]. It should be mentioned that the multiple identity approach adopted supports the principle of data minimisation of the European Parliament and Council, which requires the set of personal data disclosed to a service to exactly match the amount of data the service needs.

5.2 Context Access Control

The Node-Manager provides context access control facilities that aim to evaluate access control policies and enforce control of access to resources. In principle, the Access Control Manager (ACM) of the Node-Manager of the CDDBMS applies filtering on resources based on:

- *Subject*: The VID of the context consumer is provided to the CDDBMS escorting every context query statement. A VID representing either a single entity or a group may be used depending on the level of control required.

- *Action*: With respect to the context information required, four kinds of actions are distinguished: Read, Write, Create, and Delete.
- *Context condition*: Access to data is constrained based on the current context information.

The access policy applicable is identified and enforced by the Home Node-Manager. It is characterized by the following:

- *Access Policy Target* that contains a set of simplified conditions for the subject, target and action that must be met to apply a policy set, policy or rule to a given query.
- *Access Policy Rules* that identify the decision outcome for the specific Access Policy Target for given conditions. The obtained decision can be one of the following: Permit, Deny, Indeterminate, False, or Obfuscate. Combining decisions from multiple rules results in a single decision for the policy: Permit, Deny, or Obfuscate.

The aforementioned access control policy is based on the XACML standard [20]. A default policy of deny-all-access should be assumed for stored data, unless otherwise specified, i.e. explicitly defined in an appropriate access policy.

The access control process that takes place consists of the following steps:

1. An actor (subject) provides his VID (here assumed to be VIDx) requesting context data of VIDy (target).
2. The request is received and processed by the Local Node-Manager. As the target identifier provided is VIDy, thus not being compliant with the URL identifier of context model objects (see Section 3.2), the Node-Manager triggers the translation of VID identifiers to context identifiers (CIDs). This task is not performed locally, but is delegated to a specific remote Node-Manager that belongs in a Trusted Group of CDDBMS nodes. Once CIDy is obtained, the Trusted Node-Manager encrypts it using its public key.
3. The encrypted CIDy (encrCIDy) along with the URL of the Trusted Node-Manager is returned to the local Node-Manager. The latter replaces VIDy with encrCIDy in the context query statement and forwards it to the Trusted Node-Manager.
4. The Trusted Node-Manager decrypts the encrCIDy into CIDy. The CIDy indicates the URL of the Home Node-Manager, i.e. the one maintaining the master copy of the context information requested. Thus, the Trusted Node-Manager replaces encrCIDy with CIDy in the context query statement and forwards it to the Home Node-Manager.
5. The Home Node-Manager receives the context query, executes it and retrieves the respective result set.
6. However, VIDx may not be authorised to access the entire result set. Thus, the Home Node-Manager retrieves the context access policies that apply for CIDy and makes an access decision concerning the request of VIDx. It then enforces the access decision that may require filtering of the result set and/or obfuscation of specific Attribute values.
7. The Home Node-Manager returns the filtered result set to the Trusted Node-Manager. The latter replaces CIDy with VIDy and forwards the filtered result set to the Local Node-Manager that eventually delivers it to the context consumer.

The process described above ensures that the real CID and therefore the location of the Home Node-Manager is never disclosed to the context consumer, thus preventing the linkage of different VIDs assigned to the same context entities. Of course, in order to establish this, a Trusted Group of CDDBMSs is distinguished, which is responsible for forwarding the context requests to the Home Node-Managers. The Trusted CDDBMSs handle en-/de-cryption of CIDs and act as intermediaries between the Node-Manager at the consumer site and the Home Node-Manager maintaining the master copy of the context information requested. Of course, as the access control rights are defined per subject VID, the anonymity of the context consumer is ensured.

It should be mentioned that in order for the CDDBMS to decide on the privacy policy to be applied for the specific consumer under the current circumstances, a privacy policy negotiation process takes place. This mechanism negotiates the level of context information to be disclosed so that privacy sensitive data are not revealed to services if not absolutely necessary. Thus, it ensures that only the minimum of context information is disclosed at each external actor. The privacy policy negotiation mechanism has already been implemented and evaluated; and is thoroughly described in [21] and [22].

5.3 Query Tunelling

The routing of spatial queries outlined in Section 4.1 introduces severe security concerns, as the hierarchy requires queries to traverse Node-Managers that are not trusted or that do not have a valid federation agreement. The CDDBMS solves this problem by a tunnelling approach. Spatial queries are encapsulated within an envelope. The encrypted message body contains the original query and the sender's address. The header comprises spatial query which is extracted from the original one and describes the target Geo-D. A list of federation identifiers is also included in the publicly readable section of the message. Node-Managers that cannot decrypt the message body can only read the Geo-D description and the federation information, but they cannot access the query and sender information. Yet, this is sufficient information to make routing decisions.

6   Conclusions and Future Plans

The CDDBMS is a distributed heterogeneous multi-database system, which is built to cater for the needs of context marketplaces, while being scalable and lightweight, as it resembles more the web-server schema that makes it reliable and highly flexible. During the last years, various context management models and architectures have been proposed in the literature. The most popular of these include the Context Toolkit [23], Mediacup [24], Aura [25], Cooltown [26], Owl context service [27], Kimura System [28], HotTown [29], Solar [30], CoBrA [31], CORTEX [32], Context Stack [33], CASS [34], CONTEXT [35], SOCAM [36], ContextPhone [37], etc. Yet, none of these systems provide both semantic and spatial context queries as well as VID-based privacy and security enforcement. Furthermore, none of them meets the requirements of telecommunication systems in terms of scalability on a global level and information federation.

The proposed CDDBMS has been designed to meet the requirements of telecommunication operators and context marketplaces. As such it implements the aforementioned features which have been detailed in this paper. Other more advanced search features, such as context inference [38], query extension mechanisms and free-text based query handling [39] are also available in case the advanced Context Management layer [38] is running on top of the CDDBMS. Such sophisticated features are necessary to enable applications and application developers to discover the context information they need irrespective of the data location, to prevent them from drowning in the information glut produced by large context source infrastructures and to obtain optimal context value estimations even if the necessary context sources are not available.

Further research plans involve the extension of the context query processing described to incorporate facilities for identifying the result set demonstrating the highest possible Quality of Context [40]. Additionally, in order to further increase the retrieval performance of the CDDBMS, the Node-Manager is being extended with OWL-based semantic matching facilities. Finally, aiming to establish a global privacy protection scheme, the establishment of an infrastructure is being studied that exploits recommender systems [41] for controlled sharing of information concerning the trustworthiness of the various stakeholders in the context marketplace and for evaluating the potential privacy threats that may be introduced by specific parties.

Currently, the system is being embedded into the business platform of Digital Ecosystems [42] to enable a large number of SME participants to contribute and share context information from very heterogeneous sources [43].

Acknowledgments. This work has been partially supported by the Integrated Project Daidalos ("Designing Advanced network Interfaces for the Delivery and Administration of Location independent, Optimised personal Services"), which is financed by the European Commission under the Sixth Framework Programme. However, this paper expresses the authors' personal views, which are not necessarily those of the Daidalos consortium.

References

1. Baldauf, M., Dustar, S., Rosenberg, F.: A Survey on Context-Aware Systems. International Journal of Ad Hoc and Ubiquitous Computing 2(4), 263–277 (2007)
2. Abowd, G.D., Mynatt, E.D., Rodden, T.: The Human Experience. IEEE Pervasive Computing 1(1), 48–57 (2002)
3. Lu, H., Ooi, B.C.: Spatial Indexing: Past and Future. IEEE Data Engineering Bulletin 16(3), 16–21 (1993)
4. Yeung, A.K.W., Hall, G.B.: Spatial Database Systems: Design, Implementation and Project Management. Springer, Series: GeoJournal Library 87 (2007)
5. Vögel, H.J., Weyl, B., Eichler, S.: Federation solutions for inter- and intradomain security in next-generation mobile service platforms, AEÜ. Journal of Electronics and Communications 60(1), 13–19 (2006)
6. Open Geospatial Consortium Inc.: Simple Feature access–Part 2: SQL Option. v.1.1.0 (2005)

7. Roussaki, I., Strimpakou, M., Pils, C.: Distributed Context Retrieval and Consistency Control in Pervasive Computing. Journal of Network and Systems Management 15(1), 57–74 (2007)
8. Mondal, A.S.: Present State and Future. Springer, Series in Computer Science. Springer, Heidelberg (2003)
9. Cai, Y., Hua, K.A., Cao, G.H., Xu, T.: Real-time processing of range-monitoring queries in heterogeneous mobile databases. IEEE Transactions on Mobile Computing 5(7), 931–942 (2006)
10. Bopanna, R.B., Hastad, J., Zachos, S.: Does co-np have short interactive proofs? Information Processing Letters 25(2), 127–132 (1987)
11. Hopcroft, J.E., Wong, J.K.: Linear time algorithm for isomorphism of planar graphs. 6th annual ACM symposium on Theory of computing, Washington, USA, pp. 172–184 (1974)
12. Berglund, A., Boag, S., Chamberlin, D., Fernandez, M.F., Kay, M., Robie, J., Simeon, J.: XML Path Language(XPath) 2.0 W3C Recommendation (2007), http://www.w3.org
13. Grust, T., van Keulen, M., Teubner, J.: Accelerating Xpath Evaluation in Any RDBMS. ACM Transactions on Database Systems 29, 91–131 (2004)
14. XSB at sourceforge (2006), http://xsb.sourceforge.net/
15. Gottlob, G., Grädel, E., Veith, H.: Datalog LITE: A deductive query language with linear time model checking. ACM Trans. on Computational Logic 3(1), 42–79 (2002)
16. Conceptbase, A.: Database System for Meta Modelling and Method Engineering (v7) (2007), http://conceptbase.cc/
17. Westin, A.F.: Privacy and Freedom. H. Wolff, New York (1967)
18. Pfitzmann, A., Hansen, M.: Anonymity, Unlinkability, Unobservability, Pseudonymity, and Identity Management – A Consolidated Proposal for Terminology. Version 0.28 (2006), http://dud.inf.tu-dresden.de/Anon_Terminology.shtml
19. Porekar, J., Dolinar, K., Jerman-Blazic, B.: Middleware for Privacy Protection of Ambient Intelligence and Pervasive Systems. WSEAS Transaction on Information Science and Applications 4(2), 633–641 (2007)
20. XACML: A New Standard Protects Content in Enterprise Data Exchange (2003), http://java.sun.com/developer/technicalArticles/Security/xacml/xacml.html
21. Dolinar, K., Porekar, J., Jerman-Blazic, A., Klobucar, T.: Pervasive systems: enhancing trust negotiation with privacy support. International Workshop on Research Challenges in Security and Privacy for Mobile and Wireless Networks, Miami, Florida, pp. 1–10 (2006)
22. Jerman-Blazic, A., Dolinar, K., Porekar, J.: Enabling Privacy in Pervasive Computing Using Fusion of Privacy Negotiation, Identity Management and Trust Management Techniques. 1st International Conference on the Digital Society, pp. 30–35. Guadeloupe, French Caribbean (2007)
23. Dey, A., Salber, D., Abowd, G.: A Conceptual Framework and a Toolkit for Supporting the Rapid Prototyping of Context-Aware Applications. Human-Computer Interaction Journal 16(2-4), 97–166 (2001)
24. Beigl, M., Gellersen, H.W., Schmidt, A.: Mediacups: Experience with design and use of computer-augmented everyday objects. Elsevier Computer Networks 35(4), 401–409 (2001)
25. Garlan, D., Siewiorek, D., Smailagic, A., Steenkiste, P.: Project Aura: Towards Distraction-Free Pervasive Computing. IEEE Pervasive Computing 1(2), 22–31 (2002)
26. Kindberg, T., Barton, J., et al.: People, Places, Things: Web Presence for the Real World. ACM Mobile Networks & Applications Journal 7(5), 365–376 (2002)
27. Lei, H., Sow, D.M., Davis, II.: The design and applications of a context service. ACM SIGMOBILE Mobile Computing and Communications Review 6(4), 45–55 (2002)

28. Voida, S., Mynatt, E., MacIntyre, B., Corso, G.: Integrating virtual and physical context to support knowledge workers. IEEE Pervasive Computing 1(3), 73–79 (2002)
29. Kanter, T.: Attaching Context-Aware Services to Moving Locations. IEEE Internet Computing 7(2), 43–51 (2003)
30. Chen, G., Kotz, D.: Context-sensitive resource discovery. 1st IEEE International Conference on Pervasive Computing and Communications, Texas, USA, pp. 243–252 (2003)
31. Chen, H., Finin, T., Joshi, A., Kagal, L.: Intelligent Agents Meet the Semantic Web in Smart Spaces. IEEE Internet Computing 8(6), 69–79 (2004)
32. Biegel, G., Cahill, V.: A Framework for Developing Mobile, Context-aware Applications. 2nd IEEE Conference on Pervasive Computing and Communications, Orlando, USA, pp. 361–365 (2004)
33. Braun, E., Austaller, G., Kangasharju, J., Muhlhauser, M.: Accessing Web Applications with Multiple Context-Aware Devices. In: Matera, M., Comai, S. (eds.) Engineering Advanced Web Applications, Rinton Press (2004)
34. Fahy, P., Clarke, S.: CASS: Middleware for Mobile Context-Aware Applications. ACM MobiSys Workshop on Context Awareness, Boston, USA (2004)
35. Xynogalas, S., Chantzara, M., Sygkouna, I., Vrontis, S., Roussaki, I., Anagnostou, M.: Context Management for the Provision of Adaptive Services to Roaming Users. IEEE Wireless Communications 11(2), 40–47 (2004)
36. Gu, T., Pung, H.K., Zhang, D.Q.: A Service-Oriented Middleware for Building Context-Aware Services. Journal of Network and Computer Applications 28(1), 1–18 (2005)
37. Raento, M., Oulasvirta, A., Petit, R., Toivonen, H.: ContextPhone - A prototyping platform for context-aware mobile applications. IEEE Pervasive Computing 4(2), 51–59 (2005)
38. Pils, C., Strimpakou, M., Roussaki, I., Pfeifer, T.: A context awareness framework for telecommunication environments. eChallenges Conference, Barcelona, Spain (2006)
39. Pils, C., Roussaki, I., Strimpakou, M.: Location-Based Context Retrieval and Filtering. In: Hazas, M., Krumm, J., Strang, T. (eds.) LoCA 2006. LNCS, vol. 3987, pp. 256–273. Springer, Heidelberg (2006)
40. Zimmer, T.: QoC: Quality of Context – Improving the Performance of Context-Aware Applications. Advances in Pervasive Computing 2006, Dublin, Ireland, pp. 209–214 (2006)
41. Adomavicius, G., Tuzhilin, A.: Toward the Next Generation of Recommender Systems: A Survey of the State-of-the-Art and Possible Extensions. IEEE Transactions on Knowledge and Data Engineering 17(6), 734–749 (2005)
42. Malone, P., Pfeifer, T.: Cross-domain Context Sensing and Knowledge Sharing Ecosystem. 4th International Workshop on Managing Ubiquitous Communications and Services, Munich, Germany, pp. 165–173 (2007)
43. Pfeifer, T.: Redundant Positioning Architecture. Elsevier Computer Communications 28(13), 1575–1585 (2005)

A Taxonomy for Radio Location Fingerprinting

Mikkel Baun Kjærgaard

Department of Computer Science, University of Aarhus,
IT-parken, Aabogade 34, DK-8200 Aarhus N, Denmark
`mikkelbk@daimi.au.dk`

Abstract. *Location Fingerprinting (LF)* is a promising location technique for many awareness applications in pervasive computing. However, as research on LF systems goes beyond *basic methods* there is an increasing need for better comparison of proposed LF systems. Developers of LF systems are also lacking good frameworks for understanding different options when building LF systems. This paper proposes a taxonomy to address both of these problems. The proposed taxonomy has been constructed from a literature study of 51 papers and articles about LF. For researchers the taxonomy can also be used as an aid when scoping out future research in the area of LF.

1 Introduction

A popular location technique is *Location Fingerprinting (LF)*, having the major advantage of exploiting already existing network infrastructures, like IEEE 802.11 or GSM, which avoids extra deployment costs and effort. Based on a database of pre-recorded measurements of network characteristics from different locations, denoted as *fingerprints*, a wireless client's location is estimated by inspecting currently measured network characteristics. Network characteristics are typically base station identifiers and the received signal strength.

LF is different by the use of fingerprints to other location techniques such as lateration, angulation, proximity detection and dead reckoning [1]. Lateration and angulation techniques estimate location from measurements to fixed points with known locations. A technology example is the *Global Positioning System (GPS)* which estimate a GPS client's location from measurements to GPS satellites with known locations. Proximity detection identifies the location of clients when in proximity of fixed points. A technology example is *Radio-Frequency IDentification (RFID)* where a passive RFID tag's location is known when in proximity of a RFID scanner. Dead reckoning estimates location by advancing previous estimates by known speed, elapsed time and direction. A technology example is dead reckoning based on accelerometer measurements.

Many different LF systems have been proposed. When surveying LF systems one has to answer many different questions. For instance, how do systems differ in scale; can they be deployed to cover a single building or an entire city? What network characteristics are measured? What are the roles of the wireless clients, base stations, and servers in the estimation process? Which estimation method

J. Hightower, B. Schiele, and T. Strang (Eds.): LoCA 2007, LNCS 4718, pp. 139–156, 2007.

is used? How are fingerprints collected and used? These questions are not only important for researchers surveying LF but also developers of LF systems who have to understand the different possibilities. We believe that a taxonomy will aid LF system developers and researchers better survey, compare, and design LF systems. Being able to better survey and compare existing work also makes it possible to use the taxonomy as an aid when scoping out future research. This is especially important as research more and more moves from understanding the basic mechanisms to optimizing existing methods for non-functional properties such as robustness and scalability. Existing taxonomies such as that proposed by Hightower et al. [2] cover location systems in general and are therefore not too much help when answering the many questions specific to LF.

The taxonomy we have chosen to propose has been constructed based on a literature study of 51 papers and articles. The 51 papers and article propose 30 different systems which have been analyzed and methods and techniques grouped to form taxons for the taxonomy. The analyses of four of the 30 systems are covered as case studies in Section 7. The analysis results for all of the 30 systems are available online at [3].

The structure of the paper is as follows. The taxons of the proposed taxonomy are discussed in Section 2. The individual taxons are then presented in Sections 3 to 6. Four case studies are afterwards presented in Section 7 and a discussion is given in Section 8. Finally, conclusions are given in Section 9. Due to the limited size of this paper, the presentation level is advanced; for introductions to LF refer to books such as Küpper [1] and papers such as Krishnakumar et al. [4].

2   Taxonomy

The proposed taxonomy is built around eleven taxons listed with definitions in Table 1. These were partly inspired by earlier work on taxonomies for location systems in general and from our literature study. The four taxons: *scale, output, measurements,* and *roles* describe general properties of LF systems. We mean by scale the size of the deployment area and by output the type of provided location information. Measurements means the types of measured network characteristics and roles means the division of responsibilities between wireless clients, base stations, and servers. Only these four of our eleven taxons are covered by existing taxonomies such as Hightower et al. [2]. Their concepts for these four taxons differ by output being split over the four concepts of physical, symbolic, absolute, and relative, measurements being indirectly described by their technique concept and roles being partly described by their concept of localized location computation.

Estimation method and *radio map* describe the location estimation process. Estimation method denote a method for predicting locations from a radio map and currently measured network characteristics and radio map a model of network characteristics in a deployment area. The division into estimation method and radio map is used by many papers about LF, for instance Youssef et al. [5].

Table 1. Taxon definitions

Taxon	Definition
Scale	Size of deployment area.
Output	Type of provided location information.
Measurements	Types of measured network characteristics.
Roles	Division of responsibilities between wireless clients, base stations, and servers.
Estimation Method	Method for predicting locations from a radio map and currently measured network characteristics.
Radio Map	Model of network characteristics in a deployment area.
Spatial Variations	Observed differences in network characteristics at different locations because of signal propagation characteristics.
Temporal Variations	Observed differences in network characteristics over time at a single location because of continuing changing signal propagation.
Sensor Variations	Observed differences in network characteristics between different types of wireless clients.
Collector	Who or what collect fingerprints.
Collection Method	Procedure used when collecting fingerprints.

However, some papers use a slightly different naming for instance Otsason et al. [6] use *localization algorithm* and *radio map*.

How changing network characteristics over time, space and sensors can be handled is described by *spatial, temporal and sensor variations*. The spatial and temporal dimensions were introduced by Youssef et al. [5]. The sensor dimension was introduced in our earlier work, Kjærgaard [7]. The taxons *collector* and *collection method* describe how fingerprints are collected. These two taxons have been introduced to characterize the assumptions systems put on fingerprint collection.

The focus of the proposed taxonomy is on methods for LF and therefore the taxonomy does not cover evaluation properties for LF systems. Evaluation properties for all kinds of location systems have for instance been suggested by Muthukrishnan et al. [8], who list: precision, accuracy, calibration, responsiveness, scalability, cost, and privacy. The taxonomy proposed by Hightower et al. [2] also lists several evaluation properties: precision, accuracy, scale, cost, and limitations. In our analysis we have included the following evaluation properties: precision, accuracy, evaluation setup, and limitations. These four were chosen because this information is available from most papers. Responsiveness and cost were not included because the first is only available from very few papers and the second from none. Calibration, privacy, scalability, and scale are partly covered by our taxons scale, roles and collection method. These four properties are also listed in our case studies in Section 7.

The taxonomy does not cover non-functional system properties, because work has not yet matured in these directions for LF systems. Non-functional properties of LF systems have been addressed by several recent papers, such as system robustness by Lorincz et al. [9], server scalability by Youssef et al. [5], and minimal communication by Kjærgaard et al. [10]. Also, the taxonomy does not cover the application of LF techniques to other types of sensor measurements such as sound and light.

3 General Taxons

The proposed general taxons for LF systems are: *scale, output, measurements* and *roles*. These taxons are shown including subtaxons in Figure 1. In this and the following sections when taxons are presented up to four references are given to papers or articles that propose systems that are grouped below the particular taxon. Therefore not all papers groupped under a taxon are listed, this type of information can be found online at [3].

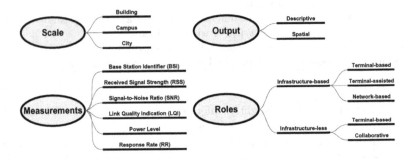

Fig. 1. Scale, output, measurements and roles

Scale describes a system's size of deployment. Scale is important because size of deployment impacts how fingerprints can be collected and some systems are limited in scale because of specific assumptions. Scale is proposed to be classified as *building, campus,* or *city*. Many LF systems have been proposed for a *building* scale of deployment [11,12,13,14]. Some systems are limited to this scale because they assume knowledge about the physical layout of buildings [15,16,17,18]; others because they assume the installation of a special infrastructure [19,20]. *Campus*-wide systems [21] scale by proposing more practical schemes for fingerprint collection. *City*-wide systems [22,23,24] scale even further by not assuming that a system is deployed by or for a single organization. City wide systems could scale to any area that is covered by base stations.

Output denotes the type of provided location information. The subtaxons for output are proposed to follow the notion introduced in Küpper [1] of dividing location information into *descriptive* and *spatial* information. Descriptive locations are described by names, identifiers or numbers assigned to natural geographic or man-made objects[1]. Spatial locations are described by a set of coordinates stated with respect to a spatial reference system. Many LF systems output *spatial* locations [11,14,24,25] but systems have also been proposed that output *descriptive*

---

[1] Some authors refer to this as symbolic locations.

locations [16,18,21]. However, a location outputted as either of the two types can be mapped to the other type given a suitable location model.

Measurements are the types of measured network characteristics. The following network characteristics have been used in existing systems: *Base Station Identifiers (BSI)*, *Received Signal Strength (RSS)*, *Signal-to-Noise Ratio (SNR)*, *Link Quality Indicator (LQI)*, *power level*, and *Response Rate (RR)*. BSI is a unique name assigned to a base station. RSS, SNR, and LQI are signal propagation metrics collected by radios for handling and optimizing communication. The power level is information from the signal sender about current sending power. The response rate is the frequency of received measurements over time from a specific base station. Many LF systems are based on BSI and RSS [11,14,18,25]; other systems have used RR in addition to RSS [15,17,24]. BSI and SNR have also been used [16] and the combination BSI, LQI, RSS, and Power level [9,26].

Roles denote the division of responsibilities between wireless clients, base stations, and servers. How roles are assigned impact both how systems are realized, but also important non-functional properties like privacy and scalability. The two main categories for roles are *infrastructure-based* and *infrastructure-less*. Infrastructure-based systems depend on a pre-installed powered infrastructure of base stations. Infrastructure-less systems consist of ad-hoc-installed battery-powered wireless clients where some of them act as "base stations". Infrastructure-based systems are following Küpper [1], being further divided into *terminal-based, terminal-assisted* and *network-based* systems. The infrastructure-less systems are divided into *terminal-based* and *collaborative* systems. The different types of systems differ in who sends out beacons, who makes measurements from the beacons and who stores the radio map and runs LF estimation, as shown in Figure 2. Most LF systems have been built as

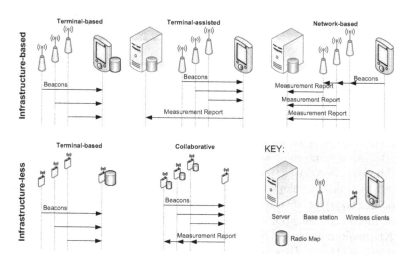

Fig. 2. Different assignments of responsabilities to wireless clients, base stations, and servers

infrastructure-based and terminal-based [5,12,24], which is attractive because this setup supports privacy. Terminal-assisted [16,21] and network-based systems [11,20] have also been built offering better support for resource-weak wireless clients[2]. Infrastructure-less LF-systems have to be optimized for the resource-weak wireless clients, which is addressed by the collaborative setup [9,26].

4 Estimation Taxons

The following two taxons describe the location estimation process: *estimation method* and *radio map*. The two taxons are shown including subtaxons in Figure 3.

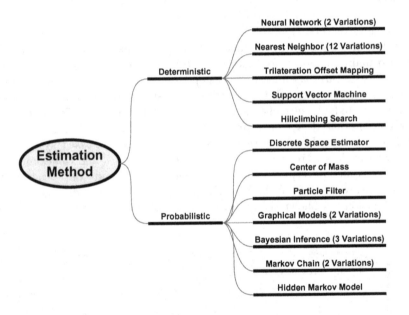

Fig. 3. Estimation method

A central part of a LF system is the *estimation method* used for predicting locations from a radio map and currently measured network characteristics. It would, however, be very challenging to taxonomize all possible methods because nearly all methods developed for machine learning (see Witten et al. [27] for a list of methods) or in the field of estimation (see Crassidis et al. [28] for a list of methods) are applicable to the problem of LF estimation. Here we follow Krishnakumar et al. [4] and divide methods only into deterministic and probabilistic methods. *Deterministic methods* estimate location by considering

---

[2] However, when only considering the basic method of each system, most can be realized in all of the three setups.

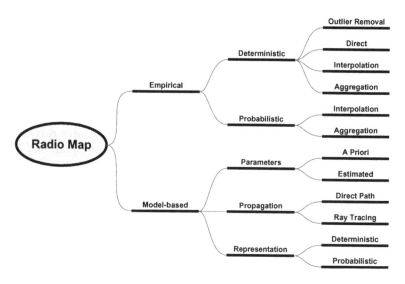

Fig. 4. Radio map

measurements only by their value [11,12,22,25]. *Probabilistic methods* estimate location considering measurements as part of a random process [5,15,16,18]. In Figure 3 examples of applied methods for LF are shown for each of the two categories, including number of identified varieties in our literature study[3]. For example, the classical deterministic technique of Nearest Neighbor was identified during the literature study in twelve different variations. A comment is that many of the studied LF systems use more than one of the listed methods.

A *radio map* provides a model of network characteristics in a deployment area. Radio maps can be constructed by methods which can be classified as either *empirical* or *model-based*. Empirical methods work with collected fingerprints to construct radio maps [5,11,15,18]. Model-based methods use a model parameterised for the LF-system covered area to construct radio maps [11,23,30,31].

Empirical methods can be subdivided into *deterministic* and *probabilistic* methods in the same manner as estimation methods, depending on how they deal with fingerprint-collected measurements. Deterministic methods represent entries in a radio map as single values and probabilistic methods represent entries by probability distributions. Both of these can be further subcategorised into *aggregation* and *interpolation* methods. An aggregation method creates entries in a radio map by summarising fingerprint measurements from a single location [11,14,18,32]. Figure 5 illustrates two aggregation methods for five RSS measurements at two locations marked with a triangle and a square on the

---

[3] However, even this simple classification is fuzzy for instance when considering the machine learning technique of support vector machines (SVMs) as applied for LF [29]. Because SVMs are defined on a probabilistic foundation but when applied for LF SVMs only consider the actual values of measurements.

figure. The first aggregation method is a deterministic mean method which takes the five measurements and finds the mean and put this value as this location's entry in the radio map. The second aggregation method is a probabilistic Gaussian distribution method which takes the five measurements and fits them to a Gaussian distribution and puts the distribution as the location's entry in the radio map. An interpolation method generate entries in a radio map at unfingerprinted locations by interpolating from fingerprint measurements or radio map entries from nearby locations [15,20,24]. Figure 5 illustrates two interpolation methods at the location marked with a circle using the square-marked and triangle-marked locations as nearby locations. The first interpolation method is a deterministic mean interpolation which finds the mean of nearby radio-map entries and put this value as the entry in the radio map. The second interpolation method is a probabilistic mean method that finds the mean of nearby radio-map entries' gaussian distributions and put the mean distribution as the entry in the radio map. Two other deterministic methods are *outlier removal* filtering away outliers [33] and *direct* creating a radio map using a direct one-to-one mapping to measurements [6].

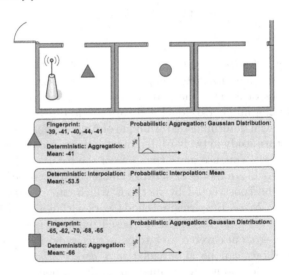

Fig. 5. Deterministic and probabilistic aggregation and interpolation

Model-based methods can be categorized based on how *parameters* for the model are specified, how signal *propagation* is modeled, and what type of *representation* is used by the generated radio map. Parameters can either be given *a priori* [11] or they can be *estimated* from a small set of parameter-estimation fingerprints [31]. Propagation can either be modeled by only considering the *direct path* between a location and a base station [11] or by considering multiple paths categorized as *ray tracing* [31]. The representation of the generated radio map can either be *deterministic* (using single values) [11] or *probabilistic* (using probability distributions) [34].

5   Variation Taxons

The three taxons for variations are: *spatial variations, temporal variations*, and *sensor variations*. The three taxons are shown including subtaxons in Figure 6.

Spatial variations are the observed differences in network characteristics at different locations because of signal propagation characteristics. Because of how signals propagate even small movements can create large variations in the measured network characteristics. The main method for addressing spatial variations is *tracking*: the use of constraints to optimize sequential location estimates. Tracking can be based on motion in terms of target *speed* [24,35], target being *still versus moving* [15], and knowledge about motion *patterns* [35]. Tracking can also be based on physical constraints such as how *connections* exist between locations [16] and the *distance* between them [15,19]. Tracking using one or several of the listed constraints is implemented using an estimation method (such as the ones listed in Section 4) that is able to encode the constraints. Spatial variations can also be addressed by *base station selection, fingerprint filtering*, and *sample perturbation*. Base station selection filters out measurements to base stations that are likely to decrease precision and accuracy [36,37]. Fingerprint filtering limits the set of used fingerprints to only those that are likely to optimize precision and accuracy [37]. *Sample perturbation* apply perturbation of measurements to mitigate spatial variations [5].

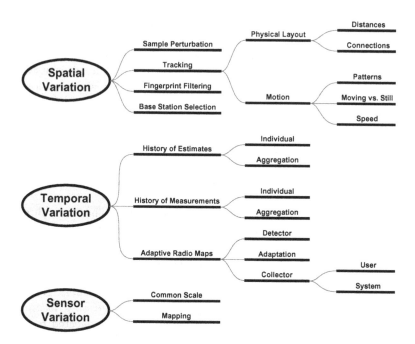

Fig. 6. Spatial variations, temporal variations, and sensor variations

Temporal variations are the observed differences in network characteristics over time at a single location because of continuing changing signal propagation. On a large-scale, temporal variations are the prolonged effects observed over larger periods of time such as day versus night. On a small-scale, temporal variations are the variations implied by quick transient effects, such as a person walking close to a client. Methods for handling temporal variations can be divided into methods that are based on a *history of estimates*, a *history of measurements*, or *adaptive radio maps*. A history of either measurements or estimates here denotes a set of estimates or measurements inside a defined time window. The alternative to a history is only to use the most recent estimate or measurements. The history of either measurements or estimates can either be used as *individual* [15,18] measurements or estimates or, using some *aggregation* [5,14], can be combined to one measurement or estimate. The adaptive radio map method introduces the idea of handling temporal variations by making the radio map adapt to the current temporal variations [19,20,32]. For this idea to work, some *collector* has to make measurements that can be used by a *detector* to control if some adaptation should be applied to the current radio map. The measurements can either be collected from the measurements a *user* collects [32] to run LF estimation on or it can be collected by some specially-installed *system* infrastructure [19,20].

Sensor variations are the observed differences in network characteristics between different types of wireless clients. On a large-scale, variations can be observed between clients from different manufactures. On a small-scale, variations can be observed between different examples of similar clients. One method for addressing sensor varations is to define a *common scale* and then, for each type of sensor, find out how this sensor's measurements can be converted to the common scale. A second approach is to use a single sensor to fingerprint with and then find a mapping from new sensors to the sensor that was used for fingerprinting [7,18].

6   Collection Taxons

The two taxons for fingerprint collection are *collector* and *collection method* as shown in Figure 7.

Collector describes who or what collect fingerprints. There are three categories: *user*, *administrator*, and *system*. A user is a person who is either tracked by or uses information from a LF system [21,24]. An administrator is a person who manages a LF system [11,18,38] and a system is a specially-installed infrastructure for collecting fingerprints [20].

The fingerprints are collected following some *collection method*. A collection method places assumptions on if fingerprints are collected on a *location* that is either *known* [6] or *unknown* [34,35]. If fingerprints are collected to match a *spatial property* such as: *orientation* [11], at a *point* [15], covering a *path* [24], or covering an *area* [18,36]. If the collected *number of measurements* for each fingerprint is *fixed* [5,14] or determined based on some *adaptive* strategy.

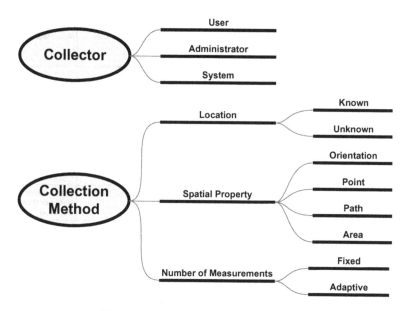

Fig. 7. Collector and collection method

7 Case Studies

To show the use of the proposed taxonomy, this section presents our analysis using the taxonomy on four of the 30 different systems identified in the literature study. Figure 8 shows the analysis results in a compact form. The four systems have been selected to highlight different parts of the taxonomy. As mentioned earlier, the analysis of the rest of the analyzed systems are available online at [3] in a similar format. In addition to the eleven taxons, four extra categories describe the systems from an evaluation perspective; these are: *accuracy, precision, evaluation setup and limitations.* The listed evaluation results have been taken from the original papers. Evaluation setup is grouped into *stationary* (meaning that the authors' test data was collected while keeping a wireless client at a static position) or *moving* (for which the wireless client was moved around mimicking normal use).

The RADAR system proposed by Bahl et al. [11] is aimed at a building scale of deployment and provides spatial locations as output. The system measures BSI, and RSS for the WaveLAN technology and roles are assigned as infrastructure-based: network. The estimation method is the deterministic k-nearest neighbor algorithm. They propose two setups, here named A and B. For A the radio map is constructed using deterministic aggregation using the mean from empirical-collected fingerprints. For B the radio map is deterministically constructed model-based considering the direct path of transmission using a priori parameters. For A an administrator will collect fingerprints at known locations standing at one point with different orientations collecting a fixed number of measurements and for B no fingerprints are collected. A limitation for setup B is that knowledge is needed of spatial locations of base stations and walls.

	Bahl et al. (2000): RADAR	Youssef et al. (2003,...,2005): Horus	LaMarca et al. (2005): Place Lab	Lorincz et al. (2005): MoteTrack
Scale	Building	Building	City	Building
Output	Spatial Locations	Spatial Locations	Spatial Locations	Spatial Locations
Measurements	BSI, RSS (WaveLan)	BSI, RSS (IEEE 802.11)	BSI, RSS, RR (IEEE 802.11 & GSM)	A: BSI, Power Level, RSS: (916 MHz FSK) B: BSI, LQI, RSS: (IEEE 802.15.4)
Roles	Infrastructure-based: Network	Infrastructure-based: Terminal	Infrastructure-based: Terminal	Infrastructure-less: Collaborate
Estimation Method	Deterministic: K-Nearest Neighbor	Probabilistic: [Discrete Space Estimator, Center of Mass]	Probabilistic: Particle Filter	Ratio-Nearest Neighbor (Manhattan Distance)
Radio Map	A: Empirical: Deterministic: Aggregation: Mean B: Model-based: [Parameters: A priori, Propagation: Direct Path: Transmission, Representation: Deterministic]	Empirical: Probabilistic: Aggregation: [Histogram Method, Kernel Distributions, Correlation Modeling]	Empirical: Deterministic: Interpolation: Mean, Probabilistic: Interpolation: Histogram Method	Empirical: Deterministic: Aggregation: Mean
Spatial Variation		Sample Perturbation	Tracking: Motion: Speed	
Temporal Variation	History of Measurements: Aggregation: Mean	History of Estimates: Aggregation: Mean History of Measurements: Aggregation: Mean		
Sensor Variation				
Collector	Administrator	Administrator	Users	Administrator
Collection Method	A: Location: Known, Spatial Property: [Point, Orientation], Number of Measurements: Fixed B: None	Location: Known, Spatial Property: Point, Number of Measurements: Fixed	Location: Known, Spatial Property: Path, Number of Measurements: Fixed	Location: Known, Spatial Property: Point, Number of Measurements: Fixed
Precision	A: 2.75m (k=5) B: 4.3m (k=1)	Site 1: 0.39m Site 2: 0.51m	Urban: 21.8m Residential: 13.4m Suburban: 31.3m	A: 2m B: 0.9m
Accuracy	50%	50%	50%	50%
Evaluation Setup	Stationary: See website for details	Stationary: See website for details	Moving: See website for details	Stationary: See website for details
Limitations	B: Spatial locations of base stations and walls		GPS (and car) for collecting fingerprints	Deployment of beacon nodes

Fig. 8. Analysis results for the four case studies

The Horus system proposed by Youssef et al. [5,39,40,41,42] also aims at a building scale of deployment and provide spatial locations as output. The system measures BSI, and RSS for the IEEE 802.11 technology and the assigned roles match infrastructure-based: terminal. The estimation method is a combination of two probabilistic techniques: discrete space estimator and center of mass. The radio-map is built using probabilistic aggregation, either based on a histogram method or on a kernel distribution method; in addition, a method for correlation modeling is also applied. To handle spatial variations sample perturbation is applied and temporal variations are handled by both mean aggregating measurements and estimates. An administrator collects fingerprints at known locations standing at one point collecting a fixed number of measurements.

The Place Lab system proposed by LaMarca et al. [24,43,44] aims at a citywide deployment and provides spatial locations as output. The system measures BSI, RSS, and RR for both IEEE 802.11 and GSM and the assigned roles match infrastructure-based: terminal. The most advanced of the system's estimation methods uses a particle filter. The radio map is built in two steps, first applying deterministic interpolation based on means and then probabilistic interpolation based on the histogram method. Spatial variations are addressed by tracking based on motion by speed constraints. The fingerprints are user collected based on paths with known location with a fixed number of measurements. A limitation is that a GPS device (and a car) is needed to practically collect fingerprints.

The MoteTrack system proposed by Lorincz et al. [9,26] targeted for sensor networks aims at building-scale deployment and provides spatial locations as output. The system has been tested in two setups, here named A and B. Setup A measures BSI, Power level, and RSS for 916 MHz FSK communication and setup B measures BSI, LQI, and RSS for IEEE 802.15.4. The roles are assigned matching infrastructure-less: collaborate with beacon nodes taking the role as base stations. The estimation method is ratio-nearest neighbor with Manhattan distance to lower computational needs. The radio map is constructed using deterministic aggregation using the mean from empirical-collected fingerprints. An administrator collects fingerprints at known locations standing at one point collecting a fixed number of measurements. A limitation is the needed deployment and maintenance of beacon nodes.

8   Discussion

During the literature study both many similarities and differences were identified between studied systems. This can be seen from just the four included case studies in Section 7. For instance, the well-known nearest-neighbor estimation method were identified in many variations of the basic method. The differences were not only in terms of improvements to the basic estimation method but also how systems address spatial and temporal variations. One system use a history of measurements and mean-aggregate them before applying nearest neighbor [11]. Another system use the measurements directly and use a history of estimates and aggregate these instead [36]. By using the proposed taxonomy these differences become clear when classifying systems. Another example also for systems based on nearest neighbor is how the radio map is built. For instance Krishnan et al. [20] builds the radio map by applying advanced aggregation and interpolation methods where as the original system proposed by Bahl et al. [11] only use a simple aggregation based on mean values. The taxonomy also here creates a better starting point when comparing and evaluating systems.

To use the proposed taxonomy for comparison too a new system, one approach would be to, first, find classifications for compared-to existing systems. As mentioned earlier a starting point for finding such classifications is to look at our classifications online at [3]. Second, one would make a classification for the new system by classifying for each of the eleven taxons the new system's methods and assumptions according to the subtaxons. Third, one would make the comparison of the new and the existing systems. For evaluation of LF systems the taxonomy can also be used to highlight the evaluated system's assumptions and methods. This can be done by providing a classification for the evaluated system which makes it explicit what methods and assummptions are evaluated. For instance, as mentioned in the discussion above many systems have been evaluation in comparison to the nearest neighbor estimation method. But this estimation method has been implemented with many different choices when considering the used radio map and methods for addressing spatial and temporal variations. This means that it is not the same baseline method that is compared-to making results incomparable.

The taxonomy can also help scoping out future research by illustrating what research topics have not yet been covered. One way to analyse this is to group systems in terms of some of the taxons. A grouping for the taxons scale and radio map is shown in Table 2. The table shows that only one system aims at a campus-size scale was identified. The table also shows that generally systems either use empirical or model-based radio maps not a combination. So an open research topic is exploring the boundary between building and city-wide systems maybe by combining empirical and model-based radio maps. A grouping for the taxons spatial and temporal variations is also shown in Table 3. The table shows that for these taxons most systems only address one of the variations. Few systems combine them and several combinations of the different methods remain unexplored.

We do not expect that the proposed taxonomy is complete in its current form. Instead, it is intended to enable better and more complete understanding of LF and to evolve as that understanding improves. At the same time, we feel that our eleven main taxons and many of the subtaxons are fairly stable. During the process of creating the taxonomy, analyzing papers and classifying systems, we

Table 2. Grouping in terms of scale and radio map

	Empirical	Model-based
Building	[5, 6, 9, 11–13, 15–20, 23, 25, 29, 32, 33, 35–38, 45–47]	[11, 29–31, 34, 46]
Campus	[21]	
City	[22,24]	[14]

Table 3. Grouping in terms of spatial and temporal variations

	None	History of Measurements	History of Estimates	Adaptive Radio Maps
None	[6, 9, 12–14, 21, 29, 30, 34]	[11, 22, 25, 33, 46]	[23]	[20, 47]
Sample Perturbation		[5]	[5]	
Tracking	[16, 24, 31, 32, 38, 45]	[18,19,35]	[15,17,18]	[18,19]
Fingerprint Filtering	[37]			
Base Station Selection	[37]			

found that all 30 systems and their methods could be classified. On the other hand, some of the subtaxons are likely to evolve as our understanding of LF evolves. An area for which it would be interesting to extend the taxonomy is for non-functional properties as mentioned in Section 2. However, only a limited number of papers have so far been published in this direction [5,9,10].

9 Conclusion

This paper presented a taxonomy for location fingerprinting. The proposed taxonomy was constructed from a literature study of 51 papers and articles about LF. The taxonomy consists of the following eleven taxons: *scale, output, measurements, roles, estimation method, radio map, spatial variations, temporal variations, sensor variations, collector,* and *collection method.* The 51 analyzed papers described 30 LF systems of which four were presented as case studies.

Valuable taxonomies can account for everything that is known so far and can predict things to come, as variations of parameters accounted for and enumerated in the taxonomy. A taxonomy first and foremost shows the depth and the breadth of our understanding. We would like others to join and based on inputs from the community further improve the proposed taxonomy.

Acknowledgements

The author would like to thank Doina Bucur, Azadeh Kushki and the reviewers for their insightful comments on earlier drafts of this paper. The research reported in this paper was partially funded by the software part of the ISIS Katrinebjerg competency centre http://www.isis.alexandra.dk/software/.

References

1. Küpper, A.: Location–based Services — Fundamentals and Operation. John Wiley & Sons, Chichester (2005)
2. Hightower, J., Borriello, G.: Location Systems for Ubiquitous Computing. Computer 34(8), 57–66 (2001)

3. Website, http://wiki.daimi.au.dk/mikkelbk
4. Krishnakumar, A.S., Krishnan, P.: The Theory and Practice of Signal Strength-Based Location Estimation. In: Proceedings of the First International Conference on Collaborative Computing: Networking, Applications and Worksharing (2005)
5. Youssef, M., Agrawala, A.: The Horus WLAN Location Determination System. In: Proceedings of the Third International Conference on Mobile Systems, Applications, and Services (2005)
6. Otsason, V., Varshavsky, A., Marca, A.L., de Lara, E.: Accurate GSM Indoor Localization. In: Proceedings of the Seventh International Conference on Ubiquitous Computing (2005)
7. Kjærgaard, M.B.: Automatic Mitigation of Sensor Variations for Signal Strength Based Location Systems. In: Second International Workshop on Location- and Context-Awareness (2006)
8. Muthukrishnan, K., Lijding, M., Havinga, P.: Towards Smart Surroundings: Enabling Techniques and Technologies for Localization. In: Proceedings of the First International Workshop on Location- and Context-Awareness (2005)
9. Lorincz, K., Welsh, M.: MoteTrack: A Robust, Decentralized Approach to RF-Based Location Tracking. In: Proceedings of the First International Workshop on Location- and Context-Awareness (2005)
10. Kjærgaard, M., Treu, G., Linnhoff-Popien, C.: Zone–based RSS Reporting for Location Fingerprinting. In: Proceedings of the 5th International Conference on Pervasive Computing (2007)
11. Bahl, P., Padmanabhan, V.N.: RADAR: An In-Building RF-based User Location and Tracking System. In: Proceedings of the 19th Annual Joint Conference of the IEEE Computer and Communications Societies, INFOCOM, IEEE Computer Society Press, Los Alamitos (2000)
12. Prasithsangaree, P., Krishnamurthy, P., Chrysanthis, P.: On Indoor Position Location with Wireless LANs. In: Proceedings of the 13th IEEE International Symposium on Personal, Indoor and Mobile Radio Communications, IEEE Computer Society Press, Los Alamitos (2002)
13. Battiti, R., Villani, A., Nhat, T.L.: Neural network models for intelligent networks: deriving the location from signal patterns. In: Proceedings of the First Annual Symposium on Autonomous Intelligent Networks and Systems (2002)
14. Roos, T., Myllymäki, P., Tirri, H.: A Statistical Modeling Approach to Location Estimation. IEEE Transactions on Mobile Computing 1(1), 59–69 (2002)
15. Krumm, J., Horvitz, E.: LOCADIO: Inferring Motion and Location from Wi-Fi Signal Strengths. In: Proceedings of the First Annual International Conference on Mobile and Ubiquitous Systems: Networking and Services (2004)
16. Castro, P., Chiu, P., Kremenek, T., Muntz, R.: A Probabilistic Room Location Service for Wireless Networked Environments. In: Proceedings of the Third International Conference on Ubiquitous Computing (2001)
17. Ladd, A.M., Bekris, K.E., Rudys, A., Marceau, G., Kavraki, L.E., Wallach, D.S.: Robotics-Based Location Sensing using Wireless Ethernet. In: Proceedings of the Eight ACM International Conference on Mobile Computing and Networking, ACM Press, New York (2002)
18. Haeberlen, A., Flannery, E., Ladd, A.M., Rudys, A., Wallach, D.S., Kavraki, L.E.: Practical Robust Localization over Large-Scale 802.11 Wireless Networks. In: Proceedings of the Tenth ACM International Conference on Mobile Computing and Networking, ACM Press, New York (2004)

19. Bahl, P., Padmanabhan, V.N., Balachandran, A.: A Software System for Locating Mobile Users: Design, Evaluation, and Lessons. Microsoft Research Technical Report MSR-TR-2000-12, Microsoft (2000)
20. Krishnan, P., Krishnakumar, A.S., Ju, W.H., Mallows, C., Ganu, S.: A System for LEASE: Location Estimation Assisted by Stationary Emitters for Indoor RF Wireless Networks. In: Proceedings of the 23th Annual Joint Conference of the IEEE Computer and Communications Societies, INFOCOM, IEEE Computer Society Press, Los Alamitos (2004)
21. Bhasker, E.S., Brown, S.W., Griswold, W.G.: Employing User Feedback for Fast, Accurate, Low-Maintenance Geolocationing. In: Proceedings of the 2nd IEEE International Conference on Pervasive Computing and Communications, IEEE Computer Society Press, Los Alamitos (2004)
22. Laitinen, H., Lahteenmaki, J., Nordstrom, T.: Database Correlation Method for GSM Location. In: Proceedings of the 53rd Vehicular Technology Conference (2001)
23. Roos, T., Myllymäki, P., Tirri, H., Misikangas, P., Sievänen, J.: A Probabilistic Approach to WLAN User Location Estimation. International Journal of Wireless Information Networks 9(3), 155–164 (2002)
24. LaMarca, A., Chawathe, Y., Consolvo, S., Hightower, J., Smith, I., Scott, J., Sohn, T., Howard, J., Hughes, J., Potter, F., Tabert, J., Powledge, P., Borriello, G., Schilit, B.: Place Lab: Device Positioning Using Radio Beacons in the Wild. In: Gellersen, H.-W., Want, R., Schmidt, A. (eds.) PERVASIVE 2005. LNCS, vol. 3468, Springer, Heidelberg (2005)
25. Smailagic, A., Kogan, D.: Location Sensing and Privacy in a Context-aware Computing Environment. IEEE Wireless Communications 9(5), 10–17 (2002)
26. Lorincz, K., Welsh, M.: MoteTrack: a robust, decentralized approach to RF-based location tracking. Personal and Ubiquitous Computing
27. Witten, I.H., Frank, E.: Data Mining: Practical machine learning tools and techniques, 2nd edn. Morgan Kaufmann, San Francisco (2005)
28. Crassidis, J.L., Junkins, J.L.: Optimal Estimation of Dynamic Systems. Chapman & Hall/CRC Press, Boca Raton, FL (2004)
29. Brunato, M., Battiti, R.: Statistical learning theory for location fingerprinting in wireless LANs. Comput. Netw. ISDN Syst. 47(6), 825–845 (2005)
30. Wallbaum, M., Wasch, T.: Markov Localization of Wireless Local Area Network Clients. In: Proceedings of the First IFIP TC6 Working Conference on Wireless On-Demand Network Systems (2004)
31. Ji, Y., Biaz, S., Pandey, S., Agrawal, P.: ARIADNE: A Dynamic Indoor Signal Map Construction and Localization System. In: Proceedings of the 4th international conference on Mobile systems, applications and services (2006)
32. Berna, M., Sellner, B., Lisien, B., Thrun, S., Gordon, G., Pfenning, F.: A Learning Algorithm for Localizing People Based on Wireless Signal Strength that Uses Labeled and Unlabeled Data. In: Proceedings of the International Joint Conference on Artificial Intelligence (2003)
33. Saha, S., Chaudhuri, K., Sanghi, D., Bhagwat, P.: Location Determination of a Mobile Device using IEEE 802.11b Access Point Signals. In: Proceedings of the IEEE Wireless Communications and Networking Conference, IEEE Computer Society Press, Los Alamitos (2003)
34. Madigan, D., Einahrawy, E., Martin, R.P., Ju, W.H., Krishnan, P., Krishnakumar, A.S.: Bayesian Indoor Positioning Systems. In: Proceedings of the 24th Annual Joint Conference of the IEEE Computer and Communications Societies, INFOCOM, IEEE Computer Society Press, Los Alamitos (2005)

35. Chai, X., Yang, Q.: Reducing the Calibration Effort for Location Estimation Using Unlabeled Samples. In: Proceedings of the Third IEEE International Conference on Pervasive Computing and Communications, IEEE Computer Society Press, Los Alamitos (2005)

36. Varshavsky, A., Lamarca, A., Hightower, J., de Lara, E.: The SkyLoc Floor Localization System. In: Proceedings of the Fifth Annual IEEE International Conference on Pervasive Computing and Communications, IEEE Computer Society Press, Los Alamitos (2007)

37. Kushki, A., Plataniotis, K.N., Venetsanopoulos, A.N.: Kernel-Based Positioning in Wireless Local Area Networks. Mobile Computing, IEEE Transactions on 6(6), 689–705 (2007)

38. Seshadri, V., Zaruba, G.V., Huber, M.: A Bayesian Sampling Approach to In-door Localization of Wireless Devices using Received Signal Strength Indication. In: Proceedings of the Third IEEE International Conference on Pervasive Computing and Communications, IEEE Computer Society Press, Los Alamitos (2005)

39. Youssef, M., Agrawala, A.: Small-Scale Compensation for WLAN Location Determination Systems. In: Proceedings of the IEEE Conference Wireless Communications and Networking, IEEE Computer Society Press, Los Alamitos (2003)

40. Youssef, M.A., Agrawala, A., Shankar, U.A.: WLAN Location Determination via Clustering and Probability Distributions. In: Proceedings of the First IEEE International Conference on Pervasive Computing and Communications, IEEE Computer Society Press, Los Alamitos (2003)

41. Youssef, M., Agrawala, A.: Handling Samples Correlation in the Horus System. In: Proceedings of the 23th Annual Joint Conference of the IEEE Computer and Communications Societies, INFOCOM, IEEE Computer Society Press, Los Alamitos (2004)

42. Youssef, M., Abdallah, M., Agrawala, A.: Multivariate Analysis for Probabilistic WLAN Location Determination Systems. In: Proceedings of the Second Annual International Conference on Mobile and Ubiquitous Systems: Networking and Services (2005)

43. Cheng, Y.C., Chawathe, Y., Lamarca, A., Krumm, J.: Accuracy Characterization for Metropolitan-scale Wi-Fi Localization. In: Proceedings of the 3rd international conference on Mobile systems, applications, and services (2005)

44. Hightower, J., Borriello, G.: Particle Filters for Location Estimation in Ubiquitous Computing: A Case Study. In: Davies, N., Mynatt, E.D., Siio, I. (eds.) UbiComp 2004. LNCS, vol. 3205, Springer, Heidelberg (2004)

45. Agiwal, A., Khandpur, P., Saran, H.: LOCATOR: location estimation system For wireless LANs. In: Proceedings of the 2nd ACM international workshop on Wireless mobile applications and services on WLAN hotspots, ACM Press, New York (2004)

46. Elnahrawy, E., Li, X., Martin, R.P.: The Limits of Localization Using Signal Strength: A Comparative Study. In: First Annual IEEE Communications Society Conference on Sensor and Ad Hoc Communications and Networks, IEEE Computer Society Press, Los Alamitos (2004)

47. Yin, J., Yang, Q., Ni, L.: Adaptive Temporal Radio Maps for Indoor Location Estimation. In: Proceedings of the Third IEEE International Conference on Pervasive Computing and Communications, IEEE Computer Society Press, Los Alamitos (2005)

Inferring the Everyday Task Capabilities of Locations

Patricia Shanahan and William G. Griswold

University of California, San Diego

Abstract. People rapidly learn the capabilities of a new location, without observing every service and product. Instead they map a few observations to familiar clusters of capabilities. This paper proposes a similar approach to computer discovery of routine location capabilities, applying machine learning to predict unobserved capabilities based on a combination of a small body of local observations and a larger body of data that is not specific to the location. We propose using the time and place of deleting items from a to-do list application to provide the local data. For reminder purposes, an area within easy walking distance is a single location, but may contain many different shops and services, collectively offering its own combination of capabilities. Truncated singular value decomposition maps the observations to combinations of features, rather than to a single cluster. Simulations, using distributions derived from real world data, demonstrate the feasibility of this approach.

1 Introduction

Everyday life includes many tasks that cannot be performed at arbitrary times and places. Some tasks require a specific place, such as the conference hotel for a given conference. Others require places with a specific relationship to the user, such as "my home" or "my office". Some tasks depend only on the context having a specific capability, such as offering a given service or selling a given product. Any location with similar capabilities is a possible location for the task. Shopping is a typical example of this kind of task.

The following scenario illustrates how a future reminder system might support context-capability dependent tasks. Joe is a college professor and a user of a reminder system, a few years in the future.

While doing his laundry, Joe notices there will not be enough detergent for next week. He runs his phone's barcode scanner over the detergent box's product code. The phone adds detergent to its shopping list. Postage stamps are already on the list. Joe has also made a note that he needs access to a copy of the Oxford English Dictionary (OED), to check the history of a word.

The next day, Joe happens to walk past his college's reference library. His phone reminds him of the word he wanted to look up in the OED.

A couple of days later, Joe's wife, Alice, phones him to say that she is running late at work, and asks him to buy some food items. Because of where he is, and the time of day, he drives to a different supermarket than he normally shops at.

J. Hightower, B. Schiele, and T. Strang (Eds.): LoCA 2007, LNCS 4718, pp. 157–174, 2007.

Nevertheless, his phone vibrates as he nears the supermarket. He looks at it, and sees text reminding him to buy detergent and postage stamps.

Without the reminders, Joe could have easily forgotten some of these tasks. The literature on prospective memory — on remembering to do things that cannot be done here and now — assumes that people do sometimes forget such tasks. For example, Farrimond et. al. mention the task of buying bread on the way home from work: "It is, however, a common experience to arrive home without the bread." [1].

This matches our personal experience. Indeed, one of us, wishing to consult a paper-only reference on prospective memory, printed out the bibliographic information and library call number, got distracted on the way to the printer by the arrival of an elevator, and did not remember to pick up the printout until outside the computer science building on the way to the library.

Most quantitative research on prospective memory uses artificial laboratory tasks, but a few do attempt to model real-world tasks. Farramond et. al. use a laboratory model of shopping tasks. Their younger control group fail to remember about 4% of the time [1]. However, comparison of similar tasks in a laboratory model and in the real-world can get different results [2].

The library reminder is relatively easy. Joe has previously carried out similar tasks at the same place. A smart reminder application that notes time and location of to-do list deletions would know where he can do that task.

Joe faces a harder problem than remembering to buy the detergent and stamps at times and places he had planned. To take advantage of the unplanned trip, he not only has to know that his location offers the items, he has to remember that fact, and his intention of buying them, while thinking about another errand.

Joe may never have bought either detergent or stamps at that location, so his phone cannot depend only on the information it can collect. It has to function as part of a larger system, as shown in Figure 1. A server can be dedicated to a single user or small group of users, or be public and widely shared. Each client device is associated with one user. Joe's deletion of "detergent" from his shopping list itself supplies data; confirmation that the location has detergent-supplying capability.

The scenario is set in the near future, not today, because it requires several advances in technology:

- Joe's phone generally knows where it is, with sufficient accuracy for Joe to be able and willing to take actions based on his phone's estimate of its location.
- The phone can decide whether Joe should be interrupted now, given an opportunity to complete a task.
- Joe's phone can interpret bar codes with high accuracy.
- The phone has access to a server that maps from a required capability to a list of nearby locations with the capability.

The last would allow Joe's phone access to a wider body of information. Given informed consent, that might include pooled to-do list deletions from many users. However, even a small shopping center may offer thousands of products and services. A system that depended exclusively on to-do list data, even if pooled

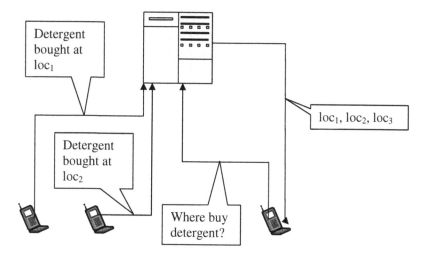

Fig. 1. A server receives reports of detergent having been bought at locations loc_1 and loc_2. loc_3 is a third location that has been found to be similar to the other two. When Joe's phone asks where detergent can be bought the server responds with all three locations.

from multiple users, would require an impractically long time to accumulate a useful body of data.

This problem is the focus of this paper. Fortunately, businesses do not make completely arbitrary choices of which products to stock and services to offer. There are clusters of products that are commonly sold together. People often use those patterns to predict which shop sells what without memorizing a list for each shop, albeit imperfectly. If experience indicates that a location is a source for dishwasher detergent and fabric softener, it is probably a valid location for Joe's laundry detergent purchase, even if there is no direct evidence.

This paper proposes applying machine learning methods to extract a mathematical representation of those patterns from a body of capability data. Ideally, if the data includes even a relatively small amount of information about a specific location, the method will use those patterns to infer its other capabilities. After experimenting with a number of approaches, we selected truncated singular value decomposition (T-SVD).

The capability prediction problem is complicated by the fact that a single location, such as a shopping center, may offer a wide range of products and services because it contains multiple businesses. Even if location detection were accurate enough to distinguish them, a reminder should be issued if a required capability is available within easy walking distance. Similarly, a shop like a supermarket combines the capabilities of a butcher, a bakery, a pharmacy, etc. T-SVD can theoretically cope with this complexity because it maps purchases at locations to combinations of capability clusters, rather than assigning the location to a unique cluster. This factoring also enables bootstrapping the training by conveniently supporting the infusion of summary capability clustering data.

Since different capabilities have different frequencies of use, and those frequencies may affect the accuracy of the algorithm, we assessed our approach using actual shopping basket data obtained from a major supermarket chain. The algorithm was effective if either the locations had simple behavior or we supplied summary capability clustering data to supplement data about the locations. In particular, with summary capability data and given 1000 observations of 135 simulated locations, equivalent to an average of 7.4 observations per location, the algorithm achieved 100% precision and 90% recall.

The next section surveys data sources for generating capability-based reminders. Section 3 develops our proposed approach. Section 4 describes our experiments, and the final section concludes.

2   Limitations of Location Capability Data Sources

There are several data sources that can be used for location capability-based reminders. Although each data source on its own has limitations for providing reminders for everyday activities, they can be used to train a machine learning algorithm for inferring place capabilities.

2.1   Direct Input of Individual Information

The simplest method of selecting a location for a reminder is to have the user name a location or point to it on a map. In effect, this method requires the user to do the mapping from capability requirements to locations having those capabilities.

Joe could have used a direct location-based reminder system, such as Place-Its, to remind himself about the detergent next time he is at his usual supermarket [3]. However, Place-Its would only remind him at the planned location, not at other locations with similar capabilities.

CybreMinder has a situation description language with power similar to a database query language [4]. Locations can be referred to by symbolic names such as "Bob's front door". This is likely to be most effective if each user has a limited number of known reminder locations or groups of locations.

Although CybreMinder's situation language may be more complicated than is appropriate for non-expert use, it would be useful to apply time restrictions to a reminder. For example, a user whose shopping list includes perishable foods would probably not wish to be reminded of it while driving past a supermarket on the way to work. The reminder would be useful, at the same location, when the user is returning home.

The main limitation of direct input is the sheer number of places that have some capabilities. A reminder system is not useful if the work of entering the data exceeds the benefit of the reminders. Yet it may be the only solution for a user in a new area, if the system does not have any local information.

2.2   Automated Entry of Individual Information

The use of a to-do list for tracking activity, as proposed in this paper, is an example of automated entry of individual information. Every task completion is a potentially observable event. With the user's consent and suitable privacy protections, the application on the phone could collect the time and location of a task check-off, and supply the data to its server. The privacy protections could include lower bounds on elapsed time and change in location between the event and its transmission to the server, so that the server would never be told the user's current or very recent location. This data collection method presents minimal cost to the user, and is applicable to non-commercial tasks.

Mankoff et. al. use cash register receipt scanning as a convenient way to help people keep track of the nutritional characteristics of the mix of foods they buy, and presumably eat [5]. Their technique could be adapted to capture the shopping data from the receipt.

Such approaches have the major advantage of capturing the information that most affects the individual user, with minimal user effort. The user's favorite shops and services will definitely be covered. However, as the sole data source, information accumulates slowly, and cannot supply any data the user did not already know or discover by other means.

2.3   Localized Web Searches

Location-limited web searching has considerable promise for finding locations by capability, but does not yet work well for many common tasks.

In practice, the user will often know the types of facilities, such as shops, that are appropriate for completing a task. A "Find businesses" search on Google Maps (maps.google.com) for "supermarket" near zip code 92126, on March 14th. 2007 got the following top results:

- A sponsored link to the home page for a supermarket chain
- A link for "Seafood City", which is a supermarket with an emphasis on seafood.
- A link to a supermarket chain pharmacy that does not exist at the indicated location.
- A link for a specialized Vietnamese market
- A link for "Slimmer Body Mall"

The nearby stores of three major supermarket chains were not shown.

The problem is harder if the user does not already know the appropriate types of facilities for completing a task, or if there are so many that entering them takes too long. Querying "Find businesses" on Google Maps for "instant coffee" near zip code 92126 was converted to "Categories: Motels & Hotels, Health & Diet Food Products", and again failed to find the local supermarkets and convenience stores at which most people would buy instant coffee.

Other web searches for common items have produced similar results. Exotic, rare, and expensive items are well represented. Large facilities such as major chain stores are well represented. Trivial items that everybody knows about such as instant coffee are not. Small facilities, such as mini-marts may be represented, depending on owner initiative and whether they are part of a chain.

2.4   Web-Accessible Database Searches

Many organizations provide web pages that in essence can query a database. For example, the US Postal Service web site (www.usps.gov) supports a search for places that sell postage stamps near a given address or zip code. The problem for a reminder system is navigating the web pages to get to the stamp-buying search. A program can be written to navigate any specific set of web pages to obtain specific data, but it would have to be done for each web site, and could stop working at any time if the web site were modified.

This problem could be ameliorated by having standard interfaces for machine-based search of location-based information. For example, the Impulse Location-based Agent Assistance project currently uses location-limited URL searches and the Wherehoo server (wherehoo.org), to identify nearby locations that might satisfy the user's "wants" [6,7]. The main difficulty is the bootstrapping problem of accumulating enough initial data to attract enough users to motivate database providers to supply data for low value tasks.

Nonetheless, databases are an attractive source for bootstrapping a machine learning algorithm. As our experiments presented later show, even a small set of accessible databases can provide useful clustering information.

3   Proposed Inference System

We propose applying the machine learning process of truncated singular value decomposition (T-SVD) to raw location-based capability data, including some general background data, to establish patterns of association between capabilities and at least a little data about each location of interest.

This proposed process is analogous to one way that many people reason about a location: Suppose Alice needs some laser printer paper. She sees a new store, with a name she does not recognize, but with posters in the windows advertising special offers on ball point pens, highlighters, ink jet printer cartridges, photocopying, and file folders. Alice uses her general experience of places offering those products and services to deduce the probable presence of an office supply store and expects to be able to buy her paper there.

Now instead suppose Alice has laser printer paper on her *digital* to-do list. Betty, another user of the system, previously visited the new store. While there, she checked off ball point pens, a highlighter, an ink jet printer cartridge, a photocopying task, and file folders. If Alice's phone depends only on directly collected data from previous shoppers like Betty, there is insufficient information for the phone to issue a reminder.

How much data would be enough, if Alice's phone had access to inferences from both the local data and a larger body of data from many other locations?

To answer that question, we built a model of location capabilities and used it to test a number of inference algorithms, eventually settling on truncated singular value decomposition.

The next two subsections describes our data model and algorithm. The final subsection outlines a possible architecture for a scalable system using this approach.

3.1   Data Model

The data model initially assigns a weight, representing the number of observations, to each combination of location and capability. The weights form a matrix, with one row for each capability and one column for each location. For example:

Table 1. Training Data

	Pete's Pets	Happy Paws	Hal's Hardware	Mike's	Stuff
Dog Food	40	153	0	0	4
Cat Food	26	95	0	0	0
Bolt	0	0	203	3	0
Nail	0	0	100	4	0
Screwdriver	0	0	23	2	0
Hammer	0	0	45	0	0

Here, each value represents a numbers of observations. For example, the data contains 153 observations of dog food selling at Happy Paws.

The frequencies of use of different capabilities at a location are useful data for predicting other capabilities. Generally, heavily used capabilities represent core characteristics, and the location is likely to continue to have those capabilities, as well other capabilities normally associated with them. On the other hand, a single observation of a capability may be an anomaly or a data entry error.

The location and product names are for reader convenience. The locations will typically only be known by GPS or similar coordinate. The product names may be product codes. Of course, a real set of training data would be much larger, with possibly tens of thousands of products and, even in small test cases, dozens to hundreds of locations. Normally, there are many more products and services than locations.

The data in this example suggests that cat food and dog food are normally sold at the same location, so it is reasonable to expect Stuff to sell cat food, despite the lack of any direct observations. A system that only uses actual history, without any generalization, would not trigger a reminder for cat food at Stuff.

This data structure can also represent seed data deduced from other data sources. A row represents a relationship among locations. A column represents a relationship among capabilities. Suppose a data source associated the label "pet store" with Pete's Pets, Happy Paws, and Stuff, and that we assigned that data source a weight of 3, given its general reliability. We would add a row containing 3 for each of those locations, and 0 in all other entries. Similarly, if we assigned weight 5 to an externally supplied list of hardware items, we would add a column with 5 for those items, and 0 for the remaining rows:

Table 2. Extended Training Data

	hardware	Pete's Pets	Happy Paws	Hal's Hardware	Mike's	Stuff
pet store	0	3	3	0	0	3
Dog Food	0	40	153	0	0	4
Cat Food	0	26	95	0	0	0
Bolt	5	0	0	203	3	0
Nail	5	0	0	100	4	0
Screwdriver	5	0	0	23	2	0
Hammer	5	0	0	45	0	0

3.2 T-SVD Algorithm

The objective of the algorithm is to infer a list of capabilities for each location that could have caused the observations, under the assumption that most of the variation between locations can be explained by a relatively small number of factors, such as the presence or absence of a bakery, as either a shop or a department in a larger shop. We map from our specialized ubiquitous computing problem into a common problem in linear algebra, find a low-rank approximation to the matrix, and then use truncated singular value decomposition, T-SVD, to solve it.

T-SVD has been applied successfully to similar linear algebra problems from other domains. For example, Deerwester et. al. applied it to text analysis [8]. Cernekova et. al. use it for detecting video shot transitions [9]. Chu notes that, if each column of X represents an unpredictable sample of a certain unknown distribution, the truncated singular value decomposition "not only is the best approximation to X in the sense of norm, but also is the closest approximation to X in the sense of statistics." [10].

T-SVD, as well as compressing data, may reduce various forms of noise that a full SVD would preserve. Our input data may have a zero for an available product because nobody has happened to report a purchase of that product at that location. It may also include false positives, because someone deleted an item from their to-do list for a reason other than completion of that task at the current location. T-SVD, by producing a lower rank approximation, removes detail that is more likely to be due to sampling or errors.

The first step in the algorithm is to build a matrix representing the data. Each location is represented by a column of the matrix containing the observed capability weights. For instance, using our original example data without the added "hardware" and "pet store" data, the column vector for "Pete's Pets" is $(40, 26, 0, 0, 0, 0)$. Similarly, each capability is represented by a row. The matrix for the example data is:

$$X = \begin{pmatrix} 40 & 153 & 0 & 0 & 4 \\ 26 & 95 & 0 & 0 & 0 \\ 0 & 0 & 203 & 3 & 0 \\ 0 & 0 & 100 & 4 & 0 \\ 0 & 0 & 23 & 2 & 0 \\ 0 & 0 & 45 & 0 & 0 \end{pmatrix}. \tag{1}$$

Despite having six rows and five columns, X only has rank four. Each of the last four rows can be generated by a linear sum of any two of them. However, if the basic hypothesis of product clustering is correct, X is a noisy, sampled approximation to a rank 2 matrix, where each column is a linear sum of a column representing an idealized pet food store and a column representing an idealized hardware store.

The general strategy is to use T-SVD to calculate a lower rank matrix Y, rank k, that is the least squares closest rank k matrix to X, and then use $Y_{i,j}$ as a score for predicting whether location j has capability i. Full singular value decomposition factorizes a matrix into USV^T such that each of U, S, and V has some useful properties, conveying information about the underlying structure of the original matrix. Nicholas and Dahlberg's work on finding topics in documents is particularly relevant [11]. Their problem is similar to ours, if we map "capability" to "term", "location" to "document", and treat a cluster of capabilities that tend to appear together, such as pet food in the example, as a "topic".

S is a diagonal matrix containing the "singular values", a list of weights related to the importance of different factors in forming the original matrix. After performing full singular value decomposition using Matlab "[U S V] = svd(X)", S is a diagonal matrix with values (231.9131, 186.3347, 2.8800, 2.3201, 0). There are only four non-zero singular values because X is rank 4, despite having 5 columns.

The full SVD result retains all noise and sampling effects in the data. The next step is to truncate, keeping only the largest k singular values. In our current algorithm, k is supplied externally. For this example, we will use $k = 2$. Note that the first two singular values, 231.9131 and 186.3347, are relatively close, but the third singular value, 2.88, is much smaller. Future work will examine selecting the truncation rank based on the singular values.

The truncation to k singular values results in a rank k approximation. The truncation could be done by running the full SVD and extracting the data relating to the first two singular values, but for large matrices it is more efficient to only obtain the required values, for example by running Matlab "[U S V] = svds(X,2)". The actual results contain several values of absolute magnitude less than 10^{-14}, due to floating point rounding error. Those numbers have been replaced by zero for clarity:

$$
\begin{matrix}
U \\
\begin{pmatrix}
0 & -0.84895 \\
0 & -0.52848 \\
0.87541 & 0 \\
0.43145 & 0 \\
0.099325 & 0 \\
0.194 & 0
\end{pmatrix}
\end{matrix}
\quad
\begin{matrix}
S \\
\begin{pmatrix}
231.91 & 0 \\
0 & 186.33
\end{pmatrix}
\end{matrix}
\quad
\begin{matrix}
V \\
\begin{pmatrix}
0 & -0.25598 \\
0 & -0.96651 \\
0.99981 & 0 \\
0.019622 & 0 \\
0 & -0.018224
\end{pmatrix}
\end{matrix}
\quad (2)
$$

We next calculate Y, the rank 2 matrix approximation to X, by multiplying the factors:

$$Y = USV^T = \begin{pmatrix} 40.493 & 152.89 & 0 & 0 & 2.8828 \\ 25.208 & 95.176 & 0 & 0 & 1.7946 \\ 0 & 0 & 202.98 & 3.9837 & 0 \\ 0 & 0 & 100.04 & 1.9634 & 0 \\ 0 & 0 & 23.03 & 0.452 & 0 \\ 0 & 0 & 44.983 & 0.88284 & 0 \end{pmatrix}. \tag{3}$$

Finally, we map the results back to our original problem domain, and use them as scores for estimating location capabilities:

Table 3. Scores

	Pete's Pets	Happy Paws	Hal's Hardware	Mike's	Stuff
Dog Food	40.493	152.89	0	0	2.8828
Cat Food	25.208	95.176	0	0	1.7946
Bolt	0	0	202.98	3.9837	0
Nail	0	0	100.04	1.9634	0
Screwdriver	0	0	23.03	0.452	0
Hammer	0	0	44.983	0.88284	0

All elements that were non-zero in Table 1 are non-zero in Table 3. Two additional elements are non-zero, representing cat food at Stuff and hammers at Mike's. The decision to issue a reminder will be made by comparing a cutoff value to the value in Table 3 for the combination of location and capability. The cutoff has to be somewhat greater than zero to avoid false positives due to rounding errors. For any cutoff below 0.452, the system would predict cat food at Stuff and hammers at Mike's, despite the lack of direct observations.

The approach can be extended to make predictions about a location that was not in the original training data, given some data about it, without relearning the result matrix. First we observe that any column of Y can be reproduced by multiplying together U, U^T, and the corresponding column of X:

$$UU^T \begin{pmatrix} 40 \\ 26 \\ 0 \\ 0 \\ 0 \\ 0 \end{pmatrix} = \begin{pmatrix} 40.4933 \\ 25.2076 \\ 0 \\ 0 \\ 0 \\ 0 \end{pmatrix}. \tag{4}$$

This operation, applied to a new or updated location column, produces an estimate of the location's capabilities. Suppose we have seen one cat food purchase and one hammer purchase at Totally Square, which could happen if Totally Square is a shopping center containing both a pet store and a hardware store. The corresponding location vector is $(0, 1, 0, 0, 0, 1)$. Then:

$$UU^T \begin{pmatrix} 0 \\ 1 \\ 0 \\ 0 \\ 0 \\ 1 \end{pmatrix} = \begin{pmatrix} 0.4487 \\ 0.2793 \\ 0.1698 \\ 0.0837 \\ 0.0193 \\ 0.0376 \end{pmatrix}. \tag{5}$$

Equation 5 predicts both hardware and pet food at Totally Square, but less strongly than for the locations with more data.

If the Totally Square data had been in the original training set, the algorithm would also have replaced some zero elements in the original result with slightly positive scores, reflecting the possibility that each location has both hardware and pet food, or that hammers are a form of pet food. This behavior creates some anomalies for the example data — Pete's Pets is unequivocally a pet food store and does not sell hammers — but may be a good reflection of the uncertainties and overlaps of the real world.

The algorithm has two parameters that are currently specified externally, the cutoff score and the truncation rank. It may be useful to adjust the cutoff according to a user selected trade-off between being notified of all possibilities, at the risk of false alarms, or being notified only when there is near certainty of a required capability. The correct choice may depend, for example, on how urgently the user wants to complete a particular task, and on the cost of an alert, given the user's context and activities.

The truncation rank is an estimate of the number of distinct factors, such as presence or absence of a facility such as a bakery, that are required to explain the data. Too low a truncation rank destroys data about real differences between locations. Too high a truncation rank preserves too much detail. At the extreme, keeping all non-zero singular values results in Y being identical, within rounding error, to X. Further work will aim to automate the truncation rank determination, and to normalize the scoring so that a given cutoff value has similar effects regardless of the volume of training data.

3.3 Scalability and Architecture

We have described the proposed system in terms of how it would be used, and have described the key algorithm. This subsection discusses how the architecture can be adjusted to scale to large problem sizes.

The configuration in Figure 1, with a single server, is sufficient for small- to medium- scale operations. Part of the workload, responding to queries and collecting data, is embarrassingly parallel. The volume of data required by each server could be limited by splitting transactions geographically.

However, the T-SVD calculation should be done with as much data as possible, so it must be centralized. Figure 2 illustrates this architecture.

Suppose there are c capabilities and l locations. There may be thousands of each. The input matrix X is has cl elements, but is sparse, having a non-zero entry only for observed combinations of location and capability.

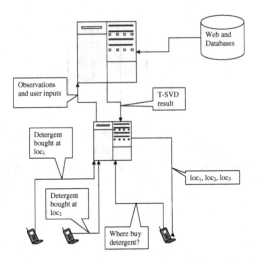

Fig. 2. The front-end server that communicates with Joe's phone also communicates with a back end inference engine server. The inference engine collects data from front-end servers and other sources. Periodically, it distributes updates to the front-end servers.

The output matrix is the same size, and may be less sparse, but does not need to be stored. As noted in the description of the algorithm, elements of it can be calculated from X and U.

Each front-end server needs a copy of the U matrix. It has ck entries, where k is the truncation rank. For 25,000 capabilities and $k = 40$, the U matrix would have one million entries and could be stored in 8 MB. A front-end server also needs the observed capability vector for each location it serves. The number of observed capability vectors could be limited by dividing work geographically, and the vectors are sparse.

Although runtime cost has not been a significant factor in our initial testing, the cost of the T-SVD calculation will tend to increase with data volume. However, the wide use of SVD has resulted in extensive work on efficient solution techniques. For example, Lin has developed an out-of-core method. [12]. In a large version of the system, the inference engine server could be effectively scaled by giving it additional memory and compute power.

The combination of geographic division of the front-end work, the gains in SVD performance from compute and memory size gains, and the potential for more sophisticated SVD methods if needed ensure that the system can scale.

4   Evaluation

We conducted simulation experiments to test the hypothesis that machine learning could fill in gaps in the observations, as well as merge different types of data.

We considered two types of input data, small numbers of random observations, such as might result from to-do list deletions, and seed data derived from bulk lists of products that are commonly stocked together, such as might be extracted from on-line databases. We tested two simulated environments, "Simple" and "Compound". In the Simple environment, each location has the capabilities of a single cluster. The Compound environment, some locations have multiple clusters of capabilities, including some that exhibit all eight clusters. In each case, we compared results to a "Null" learner that reports availability of a capability at a location if, and only if, the training data contained that combination. The traditional measures of precision and recall were used to evaluate the results.

Two important questions remain for future studies:

Group structure. These experiments are all based on eight disjoint product groups. Future experiments will use more groups, and include groups that overlap, with some products in more than one group.

False data. The training data does not include any false reports of purchases at locations that do not stock the product.

A US national supermarket chain (who asked to remain anonymous) supplied shopping basket data. The data includes classification of products into major groups. These groups provide a model of related products, and were used to model different types of shops, with unique capabilities. For our experiment, we selected the eight groups with the highest total purchase counts. We generated a table of group number and number of purchases for each product in those groups. The table contains over 40,000,000 purchases. Each group represents a set of related products, so we used each group as a model of a specialized shop type.

The training data for each location was sampled from the groups for its shop types, with the probability of each product proportionate to its frequency in the real data. We used the set of products in each group, with no frequencies, as seed data, because lists of groups of related products and services are often publicly available, but frequencies of sales are normally trade secrets.

The "Simple" environment used 8 locations per shop type, 64 locations total, where each location corresponded to a single shop. The "Compound" experiment used a mix of different types of locations. Each location has one or more shop types, as shown in Table 4. There are a total of 135 locations, 64 similar to the "Simple" experiment, the remainder modeling different types of locations, where each type has capabilities from multiple clusters.

We ran each experiment in two training data modes:

- Randomly generated samples. Each random sample is produced picking a location with equal probability, and then picking one of its capabilities with probability proportionate to the frequency of that capability in the shopping basket data.
- Randomly generated samples, as above, plus seed data derived from bulk lists of the products in each group.

Table 4. Compound Location Types

Instances	Shop Types
8	1
8	2
8	3
8	4
8	5
8	6
8	7
8	8
10	1,2
8	1,2,3
15	1,2,4
10	4,5
10	4,5,6
6	1,2,3,4,5,6,7,8
12	1,8

For T-SVD's two external parameters, we chose 8 for the rank and 10^{-6} for the cutoff. The rank was based on the expectation that at least eight singular values would be needed and an observed lack of improvement for using more. The cutoff was selected to suppress rounding error on values that should be zero.

We also ran a "Null" learner to establish a baseline. The Null learner reports a capability at a location if, and only if, that combination of capability and location appeared in the training data. It does no extrapolation. A learning method must do better than the Null learner to be worth using.

There are two ways a result can be wrong – with different consequences for a reminder system – leading to two quality measures. "Precision" is the proportion of reminder triggers that would be correct, issued at a location that affords the required capability. "Recall" is the proportion of locations affording the capability that would trigger the reminder. As an example, the simple Null learner always achieves perfect precision, at the expense of recall.

In reporting our results, we use unweighted precision and recall, a conservative approach. Some capabilities have frequencies so low that they have practically no chance of appearing in a few thousand field samples, but an error related to one of those rarities (not unlikely with our approach) carries the same error penalty as an error related to a high probability product (unlikely with our approach).

In each of the charts, the "SVD-N" line is the performance of our algorithm without the use of seed data. The "SVD-Y" line is with seed data. "Null" represents the Null learner.

Figures 3 and 4 show precision and recall for the "Simple" data, measured as a function of the number of training data samples. "Seen" in Figure 4 is the proportion of capabilities that have appeared in at least one training data sample. It is an upper bound on the recall that can be achieved without seed data. As can be seen from the chart, SVD-N achieves that bound given at least

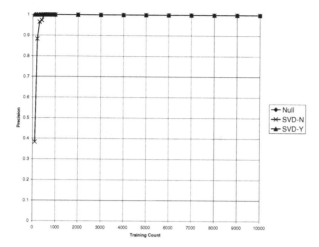

Fig. 3. Precision for simple locations

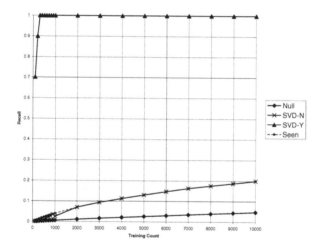

Fig. 4. Recall for simple locations

2,000 samples, an average of 31.25 samples per location. The main benefit of the seed data in the "Simple" experiment is allowing the system to make projections about capabilities that have never been observed in the training data, based on knowledge that the unseen capability is related to ones that have appeared.

Figures 5 and 6 show precision and recall for the "Compound" data. For this workload, the seed data is needed to achieve acceptable precision. Without it, the precision is about 40%. With seed data, T-SVD has 100% precision, and exceeds 90% recall given at least 1000 training data samples.

The low precision without seed data may be explained by an effect discussed in the description of the algorithm. A location with multiple shop types may

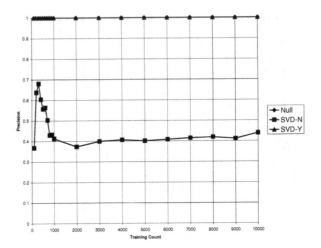

Fig. 5. Precision for compound locations

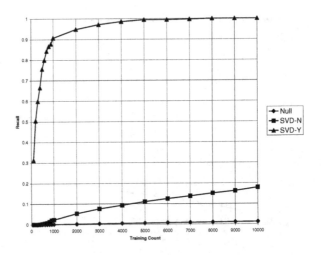

Fig. 6. Recall for compound locations

cause a low but positive score at any location with just one of its constituent
shop types. In our training data, sampled from a realistic distribution, some
observed capabilities have extremely low frequencies, leading to an overlap in
the scores for capabilities that do not exist and for capabilities that do exist, but
observed at very low frequencies. The seed data cures this by raising the scores
for existing but rarely observed capabilities.

The current T-SVD algorithm is very effective if either the locations are simple
or there is seed data to merge with the local data. As hypothesized, seed data
is needed in some cases.

5   Conclusions and Future Work

A location-based reminder system could be much more useful if the user only needed to provide the content of the reminder, without having to provide all the locations at which the reminder should be delivered. One way to achieve this is for the reminder system to learn where similar previous reminders have resulted in success in the past. Unfortunately, impractically large numbers of observations would be needed to learn anything about infrequently used capabilities from observations alone. Truncated singular value decomposition can generalize from a small number of direct observations to build high-fidelity models of locations. T-SVD's structure supports the addition of summary capability-clustering data, enabling rapid generalization in real-world situations such as the existence of hybrid store types. In our experiments based on real shopping basket data, 1000 samples randomly distributed across 135 locations gave 100% precision and 90% recall.

Future work will explore enhancements to the algorithm, such as automatic selection of the truncation rank, normalization of the cutoff score, and improved cluster detection for compound locations without seed data. Likewise, the workload will be made more realistic, for example by increasing the number of product groups. Finally, we plan to field test a small-scale reminder system based on this approach.

Acknowledgments

This research was supported in part by the UCSD FWGrid Project, NSF Research Infrastructure Grant Number EIA-0303622. It was also supported in part by a gift from Microsoft Research. We are grateful to Sanjoy Dasgupta for his consultations on machine learning. We thank the anonymous US national supermarket chain for sharing their shopping basket data, and Kevin Patrick for helping with the arrangements.

References

1. Farrimond, S., Knight, R.G., Titov, N.: The effects of aging on remembering intentions: Performance on a simulated shopping task. Applied Cognitive Psychology 20, 533–555 (2006)
2. Rendell, P.G., Craik, F.I.M.: Virtual week and actual week: Age-related differences in prospective memory. Applied Cognitive Psychology 14, S43–S62 (2000)
3. Sohn, T., Li, K.A., Lee, G., Smith, I.E., Scott, J., Griswold, W.G.: Place-its: A study of location-based reminders on mobile phones. In: Beigl, M., Intille, S.S., Rekimoto, J., Tokuda, H. (eds.) UbiComp 2005. LNCS, vol. 3660, pp. 232–250. Springer, Heidelberg (2005)
4. Dey, A.K., Abowd, G.D.: Cybreminder: A context-aware system for supporting reminders. In: Thomas, P., Gellersen, H.-W. (eds.) HUC 2000. LNCS, vol. 1927, pp. 172–186. Springer, Heidelberg (2000)

5. Mankoff, J., Hsieh, G., Hung, H.C., Lee, S., Nitao, E.: Using low-cost sensing to support nutritional awareness. In: Proceedings of the 4th international conference on Ubiquitous Computing, pp. 371–376. Springer, Heidelberg (2002)
6. Youll, J., Morris, J., Krikorian, R., Maes, P.: Impulse: Location-based agent assistance (2000)
7. Youll, J.: Wherehoo and periscope: a time & place server and tangible browser for the real world. In: CHI '01 extended abstracts on Human factors in computing systems, pp. 109–110. ACM Press, New York (2001)
8. Deerwester, S.C., Dumais, S.T., Landauer, T.K., Furnas, G.W., Harshman, R.A.: Indexing by latent semantic analysis. Journal of the American Society of Information Science 41, 391–407 (1990)
9. Cernekova, Z., Kotropoulos, C., Pitas, I.: Video shot segmentation using singular value decomposition. In: ICME '03: Proceedings of the 2003 International Conference on Multimedia and Expo, Washington, DC, USA, IEEE Computer Society, pp. 301–304. IEEE Computer Society Press, Los Alamitos (2003)
10. Chu, M.T.: On the statistical meaning of truncated singular value decomposition
11. Nicholas, C., Dahlberg, R.: Spotting topics with the singular value decomposition. In: Munson, E.V., Nicholas, C., Wood, D. (eds.) PODDP 1998 and PODP 1998. LNCS, vol. 1481, Springer, Heidelberg (1998)
12. Lin, M.H.: Out-of-core singular value decomposition (Technical report)

The Whereabouts Diary

Gabriella Castelli, Marco Mamei, and Alberto Rosi

Dipartimento di Scienze e Metodi dell'Ingegneria – Università di Modena e Reggio Emilia
Via Amendola 2 – 42100 Reggio Emilia, Italy
{gabriella.castelli,marco.mamei,alberto.rosi}@unimore.it

Abstract. The user profile is one of the main context-information in a wide range of pervasive computing applications. Modern handheld devices provided with localization capabilities could automatically create a diary of user's whereabouts and use that information as a surrogate (or a complement) of the user profile. The places we go, in fact, reveal also something about us, for example, two persons can be matched as compatible given the fact they visit the same places. Web-retrieved information, and the temporal patterns with which different places are visited, can be used to automatically define meaningful semantic labels to the visited places. In our work we used geocoding and white-pages Web-services to extract information about a place, and Bayesian networks to classify places on the basis of the time in which they have been visited. In this paper we describe the general idea at the basis of the whereabouts diary, discuss our implementation, and present experimental results. Finally, several applications that can exploit the diary are illustrated.

1 Introduction

The recent diffusion of handheld devices and smart phones equipped with localization capabilities[1] is opening new scenarios in the development of context-aware services. The location itself is an extremely useful source of information: location-based services and location-based information retrieval allow to get resources that are relevant and practically accessible given the actual location of the user [3, 4]. More than that, the places we go can reveal also something about us, and can be used as a surrogate or a complement to form a better user profile. For example, a matchmaking application could infer that two persons are compatible given the fact that they visit almost the same places. Moreover, if the places are tagged semantically (e.g., work, home, pub, etc.) the application could infer more advanced relationships among the persons. For example, two persons visiting the same "work" place could be marked as colleagues, while persons visiting the same "home" place could be marked as relatives.

In this paper we present the ideas and a first prototype implementation of the *whereabouts diary*: an application, running on a GPS-equipped handheld device that records the list of relevant places visited by the user. The diary runs autonomously without requiring user's interactions and is able to classify *semantically* the places being visited in an unsupervised way. Relevant places can be extracted by considering

---

[1] The U.S. E911 and European E112 initiatives require localization capability for calls placed to emergency services by mobile phones.

J. Hightower, B. Schiele, and T. Strang (Eds.): LoCA 2007, LNCS 4718, pp. 175–192, 2007.
© Springer-Verlag Berlin Heidelberg 2007

clusters and dropouts in the GPS signal (typically indicating the user staying in a place or entering in a building). Semantic information can be added by exploiting the structure of people daily routine. For example, the place where the user usually spends night-time can be tagged semantically as "home", while the place where the user usually goes from 8am to 6pm can be tagged as "work". Specifically, we realized a set of Bayesian networks to diagnose the kind of place given the temporal pattern of user visits. Further information can be extracted by geocoding the place and mining the Web in search for relevant information. For example, the fact that the user was at the coordinates (lon: -80.239, lat: 25.955) on the 02/04/07 evening, can be easily geocoded to infer that the user was actually at the Dolphin Stadium in South Florida. Moreover, such information could be further refined extracting from the Web the fact that the SuperBowl was actually playing that night in that stadium. The result is a diary describing the user daily life and that could provide useful profile information to other applications.

The rest of this paper is organized as follows: Section 2 describes the general idea and our current implementation of the whereabouts diary. Section 3 presents some experiments we conducted to test the effectiveness of our prototype. Section 4 discusses some applications that could be realized with the diary. Section 5 presents some related work. Section 6 concludes and presents future work diary.

2   The Whereabouts Diary

In this section we first present the conceptual idea beneath the whereabouts diary, then we detail our current implementation.

2.1   General Idea

The construction of the whereabouts diary is an incremental process. Starting from the log of the GPS readings (or of other kind of localization devices), it is possible to run segmentation and clustering algorithms to infer the places where the user spends most of his time [9]. The result of this first operation is a list of places described in terms of longitude and latitude, and a list of time intervals associated to each of the coordinates indicating when the user has been there. This first process creates a diary like the one presented in Fig. 1.

Longitude	Latitude	Time
-73.974	40.763	July, 4, 2006, 4:35pm-5:41pm
...	...	...

Fig. 1. Diary based on GPS coordinates

A simple list of coordinates is only partially informative and the need of translating from positions to places (i.e., adding semantic meaningful tags to the discovered coordinates) has been widely recognized [8]. A diary containing information like *"the user was at home*" rather than "*the user was at coordinates (10.873, 44.630)*" would be naturally much more informative and easy to use in context-aware applications.

A first step in the process of adding semantic information would be to translate from coordinates to addresses. This can be done via standard tracking and geocoding services (as common GPS navigators do). However, because of errors in GPS localization and errors in the process of segmenting and clustering the GPS readings to identify relevant places, in most of the situations, it will not be possible to identify the unique address where the user is located, and only a partial estimate can be given (e.g., all the addresses within 10 meters from a given place are actually taken into consideration). This second step converts the diary in the one depicted in Fig. 2.

Place	Time
123, 5th Ave, NY, USA	July, 4, 2006, 4:35pm-5:41pm
4,5,...,21, 26th St., NY, USA	July 6, 2006, 7:00am – 8:00am
...	...

Fig. 2. Diary based on addresses. Because of GPS errors multiple addresses can be associated to a single place.

A third step can try to mine the Web to identify what is in a particular address. The primary source of information in this context would come from yellow- and white-pages services. However, due to the aforementioned localization errors, this process will return in some of the cases a list of all the businesses performed in the geocoded addresses. Still, in some situations a single exact match could be retrieved like in the case of the user being in a big stadium or entering a big shopping mall.

Even more semantic information could derive by searching relevant events that happened in that place at that time. For example, it could be possible to extract from the Web the fact that "the 4th of July parade" took place near the geocoded location at the same time the user was there. This process could create a diary like the one depicted in Fig. 3.

Place	Time
4th July Parade	July, 4, 2006, 4:35pm-5:41pm
126, 13th St., NY, USA	July 5, 2006, 11:00pm – 7:00am
Starbucks Coffee ‖ Uno's Pizza	July 6, 2006, 7:00am – 8:00am
....	...

Fig. 3. Diary based on places. Because of errors in the previous phases, multiple businesses can be associated to a single place.

Finally, if the user activities are profiled in some way (e.g., the diary may know a priori that the user tends to stay at home at night), then the diary application can give labels to places by looking at the temporal patterns in which places are visited. For example, the place most visited at night during weekdays can be meaningfully labeled as "Home". Such kind of analysis can be also used in combination with commonsense information [13] to disambiguate between alternative retrieved places. For example, in the table in Fig. 3 the ambiguity among "Starbucks Coffee" and "Uno's Pizza" can be resolved (at least from a probabilistic point of view) in favor of the former, in consideration of the fact the place has been visited from 7:00 am to 8:00 am.

Of course, should other kind of sensing devices be available (e.g., RFID and NFC – Near Field Communication – readers), classification could use such information to better identify the places. For example, a powerful source of data could come from credit card transaction records that would identify not only in which shop the user has been, but also what he has bought (some recent proposals in the context of mobile wallet applications go in this direction [5]). In the end, the combination of all the above steps leads to a diary close to the one in Fig. 4.

Place	Time
4th July Parade	July, 4, 2006, 4:35pm-5:41pm
Home	July 5, 2006, 11pm – 7am
Starbucks Coffee	July 5, 2006, 7am – 8am
....	...

Fig. 4. Diary based on personalized places

In its final form the diary represents a powerful source of context information allowing to extrapolate user's habits, preferences and routine behavior.

2.2 Implementation

The whereabouts diary can be built incrementally and automatically on the basis of the user's trace of locations. In our current implementation the trace is acquired only via a GPS, however other localization mechanisms such as WiFi or Cell tower triangulation can be used as well [9].

The first step is to segment user's GPS trace to find "relevant" places. Following an approach similar to the one proposed in [15, 22], we tagged as relevant those places for which either one of the following conditions apply:

1. The GPS signal is lost for at least T seconds and it is re-acquired later on at a distance of less than L meters from where it was lost. This reflects the situation in which a user enters a building and leaves it after some time. Some empirical evaluations let us to set T = 20 minutes, L = 20 meters. The constraint on time is important to wash out GPS signal glitches, the constraint on space is useful to avoid those situation in which the GPS has been shut down and the user moves away.
2. The GPS readings over a time window of W seconds are clustered within a radius of R meters from each other. This reflects the situation in which the user stays for a long time in a place like a park or a square. Some empirical evaluations let us to set W = 20 minutes, R = 100 meters.

The list of relevant places is built online and incrementally. When a set of coordinates meets one of the above criteria, the system looks in the list of the already discovered places for one closer than L = 10 meters to the coordinates. If such a place does not exist, a new place is created and the time of visit is recorded. If the place exists, the place coordinates are averaged with the new coordinates, and if enough time has passed since the previous visit (30 min), the time of the new visit is recorded. The output of this algorithm is represented with Google Earth in Fig. 5.

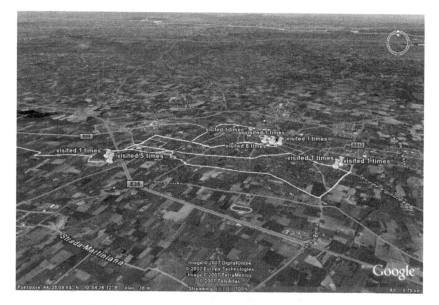

Fig. 5. Path and relevant places depicted in Google Earth

The coordinates associated to places have been translated into addresses using a geocoding service. Most of the geocoding services available online (e.g., that provided by the Google Maps API) translate addresses into coordinates. Instead, the diary needs the reverse operation: from coordinates to addresses. We developed a "reverse" geocoding for our region, on the basis of maps available from a commercial navigator software. Once such maps are available, the approach is rather straightforward: the coordinates are mapped to the closer map entry (i.e., address) being available.

To take into account GPS and geocoding inaccuracies, and the errors introduced by the place retrieving process, the diary application tries to reverse geocode all the addresses within a radius of 10m from the place being segmented. Thus, the diary actually creates a list of candidate addresses where the user has been.

The next step is to translate addresses into businesses (i.e., shops, offices, etc.). The ideal result is to have in the diary entries like "Starbuck's coffee", rather than "234, Marlborough st.". To perform this operation we screen-scraped information coming from a widely used online white-pages service[2] in our region allowing to query for who is at a given address. This operation is trivially achieved using the tools provided by the htmlparser[3] software. In particular, each geocoded address belonging to a given place (as provided by the previous step) is looked up in the white-pages and the

---

[2] www.paginebianche.it
[3] htmlparser.sourceforge.net

corresponding business is retrieved. The result of this process is a set of entries labeled with the possible businesses found in that place. Fig. 6 shows the result of this process for a given place in Google Earth. This translation process in not completely accurate, since several addresses are not listed in the white-pages (mainly due to privacy constraints). Still, the fact that most public businesses (like shops, etc.) are listed, while several private houses are not, allows to prune out a lot of unlikely addresses being discovered by the previous step. Private spaces like "home" – that are likely not to be listed in the white-pages – can be derived from other kind of analysis described below.

Fig. 6. Extracted information related to a given place

The final step in our implementation is more challenging. The diary tries to automatically extract semantic information to describe the relevant places from a personal point of view.

To this end, for each place being identified in the first phase, the diary creates a Bayesian network to analyze the temporal pattern in which the place has been visited by the user (see Fig. 7).The Bayesian network is composed of 4 nodes.

1. The *weekend* node represents a boolean variable used to represent whether a given observation takes place in the weekend or not. This node is always observed on the basis of the information stored in the GPS signal. This information represents the variability in people behavior between weekdays and weekends.
2. The *hour* node is a 24-values discrete node storing the time of day. This node is always observed on the basis of the information stored in the GPS signal.
3. The *kind of place* node is a discrete node modeling what a given place is. In our implementation, we try to classify among 5 different kind of places: home,

work, restaurant (to indicate any kind of dining place), pub (to indicate any kind of evening entertainment), and disco (to indicate any kind of late-night entertainment). This classification is rather arbitrary, and each user of the diary should provide the kinds of place that best match his habits. This node is never observed, and is inferred by probability computations.

4. The *happens* node is a boolean variable expressing whether the user visits that place at that time. This node is always observed on the basis of the outcomes of the diary localization phase.

The role of the Bayesian network is to encode the routine of the user daily life. This is done by compiling the probability distribution associated to the fact that the user, in a given moment, is in a certain kind of place. For example, the probability of the user being at home during weekdays is depicted in the table in Fig. 8.

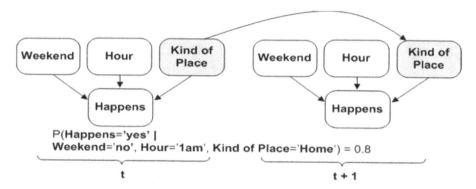

Fig. 7. Bayesian network to classify places. White nodes are those that will be provided as evidence.

Weekend = false, Kind of Place = home									
Time	**11pm-6am**	**7am**	**8am**	**9am-1pm**	**2pm-5pm**	**6pm-7pm**	**8pm**	**9pm**	**10pm**
P(happens) = true	0.8	0.6	0.4	0.2	0.2	0.4	0.5	0.6	0.7

Fig. 8. Conditional probability table describing the probability of the user being at home during weekdays

Similar tables can be created for other kind of places. In our current implementation, these tables are compiled by hand by the users that are asked to self-report the likelihood of being in a given kind of place at a given time. Such kind of data could be derived automatically also by a labeled trace of user's past whereabouts, using standard learning algorithms [18]. Once the tables are filled in, basic inference operations in Bayesian networks will be used to derive the most likely kind of place given the visit pattern.

Specifically, when the diary previous phases identify that the user is visiting a place, the corresponding Bayesian network is retrieved, and the *weekend, hour, happens* nodes are set to their actual values (the *happens* node is trivially set to *true* to indicate that there is a visit). Then, the diary computes the probability distribution of the *kind of place* node. The newly computed distribution will be used as a prior for subsequent visits. This naturally allows evidences to add up, actually enabling the Bayesian network to classify the places on the basis of the visit temporal pattern. The results of the Bayesian classifier for two places in our dataset is reported in Fig. 9.

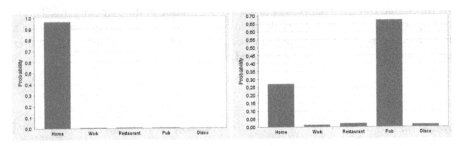

Fig. 9. Outputs of the Bayesian network classifier for two places

3   Experiments

To test the effectiveness of the whereabouts diary, we collected GPS traces for three weeks from three members of our research team (the authors) as they went about their normal lives. Each member carried either an i-mate PDA 2K smart phone, or a HP IPAQ RX3700 pda, connected with a Bluetooth GPS reader. GPS signal has been acquired at 0.1Hz and processed on the fly by the handheld device. Overall, we acquired about 90000 GPS poses amounting at 360 MB of data. Overall, this resulted in 25 places being identified as relevant.

In particular, the diary is a J2ME – personal profile application that:

1. Collects and stores the GPS trace log.
2. Runs the clustering algorithm to identify relevant places.
3. Creates a queue of the places to be resolved by the on-line (reverse) geocoding and white-pages services. Places are actually resolved whenever a WiFi connection becomes available.
4. Dynamically creates a Bayesian network for each newly discovered place.
5. When a relevant place is visited, the associated Bayesian network is retrieved, and the probability distribution to describe the kind of place is updated accordingly to the time of visit. Bayesian operations are implemented on the basis of the software described in [14].

During the data collection weeks, data collectors recorded ground-truth information about the places they have been. Such information has been collected with a simple notepad application running on the PDAs and allowing to write a textual description of where the user has been at a given time.

All the data have been recorded in our region in Italy (none of the data collectors have been abroad during that time). The region is characterized by rather small and short buildings. On the one hand, this means that GPS signal problems related to urban canyons are less severe, and it is usually easy to get fairly accurate GPS positioning. On the other hand, buildings are packed closed to each others, and thus also small errors can produce wrong address translations.

In the following, we present some results obtained by comparing the whereabouts diary entries, after some weeks of usage, with recorded ground-truth information.

In a first set of experiments, we tried to verify the accuracy of the algorithm to identify relevant places on the basis of the GPS trace log. Following an approach similar to [9], we classify the incorrect results into: *(i) wrong*: the user is in a place, but the diary reports he is in a different place, *(ii) false negative*: the user is in a place, but the diary reports he is moving, *(iii) false positive*: the user is moving, but the diary reports he is in a place. The results of this experiment are reported in Fig. 10, and they actually show the average of the results obtained by the data collectors. The results we obtained show that the algorithm is correct in 84.7% of the cases. This figure is coherent with the results presented in [9] with regard to the A-S algorithm [1] that is the one closer to our implementation. The high-percentage of false negatives (compared to the other cases) is mainly due to the fact sometimes the GPS takes a long time before acquiring the signal. Thus, it can happen that a user leaves a building, and the trace of the GPS is acquired only when he is already far away. In such a situation the place is not detected given the constraint on the maximum distance of spatial disconnection described in Sect. 2.2.

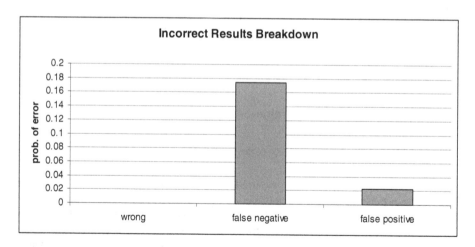

Fig. 10. Errors in the algorithm to identify relevant places on the basis of the GPS trace log. Place identification is correct in 84.7% of the cases. Errors are divided as reported in the graph.

In a second set of experiments, we tried to verify the results of the (reverse) geocoding service. Basically, the idea is to verify the impact of localization errors in the process of geocoding. It is worth noticing that the maps we used to perform this operation record only the first and the last number of a street segment and span, uniformly, all the other numbers among the segment. This of course introduces further errors in that it does not take in to account the differences in the sizes of the buildings.

Since the place discovery algorithm clusters together points that are closer than 10 meters, we counted the number of addresses retrieved within a circle of 10 meters radius centered at the relevant place. The results of this operations are displayed in Fig. 11, and highlight two aspects. On the one hand, the address of almost half of the places can be retrieved uniquely (this is the case of large buildings – like the departments of our university). On the other hand, some places produce more than 10 associated addresses. This is the case of small buildings in the center of the city. It is fair to report that these distributions are rather preliminary since they are based on a dataset of only 25 places (those identified by the diaries of the 3 data collectors). We are currently conducting a more extensive data collection process that would allow us to identify more stable distributions.

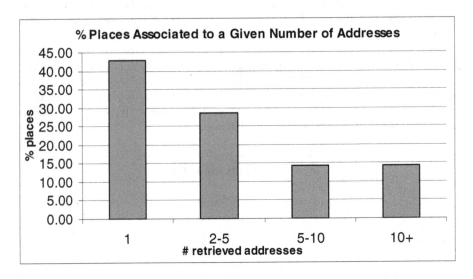

Fig. 11. Percent of relevant places corresponding to a given number of addresses

In a third group of experiments, we tried to evaluate the performance of retrieving the businesses performed on a given place via the white-pages service. Comparing the results with the ground-truth annotations, we first tried to determine whether the correct place is retrieved. With disappointment, we verified that the actual place can be retrieved in only 40% of the cases. This is either due to localization or white-pages errors. Moreover, due to the multiplicity of addresses being discovered several businesses can be assigned to a given place. In Fig. 12, we report the distribution of the number of businesses found for a given place. It is easy to see that some addresses are not listed in the white-pages, since there are no places with more than 10 retrieved businesses. In addition, It is worth reporting that the number of businesses being retrieved is almost independent of whether the correct place has been found or not. Some places, in fact, return a long list of candidate entries not containing the correct one. The main source of errors of this phase is related to the white-pages interface and how it handles street numbers. For example, one puzzling error we found, involved the Juta bar in the center of our city. Although the place was acquired correctly, the address geocoded correctly, and the Juta bar is listed in the white-pages service, the diary was not able to extract such information. We found that the problem is about places having more than one street numbers (for example, the Juta bar is a long building located from 87 to 95 of Taglio st.). Unfortunately, the Web interface to the white-pages allows only to enter a single street number, and white-pages matching mechanism does not take into account the fact that e.g., 89 Taglio st. is within the range of Juta addresses, thus it produces no results. In our future work, we plan to solve these glitches by querying multiple white- and yellow-pages services and merging the results.

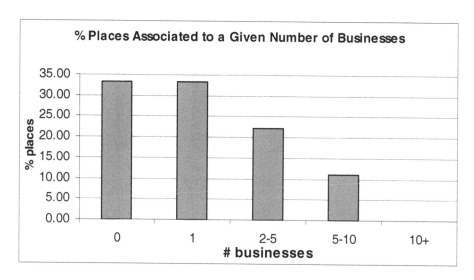

Fig. 12. Percent of relevant places corresponding to a given number of businesses being retrieved

Finally, the last set of experiments verified the results of the Bayesian classification. Overall, our approach classifies the places correctly in 64% of the cases. In order to better analyze the results we tried to assess the confidence of the diary in its own classification – most probable estimate (MPE). To this end, we compute the information entropy of the resulting distributions. The lower the entropy, the more the system is confident about the MPE (i.e., the distribution peaks on the MPE value). More in detail, we separated the entropies related to the distributions that produced a correct MPE from those that produced a wrong MPE. For each of these two categories, we averaged together the entropies of the distributions producing the same MPE (see Fig. 13). Looking at the graph it is possible to notice that entropies related to wrong MPEs and higher than entropies related to correct MPEs. This is good and reflects the fact that the distributions associated to wrong estimates are less peaked, and thus the diary is less confident about its own classification. In fact, examining the wrong distributions in a lot of circumstances the distribution is bimodal: one peak is the correct one and another slightly more probable is incorrect. In such circumstances, it is likely that more observations on the temporal pattern of visits will correct the classification outcome.

Another interesting remark about the result in Fig. 13, relates to the average entropy associated to the different kind of places. Not surprisingly, *home* and *work* places have lower entropies since their associated temporal pattern of visits is defined more precisely. On the contrary, places like *pubs*, *restaurants* and *discos* have a more flexible pattern of visits and thus they are classified less precisely and tend to produce higher entropies.

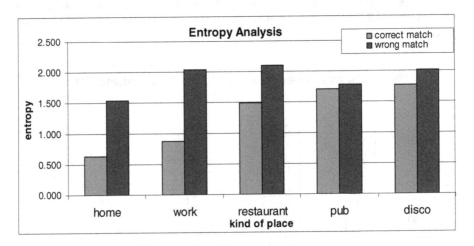

Fig. 13. Information entropy of the resulting distributions for the various kind of places. The information entropy for a 5-value discrete distribution ranges from 0 to 2.32 (flat distribution).

4 Applications

Once the diary is available, it can be used as a surrogate of the user profile in several applications.

Matchmaking. The automatic exchange of diaries between users can enforce power- ful matchmaking capabilities. An application built on top of the whereabouts diary could try to match the places visited by the users to understand whether they are visiting similar places or not. The similarity between the places being visited can be a useful measure of the affinity between the two users. Similarly to what suggested in [12], the diaries can be useful to in the process of building common ground for face to face interactions. For example, a user could be notified that the person next to her has been to the same concert one week ago. With this regard, it is important to remark that the use of diaries enriched with semantic information is really useful in this context. For example, the application can automatically discriminate among colleagues (people spending time in the same work places), relatives (people spending time in the same home places) and friends (people spending time in the same pub and disco places). It would not be possible to conduct such kind of analysis on the basis of a purely geographic diary that only computes overlapping areas among people.

Places for Tourists. Tourist scenarios have always motivated ubiquitous computing applications. These kind of applications being deeply related to user profile and context-awareness can naturally take advantage of the whereabouts diary. An application could match the places visited by the user across a database of tourist attraction and suggest possible next visits. For example, if the diary indicates that the user likes visiting museums, the application could suggest visit other museums of a city. In addition, the exchange of diaries among tourists could allow to exchange experiences, hints and recommendations. For example, backpackers traveling northward could fruitfully exchange diaries with backpackers traveling southward to obtain information about where they had just been [2]. Also in this case, the extraction of semantic information (e.g., retrieving shops and other businesses in a given area) could provide a notable added value to the information being communicated.

Shop Assistant. A shop recommendation service could try to infer users preferences on the basis of shops visited by the user. The scenario for this application could be an open-air market, for example a typical flea-market, or a city shopping district. The system can know in advance the location and the typology of goods held by any expositor and shops (as possibly provided by a sort of yellow-pages service). An application running on the whereabouts diary can trace the user's movements along the first visited places, and compose a sort of user shopping profile. Starting from this profile, the system could try to predict future user movements and indicate him the way to expositors/shops that in its opinion better fulfill his wishes. The user profile could be updated as user makes choices and moves across the area.

Pervasive Advertisement. Personalized advertisements offering users the most appropriate contents to suit their profile is a huge source of revenues for IT companies. The whereabouts diary could be a useful mechanism to apply personalized advertisement to ubiquitous computing scenarios. An application could show commercials to the user that are personalized on the basis of the diary. For example, if the user usually visits Au Bon Pain around noon, the application running on the user handheld device could present Au Bon Pain commercials at about 11am showing special offers, and indicating also those places that are in the neighborhood. In another setting, a wide screen display connected with a Bluetooth station could fetch the diaries of the people around and select the most appropriate commercials for the present population. In both these situations the whereabouts diary can provide useful information to compose the user profile. In addition, it is interesting to notice that the diary can provide useful feedback on whether the advertisement had been fruitful or not. For example, comparing the places visited by the user after seeing a commercial, it would be possible to infer whether the user followed the advertisement and actually went to Au Bon Pain.

Predict User Destination and Anomaly Detection. This application is based on the general assumption that people routinely performs repetitive actions (e.g., usually people go to work/school in the morning and come back in the evening, people have lunch around noon, etc.). On this basis, an application can learn from the whereabouts diary the user motion routine, and thus predict where the user will go next and eventually trigger alarms if anomalous deviations from the normal track are detected [18, 19]. Such a service may be very useful for very young, elder or disabled people in order to support their independent living. For example, a child goes to school by himself; the application could monitor his movements alerting himself and his parents if notable deviations from the usual track are detected (the child may got lost or may have caught the wrong bus).

Whereabouts Routing. Some interesting application related to the prediction of user next movements are presented in [1, 21]. Nodes connectivity and performance in mobile ad-hoc network scenarios could be notably enhanced by having nodes to communicate with each other their likely future movements. For example, an application could avoid initiating to exchange files with a node that is predicted to be out of the wireless range in few seconds. In another setting, this idea could be fruitfully exploited to enable network routing in the presence of large disconnections among nodes. For example, a user 'A' willing to send a message to a user 'B', that is currently not reachable because of network partitions, could inspect the motion model of the user 'B' and retrieve the fact that 'B' at that time is usually in a given place. On this basis, the user 'A' could search for other reachable users that (according to their motion model) are going to the same place and relay the message to them. This approach can create an interesting routing mechanism that allows the messages to flow also in presence of large network partitions. Of course, the diary can be fruitfully applied to this context allowing the routing algorithm to predict where the user will go next based on users' past history.

Personalized Navigation. MyRoute [17] is an application to produce personalized navigation routes with the goal of reducing route complexity and cognitive burden. This is achieved by creating user specific routes on the basis of his previous knowledge about familiar routes and landmarks. In particular, MyRoute works by compressing directions coming from traditional navigation software into a single contextualized step (e.g., drive to work). The whereabouts diary could naturally support MyRoute by providing the information about users' relevant places.

Context-Aware Instant Messaging. The messenger application Nomatic [20] proposes to exploit places' semantic labels as meaningful status information in messenger applications. Such automatic labels could be used in combination of the standard ("on line", "not at PC", "busy" labels) to better express the actual status of the user. More in general, a wide range of ubiquitous computing applications can be enhanced by incorporating information about localization. For example, mobile phones can be automatically switched off inside a theatre, or could connect with the car speakers when the user is driving. Contact-management software could be programmed to automatically exchange business cards when the current place is recognized as work by both the users. Of course, the whereabouts diary could provide all these applications with suitable information.

Memory-Aid. Memory-aid applications can take a notable advantage from the availability of the whereabouts diary. Specifically, notes, to-do-lists and reminders can be associated to specific places and be triggered by the user being in there.

Moreover, the whereabouts diary can offer predictions on where the user is going next, so that reminders can be triggered also before the user reaches his actual destination. For example, if the diary predicts that the user will be close to the library the next day, the memory-aid application can remind the user to take the books on loan when exiting the house [1].

Life Blogging. Context-aware life blogging is like writing your personal diary in an automated way. The mobile application Context Watcher [11] runs on smart phones, automatically connects to available sensors, logs the information, and generates daily summaries about user's location, activities and moods. Also in this case, the whereabouts diary could provide high-level semantic location descriptions of the identified places. This could improve the life blog by making it more semantically expressive.

5 Related Work

The recent availability of affordable localization mechanism and the recognition of location as a primary source of context information has stimulated a wealth of works addressing topics related to the whereabouts diary. In general, the originality of our work compared to others is to try to give semantic labels to places in a fully automatic way (either by mining the Web, or by classifying the places on the basis of a suitable Bayesian network).

One of the earliest work trying to automatically compose a diary of users' whereabouts is the PEPYS application [16]. This application uses IR badges and detectors to track user location in an indoor environment. On the basis of such an information, PEPYS compiles a diary of where the user has been and submits it to the user as a memory feedback. This kind of indoor localization systems, as well as its more modern incarnation (e.g., [7]) could naturally complement the proposed GPS diary to deal with indoor settings.

The work described in [9] compares three algorithms to cluster continuous GPS readings to find relevant places. Each of these algorithms could replace the clustering algorithm we described at the beginning of Section 2.2[4]. However all these algorithms are only useful to spot relevant places and identify possible recurrent visit to the sample place. The problem of adding semantic information is completely neglected.

The works in [1, 10, 15, 22] presents similar kind of clustering algorithms.

The problem of adding semantic tags is posed, at least as an open problem, in [8]. Other than clarifying the importance and the need for such a conversion from "positions" to "places", the author illustrates two viable approaches to add semantics. The first approach is based on labeling places on the basis of the activities performed in there. The author proposes using RFID tags to infer users' activities on the basis of the objects being touched (e.g., the user touches a fork and a knife, the system infers he is having dinner). Then, the system uses the activity (e.g., having dinner) to label the place (e.g., restaurant). The second approach involves humans assigning labels to

---

[4] It is worth noticing that the surveyed algorithm called BeaconPrint is more reliable and precise than the one we implemented, thus it could also improve the performance of our system.

places proactively, and exchanging such labels among users. Neither of the two approaches has been actually realized, and they are mainly left as future work. In any case, once available, they could be well complement and integrate our proposal.

The works described in [17, 18] adopt a Bayesian network to infer high-level user behaviors from low-level GPS readings. While their approach is similar to ours, their goal is different. While we try to classify the places, they try to classify user activities and eventually predict where the user will go next, on the basis of his past routes. It is worth to report that some user activities can directly identify the place in which they occur. For example, a sharp step in the user speed can reveal the user started/stopped driving the car. This automatically can be used to label that place as a parking place. Such kind of further information could improve the whereabouts diary.

The work presented in [6] presents an interesting algorithm to share labels to reach a consensus on what a place means to a given group of users. Although, this work is interesting and cloud also be someway integrated with the whereabouts diary, we think it has two main drawbacks. On the one hand, the system proposes random labels like "xyz" to places not allowing for a meaningful semantic description. On the other hand, in a lot of situations, we think it does not make sense to reach a consensus. The same place can mean different things to different people. For example, the bar tender can classify his pub as "work", while clients will classify it as "pub".

In the end, we think that a lot of ideas in related work could be used to improve the diary. However, some of the ideas discussed in the paper, like the proposed Bayesian network, are original of our proposal.

6   Conclusions and Future Work

In this paper we presented the *whereabouts diary* – an application, running on a GPS-equipped handheld device – that records the relevant places visited by the user and classifies them semantically in an automatic way. Several useful applications that can be built on the basis of the diary have been also discussed.

There are several directions to improve this work:

1. Much more information about the places could be retrieved from the Web. This could be very useful especially in the cases in which localization is precise enough to return a single or a couple of addresses. Such kind of retrieved information could be a precious source of information to estimate the user profile.
2. Commonsense data could be exploited to effectively discriminate among several candidate places [13]. For example, if a person went to a restaurant at noon, it is very unlikely that will go to another restaurant at 2pm.
3. Other kind of sensing devices and algorithms could be employed to extract more information about the place. Moreover, some GPS clustering techniques that have been used in related works [9] could improve the performance of our implementation.

In the end, accuracy will be the key measure in which the diary will be evaluated. If the diary is wrong, the applications that use it risk being rendered useless. Accordingly, improving the diary accuracy along all the above three directions is a fundamental future work. Of course, implementing some of the applications discussed in Section 4 will be an important step to evaluate the diary and to get real feedbacks of its usefulness. With this regard, we already started implementing the "places for tourist" application and we plan to test it on a large population of users.

Finally, one important aspect that should be carefully considered is related to the privacy implications involved in the diary usage. This is especially important in consideration of the fact that several applications described in the previous section involve the exchange of diaries among users. With this regard, it would be interesting to investigate the possibility of exchanging hash-based signatures of the diary entries, instead of the actual values to preserve privacy [12].

Acknowledgements

Work supported by the project CASCADAS (IST-027807) funded by the FET Program of the European Commission.

References

1. Ashbrook, D., Starner, T.: Using GPS to Learn Significant Locations and Predict Movement Across Multiple Users. Personal and Ubiquitous Computing 7(1), 275–286 (2003)
2. Axup, J., Viller, S., MacColl, I., Cooper, R.: Lo-Fi Matchmaking: A Study of Social Pairing for Backpackers. In: International Conference on Ubiquitous Computing, Orange County, Orange County (CA), USA (2006)
3. Benatallah, B., Maamar, Z.: Special issue on M-services. IEEE Transactions on Systems, Man, and Cybernetics, Part A 33(6), 665–776 (2003)
4. Castelli, G., Rosi, A., Mamei, M., Zambonelli, F.: A Simple Model and Infrastructure for Context-aware Browsing of the World, International Conference on Pervasive Computing and Communication. White Plains, NY, USA (2007)
5. Fitzgerald, M.: Your Digital Wallet, 24 August 2004. MIT Technology Review, Cambridge (2004)
6. Flanagan, J.: An Unsupervised Learning Paradigm for Peer-to-Peer Labeling and Naming of Locations and Contexts. In: International Workshop on Location and Context-Awareness, Dublin, Ireland (2006)
7. Hahnel, D., Burgard, W., Fox, D., Fishkin, K., Philipose, M.: Mapping and Localization with RFID Technology. In: IEEE International Conference on Robotics and Automation, New Orleans (LA), USA (2004)
8. Hightower, J.: From Position to Place, Workshop on Location-Aware Computing, Seattle (WA), USA (2003)
9. Hightower, J., Consolvo, S., LaMarca, A., Smith, I., Hughes, J.: Learning and Recognizing the Places We Go. In: Beigl, M., Intille, S.S., Rekimoto, J., Tokuda, H. (eds.) UbiComp 2005. LNCS, vol. 3660, Springer, Heidelberg (2005)
10. Kang, J., Welbourne, W., Stewart, B., Borriello, G.: Extracting places from traces of locations, International Workshop on Wireless Mobile Applications and Services on WLAN Hotspots, Philadelphia (PA), USA (2004)
11. Koolwaaij, J.: Context Watcher, http://portals.telin.nl/contextwatcher/index.aspx

12. Kostakos, V., O'Neill, E., Shahi, A.: Building Common Ground for Face to Face Interactions by Sharing Mobile Device Context. In: International Workshop on Location and Context-Awareness, Dublin, Ireland (2006)
13. Liu, H., Singh, P.: ConceptNet: a practical commonsense reasoning toolkit. BT Technology Journal 22(4), 211–226 (2004)
14. Mamei, M., Nagpal, R.: Macro Programming through Bayesian Networks: Distributed Inference and Anomaly Detection, International Conference on Pervasive Computing and Communication. White Plains (NY, USA) (2007)
15. Marmasse, N., Schmandt, C.: Location-aware information delivery with commotion. In: International Symposium on Handheld and Ubiquitous Computing, Bristol, UK (2000)
16. Newman, W., Eldridge, M., Lamming, M.: PEPYS: Generating Autobiographies by Automatic Tracking. In: European Conference on Computer Supported Cooperative Work, Amsterdam, Netherlands (1991)
17. Patel, K., Chen, M., Smith, I., Landay, J.: "Personalizing Routes", Symposium on User Interface Software and Technology. Montreux, Switzerland (2006)
18. Patterson, D., Liao, L., Fox, D., Kautz, H.: Inferring high-level behavior from low-level sensors. In: Dey, A.K., Schmidt, A., McCarthy, J.F. (eds.) UbiComp 2003. LNCS, vol. 2864, Springer, Heidelberg (2003)
19. Patterson, D., Liao, L., Gajos, K., Collier, M., Livic, N., Olson, K., Wang, S., Fox, D., Kautz, H.: Opportunity Knocks: a System to Provide Cognitive Assistance with Transportation Services. In: Davies, N., Mynatt, E.D., Siio, I. (eds.) UbiComp 2004. LNCS, vol. 3205, Springer, Heidelberg (2004)
20. Patterson, D., Ding, X., Noack, N.: Nomatic: Location By, For, and Of Crowds. In: International Workshop on Location and Context-Awareness, Dublin, Ireland (2006)
21. Roman, G.-C., Handorean, R., Sen, R.: Tuple Space Coordination Across Space and Time. In: International Conference on Coordination Models and Languages, Bologna, Italy (2006)
22. Schmid, F., Richter, K.: Extracting Places from Location Data Streams, International Workshop on Ubiquitous Geographical Information Services. Munster, Germany (2006)

Adaptive Learning of Semantic Locations and Routes

Keshu Zhang, Haifeng Li, Kari Torkkola, and Mike Gardner

Motorola Labs
2900 S Diablo Way, Tempe, AZ 85282
keshu.zhang@motorola.com

Abstract. Adaptation of devices and applications based on contextual information has a great potential to enhance usability and mitigate the increasing complexity of mobile devices. An important topic in context-aware computing is to learn semantic locations and routes of mobile device users. Several batch methods have been proposed to learn these locations. However, such offline methods have very limited usefulness in practice. This paper describes an online adaptive approach to learn user's semantic locations. The proposed method models user's GPS data as a mixture of Gaussians, which is updated by an online estimation. The learned Gaussian mixture is then evaluated to determine which components most likely correspond to the important locations based on *a priori* probabilities. With learned semantic locations, we also propose a minimax criterion to discover user's frequent transportation routes, which are modeled as sequences of GPS data. Finally, we describe an application of the proposed methods in a cell phone based automatic traffic advisory system.

1 Introduction

In last three decades, we have witnessed an increase in computational power and connectivity which has lead to powerful devices that deliver services in the workspace, home, and in the car. Today, people carry a variety of mobile devices with powerful computational capability and wireless connectivity, which greatly change our lifestyle. On the other side, context aware computing, emerging in recent years, will also greatly change the style of interaction between human and computing devices. Context aware applications and devices capture context information from multiple sources and learn associations of context cues with personal preferences and behaviors in order to adapt the configuration of devices, the behavior of interfaces, or to offer personalized access to services. Context awareness may also enhance the usability and mitigate the increasing complexity of mobile devices. With context aware capabilities, mobile devices such as cell phones will not only act as personal communication devices but also as gateways to services in diverse environments that support personalized interactions and proactive assistance tailored to the user preferences and behaviors.

This paper concentrates on location awareness. Several location aware applications for mobile devices have actually been developed recently [9,10,11]. Learning user's important locations (called semantic locations) is one of the most important tasks in these systems. Several batch methods have been proposed to discover semantic locations. These methods try to detect important locations through geographic information

J. Hightower, B. Schiele, and T. Strang (Eds.): LoCA 2007, LNCS 4718, pp. 193–210, 2007.

system (GIS) or machine learning techniques. For example, a landmark-based location system uses cell towers of a GSM phone network to learn important places in a user's daily routine [7]. Although this approach uses existing infrastructure and is cost-efficient, the resolution of the derived places is very coarse (from about hundreds meters to a few kilometers). Therefore, GPS receivers may be employed to identify important locations instead. Some early work on location extraction with GPS uses loss of signal to infer important indoor locations [9]. That is, if GPS signal disappears and then reappears around a small region, the region is regarded as a location. Such an approach is sufficient to identify some small indoor locations such as home. However, it does not account for larger indoor locations (e.g. office complex), and is prone to generating false positives due to many possible outdoor GPS shadows. Driving speed has been also employed to identify important locations. For example, as part of their work on identifying a user's route, Patterson *et al.* can also infer mobile places, as well as the location of parking lots and bus stops with the help of real-world knowledge of bus schedules and stop locations, along with acceleration and turning speed information [12]. Liao *et al.* use mode-changes such as GPS signal loss and acceleration peaks to identify frequent locations in an unsupervised manner [8]. [6] infers the destinations from the users driving trajectories and models personal destinations as the grid cell containing endpoints of segmented trips. Learning the important locations can also be formulated as a clustering problem [3,5,17], where traditional offline clustering methods such as K-means are employed and the staying time is clearly an important factor to identify locations. However, algorithms based on K-means approach suffers the drawbacks such as required cluster number before clustering and sensitivity to noise data. To overcome the limitation of the K-mean clustering approach, a density based clustering algorithm [2] (DBSCAN) is proposed in location discovery application [14,18]. But all of the methods require the data has to be collected in advance, which are serious limitations in Mobile device applications.

As an attempt to design an efficient and effective online learning method for semantic locations, we propose an adaptive approach that models GPS data as a mixture of Gaussians, where each component is regarded as a semantic location candidate. After incrementally estimating the model with an online algorithm, the learned Gaussian mixture is evaluated to determine which components are most likely corresponding to important locations based on *a priori* probabilities. Compared to previous batch methods, our method is time efficient and requires little memory, which are highly desired in real applications.

In the area of location awareness, the discovery of user's important transportation routes is another important topic. In the paper, we also develop a method to detect user's routes based on the learned semantic locations. In the proposed method, routes are modeled as sequences of GPS data. Considering that a route can be represented by many different sequences of GPS data that are sampled at different positions, the most critical problem in our approach is how to determine if two sequences of GPS data represent the same route. We propose an effective minimax criterion to solve the issue.

Finally, we apply our adaptive learning methods for semantic locations and routes to an automatic traffic advisory application in real life. Currently, personal or car navigation systems are accurate and easy to use for navigation purposes, and they may also

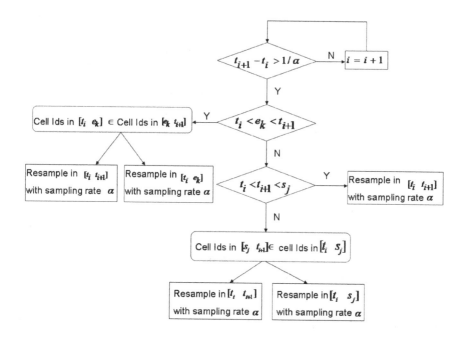

Fig. 1. Decision rule for GPS data resampling

provide real-time traffic information. However, one does not use a navigation system for daily routines – commute routes are familiar. But one typically carries a cell phone while driving. What we propose is then to let the device learn these daily commute routes and also when the routes are taken. The device will then automatically fetch traffic conditions along possible routes in anticipation (or after detection) of the user starting his/her commute, and inform the user if there are any problems. We have implemented this application with our methods on Motorola A1200/Ming cell phones and tested with different types of users, e.g. businessmen, office employees, students, etc.

The rest of the paper is organized as follows. Section 2 describes the adaptive learning method of semantic locations. In Section 3, we discuss the route learning method and minimax criterion. The automatic traffic advisory application is described in Section 4, and its evaluation in Section 5. Section 6 concludes the paper with some directions for further research.

2   Adaptive Learning of Semantic Locations

2.1   Data Preprocessing

The semantic location discovery method is based on GPS data, which include latitude and longitude[1] and are sampled every 30 seconds in our study. However, GPS signal

---

[1] Altitude, speed, and direction might also be reported by some GPS receivers.

may get lost due to various reasons, such as entering into buildings or concrete canyons in urban areas or because GPS device powers off. Therefore, re-sampling GPS data is important to obtain equally sampled data without losing the important location clusters. In the re-sampling procedure, the void GPS data are made up by repeating the last valid GPS reading, if the area where GPS signal disappeared and reappeared is covered by the same group of cell ids. The detailed re-sampling procedure is depicted in Fig. 1, where α is the GPS sampling rate , the two nearest GPS sampling times are t_{i+1} and t_i, and the corresponding GPS locations are g_{i+1} and g_i. Also, e_k denotes the time that GPS reading is invalid, and s_j denotes the last sampling time in one log file.

2.2 Adaptive Location Clustering

After re-sampling, the GPS data will be fed to the learning algorithm. Only GPS readings with speed less than 5 miles/hour will be considered to learn the stationary locations.

The adaptive algorithm is a sequential method that process only a small amount of GPS data each time. The algorithm continuously adapts the learned model with new GPS readings. More precisely, we model the GPS data as a mixture of locations with noise, where each location follows a Gaussian distribution. Given new GPS readings, an on-line algorithm is employed to update the model, i.e. adding/deleting/merging locations, updating the parameters of Gaussian mixture model, etc. Now consider a set of sequential GPS readings $\{g_1, \ldots, g_t\}$ in time order, where

$$g_i = [x_i, y_i]' \quad 1 \leq i \leq t$$

and x, y are GPS coordinates. Assume at the moment t that the true but unknown density of GPS value g is of the form

$$p(g|\theta_t) = \sum_{\ell=1}^{N_t} \pi_t^\ell \phi(g; \mu_t^\ell, \Sigma_t^\ell)$$

where $N_t < \infty$ is the number of components which may vary with time, parameter vector $\theta_t = \{\pi_t^1, \mu_t^1, \Sigma_t^1, \ldots, \pi_t^{N_t}, \mu_t^{N_t}, \Sigma_t^{N_t}\}$; the nonnegative mixing coefficients π_t^ℓ ($\ell = 1, \ldots, N_t$) sum to unity and

$$\phi(g; \mu_t^\ell, \Sigma_t^\ell) = \frac{1}{2\pi|\Sigma_t^\ell|^{\frac{1}{2}}} \exp^{-\frac{1}{2}(g-\mu_t^\ell)'(\Sigma_t^\ell)^{-1}(g-\mu_t^\ell)}$$

is the Gaussian probability density function with 2 dimensional mean μ_t^ℓ and covariance Σ_t^ℓ. For simplicity, the covariance matrix is assumed to be a diagonal matrix.

At time t, the number of Gaussians N_t in the mixture model represents the number of significant location candidates, the weight of Gaussians π_t^ℓ ($\ell = 1, \ldots, N_t$) denote the significance of the learned locations, and the mean μ_t^ℓ and variance value Σ_t^ℓ in each Gaussian specifies the important location center and size. Below, we will describe how to adapt the mixture model's parameters as well as the structures with the new coming observations.

Decision Rule

When a new GPS reading arrives, it will first be fed to the decision rule to determine if it belongs to a known semantic location (i.e. one of components in current Gaussian mixture) or a new location. If it belongs to one of known locations, update rule will be employed to update the current Gaussian mixture model with the new reading. Otherwise, a new component/location will be added to the model by creating rule. The decision can be made in a number of ways. The simplest is to check the Mahalanobis distance from the observation to the center of each component of Gaussian mixture. If the minimum of these distances exceeds a threshold (denoted T_D) then the observation point is in some sense too far away from the existing components, and a new component should be created. The square of the Mahalanobis distance between a point g_t and a component with the mean μ_{t-1}^ℓ and the standard deviation Σ_{t-1}^ℓ is defined by $M(z_t; \mu_{t-1}^\ell, \Sigma_{t-1}^\ell) = (g_t - \mu_{t-1}^\ell)'(\Sigma_{t-1}^\ell)^{-1}(g_t - \mu_{t-1}^\ell), 1 \le \ell \le N_{t-1}$. The following binary indicator function $D_t(\cdot)$ is employed in our system.

$$D_t(g_t, \hat{\theta}_{t-1}) = \begin{cases} 1 & \min_{1 \le \ell \le N_{t-1}} M(g_t; \mu_{t-1}^\ell, \Sigma_{t-1}^\ell) > T_D \\ 0 & \text{otherwise} \end{cases} \tag{1}$$

Update Rule

In this case, the number of components N_t in the mixture will not be changed. A batch method can use all observations up to the current time $\mathbf{g}_{1:t} = \{g_1, \dots, g_t\}$ to estimate the parameter vector θ_t. However, it requires that mobile devices store all historical data, which is not feasible in practice. Instead, we use a recursive EM algorithm to estimate/update the model [1,15]. Let $\beta_t = \frac{1}{t}$ and $\rho_t^\ell = \pi_{t-1}^\ell \frac{\phi^\ell(g_t)}{\hat{p}_t(g_t)}$, then

$$\pi_t^\ell = \pi_{t-1}^\ell + \beta_{t-1}\left[\rho_t^\ell - \pi_{t-1}^\ell\right]$$

$$\mu_t^\ell = \mu_{t-1}^\ell + \frac{\rho_t^\ell \beta_{t-1}}{\pi_{t-1}^\ell}(g_t - \mu_{t-1}^\ell) \tag{2}$$

$$\Sigma_t^\ell = \Sigma_{t-1}^\ell + \frac{\rho_t^\ell \beta_{t-1}}{\pi_{t-1}^\ell}\left[(g_t - \mu_{t-1}^\ell)(g_t - \mu_{t-1}^\ell)^T - \Sigma_{t-1}^\ell\right]$$

Convergence results regarding the above recursive update rule have been given in [15]. The procedure (2) is called *update rule*.

The learned weights in the Gaussian mixture model represent the size of the clusters or the number of points in a cluster. It denotes how long time the user spends at those locations. However, this definition ignores locations that user frequently visits but stays for a brief time (e.g. dropping child off for school every day). Meanwhile, a location (e.g. travel attraction) that user visits rarely but stays for a long time, would be temporarily misclassified as an important location. To solve the problem, we need also record the number of visits for each location. The weight f_t^ℓ of visit frequency for each location needs also be updated online.

Denote v_t^ℓ as the visit detection for location cluster ℓ, then

$$v_t^\ell = \begin{cases} 1 & \text{if user just enter into location } \ell \text{ boundary} \\ 0 & \text{otherwise} \end{cases}$$

Therefore, at time t, the total number of visits for all locations is $M_t = M_{t-1} + \sum_{\ell=1}^{N_t} v_t^\ell$, and $M_0 = 0$. Similarly to the update procedure for the weight in the mixture model, the weight of the visit frequency f_t^ℓ for location ℓ can also be updated as

$$f_t^\ell = f_{t-1}^\ell + \gamma_{t-1}[v_t^\ell - f_{t-1}^\ell] \tag{3}$$

where $\gamma_t = \frac{(M_t - M_{t-1})}{M_t}$.

Then the importance of a location is defind by the adjusted weight

$$\varpi_t^\ell = \alpha \pi_t^\ell + (1 - \alpha) f_t^\ell$$

where $\alpha \in [0, 1]$. With this linear combination, both how long and how often the user stays and visits in a location are considered in determining the importance of a location. Parameter α controls the compromise between the two factors, usually we use $\alpha = 0.5$ to treat the visit time and frequency with equal importance.

Creating Rule

When a new GPS reading does not belong to any current components, a new Guassian component is added to the mixture. To obtain the creating rule, $\hat{\theta}_t = \vartheta_t(g_t, \beta_t, \gamma_t, \hat{\theta}_{t-1})$, we notice the fact that the kernel estimator based on t observations is closely related to the kernel estimator based on $t - 1$ observations.

$$\mu_t^{N_t} = g_t$$
$$\Sigma_t^{N_t} = \Sigma_t^0$$
$$\pi_t^\ell = \pi_{t-1}^\ell (1 - \beta_t) \tag{4}$$
$$\pi_t^{N_t} = \beta_t$$
$$f_t^\ell = f_{t-1}^\ell (1 - \gamma_t)$$
$$f_t^{N_t} = \gamma_t$$

where $N_t = N_{t-1} + 1$ and $\ell = 1, \ldots, N_{t-1}$. Σ_t^0 may be user defined or derived from the terms in the neighborhood of the observations. Creating rule can be also used to initialize the mixture density with $\mu_1^1 = g_1$, $\Sigma_1^1 = \Sigma_t^0$ and $\pi_1^1 = 1$.

For learning the important locations, the GPS distribution is time variant due the changes of the user's daily life. When the GPS distribution changes, the new components will always be added in. The complexity may not be controlled. An intelligent system also needs to prune the unnecessary components (i.e. remove locations that user stops visiting), and merge close nearby components. In what follows, the pruning rule and merging rule for these purposes are described in detail.

Pruning Rule

The purpose of the pruning rule is to discard the redundant components in the mixture which do not entertain current observations anymore. How to select the pruning candidates is based on the Bayesian hypothesis test.

Denote C_t^ℓ the ℓth Gaussian component of current model, where $\ell = 1, \ldots, N_t$. Let $P(C_t^\ell) = \varpi_t^\ell$ and

$$p(g_t | C_t^\ell) = \frac{1}{2\pi |\Sigma_t^\ell|^{1/2}} \exp^{-\frac{1}{2}(g_t - \mu_t^\ell)'(\Sigma_t^\ell)^{-1}(g_t - \mu_t^\ell)}$$

The probability that the observation g_t belongs to the ℓth Gaussian component in the mixture is

$$P(C_t^\ell | g_t) = \frac{p(g_t | C_t^\ell) P(C_t^\ell)}{p(g_k)}$$

Therefore, for the Gaussian component ℓ_1 and ℓ_2 in the mixture, if

$$P(C_t^{\ell_1} | g_t) > P(C_t^{\ell_2} | g_t) \tag{5}$$

the component ℓ_2 is more likely to be selected as the pruning candidate. According to the 3σ property of Gaussian distribution, $\exp[-\frac{1}{2}(g_t - \mu_t^\ell)'(\Sigma_t^\ell)^{-1}(g_t - \mu_k^\ell)]$ is close to 0 when $(g_t - \mu_t^\ell)'(\Sigma_t^\ell)^{-1}(g_t - \mu_k^\ell) > 9$ for g_t that does not belong to the component ℓ. Eq. (5) can be written as

$$\pi_t^{\ell_1} > \pi_t^{\ell_2}$$

Because we adjust the location cluster weight by also considering the visiting frequency of the location, the candidate components to be discarded from the mixture model are selected from those that $D_t(g_t, \hat{\theta}_{t-1}) = 1$ with $\varpi_t^\ell < T_P$, where T_p is a preset threshold. After dropping the existing terms in the mixture, the maintained mixture model weights π_t^ℓ $(\ell = 1, \ldots, N_t)$ need to be re-normalized.

Generally, one can pre-set the largest number $N_{\max}$ of Gaussians to be allowed in the mixture model according to the system requirement. When the mixture model meets this bound, as the decision rule detects that a new component needs to be added into the mixture model, we can replace the old component with the new one. The candidate component for replacing can also be chosen by the Pruning rule.

Pruning Threshold Selection
At time t_0, when the new component ℓ is added into the mixture model, we usually allow several days of adaptation to adjust visit time weight $\pi_{t_0}^\ell$ and visit frequency weight $f_{t_0}^\ell$. To determine a reasonable pruning threshold T_p, there are some general rules. As discussed above, the initial weights $\pi_{t_0}^\ell$ and $f_{t_0}^\ell$ for the new components are often set as $\bar{\beta}$ and $\bar{f}$ respectively. Meanwhile, the current learning rates are adjusted as $\beta_{t_0} = \bar{\beta}$ and $f_{t_0} = \bar{f}$. Therefore, if the ℓth component in the mixture does not entertain the observations for T days, it has

$$\pi_{t_0+T}^\ell = (1 - \beta_{t_0+T}) \cdots (1 - \beta_{t_0+1})(1 - \beta_{t_0})\pi_{t_0}^\ell$$
$$f_{t_0+T}^\ell = (1 - \gamma_{t_0+T}) \cdots (1 - \gamma_{t_0+1})(1 - \gamma_{t_0})\pi_{t_0}^\ell$$

since $\beta_{t_0+i} = \frac{\beta_{t_0}}{i\beta_{t_0}+1}$, then

$$\pi_{t_0+T}^\ell = (1 - \frac{\beta_{t_0}}{T\beta_{t_0}+1})(1 - \frac{\beta_{t_0}}{(T-1)\beta_{t_0}+1}) \cdots (1 - \beta_{t_0})\pi_{t_0}^\ell$$
$$= \frac{(T-1)\beta_{t_0}+1}{T\beta_{t_0}+1} \cdot \frac{(T-2)\beta_{t_0}+1}{(T-1)\beta_{t_0}+1} \cdots (1 - \beta_{t_0})\pi_{t_0}^\ell$$
$$= \frac{(1 - \beta_{t_0})}{T\beta_{t_0}+1} \cdot \pi_{t_0}^\ell = \frac{(1 - \bar{\beta})}{T\bar{\beta}+1} \cdot \bar{\beta}$$

Similarly,

$$f^\ell_{t_0+T} \geq \frac{(1-\bar{f})}{T\bar{f}+1} \cdot \bar{f}$$

Therefore, we may specify the pruning threshold as

$$T_P \geq \alpha\frac{(1-\bar{\beta})\bar{\beta}}{(T\bar{\beta}+1)} + (1-\alpha)\frac{(1-\bar{f})}{T\bar{f}+1} \cdot \bar{f}$$

Merging Rule

The merging rule $\hat{\theta}_t = M(\hat{\theta}_t)$ combines two Gaussian components into a single Gaussian when the two components in the mixture model are very close to each other.

Suppose the two Gaussian components are

$$p(g|C_{\ell_1}) = N(g, \mu^{\ell_1}, \Sigma^{\ell_1})\quad P(C_{\ell_1}) = \pi^{\ell_1}$$
$$p(g|C_{\ell_2}) = N(g, \mu^{\ell_2}, \Sigma^{\ell_2})\quad P(C_{\ell_2}) = \pi^{\ell_2}$$

In probability theory, Kullback-Leibler Divergence is a quantity which measures the difference between two probability distributions. For two Gaussian distributions

$$KL(p(g|C_{\ell_1}); p(g|C_{\ell_2})) + KL(p(g|C_{\ell_2}); p(g|C_{\ell_1}))$$
$$= 0.5(|(\Sigma^{\ell_2})^{-1}\Sigma^{\ell_1}| + |(\Sigma^{\ell_1})^{-1}\Sigma^{\ell_2}|)$$
$$+ 0.5(\mu^{\ell_1} - \mu^{\ell_2})'[(\Sigma^{\ell_1})^{-1} + (\Sigma^{\ell_2})^{-1}](\mu^{\ell_1} - \mu^{\ell_2}) - n$$

When

$$KL(p(g|C_{\ell_1}); p(g|C_{\ell_2})) + KL(p(g|C_{\ell_2}); p(g|C_{\ell_1})) < \varepsilon$$

we can merge two Gaussian components $p(g|C_{\ell_1})$ and $p(g|C_{\ell_2})$ into one $p(g|C_{\ell'}) = N(g, \mu^\ell, \Sigma^\ell)$ and obviously $\pi^\ell = \pi^{\ell_1} + \pi^{\ell_2}$, $f^\ell = f^{\ell_1} + f^{\ell_2}$ and

$$\mu^\ell = E(g|C_\ell) = \frac{\mu^{\ell_1}\pi^{\ell_1} + \mu^{\ell_2}\pi^{\ell_2}}{\pi^{\ell_1} + \pi^{\ell_2}}$$
$$\Sigma^\ell = E(g^2|C_\ell) - \mu^\ell(\mu^\ell)'$$
$$= \frac{(\Sigma^{\ell_1} + \mu^{\ell_1}\mu^{\ell_1'})\pi^{\ell_1} + (\Sigma^{\ell_2} + \mu^{\ell_2}\mu^{\ell_2'})\pi^{\ell_2}}{\pi^{\ell_1} + \pi^{\ell_2}} - \mu^\ell\mu^{\ell'}$$

As we have seen, the pruning rule and merging rule are used to eliminate the unnecessary components and merge similar components. The two described procedures can keep the most efficient model for a time varying GPS distribution at the same time saving computation and memory.

Learning Rate Adjustment

In the above adaptive location clustering process, β_t is the learning rate for the parameter adaptation of the Gaussian mixture model. The convergence result regarding the recursive update formula (2) with β_t converging to 0 have been given by [15]. However, as an online location learning process, a small learning rate will result in a slow adaptation to the current situation, i.e., the new location cluster will need long time to become significant in the system, comparably, the learned location clusters are very lowly to be pruned from the system. To solve this problem, we set a lower bound for the learning rate β_t. When $\beta_t < \beta_L$, reset $\beta_t = \bar{\beta}$. Here $\bar{\beta} > \beta_L$. Also, when the system decides to create a new location cluster and $\beta_t < \bar{\beta}$, we also reset $\beta_t = \bar{\beta}$. That is, all new location clusters are adjusted with the same learning rate from beginning.

The proposed learning rate adjustment makes the system more flexible in adjusting to changes. Therefore, user's daily life will be timely updated in the system. The same technique can be applied on the learning rate γ_t to adapt the weight of visit frequency.

2.3   Identification of Semantic Locations

In location learning process, the location clusters are represented by the major components in the mixture model. The adjustment weights in the mixture model denote the significance of the locations. However, not all location clusters are significant since some location clusters are recently added to the model and need time to be justified. The location clusters only provide the candidates of the important locations. To determine the significant locations, at time t, we need evaluate the adjusted weight $\varpi_t^1 \geq \varpi_t^2 \geq \cdots \geq \varpi_t^{N_t}$, and pick the top N corresponding location clusters such that $\sum_{\ell=1}^{N} \varpi_t^\ell \geq 95\%$ and $\sum_{\ell=1}^{N-1} \varpi_t^\ell < 95\%$, where $0 < N \leq N_t$, which are regarded as important semantic locations.

3   Discovery of Routes

The discovery of transportation routes is another important topic in location awareness. Currently, most route learning methods are based on geographic information systems (GIS). Because our system runs on cell phone with limited computing and storage resources, we instead use raw GPS data sequences to represent routes. A GPS data sequence between an important location pair is denoted as a route. The starting point and ending point of the route involves detecting that the user leaves one important location boundary and enters into another important location boundary. In fact, through location clustering, the cluster boundaries also serve as the important location boundaries.

Although it is easy to extract GPS data sequence between two locations as routes, it is not straightforward to determine if two sequences represent the same routes. Note that people often have several different daily routes for the same location pair. The system has to distinguish them for providing traffic information by comparing GPS data sequences.

To solve the problem, we developed a minimax criterion to compare two routes. Suppose two routes of GPS sequences are

$$R_1 = \{g_1^1, g_2^1, \ldots, g_n^1\} \text{ and } R_2 = \{g_1^2, g_2^2, \ldots, g_m^2\}$$

The best match of R_1 in terms of R_2 is

$$\hat{R}_1 = \{\hat{g}_1^1, \hat{g}_2^1, \ldots, \hat{g}_n^1\}$$

where $\hat{g}_i^1 = \arg\min_{g_j^2} ||g_i^1 - g_j^2||$. Similarly, $\hat{R}_2 = \{\hat{g}_1^2, \hat{g}_2^2, \ldots, \hat{g}_m^2\}$ is the best match R_2 in terms of R_1, where $\hat{g}_j^2 = \arg\min_{g_i^1} ||g_i^1 - g_j^2||$.

We regarded two routes as the same if

$$\max ||g_i^1 - \hat{g}_i^1|| < d_2 \text{ and } \max ||g_j^2 - \hat{g}_j^2|| < d_1$$

where d_1 and d_2 are the largest sampling intervals of R_1 and R_2, respectively.

With the adaptive location clustering, the significant locations are gradually discovered and updated. Once an important location pairs are identified, the commute routes between them are recorded and learned. Through the route comparison, the unique ones are saved in the database. The unique routes do not distinguish the directions, i.e., the route that user moves from place A to place B or moves from place B to place A are treated as the same. The frequencies of the routes are counted in terms of the starting location and the destination in an hourly base.

4   Automatic Traffic Advisory

Based on the proposed methods of learning semantic locations and transportation routes, a software agent on cell phone to automatically notify the user of traffic conditions as the user starts driving. The system will start predicting the transportation route only when the user's driving intention is predicted. Currently, without additional information, we relay only on the GPS information. When the system finds from GPS location and speed information that the user is leaving a boundary of one of the important locations, it will start inferring the destination and transportation route of the user,

Fig. 2. Screen shots of the application. Left side depicts a textual pop-up alert, right side the map view of the alert.

which is based on current location and time (other conditions could be included in future). We have developed prototype which is a client-server system. The client collects GPS data (through Bluetooth connection to a receiver) and cell IDs and learns semantic locations and routes between them with our adaptive algorithm. An easy to use user interface is also developed to alert users about problematic traffic situations (Fig.2).

The server side provides map, real-time traffic, and other information to clients based on J2EE. The communication between clients and the server side is based on standard HTTP protocol. An option to use free traffic services available in the Internet is provided, too.

5 Experiments

We have tested our traffic advisory system and thus our adaptive learning algorithms with fourteen users who used our system on a regular basis over a period of time. In this section, we will evaluate our algorithms and compare them with existing methods.

5.1 Context Data Acquisition

Fourteen participants have taken part in this study. These participants come from three groups of interest: students, office employees, and independents. The student group consists of six undergraduate students. The office employer group consists of five persons who worked in regular business days at a fixed location. The independents group includes persons who were either stay-at-home parents or business people who did not work consistently in an office environment (e.g. realtors).

Each participant was provided with a commercially available mobile phone equipped with Bluetooth, along with a separate Bluetooth GPS receiver to acquire location data. Data logging software was installed on the mobile phone. Each participant used the phone and the GPS receiver for a two- to three-month period.

The logged context variables consist of the following:

- GPS data from a Bluetooth GPS receiver,
- Current GSM cell id,
- Bluetooth devices around the phone,
- Phone profile,
- Active phone application,
- Phone idle/active time,
- Battery status and charger status,
- Incoming/Outgoing calls, SMS-messages, multimedia messages,
- User interaction with the Phonebook and recent call log,
- Media captured with the device (photos, audio, video, text).

The data is uploaded over the air to our web server, transparent to the user. Logged data consists of events and a time stamp followed by the event. GPS data and Bluetooth status are logged every 30 seconds. Any other variable is logged as its status changes.

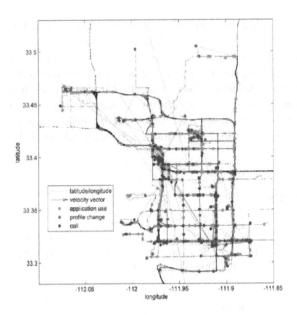

Fig. 3. Visualization of one subject's data base. User's GPS coordinates are plotted together with selected phone application events.

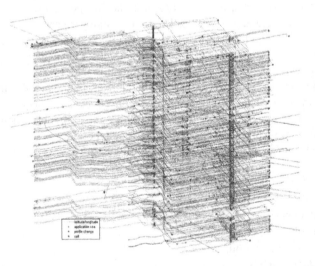

Fig. 4. Visualization of one subject's data base. User's GPS coordinates (x,y) and time (z) plotted together with certain phone application events. Time covers about five months and is increasing from bottom to top.

5.2   Data Visualization

As our focus is in user's routes, in order to visualize how and where the phone is used, GPS coordinates can be plotted together with the use of phone applications (Fig 3). GPS coordinates depict the roads on which the participant has travelled. Figure 3 is cropped to cover only the local metropolitan area.

Time can be added in the visualization as the z-coordinate (Fig. 4). This figure illustrates two important facts. First, there are a small number of seemingly important locations where the phone has been used. These become now explicit as "columns of activities" in Figure 4. We can see that there are four major location clusters of phone activities. Second, the user's daily commute routes, as well as weekend routines, become visible. Figure 4 clearly demonstrates that it is not only possible to learn the routes from the data but also to predict them.

5.3 Location Learning

To evaluate the location learning feature in the traffic advisory system, the developed adaptive location learning algorithm is compared with the batched learning method. We employ the batched algorithm, DBSCAN [2,14] (density-based clustering) algorithm, because it can automatically find the number of clusters, identify outliers, work well for arbitrary-shaped clusters, and is also very efficient for large datasets.

In the study, we first evaluate the algorithms on one office employee who worked in regular business days at a fixed location. Both batched and adaptive algorithms are applied on the re-sampled GPS data, the comparison results for important location discovery are generated for the first day (Jan-15-2006), first week (Jan-15-2006 to Jan-21-2006) and first month (Jan-15-2006 to Feb-15-2006) respectively. The visualization results of the discovered significant locations are shown in Figure 8, 9, and 10. The corresponding weight of each discovered location for both batched and adaptive methods are listed in Table 1. In fact, given the latitude and longitude of learned location, we can obtain the semantic location's geocode information (street number and name, city, etc.) by searching reverse geocode database. Then user can easily identify locations as home, office, etc. based on the geocode information and map.

Table 1. Significant location learning methods comparison

			Home	Office	Gym	University	School
First Day	DBSCAN	weight	0.8355		**0.1583**		**0.0062**
	Adaptive	weight	0.7583		0.1889		0.0474
		frequency	0.5714		0.1429		0.2857
		adjusted weight	0.6649		**0.1659**		**0.1666**
First Week	DBSCAN	weight	0.8508	0.0214	0.0235 0.0804	0.0111	0.0051
	Adaptive	weight	0.7910	0.0193	0.0965	0.0148	0.0083
		frequency	0.4359	0.1026	0.1538	0.0256	0.1795
		adjusted weight	0.6134	0.0609	0.1252	0.0202	0.0939
First Month	DBSCAN	weight	0.8333	0.0206	0.1073	0.0117	0.0049
	Adaptive	weight	0.6227	0.1283	0.0075 0.1104	0.0038 0.0193 0.0383	0.0085
		frequency	0.3557	0.1237	0.0258 0.1804	0.0103 0.0361 0.0928	0.1031
		adjusted weight	0.4892	0.1260	0.0166 0.1454	0.0071 0.0277 0.0655	0.0558

Table 2. Frequencies for routes from home to office

Route ID	4	8	25	26	27	28	29	30
frequency	0.6	0.1429	0.0286	0.1143	0.0286	0.0286	0.0286	0.0286

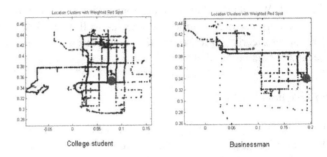

College student   Businessman

Fig. 5. Location discovery in terms of different users

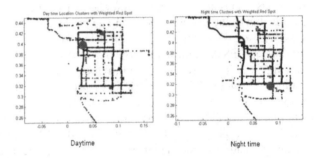

Daytime   Night time

Fig. 6. Location discovery in terms of different time intervals

After the first day, the discovered locations by both batched and adaptive methods match very well. The adjustment weight ω generated by adaptive method provides the significance measure for the locations with considering visit duration as well as visit frequencies. For example, in the first day, the adaptive method finds that "School" where the user drops his child off is comparably as important as "Gym" (Table 2). Although the visit time of the "School" is much shorter than "Gym", "School" has been visited twice for that day. In the first week, compared with the batched method, adaptive method discovered location L_0 instead of L_1 (Fig. 9). Since adaptive method adjusts the parameters online, through update, location L_1 which was visited early this week is already discarded from the significant location candidates due to the short visit time and low visit frequency (only one visit for that week). Instead, location L_0 which has been visited most recently got higher initial weight and then becomes more important than location L_1. The same reason on first month's data (Fig. 10) results obtaining location L_3 instead of L_2 from adaptive learning method. Meanwhile, both algorithms can discover several nearby locations in certain large areas, i.e. "University" campus area and "Gym".

The adaptive location discovery algorithm can also be evaluated in terms of different users, different time intervals, and different activities. Fig.5,6,7 display the prominent

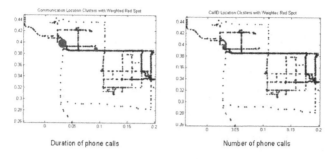

Fig. 7. Location discovery in terms of different activities

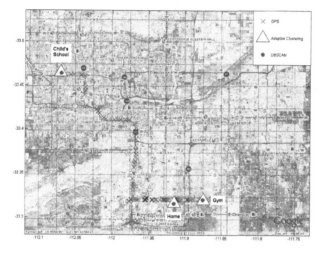

Fig. 8. Visualization of one subject's first day data. User's GPS coordinates are plotted together with important locations.

location clusters (red spots) for different cases. The size of the red spots represents the weight of the clusters.

This comparison clearly shows that the proposed location learning algorithm is effective in location identification and can adapt to the user's daily life. A further evaluation results based on the interview the users are still conducting in our lab and will be reported in our future work.

5.4   Frequent Route Learning

Once the important locations become available, the transportation routes between the location pairs, i.e. GPS sequences, are recorded in the system. With the proposed mini-max criterion, the unique routes are detected and the most frequent ones are discovered. In our study on the same user's data, after two month learning, 47 unique routes from total of 170 routes are obtained.

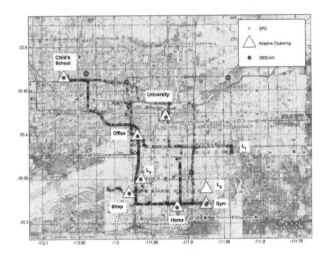

Fig. 9. Visualization of one subject's first week data. User's GPS coordinates are plotted together with important locations.

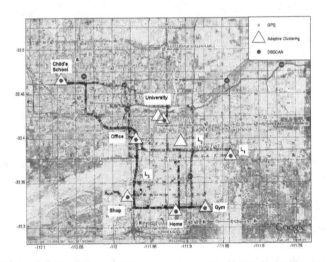

Fig. 10. Visualization of one subject's first month data. User's GPS coordinates are plotted together with important locations.

The route frequency is derived by considering all different routes starting from Location A to Location B. As an example, we show the route frequencies from "home" to "office" in Table 2, and those from "office" to "home" in Table 3.

Naturally, the most frequent route is simple to obtain once we have the frequency for each route between semantic locations. We select the most frequent routes between location A to B to cover 95% of total routes. Figure 11 displays the most frequent routes for different hour and different location pairs.

Table 3. Frequencies for routes from office to home

Route ID	8	28	35	36	37	38	39	40	41
frequency	0.4643	0.2143	0.03576	0.0357	0.0357	0.0714	0.0714	0.0357	0.0357

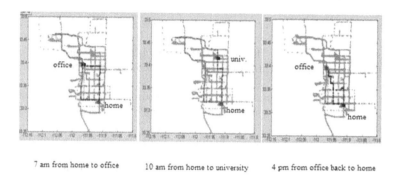

7 am from home to office   10 am from home to university   4 pm from office back to home

Fig. 11. Frequent routes

6 Conclusion

In the paper, we proposed adaptive learning methods of semantic locations and transportation routes, which are able to stably discover sematic locations and routes and
reliably track the changes of user's daily life. Based on them we have developed a cell
phone based automatic traffic advisory system. We envision that context aware and per-
sonalization features will become essential in supporting new applications and concepts
that connect consumers with media and services through multiple devices in the office,
car, or home.

References

1. Dempster, A.P., Laird, N.M., Rubin, D.B.: Maximum likelihood form incomplete data via
   the EM algorithm. Journal of Royal Statistical Society, 1–38 (1977)
2. Ester, M., et al.: A Density-Based Algorithm for Discovering Clusters in Large Spatial
   Databases with Noise. In: Proc. of KDD (1996)
3. Hariharan, R., Toyama, K.: Project Lachesis: Parsing and Modeling Location Histories. In:
   Proc. of International Conference on Geographic Information Science (2004)
4. Horvitz, E., Jacobs, A., Hovel, D.: Attention-sensitive alerting. In: Proc. of UAI'99 conference on Uncertainty in Artificial Intelligence, pp. 305–313. Stockholm, Sweden (1999)
5. Kang, J.H., Welbourne, W.: Extracting Places from Traces of Locations. In: Proc. WMASH
   (2004)
6. Krumm, J., Horvitz, E.: Predestination: Inferring Destinations from Partial Trajectories. In:
   Dourish, P., Friday, A. (eds.) UbiComp 2006. LNCS, vol. 4206, Springer, Heidelberg (2006)
7. Laasonen, K., et al.: Adaptive On-Device Location Recognition. In: Proc. of Pervasive (2004)
8. Liao, L., et al.: Learning and Inferring Transportation Routines. In: Proc. of AAAI (2004)

9. Marmasse, N., Schmandt, C.: Location-aware information delivery with comMotion. In: Proc. of International Symposium on Handheld and Ubiquitous Computing, Bristol, UK, pp. 157–171 (September 2000)
10. Marmasse, N., Schmandt, C.: A User-Centered location model. Personal and Ubiquitous Computing 6(5-6), 318–332 (2002)
11. Marmasse, N., Schmandt, C., Spectre, D.: WatchMe: communication and awareness between members of a closely-knit group. Proc. of Ubicomp 2004: Ubiquitous Computing, 214–231 (2004)
12. Patterson, D.J., et al.: Inferring High-Level Behavior from Low-Level Sensors. In: Dey, A.K., Schmidt, A., McCarthy, J.F. (eds.) UbiComp 2003. LNCS, vol. 2864, Springer, Heidelberg (2003)
13. Priebe, C.E.: Adaptive mixtures. Journal of American statistical Association, 796–806 (1994)
14. Tang, J., Meng, L.: Learning significant locations from GPS data with time window. In: Proc. of SPIE, vol. 6418 (2006)
15. Titterington, D.M.: Recursive parameter estimation using incomplete data. Journal of Royal Statistical Society, 257–267 (1984)
16. Nurmi, P., Koolwaaij, J.: Identifying meanful locations. Proc. of Third Annual International Conference on Mobile and Ubiquitous Systems: Networking & Services, 1–8 (2006)
17. Ashbrook, D., Starner, T.: Using GPS to learn significant locations and predict movement across multiple users. Journal of Personal and Ubiquitous Computing 7(5), 275–286 (2004)
18. Zhou, C., Shekhar, S., Terveen, L.: Discovering personal paths from sparse GPS Traces. In: Proc. of 1st Internatioanl Workshop on Data Mining in conjunction with 8th Joint Conference on Information Sciences (2005)

Signal Dragging: Effects of Terminal Movement on War-Driving in CDMA/WCDMA Networks

Daehyung Jo[1], Jeongkeun Lee[1], Semun Lee[1], Taejoon Ha[2], Taekyoung Kwon[1], and Yanghee Choi[1]

[1] School of Computer Science and Engineering, Seoul National University
{cdh,jklee,smlee,tk,yhchoi}@mmlab.snu.ac.kr
[2] Radiant Technologies, Inc.
tjha@radiantech.net

Abstract. In cellular networks, the signal pattern reported by a mobile terminal has been the major source for localization. In this paper we show how the signal pattern is affected by the terminal movement such as the speed and the moving direction in CDMA/WCDMA networks. When the mobile terminal is moving, its signal pattern tends to contain more signals from base stations positioned opposite of the terminal's moving direction than signals from base stations positioned in the forward. We call this phenomenon *"signal dragging"*. If the signal dragging prevails, it naturally provides a useful hint for figuring out the movement of a terminal, e.g., direction. We also show that the accuracy of the localization algorithm based on pattern matching varies greatly depending on the terminal movement. Based on these experimental results in commercial networks we suggest the practical data collection procedure, e.g., the war-driving, should consider the terminal movement. Otherwise the use of war-driving data can be harmful.

1 Introduction

[1]Recent advances in ubiquitous computing applications and location-based services (LBSs) have necessitated the network-based localization of mobile terminals. The cellular phones and many other hand-held mobile devices become the core of LBS applications such as E-911, location-aware information search, and car navigation. Although GPS provides fairly accurate location estimates in open areas, its applicability becomes very limited where line-of-sight (LOS) paths to four or more satellites are not guaranteed: for example, indoor areas, narrow street canyons of urban areas, and deep mountain valley. GPS also requires additional hardware equipments on mobile terminals, which increases manufacturing cost.

To overcome the limitation of GPS, academia and industrial communities have made great efforts for the network-based localization technologies especially for the mobile terminals in cellular networks. Every base station (BS)

---

[1] This work was supported in part by MIC & IITA through IT Leading R&D Support Project and the Brain Korea 21 project of Ministry of Education, 2007, Korea.

J. Hightower, B. Schiele, and T. Strang (Eds.): LoCA 2007, LNCS 4718, pp. 211–227, 2007.

broadcasts its own identifier (Cell-ID), which enables the mobile terminal to estimate its position roughly. For more precise positioning, a number of proposed solutions have utilized the propagation delay, time-difference-of-arrival (TDOA) [20] [22], antenna orientation or received-signal-strength (RSS). Without the LOS path between a transmitter and a receiver, the distance calculated from the propagation time can be erroneous. TDOA localization requires time synchronization among BSs, which is not fulfilled in GSM and UMTS but only in CDMA networks. The orientation and the angle opening of sector antenna can be used to increase the positioning accuracy. Many service providers, however, do not maintain the orientation, opening and tilting information of each sector antenna.

Compared to the above mentioned parameters, the RSS is commonly available parameter for all types of wireless networks. Many localization techniques proposed for cellular networks such as pattern matching (PM) [7] [10], particle filter [17] [18] [19], (weighted) centroid [6] [8], and Cell-ID [23] depend on the RSS information. In the PM localization system, for example, signal patterns are measured a priori over the entire service area and stored in a pattern database. The position of the terminal is then determined by comparing the terminal's currently reported signal pattern to the database entries and finding the best-matching location.

In this paper, however, we show that *the movement context of a mobile terminal highly affects its signal pattern, eventually the performance of some RSS-based localization systems.* From our WCDMA and CDMA measurement data obtained from two metropolitan cities: Seoul, Korea and Seattle, USA, we have observed that signal patterns measured at the same position can be highly deviating depending on the movement context such as direction and speed. In particular, our major finding is the *"signal dragging"* phenomenon: when the mobile terminal is moving, its signal pattern tends to contain more signals from the BSs positioned opposite of the terminal's moving direction than signals from BSs positioned in the forward direction. This finding indicates the caveats of using war-driving data [5]. When the accuracy of a localization system is evaluated through benchmark tests, test data set is normally obtained by war-driving: we drive a car around the test area with mobile terminals and other measurement equipments. The signal patterns for the pattern database are normally measured by war-driving, too. When a terminal requests its localization to the pattern matching system, the terminal may be stationary or moving in the opposite direction of the war-driving car, which can generate unexpectedly poor localization performance. Therefore the use of war-driving data not considering the movement context of a terminal can be harmful.

Our contributions are the following: (i) we investigate how the movement of a terminal affects its signal pattern and why this signal dragging happens, (ii) we show how localization accuracy is affected by the terminal's movement, and (iii) we demonstrate some applications of this finding: the direction of a moving terminal can be roughly estimated with only one current signal pattern without any signal pattern history.

This paper is organized as follows: Section 2 describes the concept of the signal dragging and its error metric. Section 3 and 4 present the properties and implications of the signal dragging, respectively. Section 5 explains why the signal dragging occurs from a technical perspective. Section 6 outlines related work, and we conclude in Section 7.

2   The Effect of Movement

In this section, based on our measurement data, we show how the movement of a terminal affects the signal pattern reported.

2.1   Signal Pattern Data

To prepare and perform a handover, a mobile terminal continuously measures signal strengths from both the serving BS that communicates with and other surrounding BSs. The serving BS also informs the mobile terminal of a list of adjacent cells which it should monitor. Mobile terminals automatically reports the signal pattern to the network when performing a location update procedure.[2] This signal pattern normally consists of many pairs of a BS identifier and its RSS value ([BS ID, RSS]). Thus, the signal pattern information is continuously maintained by a terminal and is accessible by a localization module in a mobile terminal.

When we seek to investigate network characteristics or to optimize the cell planning of the network, signal patterns are measured normally through war-driving. Especially if we perform the network-based localization without the help of GPS, signal patterns are the only source of information to estimate the terminal's position. Therefore understanding the characteristics of signal patterns is crucial for the localization and the network management.

Our signal pattern data used in this paper includes WCDMA measurements in Seoul, Korea and Seattle, USA; and CDMA measurements in Seoul, Korea. We used the Inno Wireless OPTis-S diagnostic module attaching SiRF3 chipset based GPS devices and mobile terminals, LG SV900 for CDMA measurements and Samsung W120 and LG CU500 for WCDMA measurements. Fig. 1 shows the measurement area in Seoul, in which we collected WCDMA data sets.[3] The positions of BSs are depicted by circles and given by operators; thus, they are fairly accurate. However, seven more BSs have been deployed in the area of Fig. 1 after we got the BS position database from the operator, which contribute to the experimental errors to some extent.

---

[2] This report is called *Network Measurement Report (NMR)* in a GSM network and NMR in GSM only contains the records of up to six or seven strongest signal strength measurements.

[3] We also have and use another WCDMA data sets measured in Seoul at different times.

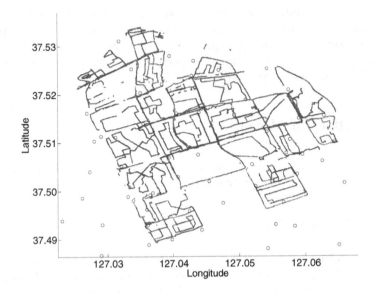

Fig. 1. The measurement area in Seoul, Korea, about $25km^2$

2.2 Signal Dragging

From our large data sets, we realized that a moving mobile terminal tends to retain signal information of old BSs than newly appearing BSs. In other words, when the mobile terminal is moving, its signal pattern information tends to contain more signals from BSs positioned opposite of the terminal's moving direction than the signals from BSs positioned in the forward direction. Fig. 2 illustrates the situation where the "*signal dragging*" phenomenon occurs. A mobile terminal is receiving signals from six BSs while the user of the mobile terminal is moving northeast-ward. The terminal's signal pattern contains four signals from the backward BSs but contains only two signals from the forward BSs.

To show the signal dragging phenomenon more effectively, we draw vectors (white arrows in Fig. 2) stemming from the mobile terminal's position to individual BSs' positions; each vector is called a BS vector. Then we sum the BS vectors to calculate the sum vector, which is illustrated by the dark gray arrow pointing toward the southwest direction in Fig. 2. Because more backward BSs are included in the signal pattern than forward ones, the sum vector tends to point toward the opposite direction of the terminal's moving direction. Thus, if we reverse the sum vector, the resulting direction vector is likely to point toward the moving direction of the terminal as described.

Fig. 3 shows that signal dragging occurs in a real driving user's circumstance. The two axes indicate the latitude and longitude, the squares are the ground truth (GT) position of a moving user, and the circles are the positions of BSs in the example area. The arrows in Fig. 3 indicate the direction estimation vector which corresponds to the reverse of sum vector (black arrow) in Fig. 2. The length

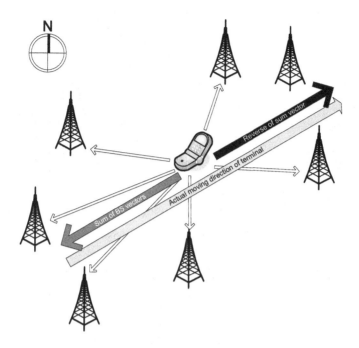

Fig. 2. A descriptive picture of the signal dragging phenomenon

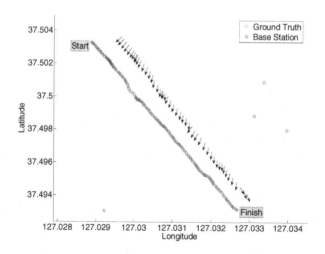

Fig. 3. An actual example of the signal dragging phenomenon from WCDMA data of Seoul, about $0.8km^2$

of all BS vectors are equalized before being summed up to remove the weighted effect of distant BSs. And the length of the sum vector is also equalized before plotting because this helps us figure out the estimated direction more easily.

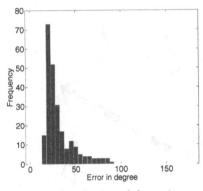 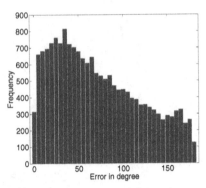

(a) SDEM distribution of the trajectory in Fig. 3, mean 31.5, median 25.8

(b) SDEM distribution of the trajectory in Fig. 1, mean 72.6, median 64.0

Fig. 4. SDEM distributions

Each arrow plotted corresponds to one GT spot estimating the current moving direction of the user.[4] Thus, if the direction of arrows matches the actual moving direction, we can say that the signal dragging phenomenon occurs notably.

Signal Dragging Error Metric (SDEM). As an intuitive metric indicating whether the phenomenon has occurred as expected or not, we can use the angular difference (absolute value) between two vectors, the actual user direction vector (i.e., difference of two consecutive ground truth (GT) positions) and the estimated direction vector (the arrows on the map in Fig. 3). We call this absolute angular difference as *Signal Dragging Error Metric (SDEM)*. Using the mean of the SDEMs at all user's position on the map, we can tell that the signal dragging phenomenon in the interested area has shown its efficacy as long as the mean value is less than 90 degrees. If the mean value is near to 90 degrees, there is no relation between the terminal's movement and the geometric distribution of BSs in the terminal's signal pattern at all. If the mean is bigger than 90 degrees, we can tell that more forward BSs tend to be contained in the signal pattern rather than the backward BSs on average: the opposite of signal dragging. Recall that the direction estimation vector is the reverse of the sum vector.

The mean SDEM of the trajectory data in Fig. 3 is 31.5 degrees while the median is 25.8 degrees. Therefore we can say that the signal dragging is apparent. The mean SDEM evaluated on the entire trajectory in Fig. 1 is 72.6 degrees and the median is 64.0 degrees. Even the mean SDEM is less than 90 degrees, we may need to further investigate the detailed distribution of the metric values. The SDEM distribution of the data set of Fig. 3 is given in Fig. 4.(a), in which no SDEM over 90 degrees is observed. Fig. 4.(b) shows the SDEM distribution of the entire trajectory of Fig. 1. In this distribution, almost two-third of SDEM values

---

[4] We draw only a half of the total arrows corresponding to GT spots in the figure to have enough spacing between adjacent arrows so that each arrow can be shown clearly.

are less than 90 degrees but also significant amount of spots show inconsistent results. Note that the median SDEM is normally smaller than the mean SDEM. This implies more number of data lie below the mean value. The reason why the average SDEM is bigger in Fig. 1 is because the trajectory and the change of moving direction is more versatile in Fig. 1, which will be explained in section 3.

In our experiments, the user GT positions are obtained by GPS and, in turn, the user moving directions are calculated from the GPS records. Because GPS position estimation is also erroneous especially in urban areas, the actual user direction we use can be erroneous. In order to reduce the effect of GPS error on SDEM, we exclude signal pattern records that are measured when the user is almost stationary. For example, in this paper, if the instant speed of the user computed from the two consecutive GPS records is less than 10km/h, the signal pattern record is excluded.

3 Properties of Signal Dragging

In this section, we enumerate interesting factors which affect the signal dragging phenomenon: speed, direction change, and BS arrangement.

Correlation with Speed

The speed of a mobile terminal affects the degree of signal dragging. In order to observe the relation, we compute the correlation coefficient between the terminal's moving speed (calculated from two consecutive GPS records) and the $(180 - SDEM)$.[5] When we test the straight trajectory data set of Fig. 3 whose average speed in km/h and deviation is 31 and 12 each, the correlation coefficient is 0.48. We argue this is sufficient to say that the moving speed of terminal is positively correlated to the effect of signal dragging. In other words, as the terminal moves faster, the signal dragging becomes more notable. Here, we exclude signal patterns with the screening threshold 4km/h instead of 10km/h in order to see the correlation between speed and signal dragging more vividly.

Direction Change

Fig. 5.(a) shows the rectangular shaped trajectory of one of our WCDMA data sets measured in Seoul, Korea, while the SDEM distribution of the data set is shown in Fig. 5.(b). As shown in the two corners marked by ovals in Fig. 5.(a), *when the mobile terminal turns its direction, the direction estimation arrows gradually converge to the changed direction of the terminal after some delay.* The arrows finally catch up with the terminal's direction as the terminal moves on the straight road about 500 meters after the turn in this example. Thus, if the terminal changes its direction frequently, the SDEM value tends to increase. The best case happens when the terminal moves in a straight line for a sufficient time as shown in Fig. 3.

---

[5] Because SDEM increases as the effect of signal dragging decreases, we subtract the calculated SDEM from 180 degrees to compute the correlation coefficient.

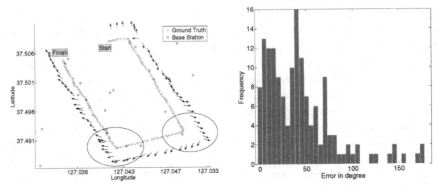

(a) WCDMA trajectory in Seoul, Korea, (b) SDEM distribution, mean 42.8, me-
about $3.5km^2$ dian 37.8

Fig. 5. Vector convergence at the change of direction

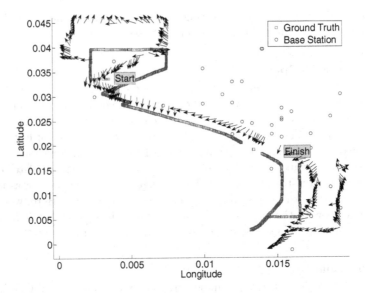

Fig. 6. The effect of uneven BS arrangement (WCDMA data in Seattle, USA, about $8.4km^2$)

We have observed a similar effect of direction change and vector convergence from many other data sets whose trajectories contain direction changes followed by straight lines. Those data sets include measurements from not only Seoul but also from Seattle, USA.

From the way how a mobile terminal updates and maintains its signal pattern, we may find the factors that attribute this convergence delay. The section 5 will convey the technical backgrounds of CDMA and WCDMA systems related to this issue.

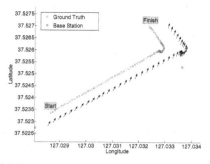
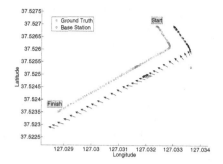

(a) Initial direction, SDEM mean 48.4, median 40.1

(b) Reverse direction, SDEM mean 88.8, median 64.0

Fig. 7. Two directional WCDMA data sets in Seoul, about $0.2km^2$

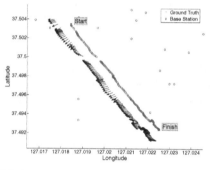
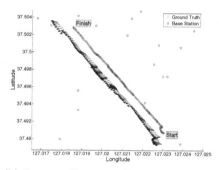

(a) Initial direction, SDEM mean 107.7, median 111.5

(b) Reverse direction, SDEM mean 68.5, median 64.0

Fig. 8. Two directional CDMA data sets in Seoul, about $0.8km^2$

Arrangement of BSs

Another interesting property is observed in Fig. 6[6]. The white area at the left bottom of the map indicates a sea in which there is no base stations. Reminding the way the arrows are drawn, if the terminal is located on the seaside, the sum vector can only indicate to the inland despite of the terminal's movement. If we reverse the sum vector, the final direction vectors will eventually point toward the sea. This specific arrangement of BSs became the major contribution to SDEM of this data set of Fig. 6 whose mean value is 79.3 degrees and the median is 65.8 degrees.

In the data sets measured in Seoul, we have observed the similar effect of uneven (or biased) arrangement of BSs. For example, if the terminal is located

---

[6] The absolute latitude and longitude values are replaced by the relative values due to the operator's request.

on the riverside or on the boundary of urban/rural area, the arrangement of BSs surrounding the terminal is highly biased toward inland or urban area. On the contrary, as the arrangement of BSs is closer to uniform, the signal dragging phenomenon tends to be more notable. *Thus, the arrangement of BSs and the geographical environment greatly affects the efficacy of signal dragging phenomenon.*

Now, we may want to know how much the moving direction of a terminal causes signal dragging despite of the influence of BS arrangement. Fig. 7 and Fig. 8 show the both effects of moving direction and BS arrangement. We measure signal patterns twice on the same road (using same measurement equipments) with two different driving directions opposite each other. For convenience, we denote one direction as *initial direction* and the other direction as *reverse direction*. If estimation arrows point toward the terminal's direction in both trajectories, we can say that the signal dragging is apparent and the influence of BS arrangement is weak. In the example of Fig. 7, arrows in both directions tend to point the direction the terminal moves toward; however, the efficacy of signal dragging in the reverse direction (Fig. 7.(b)) is not so apparent, because more BSs are placed in bottom right of the trajectory than in upper left, though most BS positions are not shown in the map.

On the contrary, the two-way direction test results in Fig.8 with CDMA measurements show one example where signal dragging hardly happens due to the uneven arrangement of surrounding BSs. The arrows in Fig.8.(a) and Fig.8.(b) are similar despite of their opposite moving directions. Although the arrows in both trajectories are similar, the signal patterns of each direction are different enough to affect localization performance. We will discuss the difference in section 4.

4   Implications of Signal Dragging

In this section, we further investigate the implications and the applications of the signal dragging with a number of example data sets.

4.1   Pattern Matching (PM)

In PM systems [7] [9] [10] operators collect signal patterns from a number of selected points in the service area and store them in a pattern database: we call a signal pattern in the pattern database as a *seed*. Based on the assumption that the signal pattern at a certain point is stable temporally and spatially, the position of a terminal is determined by comparing the terminal's current signal pattern (*sample*) to the database entries and finding the best-matching location.

To see if there exists a difference in the performance of the positioning algorithm by the movement context, we perform PM experiments using the collected signal patterns in both directions (initial and reverse) of the same road. The seed and the sample pattern data are collected in the areas in Fig. 7 (WCDMA) and Fig. 8 (CDMA). A complete description on the pattern distance metric and other

PM parameters can be found in [9]. We have total four kinds of data sets for each direction and each radio network (WCDMA and CDMA). We performed eight different PM experiments using one directional data as seeds and another directional data as samples for each radio network as the results shown in Table 1. In the case that the directions in measuring the seed and the sample data are same, the location error is much smaller than that of the case that the directions are different. This means the signal pattern can be very different depending on the moving direction in war-driving.

Table 1. 95 percentile PM errors using different seed and sample data

Seed by Sample	WCDMA (meter)	CDMA (meter)
Initial by Initial	97.87	86.71
Initial by Reverse	202.80	197.33
Reverse by Reverse	54.86	74.58
Reverse by Initial	115.30	271.21

4.2   Centroid Family

The centroid family contains three localization algorithms: centroid, weighted centroid, and cell ID. The centroid algorithm generates the resulting position as the middle point of BSs whose pilot signals are in the signal pattern regardless of the RSS value of each BS. Whereas the cell ID algorithm simply returns the position of the reference BS. In case of the weighted centroid algorithm we compute the RSS weighted average of the given BS positions in a signal pattern as explained in [8].

Table 2. 95 percentile error results of centroid family algorithms

Data	Centroid (meter)	Weighted Centroid (meter)	Cell ID (meter)
WCDMA Initial	325.37	454.44	462.85
WCDMA reverse	326.56	427.62	527.01
CDMA Initial	2103.77	412.15	274.16
CDMA reverse	1623.28	502.55	335.13

Table 2 shows the localization errors of the centroid family algorithms using the same data set in PM. We can see the similar error results in both directions irrelevant of the type of centroid algorithms, which is in contrast to the PM error results. The reason why the PM and the centroid family shows different results is that the PM algorithm is based on the similarity between the signal patterns of seeds and samples but the centroid family algorithms calculate the position of a terminal only using the current signal pattern; the centroid family algorithms do not need to compare the signal patterns. From these results we can say that the pattern database should be constructed with various terminal movement contexts considering the direction and the speed.

4.3   Direction Estimation

If the signal dragging phenomenon prevails, the signal pattern shows directional characteristics to a certain degree. We can leverage this directivity to find out the terminal moving direction: the direction estimation vector which is the reverse of the sum vector. As described in subsection 2.2, we have drawn BS vectors stemming from the terminal's true position (GT) and calculated the SDEM. The GT position of a terminal, however, may not be available to users in real application scenarios. If a terminal is equipped with GPS, we can use GPS results as GT positions. Otherwise, we should use the result of network-based localization algorithms as an alternative for the GT in calculating the SDEM. To see the applicability of signal dragging, we arbitrarily employ the RSS-based weighted centroid algorithm among the centroid family to find out the position of a terminal instead of GT. The mean and median SDEM of the area in Fig. 1 is 73.9 degrees and 65.6 degrees each. Comparing with the result of the GT based SDEM (mean 72.6, median 64.0), this proves the applicability of direction estimation.

To the best of our knowledge, this is the first work to show the possibility of direction estimation of mobile terminals without depending on previous records (history) of terminal positions. Only one single instance of a signal pattern currently available at the terminal is needed for direction estimation.

5   Technical Reasons of Signal Dragging

In order to understand why the signal dragging phenomenon happens from a technical perspective, we need to investigate the characteristics of cellular network systems we used. In this section, we overview the basics about CDMA and WCDMA systems focusing on the logical channel structure and the pilot set management policy. Based on these backgrounds we will discuss the technical reasons why the signal dragging occurs.

5.1   Basics of CDMA and WCDMA Systems

We start this section from the basics of IS-95 CDMA and CDMA2000 standards which are used for the mobile telecommunications employing the code division multiple access (CDMA) scheme. For the communications between the BS and the mobile station (MS), there are two kinds of links, the forward link from the BS to the MS and the reverse link from the MS to the BS. We are interested in the forward link because the signal information from the BS is delivered to the MS through this link. The forward link consists of a pilot channel, a synchronization (sync) channel, a number of paging channels, and traffic channels. The pilot

CDMA signal transmitted by a BS provides a reference for all MSs around. Its broadcast period is 26.66 ms due to the fixed chip rate. The pilot signals from all BSs are based on the same pseudo-random binary sequence, but each BS is identified by a unique time offset of its pseudo-random binary sequence. The MS processes the pilot channel to find the strongest pilot signals to decide when to perform handoff. Once the MS identifies the strongest pilot offset, it examines the signal on its sync channel which is locked to the pseudo-random binary sequence signal on the pilot channel and obtains the information pertinent to this particular BS. The MS now attempts to access the paging channel and listens for system information. After the acquisition of the paging channel, it listens to the assigned paging channel and is able to receive and initiate the calls.

The paging channel is subdivided into paging channel slots. In non-slotted mode in which the MS is not saving power, the MS monitors all slots on a continuous basis, thus paging and control data for the MS can be received in any of the paging channel slots. In slotted mode, the MS can stop or reduce processing activities to save battery power during the slots in which the paging channel is not monitored. The MS can specify its preferred slot cycle using the SLOT_CYCLE_INDEX field in control messages. The length of the slot cycle, in units of 1.28 seconds, is given by the two to the power of SLOT_CYCLE_INDEX. As an example, if the MS selects the SLOT_CYCLE_INDEX as two, the slot cycle becomes four meaning $1.28 * 4 = 5.12$ seconds.

The pilot channels of the BSs identified by the MS, as well as other pilot channels relayed by the serving BS are continuously categorized by the MS into four groups.

- Active Set: Contains the pilots whose paging or traffic channels are actually being monitored or used.
- Candidate set: Contains the pilots that are not currently in the active set. However, these pilots have been received with sufficient signal strength to indicate that the associated forward traffic channels could be successfully demodulated.
- Neighbor Set: Contains the pilots that are likely candidates for idle handoff. The member BSs are specified in the control or paging channel message from the BS.
- Remaining set: Contains all possible pilots in the current system, excluding pilots in the active, candidate, or neighbor sets.

The pilot channels of the BSs move among sets by the basis of the signal strength, the expiration timer, and the set capacity. The signal pattern information we obtain is from received signal powers of the pilot signals of the BSs in the above sets. The more detailed explanation can be found in [14], [15], and [16].

Wideband CDMA is a type of 3G cellular network designed to achieve higher speeds and support more users compared to the older 2G networks. The similar channel structure mentioned above is also employed in WCDMA. The primary and secondary synch channel and the common pilot channel are downlink channels which carry no user data but perform the similar role as those of CDMA. The cell search procedure is based on these three fundamental physical layer signaling channels available in every cell. The primary synch channel is used to detect the presence of cells and to give information about each cell's slot timing. The secondary synch channel serves as a means of detecting the frame start timing of cells. Other various channels for the cell broadcast and the data traffic are designed. Also the set of monitoring cells are maintained for the soft handover. Like the slotted mode in CDMA, the discontinuous reception (DRX) mode is supported in WCDMA. The MS may use DRX in an idle mode in order to reduce power consumption. When DRX is used the MS needs only to monitor one page indicator in one paging occasion per DRX cycle. The detailed specifications can be found in [11], [12], and [13].

5.2   Why the Signal Dragging Occurs, a Technical Perspective

From the information in the previous section, we can find out the reasons why the signal dragging happens.

First, the difficulty of synchronizing with a newly found BS makes the mobile terminal hard to recognize forward BSs. As we have discussed earlier, the pilot signal is broadcast by the BS every 26.66 ms. This inevitably induces delay time in reading the pilot signal from a newly found BS, which may be positioned in the forward direction with a higher probability than the backward direction. After the terminal gets the pseudo noise (PN) code from the pilot channel, it will need more time to get the PN offset from the sync channel. In addition, if the terminal is moving fast, the multipath fading effect occurs severely interfering the terminal from receiving the intended signals.

Second, if the mobile terminal is working in a slotted mode, it updates its signal pattern information with relatively long update interval time which is calculated from the SLOT_CYCLE_INDEX parameter. As explained in the previous subsection, the terminal becomes awake based on the slot cycle. From our CDMA measurement data, we found that SLOT_CYCLE_INDEX is set to be 2 in the CDMA terminal used in our measurements. In other words, the update interval of signal patterns measured in a slotted (idle) mode was about 5 seconds, which is similar to $1.28 * 2^2 = 5.12s$ as explained in the previous subsection.

The third reason of the signal dragging is that the mobile terminal tends to keep the acquired signal pattern information even after the corresponding BS's pilot channel is not detected any more. Once the terminal obtains the necessary information of BSs, it saves and manages the information according to the pilot set handling policy. Even the pilot signal strength of a BS in the active set is weakened below a certain threshold, the pilot information is not excluded from the four sets instantly but lowered the set position to candidate or neighbor or remaining set. Moreover in slotted mode, the slot cycle also contributes to the delayed discard of an old weak signal.

6   Related Work

There has been studies trying to predict the movement context of a user from the signal pattern. The movement context can be the location, direction, speed, and acceleration. The location context has been the primary concern of the academia and the industry, and the practical level of accuracy satisfying the E911 requirements are achieved using different algorithms [6] [7] [8]. Many people tried to guess the mobility status of a user from signal patterns in GSM and WiFi systems [2] [3] [4]. The basic idea is that the signal pattern varies more intensively as the terminal moving speed increases. This idea is consistent with our findings in that the signal patterns are varied by the movement context such as the speed or the moving direction. In order to extract the movement context, two are more signal patterns are compared, thus they need some history of signal patterns. But our work differs in the sense that the movement context can be extracted even from a single instance of a signal pattern.

M. Kim et al. [5] points out the hazards of using war driving trace data. According to their work, if we just drive and collect signal patterns, we may not be able to get sufficiently accurate AP position data for the subsequent localization. Even their work is based on WiFi, we argue that the same thing can happen in the cellular networks too. Due to the difficulty of getting the BS database from the provider, the researchers often build their own database, so called virtual network database [1] [6]. We point out that the errors of the localization is not just from the incorrect virtual network database but also from the mismatching movement context between the time of war-driving and that of the subsequent localization.

Many studies on the metropolitan scale localization have been done in GSM networks [1] [6] [7] or in WiFi networks [4] [21]. But we have performed our whole experiments in CDMA and WCDMA networks. The experimental results in this paper can help others understand the different properties of the CDMA/WCDMA networks.

7   Conclusion and Future Work

We have revealed that there is a significant relationship between the signal pattern and the terminal movement context. The signal patterns are very important sources for the localization, tracking, and network measurement applications. Thus understanding the nature of the signal pattern is essential for the better services. We have shown that the signal dragging occurs as an influence of the terminal movement context using CDMA/WCDMA test data in two cities. We defined an intuitive signal dragging error metric to quantify the extent of the signal dragging. Using this metric and its distribution, we exhibited how the factors affect the signal dragging. The signal dragging phenomenon illustrated how to augment the current methodology of collecting signal patterns, especially the war-driving. There can be limitations or hazards of using war-driving data without the movement context at the time of war driving. We have shown that the PM accuracy can be greatly influenced by the terminal movement context whereas the accuracy of centroid family algorithms is not affected. We suggest that we record the movement context as well as the signal patterns so that we can improve/analyze the localization accuracy. The signal dragging phenomenon itself also provides a useful direction context of the terminal, which can be a useful source of the terminal context. On the other hand, we described why the movement context of a mobile terminal influences the signal patterns based on the CDMA/WCDMA specifications.

Our work is, to our knowledge, the first analysis on the effect of the movement context on the signal patterns. We are planning to perform more experiments in various radio environments such as WiFi and GSM.

References

1. Chen, M.Y., et al.: Practical Metropolitan-Scale Positioning for GSM Phones. In: Proceedings of Ubicomp (2006)
2. Sohn, T., et al.: Mobility Detection Using Everyday GSM Trace. In: Dourish, P., Friday, A. (eds.) UbiComp 2006. LNCS, vol. 4206, Springer, Heidelberg (2006)
3. Anderson, I., Muller, H.: Context Awareness via GSM Signal Strength Fluctuation. Pervasive, Late Breaking Results, pp. 27–31 (2006)
4. Krumm, J., Horvitz, E.: LOCADIO: Inferring Motion and Location from Wi-Fi Signal Strengths. In: Proceedings of Mobiquitous (2004)
5. Kim, M., et al.: Risks of using AP locations discovered through war driving. In: Fishkin, K.P., Schiele, B., Nixon, P., Quigley, A. (eds.) PERVASIVE 2006. LNCS, vol. 3968, Springer, Heidelberg (2006)
6. LaMarca, A., et al.: Place Lab: Device Positioning Using Radio Beacons in the Wild. In: Hutter, D., Ullmann, M. (eds.) SPC 2005. LNCS, vol. 3450, Springer, Heidelberg (2005)
7. Zhu, J., et al.: Indoor/outdoor location of cellular handsets based on received signal strength. Electronics Letters, 41(1) (2005)
8. Lee, J., et al.: Distributed and energy-efficient target localization and tracking in wireless sensor networks. Elsevier Computer Communications 29(13-14), 2494–2505 (2006)
9. Lee, S., et al.: Use of AGPS call data records for non-GPS terminal positioning in cellular networks. In: Proceedings of WINSYS (2006)
10. Bahl, P., Padmanabhan, V.N.: RADAR: An In-Building RF-Based User Location and Tracking System. In: Proceedings of IEEE INFOCOM, vol. 2, pp. 775–784 (2000)
11. Tanner, R., Woodard, J.: WCDMA Requirements and Practical Design. Wiley, Chichester (2004)
12. 3GPP TS 25.221 V7.2.0. Physical channels and mapping of transport channels onto physical channels (TDD) (2007)
13. 3GPP TS 25.304 V7.1.0. User Equipment (UE) procedures in idle mode and procedures for cell reselection in connected mode (2006)
14. Vijay, K.: IS-95 CDMA and cdma2000 Cellular/PCS Systems Implementation. Prentice Hall, Englewood Cliffs (2000)
15. 3GPP2 C.S0002-D v2.0. Physical Layer Standard for cdma2000 Spread Spectrum Systems (2005)
16. 3GPP2 C.S0005-D v2.0. Upper Layer (Layer 3) Signaling Standard for cdma2000 Spread Spectrum Systems (2005)
17. Arulampalam, S., Maskell, S., Gordon, N., Clapp, T.: A Tutorial on Particle Filters for Online Non-Linear/Non-Gaussian Bayesian Tracking. IEEE Transactions on Signal Processing 50(2), 174–188 (2002)

18. Hightower, J., Borriello, G.: Particle Filters for Location Estimation in Ubiquitous Computing: A Case Study. In: Davies, N., Mynatt, E.D., Siio, I. (eds.) UbiComp 2004. LNCS, vol. 3205, Springer, Heidelberg (2004)
19. Gustafsson, F., et al.: Particle Filters for Positioning, Navigation and Tracking. IEEE Transactions on Signal Processing 50(2), 425–437 (2002)
20. Priyantha, N.B., et al.: The cricket location-support system. In: Proceedings of Mobicom, pp. 32–43 (2000)
21. Cheng, Y.C., et al.: Accuracy characterization for metropolitan-scale Wi-Fi localization. In: Proceedings of MobiSys (2005)
22. Stage 2 functional specification of User Equipment (UE) positioning in UTRAN (Release 4). 3GPP
23. Zhao, Y.: Standardization of Mobile Phone Positioning for 3G Systems. In: IEEE Communications Magazine (July 2002)

Modeling and Optimizing Positional Accuracy Based on Hyperbolic Geometry for the Adaptive Radio Interferometric Positioning System

Hao-ji Wu[1], Ho-lin Chang[1], Chuang-wen You[1], Hao-hua Chu[1,2], and Polly Huang[2,3]

[1] Department of Computer Science and Information Engineering
[2] Graduate Institute of Networking and Multimedia
[3] Department of Electrical Engineering
National Taiwan University
{b90007,b91011,f91023,hchu}@csie.ntu.edu.tw
phuang@cc.ee.ntu.edu.tw

Abstract. One of the most important performance objectives for a localization system is positional accuracy. It is fundamental and essential to general location-aware services. The radio interferometric positioning (RIP) method [1] is an exciting approach which promises sub-meter positional accuracy. In this work, we would like to enhance the RIP method by dynamically selecting the optimal anchor nodes as beacon senders to further optimizing the positional accuracy when tracking targets. We have developed an estimation error model to predict positional error of the RIP algorithm given different combinations of beacon senders. Building upon this estimation error model, we further devise an adaptive RIP method that selects the optimal sender-pair combination (SPC) according to the locations of targets relative to anchor nodes. We have implemented the adaptive RIP method and conducted experiments in a real sensor network testbed. Experimental results have shown that our adaptive RIP method outperforms the static RIP method in both single-target and multi-target tracking, and improves the average positional accuracy by 47%~60% and reduces the 90% percentile error by 55%~61%.

1 Introduction

Many ubiquitous computing applications require deployment of a sensor network infrastructure to collect a variety of data sensed from the physical world. These sensor data are then processed to implement different digital services that can exhibit intelligent context-aware behaviors by automatically adapting their services to changing environments. In order to make correct inference on these sensor data, these systems require reliable, accurate location information on the observed sensor data. This brings up the need for accurate location tracking in sensor networks.

To address this need, there have been many sensor network localization systems utilizing different sensing techniques, e.g., MoteTrack [9], Cricket [10], Spotlight [13], APIT [14], ENSBox [16], etc. Among them, the radio interferometric positioning (RIP) method from Vanderbilt University [1] has shown a promising location sensing technique for sensor network applications. Its main advantages are (1) sub-meter positional

J. Hightower, B. Schiele, and T. Strang (Eds.): LoCA 2007, LNCS 4718, pp. 228–244, 2007.
© Springer-Verlag Berlin Heidelberg 2007

accuracy (e.g., in the range of tens of centimeters), (2) a long sensing range (e.g., 50~100 meters between two anchor nodes), and (3) no additional hardware requirement (i.e., reusing the same radio module for both communication and localization).

In this work, our innovations come in two parts. First, we have developed an *estimation error model* for the RIP method, which can accurately predict the amount of estimation error given the relative positions of anchor sensor nodes and (moving) target nodes. We have also validated the correctness of this *estimation error model* empirically from an experimental sensor network testbed. Building upon this estimation error model, our second innovation is the design and implementation of an *adaptive RIP method* that dynamically chooses the best anchor nodes in locating targets and minimizes their positional error. Our experimental results have demonstrated that our adaptive RIP method outperforms the static RIP method, improving the average positional accuracy by 47%~60% and reducing the 90% percentile error by 55%~61%.

The remainder of this paper is organized as follows. Section 2 provides background on the basic RIP system, and formulates our adaptive tracking problem. Section 3 derives our estimation error model that can accurately predict the estimation error in the RIP method. Section 4 presents the design of our adaptive RIP method. Section 5 describes its implementation. Section 6 explains the experimental setup and results. Section 7 discusses related work. Section 8 draws our conclusion and future work.

2 Background on the Radio Interferometric Positioning (RIP)

We first provide a brief background on the original, single-target RIP method, followed by our multi-target tracking RIP extension. For a more detailed description of the original RIP method, we refer interested readers to [1].

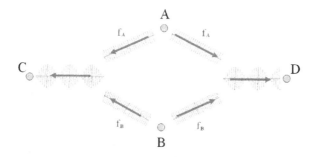

Fig. 1. The RIP method

The RIP method is a novel way of localizing targets by measuring relative phase offset. It is typically realized in a sensor network setting [1], involving at least three anchor nodes and one target node, all within a common radio communication range as shown in Figure 1. Among the anchor nodes, two of them, A and B, act as senders and transmit pure sine wave simultaneously with two nearby frequencies f_A and f_B. At nearby frequencies, these two signals interfere with each other, therefore producing a resulting signal with a low beat frequency $| f_B - f_A |$. For example, our experiments using two MICA2 Motes with 900 MHz radio showed that interference produced a signal with a low beat frequency around 350 Hz. Two sensor nodes C and D act as receivers and can use simple hardware to detect the phase of this low-beat interference wave.

Based on the relative phase difference detected on the receivers C and D, a geometric constraint among the locations of A, B, C, and D can be derived in the following equation (the details of this derivation is described in [1]):

$$\Delta\phi = \frac{2\pi}{\lambda} (d_{AD} - d_{BD} + d_{BC} - d_{AC}) \ (mod \ 2\pi) \tag{1}$$

where $\lambda = \dfrac{2c}{f_A + f_B}$, $\Delta\phi$ is the phase difference detected by receivers C and D, λ is the wavelength of the mean carrier frequency of the interference signal, and d_{XY} is the distance between nodes X and Y. Furthermore, Equation (1) can be reformulated as follows:

$$\frac{\Delta\phi}{2\pi} \lambda = d_{ABCD} \ (mod \ \lambda) \ , where \ d_{ABCD} = d_{AD} - d_{BD} + d_{BC} - d_{AC} \tag{2}$$

In Equation (2), d_{ABCD} is also denoted as q_{range}. Due to $(mod \ \lambda)$-related ambiguity of d_{ABCD}, there can be more than one values of d_{ABCD} satisfying Equation (2). In order to resolve this d_{ABCD} ambiguity, the system must take multiple measurements (e.g., N times) at slightly different frequency channels (or different wavelength $\lambda_{i=1..N}$) and obtain corresponding phase differences $\Delta\phi_i$. Since each $(\lambda_i, \Delta\phi_i)$ pair provides an instance of Equation (2), measuring N channels gives N such equations. To see how well a d_{ABCD} value fits this set of equations, an error function is defined below. By trying different values of d_{ABCD}, it is possible to find the best-fit one that minimizes this error function:

$$error \ (d_{ABCD}) = \sqrt{\sum_i (\frac{\Delta\phi_i}{2\pi} \lambda_i - mod(\ d_{ABCD}, \lambda_i \ ))} \tag{3}$$

Consider the example in Figure 2(a), node D is the tracked target, and nodes A, B, and C are anchor nodes with known locations. Then, d_{ABCD} can be transformed into the following equation:

$$d_{ABCD} + d_{AC} - d_{BC} = d_{AD} - d_{BD} \tag{4}$$

After d_{ABCD} is obtained by finding a value that minimizes Equation (3), all variables on the left hand side of Equation (4) are known. The left hand side value can then be computed and is referred to as t_{range}. Equation (4) can be further rewritten as follows:

$$t_{range} = d_{AD} - d_{BD} \tag{5}$$

Equation (5) can be drawn as a hyperbolic curve H_{AB} shown in Figure 2. It is one arm of a hyperbola with two foci A and B passing through D with the semi-major axis of the length $t_{range}/2$. In other words, D can lie anywhere on this hyperbolic curve H_{AB}. To precisely locate D, each positioning operation must take a second measurement round using a different pair of senders. In Figure 2, the second measurement round selects nodes A and C as senders, and nodes B and D as receivers. This gives another hyperbolic curve H_{AC}. The intersection of these two hyperbolic curves (H_{AB} and H_{AC}) fixes the location of D. In this example, (A, B) and (A, C) are called *sender-pair combination (SPC)*. We can think of each measurement round selects one *pair of senders* to jointly localize a moving target.

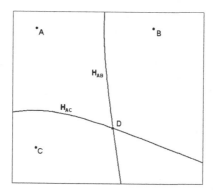

Fig. 2. Tracking the target D with intersections of hyperbolic curves

Error Components

Since the targets' locations are estimated from the intersection of hyperbolic curves, geometric properties of the curves at the intersection points can significantly impact the amount of estimation error in RIP. The reason is that these hyperbolic curves

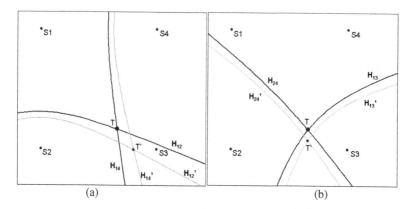

Fig. 3. Show the how different SPC selections and their produced geometric factors (the intersectional angle and the displacement of hyperbolic curve) affect the estimation error in locating the target T. Figure 3(a) selects *{(S1, S2), (S1, S4)}* as SPC, and Figure 3(b) selects *{(S1, S3), (S2, S4)}* as SPC. The black lines represent perfect hyperbolic curves that intersect on the target T. The gray ones represent hyperbolic curves with the same amount of error added to the q_{range} calculation, and intersect on T'.

inheritably have error due to imperfect measurements of q_{range} at the receivers. This error may be amplified to different amount depending on the curves' geometric properties. These geometric properties are in turn dependent on the SPC (sender pair combination) selection. Consider the examples in Figure 3(a) and 3(b). They share the same spatial layout of sensor nodes but different SPC selection: Figure 3(a) selects {(S1, S2), (S1, S4)} and Figure 3(b) selects {(S1, S3), (S2, S4)}. The black lines represent hyperbolic curves that perfectly intersect at the target T, whereas the gray lines represent hyperbolic curves with an error added to the q_{range} calculation. As shown in these examples, the same amount of q_{range} error is amplified differently, causing more estimation error in locating the target T in Figure 3(a) than in Figure 3(b). There are two geometric factors contributing to this error amplification (positional error is $|T' - T|$): (1) the intersectional angle formed between H_{12} and H_{14} is more acute than the intersectional angle between H_{13} and H_{24}, and (2) the amount of displacement between the black and gray lines is larger in Figure 3(a) than in Figure 3(b) at the intersection points.

Adaptive RIP Problem Formulation
In the RIP method, since different sender-pair-combination (SPC) gives different amount of estimation error, we can turn this tracking problem into an optimization problem as follows. Given a set of infrastructure anchor nodes with fixed known locations ($P_{1..m}$), and a target node T sharing the same radio range as these anchor nodes. Each anchor node can be assigned either a sender or a receiver dynamically. Define the estimation error as the difference between the actual (ground-truth) position and the position estimated by the radio interferometric positioning engine. Design an optimization scheme in which by dynamically selecting a set of SPC from ($P_{1..m}$) to localize a target minimizes its estimation error.

The SPC selection algorithm mentioned above is described in more details in Section 4, which must utilize an *estimation error model* that can accurately approximate the amount of error given a specific SPC selection. The following section explains this estimation error model.

3   Estimation Error Model

Given a specific sender-pair combination (SPC) selection and a target node, the estimation error model can accurately approximate the amount of estimation error from a RIP engine. To derive this estimation error model analytically, we first identify factors that contribute to the positional error: (1) q_{range} *estimation error* (q_{error}): it comes from imperfect phase difference measurements at the receivers, leading to the error in finding the best-fit d_{ABCD} from Equation (3); (2) *displacement of a hyperbolic curve*: the minimum distance from the deviated hyperbolic curve to the target; and (3) *intersectional angle of hyperbolic curves*.

To explain how these factors contribute to the estimation error, consider the examples in Figure 4. First, we describe how depending on the target T's position on the curve, a displacement *of a hyperbolic curve* can cause different amount of estimation error. In Figure 4(a), the pair of senders (A, B) can produce the perfect hyperbolic curve H_{AB} under no q_{error}, and a slightly displaced hyperbolic curve H_{AB}' under q_{error}.

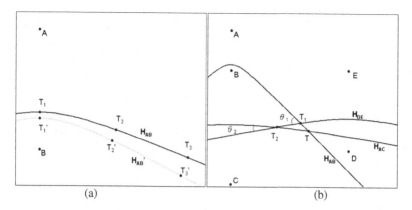

Fig. 4. (a) The displacement of a hyperbolic curve changing with target location. (b) Positional error changing with intersectional angle.

If the target is at T_1, the closest point on H_{AB}' to T_1 is T_1'. Regardless of how the other hyperbolic curve intersects with the H_{AB}', $|T_1' - T_1|$ becomes the minimum estimation error in locating T_1 under q_{error}. Next, we can observe how the estimation error grows when the target position moves to T_2 and grows even larger when it moves to T_3.

Second, we want to discuss how the intersectional angle of two hyperbolic curves can cause different amount of estimation error in locating a target T. We use the example in Figure 4(b). Suppose that the first measurement round produces a hyperbolic curve H_{DE} with q_{error}, and the second measurement round produces a perfect hyperbolic curve without any q_{error}. Consider two such perfect curves H_{AB} from the pair of senders (A, B), and H_{AC} from (A, C). From the Figure 4(b), H_{AB}/H_{AC} has a different intersection point of T_1/T_2. In addition, we can observe that because the intersectional angle θ_1 at T_1 is wider than the intersection angle θ_2 at T_2, the positional error of T_1 is smaller than the positional error of T_2.

Analytic Expression. We derive the estimation error model as follows. Consider the node layout in Figure 5, $S1{\sim}S4$ are anchor nodes, and T is the target. The $SPC:\{(S1, S2), (S3, S4)\}$ gives two hyperbolic curves of H_{12} and H_{34}. Given q_{error}, these two

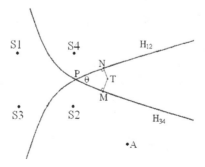

Fig. 5. Intersection of two hyperbolic curves by using SPC $\{(S1, S2), (S3, S4)\}$

hyperbolic curves intersect on P. Therefore, $\overline{TP}$ is the estimation error or the distance between the target's ground-truth position T and the estimated position P.

To solve for $\overline{TP}$, we first define two additional points N and M (shown in Figure 5) in which they are the closest points to T from H_{12} and H_{34}. If the target T is not so close to the focus of the hyperbola, i.e., the curvature of the hyperbola around the target T is relatively flat, $\overline{PN}$ and $\overline{PM}$ could be approximated as straight lines. Under such an assumption, we calculate $\overline{TP}$ by solving the geometric problem shown in Figure 6. The unknown variables are $\overline{TN}$, $\overline{TM}$ (namely, the displacement), and intersectional angle θ. Described in the following is the method to obtain the unknown values.

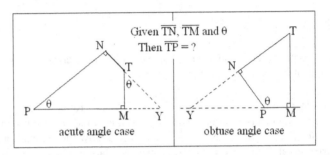

Fig. 6. Approximate the real positional error by $\overline{TP}$

Model the Displacement of a Hyperbolic Curve. In the first measurement round, $(S1, S2)$ are selected as senders, and (A,T) as receivers. This gives the first hyperbolic curve H_{12}. Since $(S1, S2)$ and A have known locations and T's location is unknown, their geometric relation, by substituting into Equation (2), is as follows:

$$d_{S1,S2,A,T} = d_{S1,T} - d_{S2,T} + d_{S2,A} - d_{S1,A} = q_{range}, \quad where \quad \begin{cases} S1 = (S1_x, S1_y) \\ S2 = (S2_x, S2_y) \\ A = (A_x, A_y) \\ T = (T_x, T_y) \end{cases} . \tag{6}$$

Rewrite Equation (6) by substituting these coordinates:

$$q_{range} - (d_{S2,A} - d_{S1,A}) = d_{S1,T} - d_{S2,T} = \sqrt{(T_x - S1_x)^2 + (T_y - S1_y)^2} - \sqrt{(T_x - S2_x)^2 + (T_y - S2_y)^2}. \tag{7}$$

If q_{range} has no error, Equation (7) is a hyperbolic curve which passes through $T(T_x, T_y)$. However, when q_{error} is added to q_{range}, its hyperbolic curve is displaced from T. We describe a method to approximate the amount of displacement. Since the only non-constant terms in Equation (7) are q_{range} and $T(T_x, T_y)$, q_{range} can be written as a function of $T(T_x, T_y)$, the gradient of $q_{range}(T_x, T_y)$ is derived as follows:

$$q_{range}(T_x, T_y) = \sqrt{(T_x - S1_x)^2 + (T_y - S1_y)^2} - \sqrt{(T_x - S2_x)^2 + (T_y - S2_y)^2} + (d_{S2,A} - d_{S1,A})$$
$$\tag{8}$$

$$\nabla q_{range}(T_x, T_y) = \left(\frac{T_x - S1_x}{d_{S1,T}} - \frac{T_x - S2_x}{d_{S2,T}}, \frac{T_y - S1_y}{d_{S1,T}} - \frac{T_y - S2_y}{d_{S2,T}} \right).$$

By the definition of gradient, $\left|\nabla q_{range}(T_x,T_y)\right|$ is the maximum changing rate of $q_{range}(T_x,T_y)$. That is, if target T is shifted by a small ε movement, the maximum q_{range} incremental change is $\varepsilon\left|\nabla q_{range}(T_x,T_y)\right|$. Equivalently, to produce this q_{error}, $\dfrac{q_{error}}{\left|\nabla q_{range}(T_x,T_y)\right|}$ is the minimum movement of the target T on the displaced hyperbola H_{12}. The minimum movement is a good approximation of $\overline{TN}$ when q_{error} is small.

Denote q_{error1} and $q_{range1}(T_x,T_y)$ as q_{error} and $q_{range}(T_x,T_y)$ measured in the first round, and q_{error2} and $q_{range2}(T_x,T_y)$ as q_{error} and $q_{range}(T_x,T_y)$ measured in the second round. By applying the above approximation to these two measurement rounds, $\overline{TN}$ and $\overline{TM}$ can be obtained as follows:

$$\overline{TN} = \frac{q_{error1}}{\left|\nabla q_{range1}(T_x,T_y)\right|}, \quad \overline{TM} = \frac{q_{error2}}{\left|\nabla q_{range2}(T_x,T_y)\right|}. \tag{9}$$

Model the Intersectional Angle of Two Hyperbolic Curves. The intersectional angle θ can be approximated by the tangent slopes for the hyperbolic curves at N and M (denote as m_N and m_M respectively) :

$$\theta = tan^{-1}\left(\frac{m_N - m_M}{1 + m_N m_M}\right). \tag{10}$$

If the coordinates of N and M are known, m_N and m_M can be obtained. Since we can approximate $\overline{TN}$ and $\overline{TM}$ and the unit vector from T to N (which runs parallel to $\nabla q_{range1}(T_x,T_y)$), we can obtain the coordinate of $N(N_x, N_y)$ by the following equation:

$$N(N_x, N_y) = T(T_x,T_y) + \frac{q_{error1}}{\left|\nabla q_{range1}(T_x,T_y)\right|} \frac{\nabla q_{range1}(T_x,T_y)}{\left|\nabla q_{range1}(T_x,T_y)\right|}. \tag{11}$$

Note that the last term is the product of $\overline{XN}$ and the unit vector from T to N. In addition, we can obtain M in a similar way:

$$M(M_x, M_y) = T(T_x,T_y) + \frac{q_{error2}}{\left|\nabla q_{range2}(T_x,T_y)\right|} \frac{\nabla q_{range2}(T_x,T_y)}{\left|\nabla q_{range2}(T_x,T_y)\right|}. \tag{12}$$

Return to our original problem – solving the length of $\overline{TP}$. First, extend $\overline{TN}$ and $\overline{PY}$ to the intersection point Y to form a triangle as shown in Figure 6. After obtaining the intersectional angle θ, $\overline{TN}$, and $\overline{TM}$ from the above approximation, $\overline{TP}$ can be solved geometrically. (ΔMTY means the triangle formed by point M, T, Y and ΔNPY means the triangle formed by point N, P, Y.)

$$For\ \Delta MTY : \begin{cases} \overline{TY} = \overline{TM}\ sec\theta \\ \overline{MY} = \overline{TM}\ tan\theta \end{cases} \tag{13}$$

$$For\ \Delta NPY : \begin{cases} \overline{NY} = \overline{PY}\ sin\theta \\ \overline{NY} = \overline{TN} + \overline{TY} \\ \overline{PY} = \overline{PM} + \overline{MY} \end{cases} \tag{14}$$

According to Equation (14), we obtain:

$$\overline{PM} = \overline{PY} - \overline{MY} = \frac{\overline{NY}}{\sin\theta} - \overline{MY} = \frac{\overline{TN} + \overline{TY}}{\sin\theta} - \overline{MY} \cdot \tag{15}$$

Substitute Equation (13) into Equation (15):

$$\overline{PM} = \frac{\overline{TN} + \overline{TY}}{\sin\theta} - \overline{MY} = \frac{\overline{TN} + \overline{TM}\sec\theta}{\sin\theta} - \overline{TM}\tan\theta \cdot \tag{16}$$

Apply Pythagorean Theory to ΔTMP and combine with Equation (16):

$$\overline{PT} = \sqrt{\overline{PM}^2 + \overline{TM}^2}$$
$$= \sqrt{\left(\frac{\overline{TN} + \overline{TM}\sec\theta}{\sin\theta} - \overline{TM}\tan\theta\right)^2 + \overline{TM}^2}. \tag{17}$$

Finally, we substitute Equation (9) into Equation (17) to obtain the final estimation error:

$$\overline{PT} = \sqrt{\left(\frac{\frac{q_{error1}}{|\nabla q_{range1}(T_x,T_y)|} + \frac{q_{error2}}{|\nabla q_{range2}(T_x,T_y)|}\sec\theta}{\sin\theta} - \frac{q_{error2}}{|\nabla q_{range2}(T_x,T_y)|}\tan\theta\right)^2 + \left(\frac{q_{error2}}{|\nabla q_{range\,2}(T_x,T_y)|}\right)^2}. \tag{18}$$

If the intersectional angle θ is obtuse, there will be some minor differences in the deduction from Equations (13) ~ (17). However, despite these differences at the intermediate steps, the solution to $\overline{PT}$ is still the same as in Equation (18).

Experimental Validation of Estimation Error Model

We have designed and conducted two experiments to validate the correctness and accuracy of the estimation error model derived above. These two experiments differ on what parameters, in the estimation error model, are considered as known (observable) values or not. For example, at localization runtime, the values of q_{error1} and q_{error2} are not observable, since they would require the knowledge of the target's ground-truth position.

To approximate these q_{error} values, we introduce a *calibration phase* prior to runtime when samples at known locations are collected. Then the average $|q_{error}|$ is calculated,

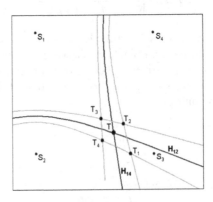

Fig. 7. Four estimation positional errors utilized $|q_{error}|$ from the calibration phase

and it can be used as the magnitude of q_{error1} and q_{error2} in our estimated error model. Note that the sign (+/-) for q_{error1} and q_{error2} is unknown. Therefore, for each position estimation, there are four possible plus/minus combinations of q_{error1} and q_{error2}. Consider the example in Figure 7. For the target T, H_{14} and H_{12} are the hyperbolic curves created from the sender pairs (S_1, S_4) and (S_1, S_2) with no q_{error}. When different combinations of plus/minus q_{error1} and q_{error2} are substituted into our estimated error model, we obtain four estimated positions $(T_1 \sim T_4)$ and estimation errors $(|T - T_1|, |T - T_2|, |T - T_3|,$ and $|T - T_4|)$. We then use the average of these four estimation errors as the target's estimation error.

In our experimental setup, six anchor nodes were placed uniformly on the ring with ten meters radius. Five targets were placed insides this circle. We measure these target nodes with 7 different SPCs. For each SPC, about 50 samples were collected. Since we had the ground-truth location of each target, the magnitude and sign of q_{error} and the estimation error were determined. Using these data, we validated the correctnesss of our error prediction model by comparing the real error and the estimation error.

All Parameters Known Case. This case considers all the parameters in the estimation error model are known. Although this is unrealistic, we conducted this experiment for the purpose of verifying the correctness of our estimation error model. Figure 8 plots the real ground-truth error vs. the estimation error (p_{error}) calculated from our model in Equation (18). The red line plots a perfect diagonal line representing perfect error prediction, and the blue dots are our measurements. The results show that our estimation error model is accurate as it falls within 6 centimeters from the real error 90 % of the time.

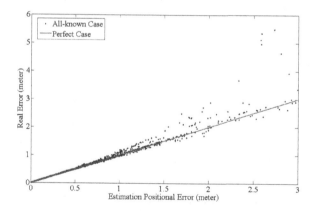

Fig. 8. Validation of the estimation error model in the all-parameters-known case

Runtime Case. At runtime, the system has no knowledge of the actual q_{error}; therefore, we use the average q_{error} obtained from a calibration phase, which is 26 centimeters, in estimation error model. Figure 9 plots the cumulative density function (CDF) of the difference between the real error and predicted error from our estimation error model. The average difference is 35 centimeters, which is not as good as in the All-Parameters-Known case, but sufficient for our error estimation purpose.

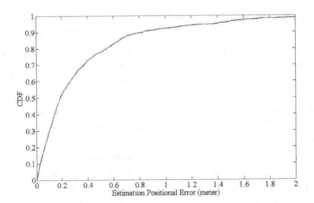

Fig. 9. CDF of the estimation error for the runtime case

4   Design of the Adaptive RIP Method

The design of our adaptive RIP method is shown in Figure 10. It consists of following components: (1) *adaptive SPC selection algorithm*, (2) *the estimation error model*, and (3) *the radio interferometric positioning engine*. In the first step, the adaptive SPC selection algorithm is invoked to find the optimal anchor nodes as sender-pair-combination (SPC) that can locate mobile targets most accurately. To find the optimal SPC, the adaptive SPC selection algorithm currently performs an *exhaustive search* through all possible SPCs, and selects the SPC that gives the minimal estimation error.

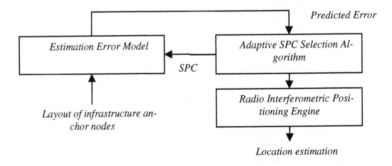

Fig. 10. System architecture of our adaptive RIP method

Specifically, for each unique SPC combination, the adaptive SPC selection algorithm invokes the Estimation Error Model in Equation (18), and calculates its corresponding estimation error. There are three notable details here. First, the exhaustive search strategy is still computationally manageable in our small testbed of 6 anchor nodes, because the estimation error computation is relatively straightforward and the number of different combinations (which grows proportional to the number of anchor nodes within the same radio range) is relatively small with 105 combinations. Second, when tracking multiple targets, the Estimation Error Model computes an error for each target. If an application considers equal importance to all targets, an optimal SPC minimizes the aggregate error from all targets. Third, the Estimation Error Model requires the knowledge of the approximate locations of mobile targets, which be obtained by using the most recently estimated locations of the mobile targets. When the optimal SPC is selected, the system invokes the RIP engine to obtain the locations of targets.

5 Implementation of the Adaptive RIP System

Our adaptive RIP system has been implemented on MICA2 Motes with 900 MHz radios made by Crossbow Inc. One MICA2 Mote connects to a laptop with MIB520 programming board and relays phase measurement packets to a positioning engine developed in Java. The MICA2 Motes are running TinyOS. We modified the Radio Interferometric Positioning (RIP) engine [20] released by Vanderbilt University and ported it to 900MHZ MICA2 Motes. In addition, we extended the RIP engine to implement multi-target tracking. In each measurement round, the base station (PC) sends a command with selected SPC information to all sensor nodes. After time synchronization is performed, the selected sender nodes transmit sine wave in predefined carrier frequency. At our test site location in Taiwan, the frequency band of GSM-900[11] also happens to be around 900MHz, overlapping with a part of MICA2 radio channels. To avoid interference from the GSM-900 up/down link channels, we selected 18 carrier frequencies between 821.277MHZ to 921.337MHZ whose ranges are away from GSM-900 channels. At the end of each measurement round, receiver nodes send back their phase measurement data to a base station. After the RIP engine collects phase measurement data from receivers, it estimates targets' locations.

6 Experimental Results

We conducted two experiments to evaluate the accuracy performance of our adaptive RIP system in a real sensor network environment. The first experiment tested the single-target tracking, whereas the second experiment tested multi-target tracking.

Both experiments were performed on a square near the sport stadium of Nation Taiwan University, which is shown in Figure 11. The tracking area is a circle with

Fig. 11. Experimental setup

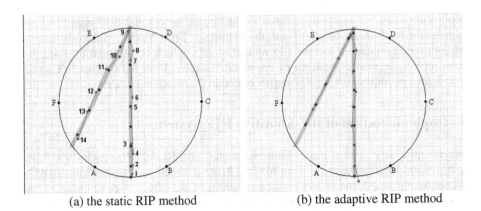

(a) the static RIP method   (b) the adaptive RIP method

Fig. 12. Results of static RIP method versus our adaptive RIP method. The blue line is the target's movement path. Blue dots indicate the target's ground-truth positions at location sampling time. Red dots show the estimated positions from static/adaptive RIP method.

10-meter radius. Six infrastructure anchor nodes were deployed uniformly on the ring, and their locations (A~F) are marked in Figure 12(a).

Single-Target Tracking Experiment. The first experiment tracked a single target, which was a person carrying a MICA2 Mote and walking under normal speed. His movement path is plotted as the blue line in Figure 12. This path was walked repeatedly 5 times for a total distance of 37 meters.

To show that our adaptive RIP can improve the positional accuracy of the original static RIP method, we repeated this experiment twice, once using the static RIP method and once using our adaptive RIP method, and then compared their positional accuracy results. Figure 12(a)/(b) shows the result from the static/dynamic RIP methods. For the static RIP method, two pairs of senders are selected a-priori and fixed to *{(B,C), (C,F)}* regardless of the changing position of the target. Blue dots indicate the target's ground-truth positions at the time of location samples, and red dots show the estimated positions from each of the RIP methods. Figure 12 shows our adaptive RIP method tracks the moving target more accurately than in the static RIP method. Table 1 shows the average positional error and the amount of improvement of our adaptive RIP method over the static RIP method: 47% reduction in average error and 55% reduction at 90% percentile error.

Table 1. Result comparison between the static and adaptive RIP methods in single-target tracking

	Average error (meter)	90%-th percentile (meter)
Static RIP	0.93	1.66
Adaptive RIP	0.49	0.75
Improvement	47%	55%

Multi-target Tracking Experiment. The second experiment tracked six targets. The first five targets are stationary with their locations marked in Figure 13(a). The 6th target is mobile and follows the same movement path as in the first experiment.

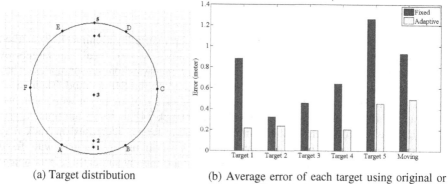

(a) Target distribution

(b) Average error of each target using original or adaptive RIP method

Fig. 13. Experimental setup and result of multi-target tracking experiment

Similar to the first experiments, we want to show that our adaptive RIP method can improve the positional accuracy of the static RIP method. Therefore, we repeated the experiment twice, once using the static RIP method and once using our adaptive RIP method, and then compared their positional accuracy results. Figure 13(b) shows the average positional error for each target using the static/adaptive RIP methods. Our adaptive RIP method reduces the average positional error in all the 6 targets. Table 2 summarizes the results, showing our adaptive RIP method with 60% reduction in average positional error and 61% reduction at the 90% percentile error.

Table 2. Performance result comparison between the static and adaptive RIP method in multi-target tracking

	Average error (meter)	90%-th percentile (meter)
Static RIP	0.75	1.41
Adaptive RIP	0.30	0.54
Improvement	60%	61%

Table 3 provides insight into why our adaptive RIP method works better than the static RIP method. At a specific time point, estimation and real errors were recorded for 6 different SPCs as if each of them were used for positioning targets. They showed a wide range. The largest estimation/real error is 1.00/0.89 meter(s), which is 4.2/4.0 times of the smallest estimation/real error 0.24/0.22 meter. Our adaptive RIP method would select the optimal SPC#6, whereas the static RIP method could pick any SPC.

Table 3. Average estimation/error for locating each of five stationary targets using different SPCs

SPC #	1	2	3	4	5	6
First Sender Pair	(D,E)	(B,C)	(B,C)	(A,C)	(B,E)	(A,D)
Second Sender Pair	(D,F)	(C,D)	(C,F)	(B,D)	(C,F)	(B,E)
Average estimation error (meter)	1.00	0.84	0.60	0.37	0.33	0.24
Average real error (meter)	0.89	0.89	0.74	0.63	0.37	0.22

7 Related Work

The most relevant related work is the Radio Interferometric Positioning (RIP) method from Vanderbilt University [1][2][3][4]. It is a novel way of localizing targets by measuring relative phase offset with inexpensive hardware on sensor nodes. They proposed a tracking system called in Track [3] based on the RIP method. Their result shows that, in 80 meters x 90 meters area, it can track a moving target with sub meter accuracy. Furthermore, they have developed mTrack [4] to track multiple targets simultaneously. However, as the number of moving targets increases, mTrack may not be able to provide good positional accuracy to all moving targets with fixed sender pairs. This motivates our adaptive RIP method that dynamically selects sender pairs given the approximate positions of targets.

There are many other sensor network positioning systems. In general, they can be classified into two broad categories of ranging-based and ranging-free methods.

Ranging-Based Methods. They commonly require signal communications between an anchor observer and a locating target. The major differences among them are the calibration methods and the usage of signal sources, such as sonic, ultrasonic, infrared, camera, RF, etc. For example, Acoustic ENSBox [16] develops a distribution acoustic sensing platform, which an acoustic embedded networked sensing box can be rapidly deployed and perform self-calibration. It claims to achieve 5 centimeters positional accuracy in a partially obstructed 80mx50m outdoor. Given that signal propagates with constant velocity, TOA (time of arrival) methods [18] estimate distance by measuring the signal propagation time. AOA (angle of arrival) [19] is a network-based solution that exploits the geometric property of the arriving signal. By measuring the angle of the signal's arrival at multiple receivers, it is able to provide an accurate location estimation. TDOA (time difference of arrival) [17] is also network-based. It infers distance by measuring the time differences. Some hybrid approaches of TOA, AOA, and TDOA have been proposed [5].

Another class of techniques measures the received signal strength indication (RSSI). These techniques exploit the decaying model of electronic-magnetic field to translate RSSI to the corresponding distance [6] [7] [9]. Also, the frequency bands used for transmission vary. For example, the well-known RADAR system [8] uses the radio frequency (RF). LADAR and SONAR use the visible light and the audible sound bands respectively. LADAR, SONAR, for instances, analyze the signal reflected from the object to estimate location. A recent innovation, Cricket [10], takes a hybrid approach, using both the RF and ultrasonic bands. But, the propagation characteristic is irregular under real environment [15]. Localization systems using RSSI information suffer from these problems and usually give meter-level accuracy.

Range-Free Methods. They are not based the range estimation between anchor nodes to localize targets. For example, APIT [14] estimates location of targets based on the connectivity information to anchor node with known location. The more anchor nodes are deployed, the narrow area that this technique could locate. In other words, the accuracy highly depends on the deployment density of anchor nodes. There is a class of techniques that detect the sequence of some artificially generated events from an event scheduler. For example, Spotlight [13] and Lighthouse [12] correlate the event detection time of a sensor node with the known spatiotemporal relationship. Then, the detection events can be mapped into a possible position. However, it is relatively difficult to generate and disseminate these events to a large-scale area, especially considering calibration efforts.

8 Conclusion and Future Work

In this paper, we have designed, implemented, and evaluated an adaptive RIP method that can enhance the positional accuracy of the static RIP method [1]. The adaptive RIP algorithm is based on the Estimation Error Model that can accurately predict the positional error of RIP method, given a specific SPC selection and the approximate location of a target. We have analytically derived the Estimation Error Model, which was then verified with its correctness through real experimental results. Furthermore, we have built upon this Estimation Error Model to devise an adaptive SPC (sender-pair combination) selection algorithm that dynamically finds the most optimal SPC according to the changing locations of targets relative to anchor nodes. Our experimental results show that the adaptive RIP method outperforms the static RIP method in both single-target and multi-target tracking, improving the average positional error by 47%~60% and at the 90% percentile error by 55%~61%.

For our future work, we would like to pursue several directions. One direction is to better estimate q_{error}, because using an average value as q_{error} in the Estimation Error Model is not so accurate. One possible improvement is to find a way to model the distribution of q_{error} at a finer-grained level, as well as further analyzing factors causing q_{error}, such as multi-path fading (environmental factor), receiving power of interference signal (deployment factors), etc. Considering these factors can help improving the prediction accuracy of our Estimation Error Model.

References

1. Maroti, M., Kusy, B., Balogh, G., Volgyesi, P., Nadas, A., Molnar, K., Dora, S., Ledeczi, A.: Radio-interferometric geolocation. In: Proc. 3rd Int'l Conference Conf. Embedded Networked Sensor Systems (SenSys 05), November 2005, pp. 1–12 (2005)
2. Kusy, B., Maroti, M., Balogh, G., Volgyesi, P., Sallai, J., Nadas, A., Ledeczi, A., Meertens, L.: Node Density Independent Localization. In: Proc. 5th Int'l Conf. Information Processing in Sensor Networks (IPSN/SPOTS 06), April 2006, pp. 441–448 (2006)
3. Kusy, B., Balogh, G., Ledeczi, A., Sallai, J., Maroti, M.: inTrack: High Precision Tracking of Mobile Sensor Nodes. In: Langendoen, K., Voigt, T. (eds.) EWSN 2007. LNCS, vol. 4373, pp. 51–66. Springer, Heidelberg (2007)
4. Kusy, B., Sallai, J., Balogh, G., Ledeczi, A., Protopopescu, V., Tolliver, J., DeNap, F., Parang, M.: Radio Interferometric Tracking of Mobile Wireless Nodes. In: Proc. 5th Int'l Conf. Mobile systems, applications and services (MobiSys 07), June 2007 (2007)
5. Cong, L., Zhuang, W.: Hybrid TDOA/AOA mobile user location for ideband CDMA cellular systems. IEEE Tran. Wireless Communications 1(3), 439–447 (2002)
6. Patwari, N.: Relative location estimation in wireless sensor networks. IEEE Tran. Signal processing 51(8), 2137–2148 (2003)
7. Niculescu, D.: Positioning in ad hoc sensor networks. IEEE Networks 18(4), 24–29 (2004)

8. Bahl, P., Padmanabhan, V.: An in building RF-based user location and tracking system. In: Proc. Conf. Computer Communications (IEEE Infocom 00), March 2000, pp. 775–784 (2000)

9. Lorincz, K., Welsh, M.: Motetrack: A robust, decentralized approach to RF-based location tracking. In: Strang, T., Linnhoff-Popien, C. (eds.) LoCA 2005. LNCS, vol. 3479, pp. 63–82. Springer, Heidelberg (2005)

10. Priyantha, N., Charkraborty, A., Balakrishnan, H.: The cricket location support system. In: Proc. 6th Int'l Conf. Mobile Computing and Networking (MOBICOM 00), August, pp. 32-43 (2000)

11. 3rd Generation Partnership Project, 3GPP TS 05.05, http://www.3gpp.org/

12. Römer, K.: The lighthouse location system for smart dust. Proc. 1st Int'l Conf. Mobile systems, applications and services (MobiSys 03), May, pp. 15-30 (2003)

13. Stoleru, R., He, T., Stankovic, J.A., Luebke, D.: A high-accuracy, lowcost localization system for wireless sensor networks. In: Proc. 3rd Int'l Conference Conf. Embedded Networked Sensor Systems (SenSys 05), pp. 13–26 (2005)

14. He, T., Huang, C., Blum, B.M., Stankovic, J.A., Abdelzaher, T.: Range-Free Localization Schemes in Large-Scale Sensor Networks. In: Proc. 9th annual Int'l Conf. Mobile computing and networking (MOBICOM 03), pp. 81–95 (September 2003)

15. Zhou, G., He, T., Stankovic, J.A.: Impact of Radio Irregularity on Wireless Sensor Networks. In: Proc. 2nd Int'l Conf. Mobile systems, applications and services (MobiSys 04), June 2004, pp. 125–138 (2004)

16. Girod, L., Lukac, M., Trifa, V., Estrin, D.: The design and implementation of a self-calibrating acoustic sensing platform. In: Proc. 4th Int'l Conference Conf. Embedded Networked Sensor Systems (SenSys 06), October 2006, pp. 71–84 (2006)

17. Savvides, A., Han, C.C., Srivastava, M.B.: Dynamic Fine-grained Localization in Ad-Hoc Networks of Sensors. In: Proc. 7th annual Int'l Conf. Mobile computing and net-working (MOBICOM 01), July 2001, pp. 166–179 (2001)

18. Patwari, N., Hero, A.O., Perkins, I.M., Correal, N.S., O'Dea, R.J.: Relative location estimation in wireless sensor networks. IEEE Tran. Signal Process, Special Issue on Signal Processing in Networking 51(9), 2137–2148 (2003)

19. Dragos, N., Nath, B.: Ad hoc positioning system (APS) using AoA. In: Dragos, N., Nath, B. (eds.) Proc. Conf. Computer Communications (IEEE Infocom 03), April 2003, pp. 1734–1743 (2003)

20. RIPS, http://tinyos.cvs.sourceforge.net/tinyos/tinyos-1.x/contrib/vu/apps/RipsOneHop/

Inferring Position Knowledge from Location Predicates

Jörg Roth

Univ. of Applied Sciences Nuremberg
Kesslerplatz 12, 90489 Nuremberg, Germany
Joerg.Roth@FH-Nuernberg.de

Abstract. Many context- and location-aware applications request high accuracy and availability of positioning systems. In reality however, knowledge about the current position may be incomplete or inaccurate as a result of, e.g., limited coverage. Often, position data is thus merged from a set of systems, each contributing a piece of position knowledge. Traditional sensor fusion approaches such as Kalman or Particle filters have certain demands concerning the statistical distribution and relation between position and sensor output. Negated position statements ("I'm *not* at home"), cell-based information or external spatial data are difficult to incorporate into existing mechanisms. In this paper, we introduce a new approach to deal with different types of position data which typically appear in context- or location-aware application scenarios.

Keywords: Location inference, probability model, position data fusion.

1 Introduction

To detect context from the user's current location, position information ideally has a high precision and is constantly available. Many positioning systems, however, have a limited coverage and availability. E.g., GPS does not work indoors and often fails in city centres. Indoor positioning systems only cover some rooms or buildings. Systems with a higher coverage (e.g. based on mobile phone cells) are often inaccurate. In reality, we thus receive a number of incomplete pieces of position knowledge such as:

- I currently receive WLAN cell ABC;
- checking my IP address, I know, I'm *not* at home;
- one minute ago, I received GPS position XY, and I have a maximum speed of 5 km/h as pedestrian.

We call such statements *location predicates*. We often still have uncertainty about the actual position, but we can at least mark some positions as *probable*. A location-aware application could request the most probable positions(s) based on incomplete knowledge to detect the context.

One research field that traditionally deals with different position information is robotics [1, 22]. Based on odometers, ultrasonic distance measurement and cameras, a mobile robot computes the most probable location (often indoors). Established approaches to compute a position from these sensors are Kalman or Particle filters.

J. Hightower, B. Schiele, and T. Strang (Eds.): LoCA 2007, LNCS 4718, pp. 245–262, 2007.

Even though these approaches are widely used, they often cannot be applied to mobile user scenarios due to significant differences: First, potential positions cover the entire Earth's surface and not only rooms or buildings. Second, position data are more complex from the viewpoint of statistics; especially we have non-Gaussian distributed sensor values. Third, we have to access external spatial data such as road maps. These differences highly complicate the task of position inference.

In this paper, we introduce a new mechanism that deals with these issues. As a first idea, every piece of position information is modelled by a standardized data structure that reflects the corresponding knowledge. Second, a mechanism processes this information and constructs a structure that represents the position probability for every location. Third, most probable positions (local maxima or centroids) are derived from these result structures.

2 General Considerations and Related Work

Any piece of information about the position such as

- not to be at home,
- a GPS receiver measured position XY,
- to drive on a road or
- to reside anywhere in the GSM cell ABC

affect the *probability* to reside at a certain position. Actually, the current position is not a random variable in the traditional sense, as it is fix but unknown. We thus formulate the problem as follows: given a position; what is the probability to get the specific list of predicates? In the case of continuous random variables, the probability of any single discrete event is in fact 0. Thus, the probabilities of all positions are represented by a *probability density function* (*pdf*). Strongly related to a pdf f, there exists a *cumulative distribution function* (*cdf*) F with

$$P(X \leq x, Y \leq y) = F(x, y) = \int\limits_{-\infty}^{x} \int\limits_{-\infty}^{y} f(a,b)dbda \qquad (1)$$

for a position (x, y) and random variables X, Y. In principle, we could express the information about the location by a cdf. But as pdfs in contrast to cdfs have small values (or even zero) for improbable positions, approximations that precisely reflect the knowledge require far less memory. Most approaches to model position information by probabilities thus use pdfs.

We first consider a fix point in time and further assume that we collect position information represented by a set of independent predicates z_i. According to the equation of conditional probabilities (Bayes rule) we get

$$f(x \,|\, z_1..z_n) = \frac{\prod f(z_i \,|\, x)f(x)}{\prod f(z_i)} \qquad (2)$$

which describes the position density according to the new information. As $f(z_i)$ does not depend on x, we can consider the denominator as constant. Thus, we do not actually compute $f(z_i)$ and instead normalize the numerator to fulfil

$$\int_{-\infty}^{+\infty} f(x \mid z_1 .. z_n) = 1 \qquad (3)$$

Here, $f(z_i \mid x)$ describes the predicate's general character, e.g., the error probability of a GPS sensor. This distribution is *predefined* and does not change over time, thus can be precomputed for each predicate.

If we had zero position knowledge (uninformative prior), but only rely on the given predicates, the equation simplifies to

$$f(x \mid z_1 .. z_n) = c \cdot \prod f(z_i \mid x) \quad \text{where } c = \frac{1}{\int \prod f(z_i \mid x)} \qquad (4)$$

To consider multiple predicates at a single point in time, we thus mainly need to multiply densities.

To model motion over time, we have to consider a density that represents the position knowledge for position p at a time t_1, say $f(t_1, p)$, and a second density that represents *relative* movement by p_Δ, say $g(t_1, t_2, p_\Delta)$. The resulting density at time t_2 can be computed using the convolution equation

$$f(t_2, p) = \int f(t_1, p - p_\Delta) g(t_1, t_2, p_\Delta) dp_\Delta \qquad (5)$$

Note that the integral is already one, thus no normalization is required.

Equations (4) and (5) form the basic toolset for any probability computation of position data. To compute densities at runtime, we have to approximate densities or assume simplifications. There exist two basic approaches:

- We assume only Gaussian densities and a linear dependency between states. As the two basic equations then significantly can be simplified, we get closed formulas. The Kalman filter is based on this idea.
- We approximate complex densities with the help of simple densities. The most popular example, the Particle filter, approximates any density by a sum of so-called *particles* which actually are Dirac densities. Dirac densities have an infinite value at the given point, 0 elsewhere and an integral of 1.

At this point, we briefly present these approaches.

2.1 Kalman Filters

The Kalman filter [13] is considered as one of the most important mathematical formalisms that deal with positioning. Detailed descriptions can be found in [9, 20]. The Kalman filter assumes a state vector x with arbitrary dimensions. For our scenarios, the state contains typical spatial state information, i.e. the position, but also orientation, speed and acceleration [2, 7, 10]. The state is unknown, but Gaussian distributed measurements y indirectly reflect information about the state. Further, two states at different points in time are linearly related, expressed by a matrix.

A resulting probability density for x is Gaussian distributed expressed by a mean (the most probably state) and an error, expressed by an error covariance matrix. A computation step contains a *time update phase* based on equation (5) and a *measurement update phase* based on equation (4). For the assumptions made for

Kalman filters, the equations can be simplified to a few matrix multiplications and one matrix inversion. These computations can be performed efficiently, even on small computers or embedded systems.

2.2 Particle Filters

Particle filters [5, 8, 11] use a set of particles; each presents a specific potential state. A particle contains a state vector p_i and a weight w_i which reflects the probability density for this state. A probability density f can be approximated by

$$f(p) \approx \frac{1}{N} \sum_{i=1}^{N} w_i \delta(p - p_i) \tag{6}$$

where δ is the Dirac delta density. In principle, a particle can have multiple dimensions, but in contrast to Kalman filters, too many dimensions dilute to result. Typical state vectors only have three dimensions (e.g. 2D position and orientation).

The so-called *Motion Model* that follows equation (5) moves all particles according to the relative movement density. This indirectly computes a convolution. The *Perceptual Model* that follows equation (4) assigns new weights according to multiple measurements at a point in time. This indirectly computes multiplying densities.

Particle filters support a huge variety of densities. Increasing numbers of particles improve the precision, but also increase the required memory and processing time. Particle filters also have to face the *degeneracy problem* [4] where all but one particle have a weight near 0. Approaches such as *Sequential Importance Sampling (SIS)* [6] and *Sampling Importance Resampling (SIR)* [19] counteract this problem applying a resampling step to particles.

2.3 Further Representations

Further representations of position knowledge are *grids, points* and *areas*. The *Position Probability Grid* [3] stores the density values for equidistant positions. Grids require a huge amount of memory space and the potential positions are limited by the initial grid border. Thus, this approach is inappropriate for our intended scenarios.

The *Area model* [15, 18] could be viewed as a simple statistical representation where the area border separates two regions with a uniform distributed position probability – inside the area the integral of probabilities is 1, outside it is 0. The computations based on this idea are quite simple (using the geometric intersection), but this simplification significantly dilutes the position knowledge, especially for Gaussian distributed sensor information.

The *Point model* is the simplest approach to model location knowledge. For any sensor input it only stores the most probably corresponding point in space. This approach is only reasonable, if all positioning systems have a high accuracy and measured values are distributed with a certain mean (i.e. this prohibits COO). Even though it is very unlikely that the measured and the true location are identical, this approach sometimes is useful: multiple pieces of position information can be processed using a weighted average. To promote more accurate sensors, the reciprocal value of the measurement variance can be used as a weight. For our intended scenarios, this approach does not provide sufficient expressiveness.

2.4 Discussion

A system that infers knowledge about the positions in order to detect context information or to support location-based services has to meet the following requirements [18]:

- As many approaches to determine the current position based on the *cell of origin* (*COO*), such information has to be considered. Beyond a certain distance to an access point (especially outdoors), signal strengths do not significantly extend knowledge about the position [21], thus we often use the entire cell as set of potential positions.
- A reasonable approach must be able to consider multiple *alternative* potential positions. E.g., consider a user is at the crossroads to two streets going in nearly the same direction. Further assume that the position data is not precise enough to detect the choice. For a certain time, we thus have to consider both paths for potential positions until further information determines the choice.
- *Negated* information should be modelled. E.g., the current IP address may indicate that an end-user device does not reside a home. *Not* to reside somewhere means to reside nearly anywhere in the world and a nearly infinite space of potential positions has to be considered.
- *External spatial data* should be integrated. A huge amount of spatial information (e.g. roadmaps, information about places) may only be accessible over network. An appropriate algorithm must be able to download additional spatial data at runtime. This especially means to limit the search space for data lookup as not an entire spatial database can be downloaded.

We now check how existing approaches meet these requirements.

If position data meet assumptions described in section 2.1, the Kalman filter extracts the maximum information about the position. Unfortunately, in some typical scenarios these presumptions are not valid:

- COO measurements do not provide a Gaussian density with a certain mean;
- negated information cannot be modelled at all;
- alternative potential paths cannot be modelled as the system always assumes a single probable position;

Particle filters relax some of the assumptions. Especially, they can follow alternative paths as some particles model one alternative and further particles a second one. However, if the number of parallel alternatives increases, the average number of particles decreases and thus the overall precision. Note that at least one particle has to be selected that follows the actual (but unknown) path of real positions. Thus, an appropriate number of particles has to be chosen *beforehand* to anticipate potential alternatives.

With a sufficient (usually high) number of particles, COO measurements can in principle be modelled. The negation, however, is difficult to express if we do not limit the potential space. Finally, both types of filters have their problems with external data as they expect to access all spatial information locally.

Surprisingly, from the approaches described above, the Area model meets a high number of requirements:

- we can model COO measurements using the cell border as modelled area;
- we approximate Gaussian distributions by, e.g., the range of 95% measured positions (the so-called *2dRMS* area for GPS [14]);
- we can describe negations using borders that mark the outer area;
- we can easily load additional data using the area as spatial index.

The main drawback of the Area model is that after a few steps, the precision decreases dramatically and important information is destroyed. We thus looked for a new approach that on the one hand combines the benefits of the Area approach and on the other hand provides sufficient precision.

3 The MAP³ Approach

MAP³ (*Multi-Area Probability-based Positioning by Predicates*) introduces a new approach that deals with problems of comparable approaches described above. The main idea:

- Any piece of information about the location at any point in time is mapped to a *location predicate*. As predicates form a kind of universal interface to any positioning system, they easily can be integrated into existing location driver structures such as the Nimbus VPS [17, 18] or the Location Stack [12].
- A predicate is mapped either to a probability *density representation* (for a predicate that describes a location of a single point in time) or a *convolution operation* (for a predicate that describes movement between two points in time).
- If all predicates are processed, we get a set of densities – one for each considered time stamp. The application now can select a specific point in time.
- Depending on the application, the most probable location (the *centroid*) or a set of local maximum values is computed.

Fig. 1 presents the corresponding data flow. Important: we execute density operations (e.g. multiplication, convolution) with the help of geometric operations widely known in the area of spatial modelling. For this, so-called *simple features* [16] are used for which efficient software libraries are available. From the variety of geometric objects (e.g. points, line strings) we only require the *multipolygon with holes* (*mph*) that represents the most common approximating two-dimensional structure. An mph contains a number of polygons representing the surface. Each of it in turn contains a number of polygons that represent the holes in the surface.

We assume that spatial information is represented in two dimensions. Table 1 presents a selection of considered predicates. We can easily extend this list in the future.

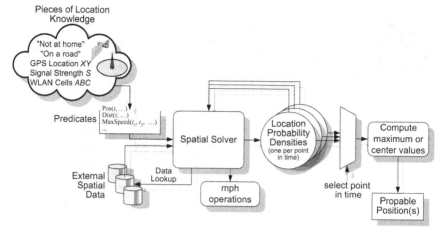

Fig. 1. Data flow in MAP[3]

Table 1. List of predicates

Predicate	Meaning	Example
$Pos(t, x, y, \sigma_x, \sigma_y, \rho)$	Gaussian distributed 2D-position	GPS
$Dist(t, p_x, p_y, d, \sigma)$	Gaussian distributed distance d to a fix point (p_x, p_y)	Runtime or signal strength measurement to a base station
$Nearer(t, p_x, p_y, d)$	The distance to a fix point (p_x, p_y) is below d	Circular cell
$InPoly(t, poly)$	The location is inside a polygon.	Map matching – car must reside on roads
$Dir(t, p_x, p_y, \alpha_1, \alpha_2, m)$	From the viewpoint of (p_x, p_y) the position has a direction inside $[\alpha_1, \alpha_2]$, maximum distance m	Segmented antenna
$MaxSpeed(t_1, t_2, v)$	Maximum speed in this time interval	Pedestrian with a maximum walking speed

Some remarks:

- σ_x, σ_y, σ are standard deviations of the respective Gaussian distribution, ρ the correlation coefficient.
- t denotes the predicate's time (i.e. of the underlying measurement), t_1, t_2 describes a time interval.
- *MaxSpeed* and *InPoly* can be defined without any point in time. In this case, they are considered as always valid.
- Some predicates (details see section 3.2) can be modified using the *Not* modifier, which means that the opposite fact is true. E.g., $Not(Nearer(t, p_x, p_y, d))$ means, the distance to the fix position is equal or more than d.

Fig. 2 illustrates the respective densities. As *MaxSpeed* leads to a special case relating two points in time, it is not shown here (see later). According to the considerations in section 2 we need at least the following operations on densities: computing the centroid and maximum values; multiplying two densities (see equation (4)) and convolving two densities (see equation (5)).

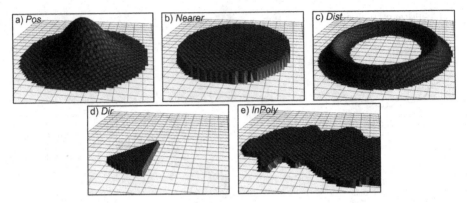

Fig. 2. Predicate densities

A density representation should allow the efficient execution of these operations. In addition, the input densities and resulting densities for (4) and (5) should precisely be presented. The MAP³ approach represents a density f with the help of *areas* as follows

$$f(p) \approx \hat{f}(p) = \sum_{i=1}^{n} w_i \Lambda(p, mph_i) \qquad (7)$$

In this equation

- p describes a point in space (x, y),
- n denotes the number of areas that approximate the density,
- w_i denotes a constant weight of an area,
- mph_i denotes the geometric description of an area and
- Λ the function $\Lambda(p, mph) = \begin{cases} 1 & \text{if } p \in mph \\ 0 & \text{otherwise} \end{cases}$

(we can consider Λ as the characteristic function of mph).

To be a density, $\hat{f}$ has to cover a volume of one, i.e. $\sum_{i=1}^{n} w_i \cdot |mph_i| = 1$. Here $|mph_i|$ denotes the surface area of the multipolygon, i.e. $|mph_i| := \int \Lambda(p, mph_i) dp$.

Two different variations fulfil equation (7):

- Variation 1: $mph_{i-1} \subset mph_i$ for every $i > 1$, i.e. we have an ordered list of areas by their size and each area is fully embedded into the next area.
- Variation 2: $mph_i \cap mph_j = \emptyset$ for every $i \neq j$. We have an ordered list of areas by their weights (from low to high).

The two variations and their influence on the weights are illustrated in fig. 3. Both variations have their pros and cons that we discuss from the viewpoint of variation 2. The advantages of variation 2 are:

- Each point p is enclosed by zero or one polygon, thus computing $\hat{f}(p)$ is very easy. That is why the computation of maximum values also is simple.
- Multiplying densities, two areas that do not overlap do not contribute to the result. Thus, the multiplication has an efficient realization.

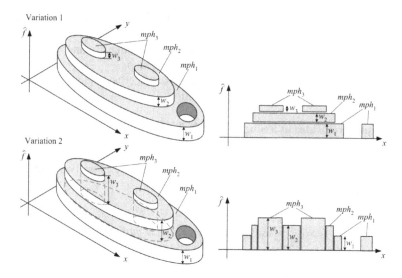

Fig. 3. Variations to present densities with the help of $\hat{f}$

Drawbacks of variation 2:

- Convolving two densities is more complex (see section 3.4).
- Comparing a variation 1 representation for the same density, variation 2 has to encode additional holes. Thus, the memory space to store the mphs nearly doubles compared to variation 1.

As these arguments nearly counterbalance, we introduce a further property into the discussion: the resampling operation. Typical multiplication and convolution operations increase the number of areas, thus, we need a resampling step that joins similar areas to a single area. We know an analogous operation for Particle filters.

We conducted a number of experiments with different resampling operations, coded for the two variations. The only suitable resample operation that is both efficient and does not remove too much information is based on variation 2. Its idea is to unite areas that have similar weights:

```
resample(density d):
as long as d.n>maxArea
    look up area k with |d.w_k - d.w_{k+areaDecr-1}| minimal
```
$$\text{create new area with } mph_{new} \leftarrow \bigcup_{i=k}^{k+areaDecr-1} d.mph_i$$

$$\text{and } w_{new} \leftarrow \left(\sum_{i=k}^{k+areaDecr-1} w_i \cdot |d.mph_i| \right) / |mph_{new}|$$

```
    replace area k by the new area
    remove areas k+1 ... k+areaDecr-1 from d
```

In this algorithm $d.n$ denotes number of areas in the density, $d.mph_i$ the multipolygon for area i, and $d.w_i$ the weight of area i. This algorithm further requires two constants: *maxArea* – the maximum numbers of areas allowed in a density and *areaDecr* – the number of areas that are united in a single resampling step.

Based on the considerations above, especially an effective resampling mechanism, we chose variation 2 for the density representation.

3.1 Multiple Predicates at a Single Point in Time

According to equation (4), we have to multiply all densities representing the same time. After normalizing, we then get the result density. For two approximated densities $\hat{f}_1, \hat{f}_2$ we use the equation

$$\hat{f}_1 \cdot \hat{f}_2 = \hat{c} \cdot \left(\sum_{i=1}^{n_1} w_{1i} \Lambda(mph_{1i}) \right) \cdot \left(\sum_{j=1}^{n_2} w_{2j} \Lambda(mph_{2j}) \right)$$

$$= \hat{c} \cdot \sum_{i=1}^{n_1} \sum_{j=1}^{n_2} w_{1i} w_{2j} \Lambda(mph_{1i} \cap mph_{2j})$$

(8)

where $mph_{1i} \cap mph_{2j}$ is the geometric intersection of two areas and $\hat{c}$ the normalization factor.

Some remarks on efficiency: First, only those mph_{1i}, mph_{2j} that overlap contribute to the result, thus an efficient algorithm first tests this, before the actual intersection is computed. As the overlapping test knows efficient implementations (e.g. using bounding boxes), this approach is reasonable.

Second, we have predicates that only contain a single area (e.g. *Nearer*). Such predicates can efficiently be multiplied by another density as the overall number of areas does not increase.

Third, even though we get $O(n_1 n_2)$ resulting areas, the actual number of overlapping mphs is far less than $n_1 n_2$. Note that low numbers of areas, e.g. 10, lead to sufficiently precise results, thus typically 20-50 areas are included in the result. But as the result may be input for further multiplications, a resampling step is required.

The multiply algorithm can be sketched as follows:

```
multiply(density d₁, density d₂):
  result ← ∅
  for i=1 to d₁.n do
    for j=1 to d₂.n
      if  d₁.mphᵢ ∩ d₂.mphⱼ ≠ ∅
          create new area with  mph_new ← d₁.mphᵢ ∩ d₂.mphⱼ
                         and  w_new ← d₁.wᵢ · d₂.wⱼ
          add new area to result
  normalize result
  resample result
```

To normalize the result, we sum up the surface areas multiplied by their weights, i.e. compute $I \leftarrow \sum w_i |mph_i|$. We then adapt all weights $w_i \leftarrow w_i / I$.

3.2 Modelling Negations

The *Not* modifier negates a predicate. Usually, this means to specify a very large area of possible positions by a single density. E.g., *Not(Nearer(t, p_x, p_y, d))* specifies all positions outside a given circle. We can consider this area as infinite, even though in reality, the respective area is limited by the Earth's surface. This means that the actual probability density at any given point is in fact 0, i.e. meaningless.

More formally: if F is the cdf and f the pdf of a predicate, the negation can be expressed by

$$1 - P(X \leq x, Y \leq y) = 1 - F(x, y) = 1 - \int\limits_{-\infty}^{x} \int\limits_{-\infty}^{y} f(a,b)dbda \qquad (9)$$

To express the negated predicate by a density, we need a density $\bar{f}$ that fulfils

$$1 - \int\limits_{-\infty}^{x} \int\limits_{-\infty}^{y} f(a,b)dbda = \int\limits_{-\infty}^{x} \int\limits_{-\infty}^{y} \bar{f}(a,b)dbda \text{ and } \int\limits_{-\infty}^{\infty} \int\limits_{-\infty}^{\infty} \bar{f}(a,b)dbda = 1 \qquad (10)$$

Unfortunately, it is not possible to provide a close description for $\bar{f}$ or $\hat{f}$. A possible solution to avoid zero densities would be to presume a limited area of potential positions. To be useful, this maximum area has to be small enough to avoid densities near to 0. The important drawback of this solution is the lack of *a priori* knowledge about potential positions. This is an important difference to the robotic (indoor) scenario.

To achieve a solution for negated predicates, we propose the following approach:

- Only predicates that have a unique density inside a finite area and a zero density outside can be negated. Such predicates are *Nearer*, *InPoly*, and *Dir*. Only such densities are reasonable densities for negations.
- The negation can only be applied inside a multiplication of two densities, where the second density has to be non-negated. This especially means, at least one non-negated predicate is required for a certain point in time.

To give a realistic example that conflicts with the second assumption: If we had three predicates stating "not at home", "not at work" and "not on any road", we still had a virtually infinite space to consider. Only with an additional *positive* predicate (e.g. "inside GSM cell XY"), we can construct an area of probable positions.

According to these considerations, we now can compute negations: let f_1 be a density and f_2 a density that should be negated. Then

$$f_{result} = c \cdot f_1 \cdot \bar{f}_2 \text{ where } \bar{f}_2(p) = \begin{cases} 1 & f_2(p) = 0 \\ 0 & \text{otherwise} \end{cases} \qquad (11)$$

Again, c is the normalizing factor. Note that $\bar{f}_2$ is not a density, as it does not produce an integral of one. Thus, we explicitly mark a density as negated and store the original non-negated density.

To actually perform this operation, we simply subtract the mph of f_2 from all areas of f_1 and normalize the result. This means, the multiply operation with a negated density knows an efficient geometric realization. We present the algorithm together with an extension to model uncertainty in the next section.

3.3 Modelling Uncertainty

In contrast to positive predicates, negative statements about the position can be uncertain. If I got sensor information stating a certain position (e.g. a *Pos* predicate), the only uncertainty can be a measurement error that is already modelled by the Gaussian distribution. In contrast, negative predicates may be uncertain in a more general meaning. If, e.g., I do not receive my home WLAN, I may be outside my home area, but also, with a small probability, I *am* at home and my WLAN router is switched off. To model these characteristics, we can append a general probability pr to the *Not* modifier. E.g., *Not(Nearer(t, p_x, p_y, d), 0.9)* means:

- with a probability of 90%, the position is outside the specified circle;
- with a probability of 10%, the position may be anywhere (i.e. inside *or* outside the circle).

We could use this predicate to, e.g., model a circular WLAN cell, where the access point's uptime is 90% on average.

For $pr=1$ we get the definite negative statement as introduced above. We can modify equation (11) as follows

$$f_{result} = c \cdot (pr \cdot f_1 \cdot \bar{f}_2 + (1-pr) \cdot f_1) \tag{12}$$

$$f_{result}(p) = c \cdot \begin{cases} pr \cdot f_1(p) + (1-pr) \cdot f_1(p) = f_1(p) & \text{if } \bar{f}_2(p) = 1 \\ (1-pr) \cdot f_1(p) & \text{if } \bar{f}_2(p) = 0 \end{cases} \tag{13}$$

Based on these equations, we can easily derive an algorithm that is fully built on geometric mph operations:

```
multiplyNegation(density d₁, density d₂, pr):
result ← ∅
for i=1 to d₁.n do
    create new area with  mph_new ← d₁.mph_i \ d₂.mph₁
        and  w_new ← d₁.w_i                // case f̄₂(p)=1
    if not empty add new area to result
    create new area with  mph_new ← d₁.mph_i ∩ d₂.mph₁
        and  w_new ← d₁.w_i · (1-pr)       // case f̄₂(p)=0
    if not empty add new area to result
normalize result
```

For every area of the first density up to two areas are created: the first area represents the case $\bar{f}_2(p) = 1$ of equation (13), the second area represents the second case.

3.4 Modelling Motion over Time

Until now, we only considered multiple predicates at a single point in time. But what, if we had multiple predicates at different times. This is the usual case for position measurements: we do not only get current sensor input, but can consider all recent sensor information to improve the current estimation. For this, we have to model spatial movement between two points in time.

Kalman and Particle filters often assume precise movement sensors such as odometers. In our intended scenarios, however, such sensors are often not available. E.g., for a pedestrian it is not possible to *explicitly* measure the direction and distance she or he walked in the last 10 seconds. Usually, the only mechanism to detect movement is to build vectors between last measured absolute positions. But these positions are already considered by the mechanisms presented before, thus they would not increase the overall position knowledge.

If no relative movement sensors are available, we only can define a maximum speed, derived from knowledge about the movement context (e.g., to be a pedestrian, or to drive a car). A maximum movement distance for a certain time is defined by a circular density with centre at the zero point, with a unique density inside the circle and 0 outside, i.e.

$$c(p,r) = \begin{cases} 1/(\pi r^2) & \text{if } x^2 + y^2 \le r^2 \text{ for } p = (x,y) \\ 0 & \text{otherwise} \end{cases} \tag{14}$$

In the following we describe how to convolve an arbitrary density with such a density c. The convolution (equation (5)) then simplifies as follows:

$$\int \hat{f}(t_1, p - p_\Delta) \cdot c(p_\Delta, r) dp_\Delta = \int \left(\sum_{i=1}^{n} w_i \Lambda(p - p_\Delta, mph_i) \right) \cdot c(p_\Delta, r) dp_\Delta$$

$$= \sum_{i=1}^{n} w_i \left(\int \Lambda(p - p_\Delta, mph_i) \cdot c(p_\Delta, r) dp_\Delta \right) \tag{15}$$

This means, we have to approximate the inner integral and create a sum. As the convolution operation is very complex, we can due to space limitations of this paper only provide the idea here.

We have to consider two cases as illustrated in fig. 4. If the area of an mph is large compared to the circle, the area that covers all points with a non-zero integral can be computed using the so-called *buffer* operation [16]. The buffer contains all points that do not exceed a certain distance to an mph. The buffer operation is available in typical geometric software libraries and can efficiently be executed.

Fig. 4 (upper right) shows the buffers for three integrals: the maximum integral (inner buffer), 50% if the maximum (second buffer) and an integral of 0 (outer buffer). With a linear approximation (that produces a maximum error of 5.8%) we can easily compute any degree between 0 and the maximum integral.

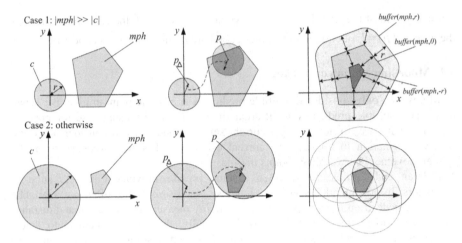

Fig. 4. Cases to convolve densities

The second case is more difficult. We can easily see that for very large circles, the area of non-zero integrals converts itself to a circle. For smaller circles we get a bulky shape as shown in fig. 4 lower right. To compute this shape, we would need a new mph operation that we call *inverse buffer*: similar to the buffer, it contains all points that do not exceed a certain distance, but in contrast to the traditional buffer, we do not use the distance with the *smallest* Euclidean value, but the *largest* one.

Unfortunately, the inverse buffer operation is usually not available as library function. Thus, we conducted some experiments using circular approximations. Usually, these approximations provide sufficient precision for our intended scenarios.

Independent from the case, we can produce a number of areas for every mph of the second density. The number defines the convolution's precision. As the overall number of areas increases, a final resampling step is required.

3.5 Generating Results

With our density representation, it is very easy to compute the *centroid* which represents the most probable position based on all processed predicates. Obviously, the centroid can be computed according to the equation

$$centroid = \frac{\sum \left(centroid(mph) \cdot |mph_i| \cdot w_i \right)}{\sum \left(|mph_i| \cdot w_i \right)} = \sum \left(centroid(mph) \cdot |mph_i| \cdot w_i \right) \quad (16)$$

Note that for mphs there exist efficient centroid functions.

Often, the centroid does not reflect the intension, especially if we follow multiple alternative paths as introduced in section 2.4. The centroid can, e.g., reside inside a hole with low probabilities. Thus, a further algorithm computes the set of local maxima. At this point we only give the idea of this algorithm:

- As the areas are sorted by their w_i, it is easy to select the absolute maximum value.
- For the selected maximum, we can delete areas that belong to this maximum going "downhill", i.e. we delete such *neighbouring* areas with smaller weights.
- From the remaining areas, we select the next maximum and so forth.

This algorithm is a typical hill climbing algorithm (even though we actually walk downhill). This approach is efficient: First, $\hat{f}(p)$ can easily be computed for every position p. Second, the neighbourhood relation can efficiently be tested using an mph *distance* operation. Note that for variation 1 (see fig. 3) this approach would be much more difficult, as "hills" would be modelled by multiple areas.

Finally, we have to argue, why MAP^3 is able to deal with external data as required in section 2.4. Consider a user with a GPS receiver. The last measured position indicates a subway station before reception fails inside the subway. We apply an *InPoly* predicate that defines all conceivable connected subway stations. As we only have *external* access to subway coordinates, MAP^3 has to generate a look-up request to the subway's spatial database.

In contrast to comparable approaches, it is easy for MAP^3 to compute all conceivable positions (i.e. those with $f(p)>0$), which is simply the geometric union of all mph areas. Kalman filters do not explicitly identify improbable positions. Affirmed knowledge about probabilities in Particle filters is only available for those positions represented by particles. Thus, a complex heuristic would be required to compute an area with non-zero probabilities.

As in our case the area of potential position can easily be computed, we get a simple mechanism to access external data: we use this area as spatial index to external databases. To get a most useful index, we process external data very late in the chain of predicates.

Considering the characteristics of all involved predicate types, we now can define the procedure to process location predicates as follows:

1. We identify the earliest time t for which non-processed predicates exist. We then multiply predicate densities for t according to the priority (1) available convolution results (2) non-negated, local predicates; (3) negated, local predicates (4) external predicates, using the prior result as spatial index.
2. For any time t_2 defined by further predicates, we produce a convolution for (t, t_2).
3. We go back to 1 until all predicates are processed.

After terminating the loop, all predicates are processed and we get a list of densities according to fig. 1. We finally can compute centroids or maximum values for a desired time stamp.

4 Experimental Results

We conducted several experiments to verify the approach. Not surprisingly, MAP^3 works well, if the position input provides a high precision such as position data from GPS. Compared to Kalman and Particle filters, our new approach leads to nearly the same results in such scenarios.

The benefit becomes apparent, if we process typical pieces of information available in location-based service scenarios. Here, we have to consider COO input, especially with negations. Kalman and Particle filters have significant problems with these data as discussed above, but our approach still works properly.

We consider a scenario as presented in fig. 5.

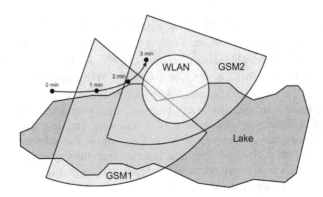

Fig. 5. The sample scenario

A walker promenades at a lakeside. Every minute, his mobile device tries to receive
GSM and WLAN cell information. We assume the device can receive up to two GSM
cells and one WLAN. The track in fig. 5 first passes cell GSM1, then the overlapping
area and finally only cell GSM2. We further know that inside GSM2 there is a
WLAN cell that we do not receive. The WLAN cell has a 90% uptime. According to
these data, we derive the location predicates as presented in table 2.

Table 2. Input predicates

Time	Predicate	Meaning
-	*MaxSpeed*(5km/h)	Pedestrians are not faster than 5km/h
-	*Not*(*InPoly*(LAKE_POLY))	Pedestrians cannot walk on water
1 min	*InPoly*(1min, GSM1_POLY)	Receiving cell GSM1
2 min	*InPoly*(1min, GSM1_POLY)	Receiving both GSM cells
	InPoly(1min, GSM2_POLY)	
3 min	*InPoly*(1min, GSM2_POLY)	Receiving only cell GSM2
	Not(*InPoly*(1min, GSM1_POLY))	Not GSM1
	Not(*Nearer*(2min, WLAN_CENTER,	WLAN cell is not in range and the WLAN
	WLAN_RADIUS),0.9)	has an uptime of 90%

These predicates undergo the MAP[3] process as presented in section 3. In summary,
the process executed 2 convolutions, 3 multiplications and 5 multiplications with
negation. Fig. 6 shows the results.

We get the first result after one minute. As we know not to be inside the lake, the
remaining cell GSM1 covers the potential positions. In this case, our maximum value
computation replies two most probable positions (fig. 6b, indicated by the arrows).
This is a typical case of two alternatives as discussed in section 2.4.

The next step (2 min) takes into account the convolution (based on the *MaxSpeed*
predicate). Looking at the last step (3 min), we see a plateau with low probability and
a peak that indicates the most probable position. The plateau is a result of the
WLAN's 10% downtime. This plateau does not significantly contribute to the result
for $t = 3$ min, but as further measurements may indicate that this area covers the only
possible positions, it is important to preserve this information.

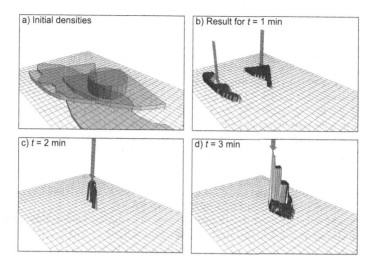

Fig. 6. Computed densities

In this example, the final position estimation considered *all* given information: the position is outside the lake, it considered the received (and not received) cells and it considered the maximum speed. The density presented in fig. 5d thus contains much more information than outputs of comparable approaches.

We chose this simple example due to presentation reasons. We conducted much more complex evaluations that in principle show similar results. With the MAP[3] approach we effectively are able to derive probable positions even from uncertain input data such as presented in this example.

5 Conclusion and Future Work

In this paper we presented the new MAP[3] approach that infers knowledge about the current position from sets of location predicates. Whereas many current approaches assume precise and reliable information, our approach is also able to derive probable positions from widely used positioning systems based on the cell of origin paradigm.

As main benefits, MAP[3] is able to deal with negated and uncertain predicates, alternative paths and non-Gaussian densities that often appear in location- or context-based scenarios. Especially, MAP[3] is able to specify spatial indices to access external spatial databases. Our approach heavily makes use of geometric operations widely available and efficiently implemented in many tool environments, software libraries and spatial databases.

Our current approach processes each unknown position separately. In the future we want to introduce predicates that relate multiple unknown positions to each others. This scenario becomes more and more important. Users may exchange their respective probabilities inside ad-hoc networks and improve their own position knowledge. If they are connected by, e.g., Bluetooth, they know to reside at the nearly same location. To incorporate this knowledge, we have to introduce a new predicate type and the respective processing mechanism.

References

1. Borenstein, J., Everett, B., Feng, L.: Navigating Mobile Robots: Systems and Techniques. A. K. Peters Ltd, Wellesley MA (1996)
2. Bruch, M.H., Gilbreath, G.A., Muelhauser, J.W., Lum, J.Q.: Accurate Waypoint Navigation Using Non-differential GPS. AUVSI Unmanned Systems. Lake Buena Vista, FL (2002)
3. Burgard, W., Fox, D., Hennig, D., Schmidt, T.: Estimating the Absolute Position of a Mobile Robot Using Position Probability Grids. IAAI 2, 896–901 (1996)
4. Doucet, A.: On Sequential Monte Carlo Methods for Bayesian Filtering. Technical Report University of Cambridge, UK Dept. of Engineering (1998)
5. Doucet, A., de Freitas, N., Gordon, N. (eds.) Sequential Monte Carlo in Practice. Springer, New York (2001)
6. Doucet, A., Godsill, S., Andrieu, C.: On Sequential Monte Carlo Sampling Methods for Bayesian Filtering. Statistics and Computing 10(3), 197–208
7. Drolet, L., Michaud, F., Côté, J.: Adaptable sensor fusion using multiple Kalman filters. In: Proc. IEEE/RSJ Intl. Conf. on Intelligent Robots and Systems (IROS), Takamatsu, Japan (2000)
8. Fox, D., Thrun, S., Burgard, W., Dellaert, F.: Particle Filters for mobile robot localization. Sequential Monte Carlo Methods in Practice. Springer, New York (2001)
9. Grewal, M., Andrews, A.: Kalman Filtering: theory and practice. Prentice-Hall, Inc, Englewood Cliffs, New Jersey (1993)
10. Hide, C.D., Moore, T., Smith, M.J.: Multiple model Kalman filtering for GPS and low-cost INS integration. In: Proceedings of ION GNSS 2004, Long Beach, CA, USA (2004)
11. Hightower, J., Borriello, G.: Particle Filters for Location Estimation in Ubiquitous Computing: A Case Study. In: Davies, N., Mynatt, E.D., Siio, I. (eds.) UbiComp 2004. LNCS, vol. 3205, pp. 88–106. Springer, Heidelberg (2004)
12. Hightower, J., Brummit, B., Borriello, G.: The Location Stack: A layered model for location in ubiquitous computing. In: Proc. of the 4th IEEE Workshop on Mobile Computing Systems and Applications (WMCSA 2002), June, pp. 22–28. Callicoon, New York (2002)
13. Kalman, R.: A new approach to linear Filtering and prediction problems. Transactions ASME Journal of Basic Engineering 82, 35–44 (1960)
14. Küpper, A.: Location-based Services. John Wiley & Sons, Chichester (2005)
15. Leonhardi, A., Kubach, U.: An Architecture for a Distributed Universal Location Service. In: Proc. of the European Wireless '99 Conference, pp. 351–355 (1999)
16. Open Geospatial Consortium Inc.: OpenGIS. In: Herring, J.R. (ed.) Implementation Specification for Geographic information - Simple feature access - Part 1: Common architecture & Part 2: SQL option. (2006)
17. Roth, J.: Flexible Positioning for Location-based Services. IADIS Journal on WWW/Internet 1(2), 18–32 (2003)
18. Roth, J.: A Decentralized Location Service Providing Semantic Locations. Computer Science Report 323, Habilitation thesis, University of Hagen (January 2005)
19. Rubin, D.B.: Using the sir algorithm to simulation posterior distributions. In: Bernado, J.M., DeGroot, M.H., Lindley, D.V., Smith, A.F.M. (eds.) Bayesian Statistics, vol. 3, pp. 395–402. Oxford University Press, Oxford (1988)
20. Sorenson, H.W.: Least-Squares estimation: from Gauss to Kalman. IEEE Spectrum, 7, 63–68 (1970)
21. Wang, Y., Jia, X., Lee, H.K., Li, G.Y.: An indoor wireless positioning system based on WLAN infrastructure. 6th Int. Symp. on Satellite Navigation Technology Including Mobile Positioning & Location Services, Melbourne, Australia, (22-25 July) (2003)
22. Weiß G., Wetzler, C., von Puttkamer, E.: Keeping track of position and orientation of moving indoor systems by correlation of range-finder scans. In: Proc. of the Intl. Conf. on Intelligent Robots and Systems, pp. 595–601 (1994)

Preserving Anonymity in Indoor Location System by Context Sensing and Camera-Based Tracking

Takeshi Iwamoto, Arei Kobayashi, and Satoshi Nishiyama

KDDI R&D Laboratories Inc.
2-1-15 Ohara, Fujimino, Saitama 3568502, Japan
{ta-iwamoto,kobayasi,tomo}@kddilabs.jp

Abstract. In this paper, we present a novel indoor location system, called Activity based Location Tracking and Identification (ALTI), which uses a combination of a camera-based tracking system in the environment and mobile devices with motion sensors. In the indoor environment, GPS-based location systems cannot offer precise location information as they fail to find the required number of GPS satellites. Therefore, many indoor location systems are proposed and developed. However, these systems still have the following two issues if they are applied for the public spaces, such as a shopping mall, an underground mall and a station where many general public visit: (1) many of location systems manage location information in centralized severs, but many people do not want to have their locations in public spaces managed by others (privacy issue) and (2) many of location systems need dedicated user devices, we can not expect that all the people in the public spaces carrying such devices (special device issue). ALTI is based on the combination of camera-based tracking system which generates anonymous user's location information and mobile phone handsets as the user's devices. ALTI solves the above issues by using mobile phone handsets as the user's devices for the special device issue and by estimating the user's location within his/her mobile phone handset assisted by anonymous location information from camera-based tracking system for the first issue. As a results, the ALTI offers fairly good user privacy. This paper describes the detailed mechanism of ALTI and shows the feasibility of it through a preliminary evaluation using the actual visual tracking system and the prototype terminal devices.

1 Introduction

Location-based services have become key ubiquitous computing applications. For example, the common three mobile phone carriers in Japan provide human navigation services, which use the Global Positioning System (GPS) to obtain location information. Although GPS is popular, thanks to its convenience and low cost, it also has a serious drawback in that precise location cannot be determined unavailable in indoor environments. For this reason, navigation services are not usable in buildings or underground, despite the strong need for such

J. Hightower, B. Schiele, and T. Strang (Eds.): LoCA 2007, LNCS 4718, pp. 263–278, 2007.

availability, even in indoor environments where GPS is inaccessible. Additionally, fine-grained location in indoor is necessary for some kind of application. For example, a museum guidance application on a mobile phone, which provide a description of works in an actual museum, should distinct which works is located in front of a user.

Recently, various techniques have been developed to locate objects in indoor environments without GPS. A typical example is an ultrasonic-based indoor location system. It provides very precise locations of users in indoor environments, however, it forces all users to carry special tags. It is feasible to have everyone carry the same special tag in certain places, such as an office and a home, as limited users use the places. In contrast, it is difficult to assume that everyone are carrying such special tag in "public spaces" such as a shopping mall, an underground mall and a station. Therefore, a method allowing objects without special devices, such as tags, to be successfully located indoors is required in public spaces,

In addition, indoor location systems in public spaces face another serious issue in privacy. In terms of privacy, the most important difference to private spaces is that users do not want to expose private information pieces to an administrator in public spaces. In the former, users can often trust a specific administrator at the private space, and therefore allow him/her to manage a certain level of the user information. In contrast however, a user cannot trust an administrator in a public space, because most users are usually visitors to such spaces, such as customers in a shop or mere passengers. In this case, users cannot accept an administrator managing their location information.

We aim to provide a solution for an indoor location system which can be used in a public space. The system requirements for an indoor location system in public spaces include avoiding the usage of special devices and protecting the privacy of located users. Our solution achieves these requirements by using only motion sensors (accelerometers) on a mobile phone and cameras that are placed in the public space. By using a mobile phone handset as the user's terminal, our solution avoids the deploying additional special devices to users. The mobile phone handset receives location information (trajectories) of anonymous users in the public space from a camera-based tracking system and estimates which trajectory is the user's one by matching the trajectory with the sensor data from the motion sensor on the handset. Therefore ALTI can locate a certain user without a centralized location management server to avoid privacy issues.

The specific contributions of our paper are twofold, as follows. Firstly, our location method is the first one which protects privacies of tracked users without special devices. Secondly, we perform experiments within an actual environment and confirm that ALTI works well as we designed it.

2   Related Work: Existing Indoor Location System

Several forms of research and products have been built for the indoor location system. We classify existing indoor location systems into 5 types, according to the technologies on which they are based.

2.1   Ultrasonic-Based System

Ultrasonic-based systems can estimate a user's location to an accuracy within a few centimeters. 3 or more receivers (or transmitters) are installed in the environment, and the systems estimate distances from the ultrasonic tag that the user has to the receivers (or transmitters) and calculate the user's location based on triangulation methods.

Basically, the systems can be separated into two types according to the respective roles of the receiver and tag. The first typical examples are Active Bat [1][2] and InterSense IS-600 [3]. Active Bat and IS-600 are similar in that several receivers are installed into an environment, typically on a ceiling, from where they detect the location of a transmitter held by a user. The second example is Cricket [4], where users carry the receivers and the transmitters are installed into an environment. Generally, the systems requires special hardware infrastructure to be installed in an environment, which costs tens of thousands of dollars for a 1000m^2 installation, and users need to carry the special tags.

2.2   Wireless LAN-Based System

The systems measure radio strength between a base station and mobile node and estimate locations of users. Basically, the systems are divided into two types, according to the sites of location management: client side management and server side management. The former system observes radio strength in client software and estimates own location. Therefore, the client software should have a map of radio strength in the space in advance before it estimates the location of the user. The latter system observes the radio strength of the users and estimates in server software. A wireless node (e.g. PC or PDA) broadcasts packets to multiple base station. The server estimates location of wireless node form the signal strength values at the base stations. Ekahau [5] and RADAR [6] are the systems using Wireless LAN.

Since wireless LAN technologies, such as IEEE 802.11a/b/g, are widely prevalent, wireless LAN-based location systems has advantage to other systems in respect to the cost.

2.3   RFID-Based System

The RFID-based system basically uses radio communication between tags and a receiver, and is usually used to identify and track tags. Various applications are actually used in the areas of logistics, security and digital money. Two different types of tags exist: "active tag" and "passive tag". The active tag has its own power supply and sends radio signal to the receiver with its ID and other attribute information, whereupon a base stations receives the information, extract the ID (and optional information) and sends it to the server. Location systems using an active tag estimate an area where the tags exists by using information from one or more receivers.

The second type of tag system, the "passive tag", differs to the active tag system on that it uses the power provided from the readers in the form of radio wave to send the ID and optional information. Therefore the communication range is relatively short compared to the active type and it is suitable for obtaining spot information of an object (or a person).

2.4   Camera-Based System

An image-recognition technique enables the system to detect the object location in camera images [7]. A camera installed in environment, such as surveillance camera, captures images of the environment, in which the system recognizes objects via image-recognition techniques. By giving the system a 3-Dimensional location model, the system can convert an object location in camera coordination system to that in 2D map coordinates.

The problem encountered by the system is difficulty in identifying a user. A typical solutions to this problem are using color histogram or face matching. In these techniques, the system needs to register the color of clothes of the users or the face of them in advance before it works.

2.5   Dead Reckoning-Based System

Dead reckoning is a method used to estimate the current position by using an accelerometer mounted on a human body. Firstly, the system estimates the speed and direction of movement from the accelerometer data. Secondly, the system advances the current position by a relative distance, calculated based on the results of estimation.

Several pieces of research [8] apply dead reckoning to human navigation. However, currently they failed to remove the influence from complicated body movements which reduces the accuracy of estimation without any condition for carrying the device. To avoid the problem, they fixed the position of the accelerometer device to the human body, such as fixing to the waist tightly.

Another difficulty of dead reckoning system is derived from an accumulation of estimation error, because a current position is estimated based upon the prior position. Therefore to achieve high accuracy, the system should utilize map-matching method and/or a high accuracy but expensive sensor.

3   Requirements for an Indoor Location System in Public Spaces

We focus on "public spaces" as the target indoor environment, such as a shopping mall, station or d underground mall. The public space is defined as a place accessed by the general public. In contrast, the "personal space" is defined as a place accessed by certain and authenticated people. As previously described, although a number of indoor location systems exist, many systems assume use in personal space, meaning several limitations are imposed when providing the same service in a public space. In this section, we describe the requirements for an indoor location system in public spaces, and point out the problems of existing location systems.

3.1 Requirement 1: No Centralized Control of Identification Information

Several indoor location systems are based on a centralized server mechanism, where location information of all the users are identified and managed using their IDs. For example, the server in RFID-based system calculates the location of the tag using the ID and the radio strength values at the base stations, hence, location and associated ID are managed in the server. The ultrasonic-based location system also manages user's location and identification in the server. These mechanism could be threats to the user privacy, exposing the users to considerable stress, since most people would prefer to keep knowledge of their activity from others.

Usually people uses the public spaces as visitors, customers or just passengers and do not want to have their locations managed in the system for the public spaces, since they do not trust the administrators or since the relationship between them and the public spaces are not stronger than those with private spaces. Therefore, the first requirement is "no centralized control of identification information". That is, any software in the environment should not be able to identify the location of a specific user in order to avoid the privacy issue.

3.2 Requirement 2: No Additional Specific Device

The second requirement is "no additional specific device". Several indoor location systems force users to have the same devices due to their nature. Ultrasonic-based and RFID-based systems assume users have specific tags, such as an ultrasonic transmitter or an RFID tag. Ensuring users are deployed with tha same devices can be assumed in a private space, because the users are limited and registered in advance, however since the users of a public space are the general public, it is difficult to deploy the special devices for them.

4 Design

We designed Activity-based Location Tracking and Identification (ALTI) as a location tracking system in public spaces. ALTI meets the requirements discusses in the previous section, which are derived from the characteristics of public spaces. In this section, we describe our design principles and the actual design of ALTI.

4.1 Design Principles

To fulfill the requirements, we decide to employ two key technologies, namely a camera-based tracking system and a mobile phone.

Solution 1: Collaboration of Camera-Based Tracking System and Personal Devices. As the solution to the requirement 1, we employ a camera-based tracking system to obtain a user's location. The camera-based tracking system is originally incapable of identifying users and just tracks the trajectories of anonymous users. This characteristic is suitable for the requirement 1, which is namely no centralized control of identification information. However, the location information obtained from the tracking system is still anonymous. ALTI solves the identification problem of anonymous trajectories by the collaboration with personal devices. The identification process is executed in the user's personal device using the motion sensor data obtained in the personal device. Therefore only the user's trajectory could be identified and the rests remain anonymous.

Solution 2: Employ Mobile Phones. To avoid the problem with deploying special personal devices, ALTI assumes the usage of mobile phone handsets. Recently, mobile phone handsets are not considered special anymore, considering that, for example, their penetration rate of over 70% in Japan. Thanks to the nature of the mobile phone, most of the users carry their handsets with them at most of time. Furthermore, handsets equipped with motion sensors are already commercially available[9] and will be more popular in near future. Recent handsets are also Java-enabled or have similar programming environment (such as BREW©[10]). Therefore, ALTI assumes that mobile phone handsets has motion sensors and software for ALTI can be easily downloaded into user's handsets.

4.2   Matching Context Sensing and Anonymous Trajectory

ALTI is an algorithm which users apply to determine their own location, based on a set of unidentified objects detected by a camera-based tracking system. The key feature of ALTI is matching an "anonymous location" from camera-based tracking system and "context sensing". The matching process enables the location of a certain user to be identified by only user's own device without any centralized location server. An overview of ALTI is shown in Figure 1.

As discussed, the camera-based tracking system cannot identify certain objects, even though the system tracks the locations of all objects. In ALTI, the tracking system broadcasts location of all objects to the mobile phone handsets continuously. On receiving the anonymous location, the handset tries to determine its own location as follows. Firstly, the user's handset recognizes his/her movements by processing motion sensor data. Recently, various small and low-cost sensors have been installed in mobile phones. We assume that a mobile phone handset has a 3-axis acceleration sensor and 3-axis geomagnetic sensor to obtain user's movement. Secondly, the handset also creates movement trajectories of all users, based on the location information received from the camera-based tracking system. Since the trajectories are also anonymous, it compares the trajectories and a user's own movements to identify the user's own trajectory from all of the trajectories. As the identification performed entirely on his/her own handset, user anonymity is guaranteed.

4.3   Trajectory Creation, Activity Recognition and Trajectory Estimation

The matching algorithm consists of 3 key processes, namely "trajectory creation", "activity recognition" and "trajectory estimation". The former two processes, trajectory creation and activity recognition are used to generate more

Camera-based Tracking System

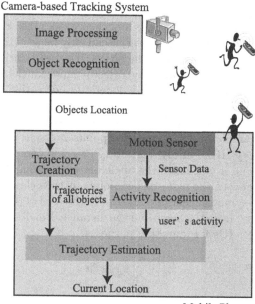

Fig. 1. ALTI Design

abstract representations of trajectories of objects and user's activities from raw data (object locations from tracking system and the sensor data), so that the computation complexity of the last process, trajectory estimation, is reduced to run in the mobile phone handsets. Currently we use very simple 4 symbols, i.e. "walk", "stop", "right trun" and "left turn", to represent the object trajectories and the user's activities. Finally trajectory estimation process compare the anonymous object trajectories with the user's activities and estimates which is the user's one.

Another approach, dead reckoning techniques, may be used for the trajectory estimation as another candidate. The trajectory of user's movements can be calculated by the twice-integral of acceleration equivalent to the dead reckoning-based systems described above. Comparison of the form of user's movement and trajectories allows a system to find a certain trajectory. However, we use the above approach, since measurable error could be occurred in dead reckoning approach due to the influences of gravity to acceleration data and limitation of the posture of the motion sensor does not meet our assumption, i.e. motion sensor on mobile phone handsets.

Trajectory Creation. The location information from camera-based tracking system is assumed to be represented by X-Y coordinates, meaning the current location of an object is associated with a single point. Because it is difficult to deal with the a cluster of points for the matching, "trajectory creation" process accumulates the location information in the X-Y coordinates and makes them into a set of trajectories. ALTI assumes that the camera-based tracking system outputs only location of moving objects and their object IDs. Since each "object ID" is not associated with any actual user, it can only be used to manage objects. The trajectory creation accumulates the object IDs and locations continuously, recognizes trajectories and extracts the trajectory movements.

The process flow is as follows. Firstly, location information provided by X-Y coordinates is accumulated(Figure 2 (A)). Secondly, series of point belonging to the same object ID are aggregated into trajectories by using the least-square method. In the example of the figure, five points are selected and aggregated into single trajectory (B). Thirdly, trajectory creation chooses two trajectories at fixed intervals, and it calculates the angle between them. Based on the angle and the distance between the first and last points, it then classifies the trajectory movement into the symbols mentioned above. In the case of (C), the process may estimate "turn right" from the angle and the distance. Finally, the result is stored and sorted by object IDs for matching purposes.

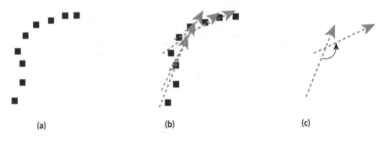

(a)   (b)   (c)

Fig. 2. Trajectory Creation

Activity Recognition. The "activity recognition" process involves analyzes sensor data to recognize a user's movement. With path estimation taken into account, we also use the same 4 types of user activity identical to trajectory movement. As described previously, we avoid using raw acceleration data and instead focus on the Fast Fourier Transform(FFT) of acceleration data. The process of activity recognition analyzes the sum of 3-axis acceleration and finds a cycle of transition of the accelerometer data, which then used to decide the user's activity.

Firstly, the activities of walk and stop are recognized by using FFT. We choose 2 seconds as window size at sampling frequency of 128Hz, thus, it leads to 256 samples in a single window. To decide on the parameter of estimation, we performed experiments to collect acceleration data from several subjects and executed FFT to the data(shown in Figure 3). Following the evaluation, the frequency peak is about 2.0Hz and many of the major FFT frequencies are between 1.5Hz-2.5Hz when the subjects walk. We discovered that the power spectrum of 1.5Hz-2.5Hz is approximately 2-3 times greater than that of other frequencies, hence, we decided 2.5 times as the threshold value. Based on the evaluation, ALTI compares a power spectrum between 1.5Hz-2.5Hz with others and then decides whether the activity is walk, otherwise, the activity is considered to be stop.

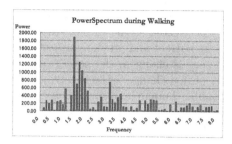 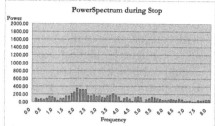

Fig. 3. FFT Experiment Results

Secondly, the process involves the observation of geomagnetic data within a certain period of time to recognize left and right turns. The process calculates the position and azimuth of the device, and it utilizes azimuth data to estimate the activity of left and right turns using a threshold value. When the total extent of changes of the azimuth within 1 second and in one direction exceeds the threshold, defined as 90 degrees, the process decides that the user has turned left or right according to the relevant direction.

Trajectory Estimation. Trajectory estimation is performed by estimating all anonymous trajectory with sensor data in order to locate the user him/herself. We designed two phases for estimation, i.e. short-term comparison and long-term comparison. The difference is in the length of the period used to estimate the trajectories.

The short-term comparison focuses a shor-time period to compare sensor data and trajectories. According to the nature of the ALTI concept, it is impossible to identify a user's trajectory when more than one objects are recognized as performing the same movement. Therefore, the comparison initially finds a "unique trajectory", which is only a single trajectory which performs a different movement from others within a period. When the unique trajectory is found, the process subsequently compares a user's activity occurring in the same period. If the unique trajectory and user's activity are matched, the process determines that the trajectory is user's one and it represents current user's location.

If a unique trajectory can not be identified by the short-term comparison, the long-term comparison decides user's trajectory in accordance with the scores of the trajectories in a long-term period. The scoring and selection of trajectory is performed by following rules.

1. Simple Match
   Unlike finding a unique trajectory as with short-term comparison, all trajectories matching the sensor data obtain a certain score and the score during a certain period is stored with each object.
2. Consecutive Match
   When a trajectory matches continuously, the trajectory is given an additional score.

3. Distance Based Threshold

   Basically, the highest scoring trajectory is selected as the correct trajectory with consideration of distance between the current and previous trajectories. Even though the highest scoring trajectory is changed, the new trajectory should not be a correct trajectory in case of that change to the new trajectory from previous trajectory require impossible human movements. By using a distance-based threshold, the algorithm can eliminate the case where a change to new trajectory is not practical.

5   Implementation

ALTI system consists of mainly 2 components, i.e. mobile device and camera-based tracking system, as shown in Figure 4.

   We build the camera-based tracking system and installed into our laboratory. We also build an experimental mobile device which has a 6-axis motion sensor, WiFi and bluetooth connectivity, and deals with most of the operation of ALTI, as the attachment to a mobile phone handset. Moreover, we implemented logging software executed on a PC, which captures the tracking and estimation results of ALTI algorithm for analysis.

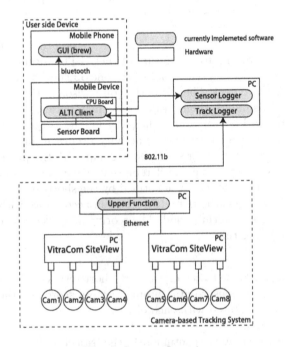

Fig. 4. System Overview

5.1   Mobile Device

The experimental mobile device consists of CPU board and a sensor board, shown in Figure 5. We utilized gumstix [11] as CPU board.

The sensor board is proprietary implementation, which has a 6-axis sensor and geomagnetic sensor. The mobile device performs sensor data processing for location detection and it sends the result to an actual mobile phone which provides GUI via bluetooth. The detailed specifications of the mobile device is indicated in Table 1.

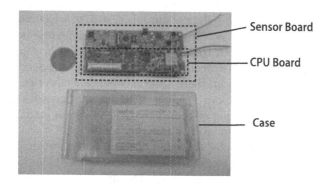

Fig. 5. Mobile Device

Table 1. Specification of the mobile device

CPU board		
	CPU	XScale 400MHz
	OS	Linux 2.6.11
	Connectivity	802.11bCbluetooth
Sensor board		
	Accelerometer	Hitachi H34B
	Geomagnetic	Asahi-Kasei AK8971N
	I/O	I^2C
Power supply		
	Li-ion battery	1200mAh

ALTI Client. The ALTI client is executed on the mobile device, which recognizes the user's context (movement), analysis of trajectory and matching them for personal identification. The client read sensor data from a device driver implemented on linux and it process data for activity recognition. Also it obtains tracking data periodically sent from camera-based tracking system and perform trajectory estimation. These results are sent to the logger executed on other PC to records these processes. The client finally sends the result of locations of all anonymous object and estimated user's trajectory to mobile phone for display purpose.

5.2 Camera-Based Tracking System

We installed 8 cameras in our laboratory to cover the entire room area, due to the limitation of the area covered by a single camera. Our camera-based tracking system consists of two functions, namely a lower function which detects an objects within a single camera image, and an upper function, which integrates the multiple camera views and creates locations of objects in a single X-Y coordinate system.

We utilized Vitracom Siteview [12] as the lower function, which is capable of handling images from single camera, and detects the locations of moving objects. We installed 8 cameras in the ceiling of our office, each of which pointed directly downwards to prevent any objects from being hidden behind others. The location information which is generated by Vitracom is represented by separated "lower coordinate system". As each camera is processed by an independent Vitracom due to the system specification, there are 8 independent lower coordinates. We chose 200 milliseconds of temporal granularity to output the location information from the camera-based tracking system. The ALTI targets is human movements, therefore, we assume the granularity to be sufficient.

The upper function integrates a number of coordinates into single "integrated coordinate system", because each lower function outputs object location, which are represented in each lower coordinates. The upper function provides configuration tools for an alignment of a number of coordinates by using GUI. It converts each objects location represented in each lower coordinates into single coordinates according to the configuration. The upper function manages the location of objects in integrated coordinates and integrated object ID numbering. Meanwhile, the object location from the lower function may be duplicated, because the visible ranges of each camera overlap, as shown in Figure 6. The upper function removes duplicated objects according to the distance between two. When each of two lower functions detect an object and they are near to

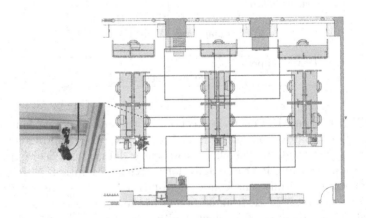

Fig. 6. Camera Arrangement

each other in integrated coordinates, the upper function considered that a single object is caught by two cameras and merged them into one.

5.3   Logger and Viewer Tool

We also implemented two support tools for viewing and analyzing a result, i.e. "logger tool" and "viewer tool". Figure 7 shows a screen shot of viewer tool executed on PC.

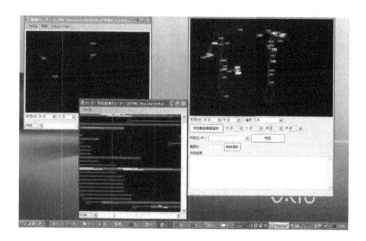

Fig. 7. Viewer Tool

Logger tool captures result of recognition in the mobile device and the camera-based tracking system. The both of logs are recorded separately into two XML formatted files: sensor result log and track log. Sensor result log is created for each mobile device and it has records of the mobile devices operations, which are activity recognition, trajectory creation and identification. Track log has outputs of camera-based tracking system. By loading both types of files, viewer tool provides an overview of whole system operations.

6   Evaluation

We evaluated prototype system of ALTI by using the implementation described above. We performed two evaluations. The first evaluation shows the basic performance of ALTI, and the second one shows results in actual environment. In all evaluations, we made subjects to have the mobile device in their hands and to hold it in front of their body.

6.1   Basic Performance

As the preliminary evaluation, we evaluated the accuracy of detecting a user's trajectory. The evaluation is performed off-line, using 6 movement trajectories

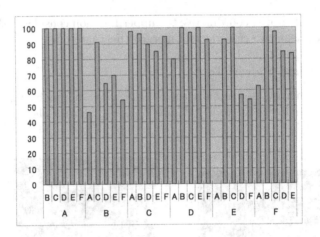

Fig. 8. Basic Performance

and associated sensor data for each trajectory obtained in advance. We fed two movement trajectories from any combination and one of the object sensor data associated to the trajectories to the ALTI system. If the system chose a right trajectory associated to the given sensor data, the recognition was considered a successful.

Figure 8 shows the result of the evaluation. In the figure, the labels written in the lower column, on the X-axis, represent the correct trajectory. While during the preliminary evaluation, we used a short-term comparison to find the trajectories and set length of period was 500ms. Accuracy is indicated in the figure as a proportion of the number of periods in which the system chose correct trajectory. The figure shows the accuracy of the recognition of the pattern labeled in lower column. The results was fairly positive (more than 50% and mostly 80% or 90%) except for the cases of combination with pattern B. However, we consider that the length of the pause (3 seconds) is not long enough to eliminate the effects of the window size of the FFT (2 seconds) when the mobile device distinguishes the user's activities of move straight and stop using the motion sensor data.

6.2 Evaluation in Actual Environment

We evaluated ALTI on-line in the actual environment, prepared in our office room. We performed 8 experiments of 60 seconds for each. In each experiment, we made two subject A and B move around in separated areas of our room. We also allowed both of subjects freely to execute the any sequence of 4 movements, namely stop, walk, turn right and turn left. The observed trajectories in one of experiment are shown in left side of Figure 9. The evaluation counts the number of unique trajectory found, the number of identified trajectories and the results of ALTI. The table in right side of the figure indicates the number of correct, wrong and unmatched trajectories in each result. The overall accuracy is about

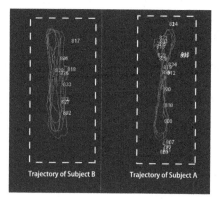

Correct Match(a)	Wrong Match (b)	Unmatched (c)	Accuracy (a/(a+b))
768	252	530	75%
895	221	404	82%
868	154	466	85%
825	357	432	70%
1001	301	452	77%
940	316	609	72%
983	213	533	82%
997	157	548	86%
9207	2516	4886	78%

Fig. 9. Trajectories and Results

80%, therefore, we can conclude that the short-term comparison already gives fairly good results. And if we apply the long-term comparison for the sequence of the results from the short-term comparisons, it would be precise results.

6.3 Future Work

The main reason to reduce accuracy of trajectory is fragmentation problem. Due to the problem, a movement of single object is recognized as the separated several trajectories. When fragmentation is occurred, current ALTI algorithm re-starts the process of identification even the correct trajectory is selected. This causes unidentified blank periods during the search of the correct trajectory again. The reason of the problem is that the camera-based tracking system fails at recognition of moving object, especially, the upper function fails to integrate duplicated objects. Therefore some kinds of trajectory connection methods should be introduced to solve the problem in future work.

There is another problems with camera-based tracking system. When the two people are near each other, the camera tracking system, in particular the lower function, often recognizes them as one object. This problem, called "occlusion problem", is derived from a nature of the image recognition scheme. When two trajectories come close to each other and occlusion is happened, the system may detect them as a single new object and delete previous two trajectories. To solve this problem, the system should detect occlusion and carry over previous trajectories into a new object. This is also another future work of our system.

7 Conclusion

We proposed ALTI to provide an indoor location tracking system which would be suitable for public space environment. The characteristic of the ALTI system is its ability to match anonymous location information from a public tracking system with the user's activity obtained from the mobile device. This approach allows easy installation and avoiding privacy problems. We developed the prototype system of ALTI including the dedicated mobile device to act as a mobile phone handset. Through the empirical evaluation of ALTI, we showed the algorithm works well in the actual camera-based tracking system and movement data from motion sensors on the mobile device. In the future, we will improve our algorithm to gain more precise location estimation and deploy ALTI into the actual usage.

References

1. Ward, A., Jones, A., Hopper, A.: A new location technique for the active office. IEEE Personnel Communications 4(5), 42–47 (1997)
2. Harter, A., Hopper, A., Steggles, P., Ward, A., Webster, P.: The anatomy of a context-aware application. Mobile Computing and Networking, 59–68 (1999)
3. InterSense: IS-600, http://www.isense.com/products/prec/is600/
4. Priyantha, N.B., Chakraborty, A., Balakrishnan, H.: The cricket compass for context-aware mobile applications. In: Proc.7th ACM MOBICOM (2001)
5. Ekahau: Ekahau rtls, http://www.ekahau.com/?id=4200
6. Bahl, P., Padmanabhan, V.N.: RADAR: An in-building RF-based user location and tracking system. In: INFOCOM, vol. (2), pp. 775–784 (2000)
7. Krumm, J., Harris, S., Meyers, B., Brumitt, B., Hale, M., Shafer, S.: Multi-camera multi-person tracking for easyliving. In: VS '00: Proceedings of the Third IEEE International Workshop on Visual Surveillance (VS'2000), vol. 3, IEEE Computer Society, Los Alamitos (2000)
8. Kourogi, M., Kuratal, T.: Personal positioning based on walking locomotion analysis with self-contained sensors and a wearable camera. In: Proc. ISMAR03, pp. 103–112 (2003)
9. DoCoMo, N.T.T.: Press Release: 904i series, http://www.nttdocomo.com/pr/2007/001335.html
10. QUALCOMM: Brew home, http://brew.qualcomm.com/brew/en/
11. Gumstix Inc.: Gumstix, http://gumstix.com
12. VitraCom: Siteview, http://www4.kke.co.jp/siteview/

Localizing Tags Using Mobile Infrastructure

Ying Zhang, Kurt Partridge, and Jim Reich

Palo Alto Research Center
3333 Coyote Hill Road, Palo Alto, CA, 94304, USA
{yzhang,kurt,jreich}@parc.com

Abstract. This paper presents algorithms, simulations, and empirical results of a system that finds relative tag positions in 3D space using a new approach called "mobile infrastructure." Mobile infrastructure consists of one or more sensors in a fixed configuration on a mobile platform, and a set of tags affixed to objects or locations in the environment which the users want to localize. It is especially useful in cases where infrastructure is needed only temporarily, such as during installation, calibration, or maintenance. Mobile infrastructure can cover a much larger area than installed infrastructure with the same number of sensors, and is especially useful in cases where localization hardware costs are asymmetric, with expensive sensors and inexpensive tags. The data collected at various positions are combined by a simple "leapfrog" procedure, with constrained optimization to obtain better accuracy. Our system achieves about one foot (0.3 meter) accuracy with 90% confidence in indoor environments.

1 Introduction and Related Work

Location-awareness is a key component for achieving context-awareness. In most cases, a ubiquitous computing system must know the locations of its sensor and actuator devices. However, few systems bootstrap the locations of devices in a way that is acceptable to end-users. Often, users are expected to manually enter room names or manually survey geometric coordinates. This greatly increases the barrier to entry of ubiquitous computing systems and location based services, due to the expense of skilled installer labor, high probability of data-entry error and difficulty of troubleshooting configuration errors.

There are two general approaches to automatically bootstrap device positions. The first approach is to use an already-available positioning system. However, GPS only works reliably outdoors and outside of city centers, GSM [15] or TV-signal based [20] localization are precise only to tens of meters, and WiFi either has similar precision problems [9,10,11] and/or requires extensive preparatory manual surveying and calibration [5,8]. Powerline positioning [16] has also been proposed, but it also requires a manual survey.

The second approach is for devices to self-localize by collectively determining their positions relative to each other. Time-Of-Arrival (TOA) and Time Difference of Arrival (TDOA) ultrasonic-based systems, while accurate to a few centimeters [14,23], are limited to a roughly five meter range and are subject

J. Hightower, B. Schiele, and T. Strang (Eds.): LoCA 2007, LNCS 4718, pp. 279–296, 2007.
© Springer-Verlag Berlin Heidelberg 2007

to reflections, obstructions, and directionality restrictions. In many cases, they only work in 2D spaces [19,25]. Radio Signal Strength (RSS) systems [7] are also subject to environmentally-determined attenuation, and are precise only to several meters. Ultrawideband (UWB) systems have better range (up to 100m) and accuracy (down to 15cm), but these systems are either not commercially available [1], or are still too expensive for many applications [2,3], since they require the developer to embed an expensive wireless chip in each device.

In this paper, we introduce a third approach to bootstrapping device locations. Our approach is based on taking a series of measurements from ultrawideband Angle-of-Arrival (AOA) sensors mounted on a mobile cart. UWB provides the high-accuracy localization in the presence of clutter and environmental variation, while the cart's mobility allows our platform to act like a set of "virtual nodes," covering many positions.

Our experiments test this approach using Ubisense's localization hardware [4]. Unlike other UWB positioning systems, Ubisense has two types of nodes: UWB transmitters ("Ubitags"), which are small (6cm x 9cm x 1cm), light (50g), and cheap), and UWB receivers ("Ubisensors"), which are larger (21cm x 13cm x 7cm), heavier (690g), and more expensive. Ubisensors determine the position of the Ubitags. The Ubisense system is designed to be a general-purpose location infrastructure. In its intended use, the Ubisensors are permanently installed in the upper (usually four) corners of a room, and their relative positions are carefully measured and manually input by a skilled technician.

In our system, we reverse the roles of the Ubisense hardware: the Ubisensors are attached to the a moveable cart (see Fig. 7), and the Ubitags are assumed to be embedded or attached to the non-moving devices that are to be localized. As the cart is wheeled around, it computes the positions of the tags it sees. Provided that different perspectives detect enough overlapping tag sets, it is possible to determine the positions of all the tags in a single, common reference frame, which may span a space far larger than could be covered by a comparable set of Ubisensors. Furthermore, the cart can be later reused for a completely different installation. We call this approach "mobile infrastructure."

Our work contributes an algorithm for static tag localization based on AOA measurements, evaluates the effectiveness of this algorithm both in simulation and in practice, and evaluates improvements to the simple leapfrog algorithm with constrained optimization technique. We also study AOA data obtained from Ubisensors, to preprocess and pre-filter the raw data to get better and more robust localization results.

There are similarities between our approach and mobile-assisted localization (MAL) [17,18,21,22,24]. Generally, MAL algorithms estimate relative distances rather than angles and assume that all nodes, mobile and static, can both transmit and receive; generally, they have assumed homogeneous installations in which the mobile nodes are identical to the static nodes. Our work also differs from SLAM [13] in the robotics community, in which one or more robots simultaneously produce a map of the walls and obstacles in the environment (often through laser scanners or vision) while navigating. However, SLAM is not focused on determining the relative locations of tagged objects, and is specifically intended for autonomous mobile platforms rather than human-controlled ones.

The rest of the paper is organized as follows. Section 2 provides a system overview for tag localization using mobile infrastructure. Section 3 presents the algorithms, a leapfrog procedure and refinements to it using constrained optimization. Section 4 presents simulation results that evaluate the algorithms given different sensor configuration and noise parameters. Section 5 demonstrates the system using a real hardware deployment, with an emphasis on preprocessing and pre-filtering AOA data from the Ubisense System. Section 6 concludes the paper and suggests future directions.

2   System Overview

Each AOA sensor has six degrees of freedom in space: $x_s, y_s, z_s, a_s, b_s, r_s$ where x_s, y_s, z_s are 3D coordinates and a_s, b_s, r_s are yaw, pitch and roll angles, respectively. In the rest of this paper, we assume $r_s = 0$. Tags have x_t, y_t, z_t locations, but no orientation. Each AOA sensor's parameters $(x_s, y_s, z_s, a_s, b_s)$ define its own reference frame. The position of a tag in a sensor's reference frame uniquely determines the AOA: yaw α and pitch β (Fig. 1). Each tag/sensor pair introduces two equations. Let x_t^s, y_t^s, z_t^s be the location coordinates of a tag in the sensor's reference frame, and α and β be the yaw and pitch angles, respectively. From these, the following two equations may be deduced:

$$x_t^s \sin(\alpha) - y_t^s \cos(\alpha) = 0 \qquad (1)$$
$$x_t^s \sin(\beta) - z_t^s \cos(\beta) \cos(\alpha) = 0 \qquad (2)$$

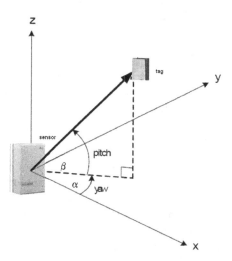

Fig. 1. Local reference frame for a sensor and AOA of a tag

where x_t^s, y_t^s, z_t^s can be obtained given the sensor's position x_s, y_s, z_s, a_s, b_s and the tag's position x_t, y_t, z_t in a global reference frame according to a standard coordinate transformation [6]:

$$
\begin{pmatrix} x_t^s \\ y_t^s \\ z_t^s \\ 1 \end{pmatrix} = \begin{bmatrix} T' & -T' \begin{pmatrix} x_s \\ y_s \\ z_s \end{pmatrix} \\ 0\ 0\ 0 & 1 \end{bmatrix} \begin{pmatrix} x_t \\ y_t \\ z_t \\ 1 \end{pmatrix} \tag{3}
$$

where T is the rotational transformation matrix for the sensor frame:

$$
\begin{bmatrix} \cos(a_s)\cos(b_s) & -\sin(a_s) & \cos(a_s)\sin(b_s) \\ \sin(a_s)\cos(b_s) & \cos(a_s) & \sin(a_s)\sin(b_s) \\ -\sin(b_s) & 0 & \cos(b_s) \end{bmatrix} \tag{4}
$$

Using the set of equations (Eqs. 1 and 2 for each tag/sensor pair), one can compute a tag's location x_t, y_t, z_t given AOA data from two sensors with known locations (four equations, three unknowns). Or one can compute a sensor's orientation (a_s and b_s) given AOA data from a fixed tag at a known position relative to the sensor (two equations, two unknowns).

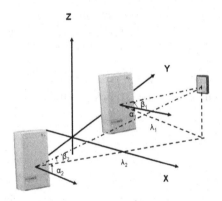

Fig. 2. Two sensor platform with the local frame in the center between the sensors

Our problem is to localize a set of static tags in 3D space. The sensor pair on the cart is depicted in (Fig. 2), and for simplicity, we set $b_s = 0$. The distance between the two sensors is fixed. The cart can move in four degrees of freedom, x_c, y_c, z_c and yaw a_c. A simple, fixed transformation exists between the cart coordinates and sensor coordinates. At each cart position, only a subset of tags can be seen by the sensors, however, we assume each tag can be seen by the sensors at least once at some cart position.

We roughly estimate how many cart positions are needed for tag localization as follows. Let the first cart position be the global reference frame. Each new cart position adds four unknowns. If at least k tags can be seen at a cart position, at least $4k$ equations are added. Let n be the total number of tags and m be the number of extra cart positions. There are $3n + 4m$ unknowns and at least $4k(m + 1)$ equations. One may solve the set of equation for the unknowns if $4k(m + 1) \geq 3n + 4m$, i.e., the number of equations is greater than the number of unknowns.

Note that the number of cart positions is only one factor in determining whether the equations can be solved. Another important factor is the connectivity of the overall tag/sensor pairs. A tag is *connected* to a sensor at a position if it can be seen by the sensor at that position. There are $2(m + 1)$ sensor nodes and n tag nodes for $m + 1$ positions and n tags, which constitute a bipartite graph. Such a graph has to be at least connected to have all coordinates in the same reference frame. For example, if three tags are seen by the sensors in the first cart position, and a totally different three sensors are seen by the sensors in the second cart position, one cannot obtain the six tag locations in a common reference frame, although $4 \times 3 \times 2 \geq 3 \times 6 + 4$. Let $c \geq 1$ be the minimum number of tags in common for a new location. Given n tags, if at most K tags can be seen at a time, i.e., at most $K - c$ new tags can been seen at each extra location, we need $K + (K - c)m \geq n$ to see all the tags. In the previous example, we have $3 + (3 - 1) < 6$.

The inputs to our algorithm are AOA data at each cart position, i.e., α and β, where $\alpha(i, j, l)$ and $\beta(i, j, l)$ are the yaw and pitch angles, respectively, from sensor j to tag i at l'th position. AOA sensing scope is limited by both distance and angles. If tag i is out of range of sensor j at position l, $\alpha(i, j, l)$ and $\beta(i, j, l)$ are set to infinity. Given the input data α and β, we first filter out bad cart positions. A cart position is bad if it does not have at least two sensor/tag connections. We remove such cart positions since each position adds four variables and one pair of sensor/tag connection adds two equations; a good cart position must add more equations than variables.

3   Localization Algorithm Using the Mobile Sensing Pair

We can plug the data α and β into the equations (1) - (2) in the previous section, and use a nonlinear solver to find the n tag locations and m cart positions. However, since the constraints are nonlinear and the size of the problem is large ($4m + 3n$ variables for m positions and n tags), the solution in practice is intractable. Fortunately, due to the special configuration of the sensor platform, we can get a complete or partial solution using a set of linear equations.

3.1   Closed-Form Solutions

The procedure consists of two components: from sensors to tags, and from tags to sensors.

From Sensors to Tags. Given a position of the two-sensor frame (Fig. 3), x, y, z, a, the two sensor locations are x_1, y_1, z, a and x_2, y_2, z, a, respectively,

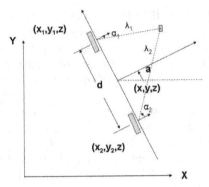

Fig. 3. 2D projection of the two sensor platform

with $x_1 = x - d\sin(a)/2$, $y_1 = y + d\cos(a)/2$ and $x_2 = x + d\sin(a)/2$ and $y_2 = y - d\cos(a)/2$ where d is the distance between the two sensors.

Let λ_1 and λ_2 be the distances from a tag to the two sensors in the XY plane, respectively. We have

$$x_t = x_1 + \lambda_1 \cos(\alpha_1 + a) \tag{5}$$
$$y_t = y_1 + \lambda_1 \sin(\alpha_1 + a) \tag{6}$$

$$x_t = x_2 + \lambda_2 \cos(\alpha_2 + a) \tag{7}$$
$$y_t = y_2 + \lambda_2 \sin(\alpha_2 + a) \tag{8}$$

and from

$$\lambda_1 \cos(\alpha_1 + a) - \lambda_2 \cos(\alpha_2 + a) = x_2 - x_1 = d\sin(a)$$
$$\lambda_1 \sin(\alpha_1 + a) - \lambda_2 \sin(\alpha_2 + a) = y_2 - y_1 = -d\cos(a)$$

one can solve for λ_1 and λ_2. Setting these values in Eqs. (5) and (7), we have

$$x_t = \frac{1}{2}[(x_1 + \lambda_1 \cos(\alpha_1 + a)) + (x_2 + \lambda_2 \cos(\alpha_2 + a))] \tag{9}$$

and similarly,

$$y_t = \frac{1}{2}[(y_1 + \lambda_1 \sin(\alpha_1 + a)) + (y_2 + \lambda_2 \sin(\alpha_2 + a))] \tag{10}$$

Using equations

$$z_t = z + \lambda_1 \tan(\beta_1) \tag{11}$$
$$z_t = z + \lambda_2 \tan(\beta_2) \tag{12}$$

we have

$$z_t = z + \frac{1}{2}(\lambda_1 \tan(\beta_1) + \lambda_2 \tan(\beta_2)) \tag{13}$$

From Tags to Sensors. If the pair of sensors can see multiple tags with known positions, the sensor frame position x, y, z, a can be obtained. Let α_{ik} and β_{ik} be yaw and pitch angles from sensor k to tag i, respectively, and let λ_{ik} be the projected distance between tag i and sensor k on the XY plane. If a tag i can be seen by both sensors, we have

$$-\lambda_{i1}\sin(\alpha_{i1}) + \lambda_{i2}\sin(\alpha_{i2}) = d \qquad (14)$$
$$\lambda_{i1}\cos(\alpha_{i1}) - \lambda_{i2}\cos(\alpha_{i2}) = 0 \qquad (15)$$

and we can compute λ_{i1} and λ_{i2}. Given a pair of tags i and j, and a sensor at x_k, y_k, z_k, a, where $k = 1$ or 2, we have

$$x_k = x_i - \lambda_{ik}\cos(\alpha_{ik} + a) \qquad (16)$$
$$y_k = y_i - \lambda_{ik}\sin(\alpha_{ik} + a) \qquad (17)$$

$$x_k = x_j - \lambda_{jk}\cos(\alpha_{jk} + a) \qquad (18)$$
$$y_k = y_j - \lambda_{jk}\sin(\alpha_{jk} + a) \qquad (19)$$

and

$$x_i - x_j - \lambda_{ik}\cos(\alpha_{ik} + a) + \lambda_{jk}\cos(\alpha_{jk} + a) = 0 \qquad (20)$$
$$y_i - y_j - \lambda_{ik}\sin(\alpha_{ik} + a) + \lambda_{jk}\sin(\alpha_{jk} + a) = 0 \qquad (21)$$

Let $(20)\cos(a) + (21)\sin(a)$ we have

$$(x_i - x_j)\cos(a) + (y_i - y_j)\sin(a) = \lambda_{ik}\cos(\alpha_{ik}) - \lambda_{jk}\cos(\alpha_{jk}) \qquad (22)$$

and let $(20)\sin(a) - (21)\cos(a)$ we have

$$(x_i - x_j)\sin(a) - (y_i - y_j)\cos(a) = -\lambda_{ik}\sin(\alpha_{ik}) + \lambda_{jk}\sin(\alpha_{jk}) \qquad (23)$$

If a sensor sees n tags, there are $2(n-1)$ linear equations with two variables $\cos(a)$ and $\sin(a)$. When $n \geq 2$, one can solve the set of linear equations and obtain $\cos(a)$ and $\sin(a)$. Therefore $a = \arctan(\frac{\sin(a)}{\cos(a)})$. Using Eq. (16) and (17) for each tag i, we have

$$x_1^i = x_i - \lambda_{i1}\cos(\alpha_{i1} + a)$$
$$y_1^i = y_i - \lambda_{i1}\sin(\alpha_{i1} + a)$$
$$x_2^i = x_i - \lambda_{i2}\cos(\alpha_{i2} + a)$$
$$y_2^i = y_i - \lambda_{i2}\sin(\alpha_{i2} + a)$$

and also

$$z_1^i = z_i - \lambda_{i1}\tan(\beta_{i1})$$
$$z_2^i = z_i - \lambda_{i2}\tan(\beta_{i2})$$

Therefore, the estimated locations for sensor 1 and 2 seeing n tags are

$$(\frac{1}{n}\Sigma_{i=1}^{n}x_1^i, \frac{1}{n}\Sigma_{i=1}^{n}y_1^i, \frac{1}{n}\Sigma_{i=1}^{n}z_1^i)$$

and

$$(\frac{1}{n}\Sigma_{i=1}^{n}x_2^i, \frac{1}{n}\Sigma_{i=1}^{n}y_2^i, \frac{1}{n}\Sigma_{i=1}^{n}z_2^i),$$

respectively. The center of the sensor frame is at: $(\frac{x_1+x_2}{2}, \frac{y_1+y_2}{2}, \frac{z_1+z_2}{2})$.

3.2   Leapfrog Algorithm

The leapfrog algorithm is the approach we use to calculate all tag positions in a common reference frame. Starting from the position from which we can see the maximum number of tags (this will be used as the reference frame), the

Table 1. Leapfrog algorithm for tag localization using a mobile infrastructure

Inputs:
   $\alpha_{ijl}, \beta_{ijl}$: angles from tag i to sensor j at cart position l

Outputs:
   x_i, y_i, z_i: locations for all tags;
   x_l, y_l, z_l, a_l: positions of the mobile sensor frame;

Notations:
   l: current sensor frame
   kTs: the set of tags with known locations
   cTs: the set of tags connected to the current sensor frame

Initialization:
   $l \leftarrow 1$: the first sensor frame is the reference frame,
   $kTs \leftarrow \emptyset$: all tags are unknown position

0. **while there is a sensor frame** l:
1. Let cTs
     be the set of tags connected to frame l;
2. Let $cnTs \leftarrow cTs \backslash kTs$
     be the set of connected tags with unknown locations
3. Compute tag locations for each tag in $cnTs$
     using the closed-form solution in Section 3.1
4. $kTs \leftarrow kTs \cup cnTs$
5. Let l be the next unknown sensor frame
     with the maximum connections to known tags
6. Compute the position of the sensor frame
     using the closed-form solution in Section 3.1
7. **end while**

leapfrog algorithm alternates between computation of tag locations and cart locations, using the closed-form solutions from the previous section, until all the locations are obtained. In particular, after locating the tags using the in the current sensor frame, it then selects as the next frame the sensor frame with the maximum number of *known tags* (i.e. those which have been observed by any of the sensor frames we have already processed). It computes the location of this new frame, and proceeds iteratively. The pseudocode is shown in Table 1.

The leapfrog algorithm is simple, but it may only give a partial solution if there are not enough connections. For example, in line 1 of the algorithm, there may be no tags connected to both sensors, i.e. $cTs = \emptyset$, although there may be tags connected to one sensor. Also, in line 5, there may be no next unknown sensor frame that can see at least two known tags. Another potential weakness of this algorithm is that errors in localization of the previous tags will propagate into the localization of the next frame, accumulating over time. How to select the best next sensor frame to reduce error propagation is an open question for future research. Some techniques in error control for self-localization similar to those in [12] may be employed. This error accumulation might also be limited by adding a small number of anchor points with known locations, e.g., using a blueprint of the building.

3.3   Optimization-Based Algorithms

The leapfrog algorithm does not work well when connectivity is low and when inputs are noisy. The optimization-based algorithms below are more robust and work by minimizing the least-square errors for all equations.

Let $e_k = 0$ be an equation from one tag/sensor pair. One can minimize $\frac{1}{2}\Sigma_k e_k^2$ for all tag/sensor pairs. We found the constrained optimization (fmincon in Matlab) works particularly well for this problem, where constraints are ranges for locations ($[-b, b]$ where $2b$ is the size of the x, y or z dimension) and angles $[-\pi, \pi]$).

We have tried two variations of this approach. The first variation (LSLeapfrog) is to apply the optimization procedure at each leapfrog step, i.e., at each step, from sensors to tags or from tags to sensors, using the closed-form solution first, and then apply the least-square minimization with the closed-form solution as the initial value. The second variation (LeapfrogLS) uses the original leapfrog solution as the initial value for least-square minimization of all equations.

In the next section, we compare the performance of these three algorithms (Leapfrog, LSLeapfrog, LeapfrogLS) with two different tag configurations and analyze their robustness in the presence of noise.

4   Simulation Results

In this section, we analyze the localization performance in two scenarios: "Wall," in which tags are put on four walls of a room, and "Hallway," in which tags are distributed along two walls of a narrow hallway. A total of 12 tags are used, in

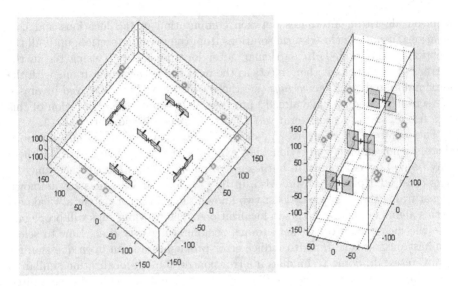

Fig. 4. The "Wall" scenario (left) and "Hallway" scenario (right)

an area bounded by $[-150, 150]$ inches[1]. Figure 4 shows the wall and hallway scenarios.

In our simulations, we use sensors separated by either 25 inches or 40 inches, with additive sensor noise modeled by a uniform distribution[2] in $[-m, m]$ where m is either 0.01 or 0.02 radians, a value based on the measurements of Section 5.1. The algorithm itself does not require an explicit noise model; this is for performance analysis only. The AOA sensing range of the sensor is [-1.2, 1.2] radians for yaw angles and [-1.0, 1.0] radians for pitch angles, the limits of the actual Ubisense hardware.

We then compare the three algorithms of the previous section are compared using *average estimation accuracy*. The estimation accuracy for one tag is the distance between the true and estimated location; the *average estimation accuracy* across all tags is used as the overall performance metric of localization.

Figure 5 shows samples of the 2D projections onto the XY plane for these two cases (where the noise is 0.02 radians and the distance between two sensors is 40 inches) resulting from LeapfrogLS; the lines from the tags and sensors indicate the displacements between the actual and estimated locations.

For the wall case, each of the four walls has three tags placed in random positions, and for the hallway case, each side has six tags in random positions. In both cases, the heights are uniformly randomly distributed in [-24, 24] inches. For the wall case, there are five cart positions, with the first position in the middle of the room. In the hallway case, there are three cart positions, with

---

[1] In this paper, distances are measured in inches (1 in = 2.54 cm) and angles are measured in radians (1 radian = $180/\pi$ degrees).

[2] In other simulations, normal distributions gave similar results.

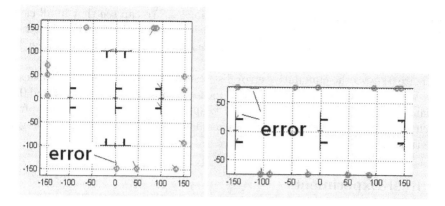

Fig. 5. localization results, left: wall tags, right: hallway tags

Table 2. 90% confidence level for all algorithms on wall case

algorithms	25 in; 0.01	40 in; 0.01	25 in; 0.02	40 in; 0.02
Leapfrog	107 in	68 in	143 in	95 in
LSLeapfrog	54 in	31 in	67 in	58 in
LeapfrogLS	15 in	11 in	39 in	15 in

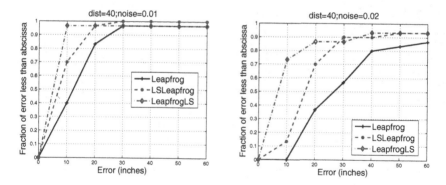

Fig. 6. Error distribution for hallway case with distance 40in, left: noise 0.01, right: noise 0.02

the first one in the middle of the hallway. Note that we use fixed, rather than random, cart positions to reduce run-to-run variations since cart positions can affect the localization results significantly. We generate 30 random cases for each selection of sensor separation and noise range, and run the three algorithms on each of the 30 cases. Location accuracies of 90% confidence level for the wall case is shown in Table 2, where $d; m$ indicates the distance between the sensors d in inches and angle noise range m in radians. Each entry x represents at least 27 out of 30 runs (i.e. 90%) have error less than x inches. We can see that in all cases, LeapfrogLS is better than LSLeapfrog, which is in turn better than Leapfrog. The distance between the sensor pair also matters: the larger the distance, the smaller the error.

Figure 6 shows the cumulative error distribution function for the hallway case, with distance between the sensor pair 40 inches, and noise of angles 0.01 and 0.02 radians, respectively. Again, we see that LeapfrogLS is better than LSLeapfrog, which is in turn better than Leapfrog, and the larger the angle noise, the bigger the error.

5   Real Experiments

We tested our algorithms using the Ubisense Location System. Figure 7 left shows a prototype of the system: two Ubisensors are mounted vertically on the poles with distance 40 inches. Our initial test had eight tags on two walls, and the space between neighboring tags was about 24 inches (Fig. 7 right).

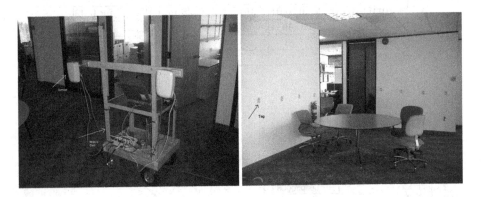

Fig. 7. Left: the mobile cart with two Ubisensors, right: 8 Tags on two walls

The simulated and real experiments differed in their source of input data. For simulated cases, data were generated given the tag sensor positions and the noise model. For real experiments, data were generated from continuous AOA sensor readings during operation. In order to get a set of good data inputs corresponding to a set of cart positions, we moved the cart to multiple locations and stopped at each location for 5 to 10 seconds to get stable angle readings. The next section describes how to get a clean set of angle data for each location of the cart.

5.1   Data Preprocessing

In order to understand the noise characteristics of Ubisense data, we performed a series of experiments. The results from these experiments guided us to develop a robust data extraction algorithm from a continuous source of input data.

We first studied horizontal and vertical angle variations given a static pair of a sensor and a tag. We put a sensor and a tag in a fixed position, and measured AOA data in a given time period. Although details depended on the relative positions of the sensor and the tag, we found that error distributions with respect to the mean were very similar. Figure 8 shows the histogram from one data set. The standard deviations are between 0.01 and 0.03 radians for both yaw and pitch angles in our experiments. The distribution seemed not to be affected by distance or angle, although angles approaching the boundary of the valid range (about +/- 1.2 radians in yaw and +/- 1.0 radians in pitch) sometimes did result in readings with large variations. We filtered out data at large angles for robustness. To reduce variations in angle readings, we also averaged multiple data points for a stable position.

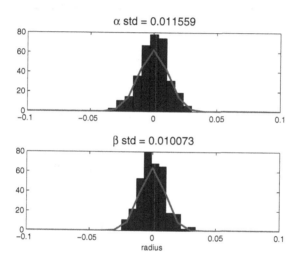

Fig. 8. Histogram of error distribution with respect to mean for a fixed sensor/tag. Errors are measured in radians.

The raw AOA input to our algorithm is a continuous series of data points, with each entry: $timeslot, sensor, tagID, \alpha, \beta$, where $timeslot$ is the time slot in which the data is taken (one slot is about $1/40$ second), $sensor$ and $tagID$ indicate from which pair of Ubisensor and Ubitag the data were obtained, and α and β are the pitch and yaw angles, respectively. Although in a stable position the angle variations are small, when the sensors are moving, readings are generally not reliable. In our system, we attempt to use only data from *stationary* points, where the data are relatively stable.

First, we segment the input data so that consecutive data points with both α and β variations less than ϵ are grouped. Only groups with the number of data points more than n are kept. In our experiments, we set $\epsilon = 0.05$ and $n = 5$. Each group has a starting time slot s and ending time slot e, and an average α and β in the period of $[s, e]$. Figure 9 shows the original and grouped data

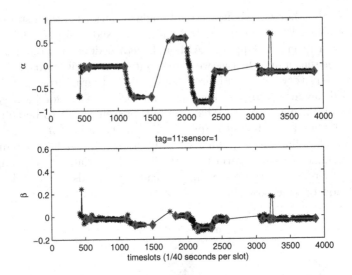

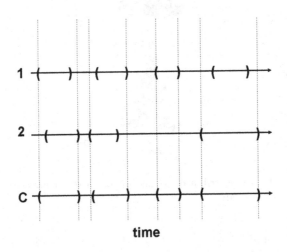

Fig. 9. The original (star) and grouped (diamond) data points for a sensor/tag pair

Fig. 10. Obtaining common data points from two separate sources. Note that source 2 does not have data at the third time period.

points for a sensor/tag pair. Note that, as seen in the figure, this process also removes some isolated bad data. After grouping data points for each tag/sensor pair, the next step is to find a common set of data points which are consistent for all tag/sensor pairs. Such a set of points corresponds to the set of stationary positions in the trajectory of the mobile sensor platform. Figure 10 illustrates this process for two data sources. Let the start and end time of a period be represented as a left and right parenthesis, respectively. We first order all the parentheses along the time line and then search for periods with balanced left and right parenthesis. Note that it is possible that not all sources have data in a given time period.

5.2   Experiment Results

Figure 11 shows 2D and 3D views of the estimated locations of the 8 tags in Fig. 7 (right) using LeapfrogLS. To get a sense of the error in these experiments, we use the mean square error (MSE) of the model fitting error. Note that this is not the error from the ground truth, but merely the residual error remaining in equations 1 and 2 once the algorithm terminates.

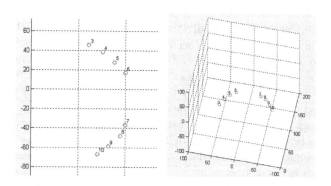

Fig. 11. Results of 8-tag localization (units in inches)

Let $e_k = 0$ be an equation from one tag/sensor pair. We use $\sqrt{\frac{1}{2n}\Sigma_{k=1}^{n}e_k^2}$, where n is the number of equations, for error estimates for real experiments. For the above example, the MSE of LeapfrogLS is 2.7 inches, and the MSE for LSLeapfrog and Leapfrog are 4.7 inches and 11 inches, respectively. In general, we find that the smaller the MSE, the smaller the position error. In cases where more than one solution exists, one may get a small MSE with large position error. However, we can usually avoid such cases by moving to a sufficient number of positions and taking enough data to guarantee a unique solution.

6   Conclusions and Future Work

We have presented an algorithm, and simulation and empirical studies of our approach to localizing static tags using mobile infrastructure to cover an area far larger than the sensor range. We show how a closed-form solution can be used to yield approximate results, and to what extent further optimizations improve these results when applied iteratively (LSLeapfrog) and when applied globally (LeapfrogLS) (e.g., location accuracy of 1 ft. (0.3 m) vs. 3 ft. (1 m) or 5 ft. (1.5 m)).

Note that although errors accumulate in the leapfrog procedure, the global optimization for the solution refinement minimizes the overall errors. In describing our experiments, we have used the MSE of the data fitting error rather than the MSE of the deviation from ground truth. Future experiments will measure both the accuracy of our localization and its growth as we use the mobile infrastructure over increasingly large areas.

One advantage of our approach is that no computer control of cart movement is needed; the natural movement of the cart during an installation process should be sufficient, although a few extra stops might be needed. Our algorithm automatically filters out bad cart positions in which too few tags are in view. In general, the more good cart positions, the more data, and the better the results. Compared to the Ubisense Location System with static sensors, our system achieves similar results as a fully "untethered" (i.e. without TDOA measurements) configuration, which has an accuracy of about 0.4 m with 90% confidence.

One way to extend this work would be to incorporate other kinds of motion data, using inertial sensors or odometry. A cart with an inertial or wheel sensor could provide an alternative way to know when the cart was stationary. A wheel-mounted odometric distance measurement could also be combined with the tag readings to improve the overall system accuracy. Our system's performance would also improve if the extra TDOA data from the Ubisense hardware were used to augment the AOA data, or if greater numbers of sensors could be used to achieve better connectivity.

Although the approach presented in this paper used two sensors on the cart, it is theoretically possible to localize static tags with only a single AOA sensor, if distance data of the mobile sensor are available. Such a system would be smaller and perhaps could be integrated into a portable device such as a cellphone with an embedded accelerometer and would enable a greater set of applications. One example would be for home assistant robots. A robot with an AOA sensor could localize a set of tags, and at the same time, localize itself using the static tags as landmarks. On the other hand, rather than using only a single sensor, a system with more than two sensors could have a larger detection field, could collect data in fewer steps, and could allow for greater tag connectivity.

A greater set of applications would also be enabled by allowing some tags to be mobile, provided that enough tags remain stationary when the mobile infrastructure is moved. Furthermore, it should be possible to reuse tags as the process proceeds. Alternatively, localized tags might be left behind as a persistent localization infrastructure, allowing a single mobile sensor to be localized anywhere in the space. These classes of system can provide generalized precise positioning when it matters, without the cost of a permanently installed infrastructure.

Acknowledgement

We would like to thank Dr. Patrick Cheung for helping to build the mobile sensor infrastructure. We also like to thank the regional sales and technical support personnel from Ubisense for providing valuable information and assistance.

References

1. MERL project on UWB ranging and locating,
   http://www.merl.com/projects/uwbranging/
2. Multispectral solutions, inc., http://www.multispectral.com/
3. Time domain, http://www.timedomain.com/
4. Ubisense precise real-time location, http://www.ubisense.net
5. Bahl, P., Padmanabhan, V.N.: An in-building RF-based location and tracking system. In: IEEE InfoComm (2000)
6. Craig, J.J.: Introduction to Robotics: Mechanics and Control. Addison Wesley, London, UK (1989)
7. Genco, A.: Three step BlueTooth positioning. In: Strang, T., Linnhoff-Popien, C. (eds.) LoCA 2005. LNCS, vol. 3479, Springer, Heidelberg (2005)
8. Kaemarungsi, K., Krishnamurthy, P.: Properties of indoor received signal strength for WLAN location fingerprinting. In: IEEE MobiQuitous (2004)
9. LaMarca, A., Chawathe, Y., Consolvo, S., Hightower, J., Smith, I., Scott, J., Sohn, T., Howard, J., Hughes, J., Potter, F., Tabert, J., Powledge, P., Borriello, G., Schilit, B.: Place lab: Device positioning using radio beacons in the wild. In: Proceedings of Pervasive (2005)
10. Letchner, J., Fox, D., LaMarca, A.: Large-scale localization from wireless signal strength. In: Proceedings of the National Conference on Artificial Intelligence (AAAI 2005) (2005)
11. Lim, H., Kung, L.C., Hou, J.C., Luo, H.: Zero-configuration: Robust indoor localization: Theory and experimentation. In: IEEE InfoComm (2006)
12. Liu, J., Zhang, Y., Zhao, F.: Robust distributed node localization with error management. In: ACM MobiHoc 2006 (2006)
13. Montemerlo, M., Thrun, S.: The FastSLAM Algortihm for Simultaneous Localization and Mapping. In: Springer Tracts in Advanced Robotics (forthcoming, 2007)
14. Muller, H.L., McCarthy, M., Randell, C.: Particle filters for position sensing with asynchronous ultrasonic beacons. In: Hazas, M., Krumm, J., Strang, T. (eds.) LoCA 2006. LNCS, vol. 3987, Springer, Heidelberg (2006)
15. Otsason, V., Varshavsky, A., LaMarca, A., de Lara, E.: Accurate GSM indoor localization. In: Ubicomp 2005 (2005)
16. Parel, S.N., Truong, K.N., Abowd, G.D.: Powerline positioning: A practical sub-room-level indoor location system for domestic use. In: Dourish, P., Friday, A. (eds.) UbiComp 2006. LNCS, vol. 4206, Springer, Heidelberg (2006)
17. Pathirana, P.N., Bulusu, N., Savkin, A., Jha, S.: Node localization using mobile robots in delay-tolerant sensor networks. IEEE Transactions on Mobile Computing, 4(4), (July/August 2005)
18. Priyantha, N.B., Balakrishnan, H., Demaine, E.D., Teller, S.: Mobile-assisted localization in wireless sensor networks. In: IEEE Conference on Computer Communications (InfoCom05) (2005)
19. Priyantha, N.B., Chakraborty, A., Balakrishnan, H.: The cricket location-support system. In: Proc. of the Sixth Annual ACM International Conference on Mobile Computing and Networking (MOBICOM) (2000)
20. Rabinowitz, M., Spilker Jr, J.: A new positioning system using television synchronization signals, http://www.rosum.com/
21. Taylor, C., Rahimi, A., Bachrach, J.: Simulatenous localization, calibration and tracking in an ad hoc sensor network. In: 5th International Conference on Information Processing in Sensor Networks (IPSN06) (2006)

22. Wang, C., Ding, Y., Xiao, L.: Virtual ruler: Mobile beacon based distance measurements for indoor sensor localization. In: The Third International Conference on Mobile Ad-hoc and Sensor Systems (MASS06) (2006)
23. Ward, A., Jones, A., Hopper, A.: A new location technique for the active office. IEEE Personal Communications 4(5), 42–47 (1997)
24. Wu, C., Sheng, W., Zhang, Y.: Mobile sensor networks self localization based on multi-dimensional scaling. In: IEEE ICRA07 (2007)
25. Zhang, Y., Yim, M., Ackerson, L., Duff, D., Eldershaw, C.: Stam: A system of tracking and mapping in real environments. IEEE Wireless Communications (Decemeber 2004), http://www.parc.com/era/nest/STAM

Author Index

Lecture Notes in Computer Science

Sublibrary 3: Information Systems and Application, incl. Internet/Web and HCI

For information about Vols. 1– 4275
please contact your bookseller or Springer

Vol. 4526: M. Malek, M. Reitenspieß, A. van Moorsel (Eds.), Service Availability. X, 155 pages. 2007.

Vol. 4524: M. Marchiori, J.Z. Pan, C.d.S. Marie (Eds.), Web Reasoning and Rule Systems. XI, 382 pages. 2007.

Vol. 4519: E. Franconi, M. Kifer, W. May (Eds.), The Semantic Web: Research and Applications. XVIII, 830 pages. 2007.

Vol. 4518: N. Fuhr, M. Lalmas, A. Trotman (Eds.), Comparative Evaluation of XML Information Retrieval Systems. XII, 554 pages. 2007.

Vol. 4508: M.-Y. Kao, X.-Y. Li (Eds.), Algorithmic Aspects in Information and Management. VIII, 428 pages. 2007.

Vol. 4506: D. Zeng, I. Gotham, K. Komatsu, C. Lynch, M. Thurmond, D. Madigan, B. Lober, J. Kvach, H. Chen (Eds.), Intelligence and Security Informatics: Biosurveillance. XI, 234 pages. 2007.

Vol. 4505: G. Dong, X. Lin, W. Wang, Y. Yang, J.X. Yu (Eds.), Advances in Data and Web Management. XXII, 896 pages. 2007.

Vol. 4504: J. Huang, R. Kowalczyk, Z. Maamar, D. Martin, I. Müller, S. Stoutenburg, K.P. Sycara (Eds.), Service-Oriented Computing: Agents, Semantics, and Engineering. X, 175 pages. 2007.

Vol. 4500: N.A. Streitz, A. Kameas, I. Mavrommati (Eds.), The Disappearing Computer. XVIII, 304 pages. 2007.

Vol. 4495: J. Krogstie, A. Opdahl, G. Sindre (Eds.), Advanced Information Systems Engineering. XVI, 606 pages. 2007.

Vol. 4480: A. LaMarca, M. Langheinrich, K.N. Truong (Eds.), Pervasive Computing. XIII, 369 pages. 2007.

Vol. 4471: P. Cesar, K. Chorianopoulos, J.F. Jensen (Eds.), Interactive TV: A Shared Experience. XIII, 236 pages. 2007.

Vol. 4469: K.-c. Hui, Z. Pan, R.C.-k. Chung, C.C.L. Wang, X. Jin, S. Göbel, E.C.-L. Li (Eds.), Technologies for E-Learning and Digital Entertainment. XVIII, 974 pages. 2007.

Vol. 4443: R. Kotagiri, P. Radha Krishna, M. Mohania, E. Nantajeewarawat (Eds.), Advances in Databases: Concepts, Systems and Applications. XXI, 1126 pages. 2007.

Vol. 4439: W. Abramowicz (Ed.), Business Information Systems. XV, 654 pages. 2007.

Vol. 4430: C.C. Yang, D. Zeng, M. Chau, K. Chang, Q. Yang, X. Cheng, J. Wang, F.-Y. Wang, H. Chen (Eds.), Intelligence and Security Informatics. XII, 330 pages. 2007.

Vol. 4425: G. Amati, C. Carpineto, G. Romano (Eds.), Advances in Information Retrieval. XIX, 759 pages. 2007.

Vol. 4412: F. Stajano, H.J. Kim, J.-S. Chae, S.-D. Kim (Eds.), Ubiquitous Convergence Technology. XI, 302 pages. 2007.

Vol. 4402: W. Shen, J.-Z. Luo, Z. Lin, J.-P.A. Barthès, Q. Hao (Eds.), Computer Supported Cooperative Work in Design III. XV, 763 pages. 2007.

Vol. 4398: S. Marchand-Maillet, E. Bruno, A. Nürnberger, M. Detyniecki (Eds.), Adaptive Multimedia Retrieval: User, Context, and Feedback. XI, 269 pages. 2007.

Vol. 4397: C. Stephanidis, M. Pieper (Eds.), Universal Access in Ambient Intelligence Environments. XV, 467 pages. 2007.

Vol. 4380: S. Spaccapietra, P. Atzeni, F. Fages, M.-S. Hacid, M. Kifer, J. Mylopoulos, B. Pernici, P. Shvaiko, J. Trujillo, I. Zaihrayeu (Eds.), Journal on Data Semantics VIII. XV, 219 pages. 2007.

Vol. 4365: C.J. Bussler, M. Castellanos, U. Dayal, S. Navathe (Eds.), Business Intelligence for the Real-Time Enterprises. IX, 157 pages. 2007.

Vol. 4353: T. Schwentick, D. Suciu (Eds.), Database Theory – ICDT 2007. XI, 419 pages. 2006.

Vol. 4352: T.-J. Cham, J. Cai, C. Dorai, D. Rajan, T.-S. Chua, L.-T. Chia (Eds.), Advances in Multimedia Modeling, Part II. XVIII, 743 pages. 2006.

Vol. 4351: T.-J. Cham, J. Cai, C. Dorai, D. Rajan, T.-S. Chua, L.-T. Chia (Eds.), Advances in Multimedia Modeling, Part I. XIX, 797 pages. 2006.

Vol. 4328: D. Penkler, M. Reitenspiess, F. Tam (Eds.), Service Availability. X, 289 pages. 2006.

Vol. 4321: P. Brusilovsky, A. Kobsa, W. Nejdl (Eds.), The Adaptive Web. XII, 763 pages. 2007.

Vol. 4317: S.K. Madria, K.T. Claypool, R. Kannan, P. Uppuluri, M.M. Gore (Eds.), Distributed Computing and Internet Technology. XIX, 466 pages. 2006.

Vol. 4312: S. Sugimoto, J. Hunter, A. Rauber, A. Morishima (Eds.), Digital Libraries: Achievements, Challenges and Opportunities. XVIII, 571 pages. 2006.

Vol. 4306: Y. Avrithis, Y. Kompatsiaris, S. Staab, N.E. O'Connor (Eds.), Semantic Multimedia. XII, 241 pages. 2006.

Vol. 4302: J. Domingo-Ferrer, L. Franconi (Eds.), Privacy in Statistical Databases. XI, 383 pages. 2006.

Vol. 4299: S. Renals, S. Bengio, J.G. Fiscus (Eds.), Machine Learning for Multimodal Interaction. XII, 470 pages. 2006.

Vol. 4295: J.D. Carswell, T. Tezuka (Eds.), Web and Wireless Geographical Information Systems. XI, 269 pages. 2006.

Vol. 4286: P.G. Spirakis, M. Mavronicolas, S.C. Kontogiannis (Eds.), Internet and Network Economics. XI, 401 pages. 2006.

Vol. 4282: Z. Pan, A. Cheok, M. Haller, R.W.H. Lau, H. Saito, R. Liang (Eds.), Advances in Artificial Reality and Tele-Existence. XXIII, 1347 pages. 2006.

Vol. 4278: R. Meersman, Z. Tari, P. Herrero (Eds.), On the Move to Meaningful Internet Systems 2006: OTM 2006 Workshops, Part II. XLV, 1004 pages. 2006.

Vol. 4277: R. Meersman, Z. Tari, P. Herrero (Eds.), On the Move to Meaningful Internet Systems 2006: OTM 2006 Workshops, Part I. XLV, 1009 pages. 2006.

Vol. 4276: R. Meersman, Z. Tari (Eds.), On the Move to Meaningful Internet Systems 2006: CoopIS, DOA, GADA, and ODBASE, Part II. XXXII, 752 pages. 2006.